Praise for Perspectives on Canadian Educational Law and Policy

Smale has convened a group of Canadian experts from the academy, classroom, and courtroom who have provided a detailed yet accessible review of legal issues affecting K-12 and post-secondary education environments. The review of contemporary *Charter* cases, in tandem with scholarly insights into the ever-evolving legal aspects of diversity rights, intellectual property, and professional conduct, has resulted in an informative collection suitable for pre-service and practicing teachers, educational administrators, policy makers, and instructors of educational law. This book provides a much-needed Canadian perspective on legal matters in schools. **–Dr. Bonnie Stelmach, Associate Professor, Department of Educational Policy Studies, University of Alberta.**

This book provides key insights on how educators in educational institutions experience law and policy. This collection provides sample cases and commentary with relevance for educators who work daily in legal and policy contexts, as well as for scholars who study education and the law. The essays in this collection blend notions of the moral, legal, and ethical work of educators and situate these concepts within a context where the educators' discretion is at the centre of educational practice. Smale has gathered together some of the best Canadian writers on education and the law and has delivered an engaging and eminently readable collection of essays on educational law and policy.
–Paul Newton, PhD, Department Head, Educational Administration, Acting Department Head, Educational Psychology and Special Education, College of Education, University of Saskatchewan, Co-editor, the *Canadian Journal of Educational Administration and Policy* (CJEAP).

Perspectives on Canadian Educational Law and Policy, edited by Dr. William Smale, is an outstanding and timely collection of writing and research about diverse legal and policy issues currently facing both K-12 and post-secondary educational communities. The authors represent a highly qualified cross-Canadian panel of experts, who explore a variety of current issues facing educators today. This timely volume will provide insight and information for ͡ discussions, university classrooms, school staff meetings, and ͡ to anyone interested in understanding the intricacies ͡ current political and social environments. **–Jacq͡**

Professor and Chair of the Department of Leadership and Educational Administration at Brandon University, and President of the Canadian Association for the Study of Educational Administration.

Dr. Smale and his impressive array of diverse authors are to be congratulated in producing this thoughtful and interesting book which is an excellent supplement to my Teachers and the Law book, with its useful exploration of the interconnected worlds of education law and policy. I particularly applaud the foray into the newer frontiers of post-secondary education. –**Dr. A. Wayne MacKay Professor Emeritus at the Schulich School of Law at Dalhousie University.**

This book is a first in the area of education and the law in Canada. Well over twenty authors contributed to this exciting, comprehensive volume. Page after page presents the reader with provocative descriptions or interpretations, each to be challenged or agreed with. Every chapter deserves to be read thoughtfully and carefully and even reviewed separately. This collection is the product of the coming together of an immense amount of energy and intelligence from all across the country – a tribute to the persistence and commitment of the editor - and is a superb contribution to further developing our understandings of the interfaces of law and education in Canada. -**Dr. Frank Peters, Professor Emeritus, Department of Educational Policy Studies, University of Alberta.**

A hands-on approach to Canadian Education law and Policy, *Perspectives on Canadian Educational Law and Policy* is a highly readable, timely volume containing valuable insights for all interested in this essential topic, whether they are newcomers to the field or experienced in it. This well organized, researched, and written volume provides contributions from leading authorities on Education Law and Policy in Canada, including many from the premier organization for the topic, the Canadian Association for the Practical Study of Law in Education (CAPSLE). This book covers a wide range of current and emerging topics concerning the Canadian Charter of Rights and Freedoms, as well as education in both K-12 and higher education settings. In light of the quality and timeliness of the analysis, *Perspectives on Canadian Educational Law and Policy* is an invaluable addition to the libraries of educators, policy makers, and all interested in the study of Education Law and Policy in Canada. –**Charles J. Russo, J.D., Ed.D., the Joseph Panzer Chair in Education in the School of Education and Health Sciences and Adjunct Professor of Law at the University of Dayton, Ohio, and a Past President of the (American) Education Law Association.**

Perspectives

on

Canadian Educational Law and Policy

Edited by

William T. Smale, PhD

Word & Deed Publishing Incorporated
1860 Appleby Line, Suite #778
Burlington, Ontario, Canada, L7L 7H7

Edited by William T. Smale, PhD
Book design by Jim Bisakowski – www.bookdesign.ca

ISBN 978-0-9959782-1-8

Word & Deed Publishing Incorporated
1860 Appleby Line, Suite #778
Burlington, Ontario, Canada, L7L 7H7
(Toll Free) 1-866-601-1213

Visit our website at
www.wordanddeedpublishing.com

Acknowledgments

I want to extend my sincere thanks and gratitude to the 18 chapter contributors to this book, who agreed to share their knowledge and wisdom: Dr. Fiona Blaikie, David Boulding, Dr. Ken Brien, Dr. Dawn Buzza, Dr. Paul T. Clarke, Kelly Clement, Dr. José L. da Costa, José R. da Costa, Dr. Yvette Daniel, Dr. Jerome G. Delaney, Dr. Nora M. Findlay, Dr. Tatiana Gounko, Dr. André P. Grace, Dr. Luigi Iannacci, Terry Kharyati, Dr. Benjamin Kutsyuruba, Dr. Kevin McDonough, Dr. Bruce Maxwell, Danielle McLaughlin, Dr. Jackie Muldoon, Frank Muia, James Murray, Dr. Blair Niblett, Vanessa Piccinin, Mauro Porco, Dr. Carole Richardson, and Dr. Shaheen Shariff.

I gratefully acknowledge and thank those individuals who helped bring this book to completion. To colleagues and friends, a very special acknowledgement is due for their continued support. I would like to express my appreciation to Dr. Keith Walker, University of Saskatchewan, for writing the Foreword to this book. Likewise, I want to thank Dr. Jacqueline Kirk, Brandon University; Dr. A. Wayne MacKay, Dalhousie University; Dr. Paul Newton, University of Saskatchewan; Dr. Frank Peters, University of Alberta; Dr. Charles J. Russo, University of Dayton; and Dr. Bonnie Stelmach, University of Alberta, who provided testimonials for the book.

I want to acknowledge the contribution of Eric W. Smale, University of Toronto, who spent a great deal of time carefully editing and reviewing various drafts of the chapters. His constructive comments and helpful suggestions improved the overall quality of the book. I would also like to express my appreciation to Max Moloney, Queen's University, who spent many hours proofreading each chapter. His suggestions, edits, and corrections were greatly appreciated. I would similarly like to thank the team at Word & Deed Publishing, particularly Dr. Darrin Griffiths for his editorial assistance and guidance in the production of this book. Finally, I am grateful for the financial support I received from Trent University's School of Education and Professional Learning.

Contents

SECTION ONE

Legal Issues Related to K-12 Education

SECTION TWO

Fundamental Freedoms and Charter Rights

SECTION THREE

Higher Education and the Law

Foreword

Isn't it true that almost everything that we engage in is governed in some way or another by rules, laws, or policies? Our perspectives on these constraints tend to bind us together with some people and separate us from others. The pressure and obligations of these norms can result in our experiencing either freedoms or limits. Some of these governing precepts are rules for everything we do. These rules tend to be articulated as self-evident, idealized, universal, and even absolute statements (i.e., always try to care for people and try to help them out; always play fairly; be law-abiding).

With a relatively low tolerance for imposed conformity, or for anything that might quench, hinder, or limit autonomy, it is understandable that not many of these foundational-type rules have been agreed upon – but there are some. There are also rules of tradition, prudence, and social propriety that help people to act with civility. These are meant to make life more pleasant and predictable. There are many of these rules because they are derived in diverse cultures, rooted in long-standing religions and traditions, and supported by practices connected with socialization, normalization, and sustainability. Varieties of "tribes," histories, and experiences partially explain the sources of these rules, laws, and policies, across sectors, space, and time. Of course, one has to pay respect and attention to how these rules are interpreted in different circumstances because, given their variability, any lack of attention may result in one's life becoming rather uncomfortable, and one's relationships becoming significantly strained. Insiders and outsiders are often identified by their relative alignment - or misalignment - to such rules.

We also have rules of organizations, strategies, and operations. Typically not moral, ethical, or binding rules, these are tied to perspectives and discrete thresholds for diligence, direction, accountabilities, role expectations, and the achievement of goals. For example, some rules dictate the requirements for fostering effective teamwork or improving our lives. Some promising practices, commended behaviours, and prescriptions become rules or policies and, if followed, promise to help us to cope, to generally perform better at a task, or interact with others. This short recitation of the various forms of rules, laws, and policies could go on, but I will mention just one other type. As I do so, you will notice that these forms are not always distinctive, but blend into one another. My last category of rules, laws, and policies pertains to specific locations, fields of practice, contexts, or circumstances. For example, certain professions, sectors, villages, cities, provinces, or nations have rules, laws, and policies set forth for their particular constituents, populations, or circumstances. These particular rules make professions, functions, places, and practices special. Associated constitutions, statutes, regulations, policies, and patterns interact to provide authority; assign power, rights, and responsibilities; and distribute burdens and benefits.

I mention the pervasiveness of rules, laws, and policies and identify these four forms to commend the editor, Bill Smale, and the contributing authors of the chapters in this book for touching on all four forms of rules, laws, and policy. Especially commendable is their focus on the particular rules, laws, and policies related to K-12 and post-secondary education, together with the anchoring fundamental freedoms and Charter rights in Canada. I know of no other recent work that has even attempted to bring together work from these two educational sectors, and, certainly, no group of scholars has done so with such finesse. This fine group of well-known, regionally dispersed, and highly respected scholars and practitioners has engaged in description, analysis, and critical consideration of practices, processes, precedences, and perspectives involving highly relevant issues pertaining to educational law and policy in Canada and beyond.

Both the world-wide and the Canadian landscapes of education in this second decade of the 21st century have aptly been described as volatile, uncertain, complex, and ambiguous (VUCA). Nevertheless, in this same context and with limited (even shrinking) resources, those working in the education sectors are tasked with the daunting responsibilities associated with providing safe, high-quality, closely scrutinized, reliable, predictable, consistent, reasonable, and appropriate educational access to services and learning opportunities for all. With others, I believe that we need well-designed, clearly understood, and carefully implemented laws and policies to bring order to the educational sectors. These governing principles, precepts, precedents, and ensuing practices effectively bring order to some of the chaos. Good people and good laws and policies help to move us forward in the quest to dare and to do what is right, good, just, and virtuous, as we seek to support the best interests of all. Well-conceived educational laws and policies contribute to the mediation of diverse demands and firmly anchor our educational purposes and practices in response to the storms of change. Given the increasing cynicism, subtle culture wars, desperate and overdue needs to reconcile, the need to promote equity for all, and the ongoing collisions of values and interests, educational leaders need to be equipped and empowered to convince their constituents about the integrity of educational systems and services.

This volume is a treasure trove of helpful exploration, careful analysis, thick description, and highly relevant legal and educational research, as well as invitations to engage in critical thinking. The authors' discussions help us to navigate through the current quagmires in our education systems, enabling us to describe and face some uncomfortable realities and providing insights as the authors observe and unpack emerging and contemporary challenges. I know Bill Smale, as do others, to be an extraordinary educator who has a passion for empowering others by enhancing our understanding of the laws and policies that govern us. Along with the authors of this book, he has provided an outstanding resource, one I commend to all those who believe that various forms of rules, laws, and policies permeate our lives and who appreciate the importance of principled practice in the education sectors and civil society.

Keith D. Walker, PhD, D.D.
Professor
Department of Educational Administration
University of Saskatchewan
28 Campus Drive, Saskatoon, Saskatchewan

CHAPTER 1

Introduction: Perspectives on Canadian Educational Law and Policy

William T. Smale

Given the constantly-evolving nature of educational law and policy in Canada, and the speed with which existing legal and policy frameworks are challenged by emerging issues involving new knowledge, new technology and previously-unexamined ethical considerations, the motivation for this anthology is to present the most current thinking on Canadian educational law and policy. This book presents a review of topical and important legal issues affecting various stakeholders in the K-12 and post-secondary education system, including students, parents, teacher candidates, graduate students, educators, lawyers, judges, policymakers, administrators, and other caring professionals involved in the related fields of education, law, and medicine. *Perspectives on Canadian Educational Law and Policy* consists of eighteen thought-provoking chapters, each exploring a specific facet of educational law and policy. While this book examines the above issues primarily in the context of Canadian law, the authors also draw on American case law and jurisprudence. The contributors present a comprehensive collection of topics covering a diverse range of emerging issues in educational law, all of which intersect on questions related to the moral and ethical dimensions of education, democracy, civil liberties, equality and diversity, social justice, human rights, and the *Canadian Charter of Rights and Freedoms*.

The book is divided into three main sections: the first addresses topics related to K-12 education; the second section focuses on fundamental freedoms and *Charter* rights; and the third investigates contemporary legal issues surrounding higher education. The reader will learn about the principal's discretion in disciplinary decision-making, teacher misconduct in Canada, legal and policy issues arising from professional learning communities, fetal alcohol and the legal system, legal and policy issues related to inclusion, and touch/no-touch discourse in the K-12 school environment. The chapters also examine the recent decision of the Supreme Court of Canada (SCC) in *Loyola High School v. Quebec (Attorney General)*, copyright in the Canadian education context, reasonable limits on teachers' freedom of expression in the classroom, the full recognition of sexual and gender minority youth in Canadian schooling, teaching for democracy and social justice in Canadian classrooms, and the impact of Quebec's *Bill 56* on school administrators' work in maintaining a positive school climate. Other topics include clarifying institutional legal responsibilities to address sexual violence as university contexts expand beyond campus borders to the online realm, professional practice and mental health accommodations for teacher candidates, mental health accommodation for graduate students, legal issues in Canadian higher education, pre-service teachers' legal literacy and experiences with legal issues in the practicum setting, as well as educational institutions' jurisdiction over students' off-campus behaviours. Written in a non-legalistic language, and including a combination of court decisions, legislation, social policy documents, case studies, research literature, qualitative and quantitative research, interviews, personal narratives, reflection pieces, and newspaper articles, *Perspectives on Canadian Educational Law and Policy* is a valuable resource that could be used as a primary or supplementary course text for a senior undergraduate course, teacher education course, or graduate-level education law course.

As noted above, the first section of the book focuses on emerging legal issues related to elementary and secondary education. Nora M. Findlay, who served more than twenty-five years as an educator and school-based administrator in Saskatchewan, Canada, explores the intriguing concept of administrative discretion in disciplinary decision-making. Findlay considers how elementary school principals interpret their ability to exercise discretion and negotiate within these legal parameters, as delegated to them through legislation, case law, and policy, as a means of maintaining their own value systems in matters of student discipline. Two findings of Findlay's investigation - involving the appropriate exercise of discretion in policy implementation and the exercise of discretion to balance competing rights in the school setting - are the focus of the analysis in this chapter.

Jerome G. Delaney, an Associate Professor of Educational Administration in the Faculty of Education at Memorial University of Newfoundland, St. John's, Newfoundland, addresses an important topic in contemporary educational law: teacher misconduct in Canada. Delaney's chapter examines teacher misconduct, mainly in the provinces of British Columbia and Ontario. The author presents his four categories of teacher misconduct and includes their definitions, statistics, and real-life examples. Finally, this chapter presents some concrete strategies for curbing teacher misconduct and briefly describes four organizations involved with education law.

Ken Brien, an Associate Professor of Educational Administration and Leadership at the University of New Brunswick, Fredericton, New Brunswick, Canada, who worked previously as a high school teacher and administrator in Northern Ontario, explores Professional Learning Communities (PLCs). Brien notes that PLCs have been widely promoted and implemented by school systems in recent years. As they represent a significant culture change from the traditional bureaucratic model of schooling, PLCs challenge existing laws and policies in education. With reference primarily to New Brunswick legal and policy documents, Brien's engaging chapter examines the principles of PLCs and the legal and policy implications of their implementation at the school, district, and provincial levels of the school system.

David Boulding, a former trial lawyer with a practice now restricted to writing, speaking, and training about fetal alcohol, examines the potential applicability of lessons learned through experiential outdoor education to the context of educating judges on the topic of fetal alcohol. Boulding argues that the current judicial system is failing with respect to people with fetal alcohol charged with a criminal offence. The author notes the many ways in which people with fetal alcohol can be cognitively and behaviourally affected on the level of brain development, and advances the argument that the current legal and judicial system simply does not adequately compensate for people with these types of developmental difficulties. The author then goes on to describe personal success stories that applied lessons in experiential education gathered from outdoor education to teaching judges key facts about fetal alcohol and its relation to criminality.

Luigi Iannacci, an Associate Professor in the School of Education and Professional Learning at Trent University in Peterborough, Ontario, Canada; Frank Muia, a Teacher with the Dufferin-Peel Catholic District School Board in Ontario, Canada; and Mauro Porco, a Special Education and Resource Teacher in the Simcoe Muskoka Catholic District School Board, Ontario, Canada, critically explore a variety of perspectives regarding inclusion. Misunderstandings about inclusion that have depicted it as only achievable within the confines of the regular classroom are also questioned. This illuminating chapter begins by exploring the legal perspectives that govern and mandate inclusion, and then uses philosophical, epistemological, organizational, practical, pedagogic, and economic perspectives to form an ethical and responsive model of, and operational framework for, inclusion. This critical exploration aims to encourage educators to re-think what they understand about inclusion, and to then provide dynamic leadership that supports it. The dominant and under-theorized misconceptions of what "inclusion" means are destabilized throughout this critical exploration. The chapter provides information that can be applied to a variety of educational contexts such as school boards, schools and in-/pre-service teacher education. The authors give educational leaders a clear framework for critically thinking about inclusive practices that will support the learning of students with special needs and students identified as exceptional.

Blair Niblett, an Assistant Professor in the School of Education at Trent University, Peterborough, Ontario, Canada, critically and insightfully discusses touch/no-touch discourse in the K-12 school environment. Inspired by a 2013 composite case study in the Ontario College of Teachers' magazine, *Professionally Speaking,* this chapter introduces a heuristic for thinking about the dynamics of touch between teachers and students, arguing for more clear legal direction on what kinds of touch are professionally appropriate. Using a 'stoplight' metaphor, the heuristic is developed as a continuum from red through amber to green zones.

Red zone touching is harmful, and clearly prohibited in law and policy. Amber zone instances are contested, with little clarification offered by law and policy. Green zone touching, Niblett argues, is a positive and important element of teaching and learning and should be clearly condoned by law and policy in order to develop effective pedagogies that depend on touch. The heuristic is further explained by discussing the mediating dimensions that complicate the assigning of instances of touch to fixed zones.

The second section of the book presents five concise chapters focusing on fundamental freedoms and *Charter* rights. Paul T. Clarke, a Professor of Educational Law and Leadership at the University of Regina, Regina, Canada, and the Associate Dean of Faculty Development and Human Resources in the University of Regina's Faculty of Education, investigates the *Loyola* decision. In this detailed and important contribution, Clarke examines the recent decision of the Supreme Court of Canada (SCC) in *Loyola High School v. Quebec (Attorney General)*. In the first part of the chapter, the author explains the case's context. In the second part, he explains the reasons for the judgment of the majority, penned by Justice Abella, along with the reasons for the partial concurrence of the minority, as authored by Chief Justice McLachlin and Justice Moldaver. In the third part of the chapter, the author considers the implications of this decision for those interested in contemporary education law. This consideration includes a critique of the majority's call for teachers at Loyola High School to teach ethics in an objective and neutral manner. This critique is followed by concluding remarks offered by Clarke.

José R. da Costa, a Librarian employed by the Kamloops Public Library, and José L. da Costa, a Professor of Educational Administration and Leadership in the Department of Educational Policy Studies, Faculty of Education at the University of Alberta, Edmonton, Canada, comprehensively examine the timely issue of copyright in the Canadian education context. The last two decades have seen sweeping changes to intellectual property rights throughout the world. In Canada, the 1996 *Copyright Act* and the 2012 *Copyright Modernization Act* reflect this shift. These acts, along with two landmark Supreme Court of Canada decisions, provide the context for understanding copyright for educators in contemporary Canadian schools. The first of these cases, *CCH Canadian Ltd. v. Law Society of Upper Canada* (2004), clarified the criteria for determining fair dealing. The second case, *Alberta v. Canadian Copyright Licensing Agency* (2012), helped define fair dealing in the context of photocopying materials for educational purposes. This revealing chapter also explores the current balance between intellectual property rights and teacher rights for use of copyrighted materials.

Bruce Maxwell, an Associate Professor of Education at the University of Quebec at Trois-Rivières, Quebec, Canada, and Kevin McDonough, an Associate Professor of Philosophy of Education at McGill University, Quebec, Canada, identify five principles, derived from an analysis of U.S. and Canadian jurisprudence, which together provide the contours of permissible teacher speech in the classroom, particularly in cases involving controversial and contested curricular issues. In their thoughtful examination of teachers' freedom of expression, Maxwell and McDonough argue that greater clarity about the principles in question – curricular alignment, teacher even-handedness, consistency with *Charter* principles, avoidance of foreseeable inflammatory speech, and age-appropriateness – has at least two important benefits for educators. First, the principles serve as guidelines for responsible teacher decision making in the classroom; and second, they serve as a potential basis for resolving disputes among various stakeholders – teachers, school administrators and other school officials, and parents – which might otherwise lead to long, costly, and protracted legal conflicts.

André P. Grace, a Canada Research Chair in Sexual and Gender Minority Studies (Tier 1) in the Faculty of Education, University of Alberta, Edmonton, Canada, authoritatively examines the full recognition of sexual and gender minority – lesbian, gay, bisexual, trans-spectrum, intersexual, and queer Indigenous (or, more commonly, Two-Spirit Aboriginal) – youth in Canada. In schooling, matters of access, adjustment, and accommodation continue to take educational policymaking and its implementation in ethical and caring practices into the messy intersection of the moral and the political. This sensitive and thought-provoking chapter begins with a reflection on realities and consequences for sexual and gender minority (SGM) youth who are navigating education and healthcare. From this perspective, Grace considers the importance of synchronizing research, policy, and practice to enhance the possibilities for recognizing and accommodating SGM youth across the institutions charged with their care. Next, the chapter explores the dire sexual health predicament of youth, including SGM youth, highlighting the need for comprehensive sexual health education for all to be included in the core curriculum and instruction. Here, Grace reflects on the Canadian guidelines while problematizing the current sexual health curriculum in Alberta's high schools. The chapter concludes by discussing the recently passed *Bill 10*, which has advanced SGM recognition and accommodation in schooling in Alberta while paradoxically leaving schools with a key roadblock to universalizing comprehensive sexual health education for all students.

Yvette Daniel, an Associate Professor in Educational Leadership and Policy Studies at the Faculty of Education and Academic Development, University of Windsor, Ontario, Canada, and Danielle McLaughlin, who was Director of Education of the Canadian Civil Liberties Association and Education Trust (CCLA/CCLET) from 1988 to 2016, discuss the important issue of human rights and social justice. This chapter underscores the links between critical thinking and critical pedagogy in teaching for democracy and social justice. Daniel and McLaughlin report on their exploration of the challenges teacher candidates face when they try to implement strategies for critical thinking into lesson plans in their practice teaching. This chapter is the result of a collaborative initiative between the Faculty of Education, University of Windsor and the Canadian Civil Liberties Education Trust (CCLET). The authors introduced an assignment for their teacher candidates to implement in their practicum classrooms. One component required the teacher candidates to reflect upon the realities of practice. Five themes emerged from the analysis of these documents, in terms of common factors influencing teacher candidates' ability to implement critical thinking strategies into practice teaching lessons: (1) making connections and relating the activities to student's experiences; (2) showing alternative viewpoints/perspectives; (3) lack of experience and understanding of critical thinking for social justice; (4) resistance from associate/mentor teachers; and (5) teacher candidates' underestimation of students' abilities based on the candidates' perceptions of age and grade level.

Terry Kharyati, a Teacher, Vice-Principal, and Principal for 23 years, now the Director of Human Resources at the Western Quebec School Board, and Benjamin Kutsyuruba, an Associate Professor in Educational Policy, Leadership, and School Law and an Associate Director of Social Program Evaluation Group (SPEG) in the Faculty of Education at Queen's University, Kingston, Ontario, Canada, address the impact of Quebec's *Bill 56* on school administrators' work in maintaining a positive school climate. The authors note that the implementation of new laws and policies in contemporary education often poses significant challenges for school administration. In June 2012, the province of Quebec enacted *Bill 56: An act to prevent and stop bullying and violence in schools.* This timely chapter examines Quebec school administrators' perceptions of the impact of *Bill 56* on their work in maintaining a positive school climate. Kharyati and Kutsyuruba discuss the goals and mandates of the anti-bullying *Bill 56* in the province of Quebec, both as stated in the document and as perceived by Quebec school administrators, report on how Quebec school administrators see their responsibilities and roles changing in regards to the mandates of *Bill 56*, and describe school administrators' perceptions of the existing challenges to the bill, as well as the various supports put in place regarding the anti-bullying legislation *Bill 56* in the province of Quebec.

The third section of this book presents six chapters addressing the topic of higher education and the law. Shaheen Shariff, an Associate Professor at McGill University, Quebec, Canada, insightfully discusses institutional legal responsibilities to address sexual violence as university contexts expand beyond campus borders to the online realm. Within universities across Canada, the issues of sexual violence, sexually offensive online comments, and the distribution of non-consensual images online have attracted significant attention from news media, social media, legislators, and educational policy makers. Specifically, this chapter addresses policy dilemmas confronted by university administrators as they attempt to balance free expression, safety and protection, accountability and regulation with due process and discipline when incidents of sexual violence occur in the "university context." Shariff's chapter also unpacks the notion of what a "university context" means if the definition of rape culture is taken to include the online context and the continuum of sexual violence that includes sexist and misogynist online comments, threats, non-consensual distribution of intimate images, peer rating of female or LGBTQ classmates, and sexist jokes about disabled or international students. Shariff also addresses the policy vacuum and the increasingly blurred lines involving institutional responsibilities to address off-campus and/or on-line sexual violence. The author also explores legal accountability through case law analysis and analysis of media-reported incidents of sexual violence on Canadian campuses, and the subsequent university responses or lack thereof. The chapter concludes by recommending a multi-sector partnership approach to reclaim the role of universities in developing educational responses that will help to educate society on issues such as sexual violence and civil responsibility.

Fiona Blaikie, a Professor in the Faculty of Education at Brock University, St. Catharines, Ontario, Canada; Dawn Buzza, a Professor of Education at Wilfrid Laurier University, Waterloo, Ontario, Canada; Jackie Muldoon, the Provost and Vice President Academic at Trent University, Peterborough, Ontario, Canada; and Carole Richardson, the Dean of the Schulich School of Education at Nipissing University in North Bay, Ontario, Canada, discuss professional practice and mental health accommodations for teacher candidates. In this very important contribution to higher education and the law, the authors offer a common set of defining principles and a policy that focuses on mental health in relation to our expectations of teacher candidates and their professional practices. In the context of the *Ontario Human Rights Commission Policy* (2014), which prohibits discrimination based on mental health disabilities and addictions, all accommodations must provide equitable opportunities to teacher candidates with human-rights-protected needs. Needs cannot impede the teacher candidate's ability to meet the standards of professionalism and competency which are required to graduate, given that faculties of education, school boards, and other agents are not at liberty to modify the policy-defining standards and ethics of professional practice. The issues discussed include the need to uphold the ethics of the teaching profession; mutual respect, dignity and reasonableness; the importance of collaboration with stakeholders; the duty to accommodate; the limits of accommodations; the need for teacher candidates to declare a limitation/disability (professional discernment suggests a duty to disclose and an ability to discern if, when, and how to disclose); and the duty to educate teacher candidates on the ethics of practice beyond the curriculum and classroom management.

Tatiana Gounko, an Associate Professor in the Department of Educational Psychology and Leadership Studies at the University of Victoria in Victoria, British Columbia, Canada, discusses the existing institutional strategies related to the accommodation of graduate students with mental health issues in order to understand their complexity and associated challenges. In this important and multifaceted discussion, Gounko examines the central issues in the academic accommodations, institutional strategies, and challenges faced by graduate students with mental health disabilities. As no specific federal or provincial governmental standards exist in Canada, the policies and procedures for accessing accommodations vary across universities, as do the staffing and budgets for disability services, and the level of understanding among administrators and faculty. Universities are still trying to develop best practices while dealing with declining public resources and increasing demands for student services. Gounko also observes that this task is exceptionally complex and requires the entire university community to participate in implementing a student mental health strategy in order to create an inclusive and accessible learning environment.

William T. Smale, an Associate Professor in the School of Education and Professional Learning at Trent University in Peterborough, Ontario, Canada, and Kelly Clement, the College Secretary for Governance Matters in the College of Graduate and Postdoctoral Studies at the University of Saskatchewan, Saskatoon, Saskatchewan, Canada, explore the question of bias and procedural fairness in the admissions process for the post-secondary education system. Specifically, the chapter examines the extent to which universities' discretionary decision-making regarding admissions can be construed as being biased or unfair. Through a review of relevant case law, the authors examine factors involving faculty research funding requirements and conditional admission offers. The chapter also considers the legal implications of case law regarding the contractual nature of educational institutions' requirements to use factual and accurate information regarding their programs. The authors emphasize the importance of the legal distinction between academic issues, which are typically decided internally by the university, and contractual issues, which are subject to intervention by the courts. The authors further consider the requirement to provide due process and procedural fairness. Finally, the chapter looks at students' right to freedom of expression as defined in the *Canadian Charter of Rights and Freedoms*, and the definition of these rights in cases where students are thought to be violating the university code of conduct.

Benjamin Kutsyuruba, an Associate Professor in Educational Policy, Leadership, and School Law and an Associate Director of the Social Program Evaluation Group (SPEG) in the Faculty of Education at Queen's University, Kingston, Ontario, Canada, and James Murray, a fourth-year Ph.D. student in the Faculty of Education at Queen's University, who holds an M.Ed., L.L.B., and B.A. Honours (Political Studies) from Queen's University, discuss pre-service teachers' legal literacy. According to Kutsyuruba and Murray, pre-service teachers' legal literacy refers to the knowledge level that teacher candidates in teacher education programs have with respect to educational law and policy, and considers how their knowledge affects their preparation for entering the teaching profession. Their chapter presents findings from an exploratory qualitative study examining teacher candidates' (n=744) observations of and experiences with legal issues while on practicum placements in a teacher education program in a southeastern Ontario university (during the 2014-2015 academic year). In this chapter, Kutsyuruba and Murray identify the most frequently occurring aspects of school law and policy, analyze teacher candidates' awareness of school laws and policies pertaining to those aspects, and, finally, explore the candidates' preparedness to deal with the legal issues occurring in their practicum placements. The authors conclude by discussing their findings and the research implications for teacher education programs.

Vanessa Piccinin, a Doctoral Candidate in Educational Leadership and Policy in the School of Leadership, Higher, and Adult Education, at the Ontario Institute for Studies in Education (OISE), University of Toronto, Ontario, Canada, examines a specific case of civil disobedience that occurred in the immediate vicinity of an Ontario community college. Piccinin employs a case study approach to critically examine and contextualize the key issues pertaining to students' rights, particularly the right to due process. Specifically, the author asks, to what extent can educational administrators enact policy to impose disciplinary measures over students' off-campus behaviours? Moreover, how are social media used to monitor and govern students? In this insightful chapter, the competing interests of higher-level administrators, students, local police, and the greater community are also considered in discussing the implications for future policy and practice.

Legal Issues Related to K-12 Education

CHAPTER 2

Principals' Discretion in Disciplinary Decision-Making: Charting a Course between Charybdis and Scylla?

Nora M. Findlay

"Teachers and those in charge of our schools are entrusted with the care and education of our children. It is difficult to imagine a more important trust or duty." –(*R. v. M.R.M.*, para. 1)

Abstract

This chapter presents research based on the study conducted for the author's doctoral dissertation. Exploring the concept of administrative discretion in decision-making, she considers the ways in which elementary school principals interpret their exercise of discretion and how they negotiate within the legal parameters of discretion, as it is delegated to them through legislation, case law, and policy, in order to maintain their own value system in matters of student discipline. As seen through a legal lens, two findings of that investigation—the appropriate exercise of discretion in policy implementation and the exercise of discretion to balance competing rights in the school setting—are the focus of the analysis in this chapter.

Introduction

In two simple words, the Supreme Court of Canada identified many of the complexities and challenges facing Canadian educators in the twenty-first century. The notions of "trust" and "duty" reside at the heart of education and speak to the significance of educators' roles. Not coincidentally, La Forest (1997), a former Justice of the Supreme Court of Canada, also highlighted the importance of trust and duty when he described the "fiduciary obligations" found in many different types of relationships, such as "banker-customer, solicitor-client, doctor-client," (p. 122) and "teacher-student" (p. 128). He identified two features common to fiduciary relationships as "'trust and confidence'" (p. 122), wherein "the fiduciary has scope for the exercise of a discretion or power," "the beneficiary is peculiarly vulnerable to or at the mercy of the fiduciary," (p. 123) and the fiduciary "has a duty to act in that person's best interests" (p. 120). La Forest (1997) added that educators' "responsibilities stem from their special position in our society and from the particular vulnerability of children to those in positions of authority over them" (p. 120).[1] One way in which principals can build trust with students, parents, and the school community while working to fulfill their many obligations, is through their discretionary decision-making in student disciplinary issues.

Significance of Student Discipline

As I have argued elsewhere (Findlay, 2012a), some of the most difficult issues facing school principals are related to discipline and student behaviour. Indeed, Cornell and Mayer (2010) claimed that "few issues have more impact on educators and students" (p. 11) than school discipline. Even the Supreme Court of Canada has grappled with the notion of discipline; in *Canadian Foundation for Children, Youth, & the Law v. Canada (Attorney General)*, Chief Justice Beverley McLachlin

---

1 La Forest (1997) also maintained that "discretion, influence and vulnerability are *inherent* in the teacher-student dynamic [emphasis in original]" and, consequently, "there is a rebuttable presumption that teachers owe a fiduciary obligation to their students" (p. 125).

acknowledged the "unclear and inconsistent" messages sent by courts which have endeavoured to define what is "reasonable under the circumstances" in cases of child discipline (para. 39). She admitted, however, that "on occasion, judges erroneously applied their own subjective views on what constitutes reasonable discipline—views as varied as different judges' backgrounds" (para. 39). What is more, Gall (2010) found that school discipline may not foster "collaboration between school authorities and students" (p. 137) and suggested "the disconnect between school authorities and students (whether real or perceived) as caused by many practices of school discipline is a problem" (p. 138).

Principals wield significant authority over students, especially in matters of student discipline, and their responses to student behaviour are of special concern. Webb (2012) noted how "students are highly impacted by the discretionary decisions educators make in regard to student discipline, and those about whom decisions are made bear the greatest consequences" (p. 98). For example, certain types of approach to student misbehaviour have been found to result in "antisocial behavior...increased vandalism ... school disengagement, lost opportunities to learn, and dropout" (Osher, Bear, Sprague, & Doyle, 2010, p. 48). Cornell and Mayer (2010) also highlighted the "*school discipline gap* [emphasis in original]" identified in research which reveals "disturbing findings of racial and ethnic inequities in school discipline" (p. 11). Similarly, Gregory, Skiba, and Noguera (2010) found a possible correlation between widely-used "school disciplinary practices," such as school suspensions in the United States, and "lowered academic performance" among certain student racial groups (p. 60). These researchers observed that "when taking into account grade point average, race remains a predictor of suspensions" (p. 61). Similarly, when discussing Aboriginal and non-Aboriginal students' different achievement levels in Saskatchewan, Canada, French (2013) identified a school division where Aboriginal students comprised "16% of the school division" but "accounted for one-third of all school suspensions in October and November 2012" (p. 41). Arguably, student discipline should be "corrective, supportive, educative, and equitable" (Findlay, 2012b, p. 41) and, for many principals, disciplinary decision-making can be exceedingly difficult. Indeed, principals often wrestle with the tension between being, and/or being perceived by stakeholders as being, either too harsh or too weak in dealing with disciplinary issues, since students, staff, and parents might use this perception to evaluate their effectiveness as school leaders (Axelrod, 2010).

Concept of Discretion

Discretion, in its legal sense, typically resides in the field of Administrative Law and is defined in *Black's Law Dictionary* as "wise conduct and management; cautious discernment; prudence; individual judgment; the power of free decision-making" (Garner, 2009, p. 534). Hawkins (1992) maintained that discretion is either "formally granted" or "assumed" (p. 11) and succinctly defined it as "the means by which the words of law are translated into action" (Hawkins, 1997, p. 140), while Handler (1992) described discretion as that which gives an official "choice" (p. 333). Discretion may be alternatively regarded in a more informal sense, as latitude, or flexibility (Findlay, 2012a, pp. 47–48). Paquette and Allison (1997), however, contended that discretion is "ultimately the power to do what one wants or believes best given one's particular mix of motives, values, and cultural context, in a particular case or set of similar cases" (p. 173). Nonetheless, discretion appears to be an elusive notion, and has been variously described as "sponge-like because it absorbs the values, assumptions, and preferences to which it is exposed" (Sossin, 2005, pp. 438–439); a "calculus of decision making" (Manley-Casimir, 2012, p. 6); or as being exercised within a "matrix of influences," obligations, and responsibilities (Vinzant & Crothers, 1998, p. 9) that shape decision-making. Paquette and Allison (1997) described discretion as "many-faceted and eminently situational;" consequently, what it is "depends on where [one sits]" (p. 179).

Discretion and Moral Decision-Making

School administrators exercise discretion in their decision-making as a response to ethical dilemmas (Cranston, Ehrich, & Kimber, 2006). Hall (1999) found that school administrators "rely on their core values in their use of discretion" (p. 96), while Young and Meyer (2011) asserted that the "employment and deployment of discretion is a fundamental pillar of leadership" (p. 76). In their analysis of special education litigation, they determined that "the capacity to exercise discretion is important for educators because of the assumption made by some that all decisions are by their nature moral decisions" (p. 82). They concluded that "educational leaders must make a moral decision based on their conscience, specifically, their sense of defining a moral implication of educational purpose" and that their use of both "discretion and conscience, because of their blatant choice components, puts any decision into a moral context" (Young & Meyer, 2011, p. 83). Thus, the link between discretion, values, morals and ethical behaviour may be considered in the following way:

> "[J]udgement" or "discretion" (terms that are usually treated as synonyms) lie at the heart of responsible and defensible decision making. Discretion conveys legally approved or delegated latitude that empowers administrators to use their best judgment in the circumstances they face. And it is through discretionary [sic] decisions that administrators aspire to excellence in their work. Discretion and its exercise are normative—that is, it invokes considerations of morality and right action on the part of the administrator. Inevitably, therefore, such discretion forms a nexus with ethics, and with recognition of a personal categorical imperative or conscience on the part of the decision maker (Manley-Casimir, 2012, pp. 258–259).

Advantages of Discretion

In an insightful analysis, Hawkins (1997) contended discretion is pervasive and is part of the daily decision-making behaviour of administrative officials. Discretion is especially helpful to administrators when policy does not provide adequate or sufficient direction, or when precedent does not prove illustrative. Schneider (1992) identified what he saw as the many advantages discretion allows: discretion permits "the decision-maker to resolve the conflict in ways that accommodate all the interests involved" and can be "tailored" to the special circumstances of each case (p. 61). It can let the decision-maker "do justice" (p. 67) and deal with highly complex situations. Moreover, discretion can be used to form compromises, to allow for a more expansive interpretation of circumstances than was envisioned by the rules, to allow more readily than legislative changes for incremental adjustments to changing societal norms, and to take the standards of the decision-maker's community into account (pp. 62–68). Manley-Casimir (1977–78) also identified the "flexibility" and creativity afforded by the exercise of discretion, claiming it is "vital" to administrators in their decision-making (p. 84).

Disadvantages of Discretion

On the other hand, however, Schneider (1992) saw discretion as "a kind of power" that seems "conducive to an arrogance and carelessness" in dealing with the lives of others (p. 68). He also argued that the exercise of discretion may appear to violate the assumption that "like cases should be treated alike" and may lead an individual to question whether he or she has been treated fairly (Schneider, 1992, p. 74). Pointing to research, for instance, which indicated officials' decision-making in the criminal justice system may be influenced by "arbitrary or irrelevant standards" such as "race" or "sex or sexual orientation," Gelsthorpe and Padfield (2003) underscored the notion of power—the "power to decide, to choose, to discern or to determine"—and suggested the power to exercise discretion also includes the potential for abuse (p. 9). Davis (1969), too, warned that discretion can provide the opportunity for "beneficence or tyranny, either justice or injustice, [or] either reasonableness or arbitrariness" (p. 3), and, citing disproportionate sentencing decisions in capital and domestic violence cases in the United States, Baumgartner (1992) argued that discretion's true nature is "socially patterned and socially predictable" (p. 156) and allows for favouritism in decision-making.

Discretion in Schools

School administrators are delegated discretion through provincial legislation and regulations, case law, and school board policies and through legal doctrines (Findlay, 2014), such as the fiduciary principle (Brien, 2005) noted above. Sitch and McCoubrey (2000) maintained the courts hold that "learning takes place in an orderly environment" and that it is thought to be "in the best interest of students to extend broad discretion to those administering education to preserve this orderliness" (p. 191). Certainly, much of the legislation under provincial statutes directing principals' actions does relate to maintaining order and discipline in schools, and principals are delegated discretion in order to achieve these goals. For example, Section 175(j) of Saskatchewan's *Education Act*[2] outlines the duties of a principal, one of which is to "administer or cause to be administered any discipinary measures that are considered proper by him or her and that are consistent with this Act." The same legislation also describes the duties of students, one of which is to "submit to any discipline that would be exercised by a kind, firm and judicious parent" (s. 150(3)(f)). Section 154 deals with student suspension; the principal "may suspend a pupil from school for not more than three school days at a time for overt opposition to authority or serious misconduct" (154) (1)(a). Clearly, the language of discretion is broad, subjectively-worded, open to various interpretations and appears to assume much about the good faith, judgment, and common sense of administrators in making decisions and applying rules.

Interestingly, MacKay (2008) noted "'the good old days' of open-ended administrative discretion for teachers and principals are gone"

---

2 *The Education Act*, S.S. 1995, c. E-0.2.

(p. 32). He pointed to what he saw as the benefits of the expanded "judicial role in education," since the entrenchment of the *Charter*,[3] as contributing, in part, to the need for the clarification of school rules in order to meet the "justification standard" of the *Charter*, "thereby diminishing [administrators'] discretion" (MacKay, 2008, p. 32). However, MacKay (2008) also asserted that since the *Charter's* adoption, "the courts and most administrative tribunals" have shown "considerable deference to the educational experts" in matters of educational policy, "mindful of the practical demands of the school context" (p. 23). Similarly, Torres and Chen (2006) predicted that courts in the United States generally would continue to defer to the "expertise and judgment" (p. 191) of school officials as they exercise discretion in dealing with students. In arguing for greater awareness and understanding of the "extent and nature of human rights," (p. 174) however, Sitch and McCoubrey (2000) believed that "administrators are reluctant to discuss changes to their discretionary authority" because they may fear that "*Charter* scrutiny" could "lead to the erosion or complete removal of that authority" (p. 197).

Nonetheless, discretion is exercised by school administrators throughout all aspects of their practice. For example, Handler (1986) suggested that in cases of special education, which require programs that are "judgmental, professional, flexible, [and] experimental" (p. 3) student placement decisions "should be discretionary" (p. 3) because of knowledge gaps about student performance and achievement, while Larsen and Akmal (2007) identified the implementation of student retention policies as being another area where administrative discretion is required. School administrators' exercise of discretion in student discipline has been identified (e.g., Clark, 2002; Hall, 1999), and it may be reasoned that in disciplinary issues principals exercise their discretion within a quasi-legal system (e.g., Arum, 2003; Kajs, 2006). Judge-like, principals are required to make decisions in cases of student misbehaviour in light of specific circumstances, a student's history, and the effects of specific incidents upon others. In their investigation of these matters, then, principals may determine guilt or innocence and assign the appropriate

---

3 *Canadian Charter of Rights and Freedoms.* Part 1 of the *Constitution Act, 1982,* being Schedule B to the *Canada Act 1982* (U.K.), 1982, c. 11.

consequences. Arguably, discretion in school discipline demands special consideration because it is through administrators' exercise of discretionary power in matters of student discipline that "the school's recognition or denial of student rights and interests assumes sharpest focus" (Manley-Casimir, 1977–78, p. 84).

Study of Principals' Discretion in Disciplinary Decision-Making

My research for my doctoral dissertation examined how principals made sense of and interpreted their exercise of discretion, and also how they negotiated within the legal parameters of discretion in order to maintain their value system in student disciplinary matters (Findlay, 2012a, p. 17). Ten Western Canadian urban elementary school-based administrators with from one to ten years' experience as principals participated in the qualitative study. The method consisted of semi-structured interviews wherein the six female and four male principals responded to a vignette involving a student behavioural incident. The interview protocol also included fifteen specific questions which sought to determine their understanding of their exercise of discretion (Findlay, 2012a, pp. 443–445). Two findings of that investigation—involving the appropriate exercise of discretion in policy implementation and the exercise of discretion to balance competing rights—are the focus of the present discussion.

Appropriate Exercise of Discretion in Policy Implementation

Shipman (1969) asserted that "there can be no sharp separation between policy and administration. Policy is the value content of the administrative process" (p. 122). LaRocque and Coleman (1985) identified policies in administration as forming "the critical link between the policy realm and the realm of programs and practices" (p. 152) while highlighting the "critical importance of administrators, both district and school level, to the success of policy implementation efforts" (p. 155). Hall (1999) contended discretion is a central element in school administrators' "interpretation and implementation of district policy" (p. 162), while Hawkins's (1992) assertion that "interpretive behavior is involved in making sense of rules and in making choices about the relevance and use of rules" (p. 13) was borne out in the findings of my study.

Some of the administrators in my study (Findlay, 2012a) perceived either that school policies were too constricting or limiting upon their discretion (i.e., a specific policy might have been overly rigid or strict), or that certain legislation, such as that outlining reasons for student suspensions, did not align with their own beliefs or values. In this latter situation, the principals appeared to think they could determine whether or not to enforce the policy. On the one hand, a principal maintained, "I follow school board policy ... that's the school board policy, and if he [the student's father] doesn't agree with it, then I'm sorry, but that's the policy ... I don't have any say" (p. 331). Another principal, on the other hand, believed policy to be a "starting point" and asked himself, "Does this policy make any sense whatsoever in the context I am dealing in right now?" (pp. 331-332). One of the female principals said that although she was familiar with the policies on suspension and expulsion in the school division, she did "not feel bound [to implement them], as [she felt principals] are given discretion depending upon circumstances and context" (p. 332). While they also may have been reluctant to "reflect on the appropriateness of the basic assumptions underlying established policy and practice in specific instances," (p. 332) some of the principals simply may have adhered to what they perceived was the school division policy, or what they thought was best for the student based on "unconscious assumptions" (Roche, 1999, p. 267). For instance, despite having been in school-based administrative roles for almost twenty years, one principal revealed he did not know whether there was a policy on weapons in the school division. All the principals appeared to understand they possessed the personal skills or abilities (LaRocque & Coleman, 1985) needed to implement policy. However, they interpreted that relying solely upon policies as a basis for decision-making was an inappropriate exercise of discretion, whether or not they believed they possessed the personal ability or skill to do so.

Policies and Principals' Values

Furthermore, in line with the conclusions of LaRocque and Coleman's (1985) research on the implementation of community policy relations in public schools, if the values articulated in a policy aligned with the principals' own values, the administrators were more inclined than they would have been otherwise to accept and internalize the "values and goals of the policy," support it, and change their "role behaviors and role relationships" to be consistent with it (p. 157). As one male principal concluded, he did not "feel any obligation" (p. 333) to enforce a policy he believed was "counterintuitive to what a child needs," (p. 333) although in specific cases, he did feel somewhat constrained by school board policies for a student search because it was a "legality issue" (p. 333). Two principals commented on their belief that the prevailing provincial legislation was outdated, a notion which may have provided them with some justification for their decision to enforce the legislation as they "saw fit" (p. 333). The principals appeared to be guided by their own interpretation of what was good for a student, despite rules or policies to the contrary (Findlay, 2012a). Unlike the principals in Roche's (1999) inquiry, who felt they needed to be consistent in their application of policy, the principals in my study did not appear to believe they needed to apply policies consistently. They seemed to support Hawkins's (2003) maxim that "rule breaking may be a threat to order, but rule enforcement is not necessarily conducive to order" (p. 207). Instead, they believed they had to apply policy differentially based on circumstances, and that consistency in policy implementation was not necessarily a good thing and could bring about disparity in outcomes for students. As a result, discretion, as these principals exercised it, could undermine the "intent of the statute" or policy (Vorenberg, 1976, p. 665).

In her study of values in principals' decision-making, Campbell-Evans (1988) discovered that "where policy conflicted with their values, principals responded by implementing the policy and then worked to change or amend it to correspond to their value position. In cases of internal conflict, value choice preceded decision action" (p. 86). Similarly, most of the principals in my study either appeared to ignore a policy's intent entirely if it conflicted with their own espoused, or even unconscious values, or worked to "ameliorate" what they interpreted as the "negative" effects of a policy (Haynes & Licata, 1995, p. 23) upon students by adapting it to their own value position. This avoidance of policy implementation may have resulted from any one of a number of considerations, such as misinterpretation, misunderstanding, or uncertainty about a policy's intent; a subjective evaluation of the policy's importance for the school; the policy's impact on the best interests of a student or students in general; or simply a desire to undermine central office dictates for personal reasons.

Selective Enforcement of Policy

When enforcing a policy served their purpose, however, the principals would selectively choose to do so, especially when school safety was an issue or when they feared that their decision-making might have been subject to legal scrutiny. In many ways, their decision-making mirrored Walker's (1998) belief in policy implementation based on utilitarian principles, whereby administrators selectively implement that part of a policy which will bring the "greatest benefit" (p. 300) and the least detriment for the greatest number of students. Similarly, the research of Marshall, Patterson, Rogers, and Steele (1996) on "*career assistant principals* (CAPs) [emphasis in original]" (p. 272) revealed they would "often find policy, orders, roles, rules, and resources inadequate" (pp. 287–288); consequently, in order to maintain relationships with their students and to resolve conflicts, the assistant principals would "make their own judgments" rather than follow the dictates of a policy (p. 288). However, as Torres and Chen (2006) observed, different policies and their different intents may "demand different levels of discretion" (p. 190); thus, the principals' exercise of discretion varied, as did their need to adhere to rules and policies. They did not appear to assume the rules operated "in a simple causal way," or to believe that "'the rule is this, therefore I must do that'" (Hawkins, 2003, p. 206).

Smith and Foster (2009) contended that "school policy and practice" must "provide equal opportunities to students," a process which involves taking "a hard look at the extent to which they [educators] are accommodating students of diverse backgrounds, needs, and aspirations" (pp. 35–36). The principals in my study emphasized that their decision-making, through the exercise of discretion, had to accommodate for the diversity in their schools. These school leaders avoided implementing a policy when they believed it would not result in fair or just outcomes for students or when it did not "make sense" (Findlay, 2012a, p. 337) to them. The principals indicated that they would alter a policy in order to act fairly on the basis of such personal circumstances as poverty or ethnicity, but they did not appear to realize they were imposing their own values in their decision-making or to be aware of some of their assumptions. Nothing indicated, however, whether the principals' interpretation of a policy would guard against the negative effect of its implementation, or whether selective enforcement or avoidance of a policy may have adversely impacted their students.

Enforcement of Policy to Meet Perceived Needs

Research has indicated that policy implementation will be "more successful" if "the beliefs and attitudes inherent in the policy" are close to "existing norms," and that educators are most likely to implement a policy if they feel it offers a solution that is "an improvement to the status quo" (LaRocque & Coleman, 1985, p. 156). The decision-making practices of the principals interviewed in my study (Findlay, 2012a) are consistent with this finding, although in some cases individual principals may have interpreted successful policy implementation differently. For example, one principal's declaration that he would not "purposely be going out and finding ways to break" (p. 338) a policy, but that he was "not going to go out and follow it to the 'T' just to follow it to the 'T'" (p. 338) may reflect this finding. A principal's acceptance of a policy could be "related to compliance," while non-acceptance could be related to "noncompliance, symbolic compliance, or co-optation" (LaRocque & Coleman, 1985, p. 160). For instance, one principal found she could not support the implementation of a hat policy in her school. In other words, she "saw no need for it, judged the goals and assumptions of the policy to be incompatible with [her] own, and derived no sense of challenge or satisfaction" from its implementation (LaRocque & Coleman, 1985, p. 156). She indicated that "rules have to be established through kids ... if you don't want hats, you better have a reason why. I am not ignoring it. I will say no hat in the hallway ... if the hat goes by me, it is not going to be my first priority, frankly," and added that such rules were "stupid" and that she would exercise discretion in her decision whether or not to implement the hat policy (Findlay, 2012a, p. 338). As LaRocque and Coleman (1985) contend, educators are more likely to implement a policy if they feel it addresses "a real problem or need" (p. 156). Because the hat policy did not appear to align with an identified problem or need for their students, the principals were noncompliant. In much the same way, another administrator said he did "not feel any obligation" to enforce a policy that "is counterintuitive to what a child needs" (Findlay, 2012a, p. 339).

The principals' modification, adaptation, or overturning of system policies perceived to be impinging "unfairly on teachers, children, and families in their school community" was consistent with the results of Roche's (1999) investigation (p. 264).

Principals as Implementers of Policy

The findings of my study also supported LaRocque and Coleman's (1985) assertion more than twenty years ago that "there is little reason to believe that [educational] administrators, as part of their training, have developed a keen sense of their responsibilities as policy implementers" (p. 155). However, the principals in the study may have had a sense of their responsibilities as implementers of any given policy, but simply chose not to implement it for any number of reasons. Alternatively, perhaps they used "policy and regulations to evade decision responsibility" (Manley-Casimir, 2003, p. 271). If, however, policy-making is, as

Hodgkinson (1996) maintained, "decision making writ large" (p. 49) then administrators "directly or indirectly, formally or informally, by persuasion, influence, manipulation [or] control of information ... do in fact determine policy decisions" (p. 58).

Discretion Exercised to Balance Competing Interests

My research findings also suggested the principals understood discretion as a mechanism enabling them to balance individual and group interests in the school setting. Most administrators emphasized that finding this balance was a critical, ongoing aspect of their decision-making; they believed that the differentiation afforded them through the exercise of discretion allowed them to treat everyone fairly, or equitably, although not necessarily equally, and helped them to resolve the tension between competing rights and interests. Some principals appeared to believe that by exercising discretion in disciplining students, they could achieve a balance by supporting either equity or fairness. As one principal said, "I think that sometimes if we treat...what's the old thing about the difference between equality and equity? We cannot treat every kid the same and if we have a hard and fast rule we are not really teaching reality" (Findlay, 2012a, p. 260). Another principal suggested, "Equal is not always equitable. So I think I make it [a decision] based on what I know about the child...but I also see how it affects the rest of the school" (p. 260). In seeking to strike a balance between the rights of the individual and those of the rest of the school population, most principals indicated they exercised discretion in their decision-making based on what they thought was best for the entire group, depending upon the seriousness of the situation. One principal indicated her decision was "always for the greater good ... the safety and concern of all students," while another said he felt "it's not hard to bring them [stakeholders] to understand that it's not the rights of three or four people, it's the rights of the whole school" (p. 260). For the principals, finding a balance also depended upon their short- and long-term goals for individual students and for the advancement of the learning agenda, as well as for as the overall mission of the school. To this end, the principals understood they needed to maintain their authority and, more importantly, to be seen as maintaining it, in addition to building consensus, gaining support, and being reasonable. Other considerations affecting their decision-making as they sought to balance interests were the level of acceptability of the behaviour; the need for consistency in their decision-making; the reasonableness of the application of applicable rules, legislation, or policy; the seriousness of the disciplinary issue; and the availability of resources such as time and personnel.

Notion of Student Rights

Brown and Zuker (2007) briefly provided a historical context for children's rights when they described them as evolving from a pre-industrial society in which children were viewed as chattels or property of their parents, through an age of industrialism when children were seen as needing protection, to a post-industrial age when they are now seen as persons with human rights. Sitch and McCoubrey (2000) agreed, stating that "recognition of children as persons under the law is a twentieth century phenomenon," and that "children are currently accorded not only legal personhood but also the status of individual rights holder" (pp. 174–175) as set out in the *United Nations Convention on the Rights of the Child*.[4]

Interestingly, none of the principals indicated knowledge or awareness of the Canadian *Charter*, and few mentioned the notion of students rights in their discussion of balancing rights and interests, although these omissions do not mean the principals were unaware of rights or did not consider them while seeking to reconcile competing claims. When asked whether the rights of students would inform his decision-making, one of the principals replied that students "have the basic rights that every human being does. Do we need to have a *Charter of Rights* for students? Maybe, for some of those hardliners, but for me, no" (Findlay, 2012a, p. 345). Generally, the principals appeared inclined to interpret rights not as an entitlement, but in terms of a dominant notion of corresponding student responsibilities. They expected students to be responsible and

---

4 *United Nations Convention on the Rights of the Child*, 20 November 1989, United Nations General Assembly, Res. 44/25 [CRC].

to regulate their own behaviour so as not to infringe upon the rights of others in the school setting. Sitch and McCoubrey (2000) argued that "promoting and respecting students' rights might eliminate discipline issues through increased responsibility and respect for the rights of others" (p. 195). The principals, however, seemed to understand student rights as being limited, rather than supported, by their discretionary decision-making.

Trumping Rights for the Greater Good

In the realm of school safety, the principals appeared quite willing to trump individual student rights for a greater good—that of the entire school population usually, but not solely—and most principals indicated this norm or standard would be the basis for decision-making in order for the school to accomplish its goal of educating students. MacKay (2008) made this same point when he observed that administrators are apt to be "focused on the collective good and to be generally more comfortable in limiting individual rights in the name of the larger good" (p. 4).

The principals also firmly indicated their decision-making should send a message to the student body. One principal said that occasionally, "there is an individual in the building that, perhaps, is not keeping things for the general good ... kids have to learn that it is not always about me," (p. 346) whereas another affirmed her decision-making "is always for the greater good" (p. 346). These decisions could also be the path of least resistance. The principals' perception of the greater good is consistent with the study of Frick and Faircloth (2007), in which one participant believed that "the balance between the individual and the group was skewed more toward the group" and, that in fact, the "uniform treatment of all students" helped to meet the administrator's purpose (p. 26). The principals did not appear to consistently question whether the decision to support this greater good was, in fact, the least detrimental decision for all students involved and, if so, whether the decision was the correct way to achieve their own goal or purpose (Walker, 1998). In their decision-making, the "collective justification" (Hodgkinson, 1991, p. 98) of the principals may not have benefitted the individual student, respected his or her rights, or benefitted all members of the group, even though the principals assumed it did so.

Desire to Send a Message

The principals' desire to send a message about misbehaviour echoes, to some extent, the sentencing principles of deterrence and denunciation,[5] especially as these principles relate to youth justice under the *Youth Criminal Justice Act*.[6] This need to send a message was also linked to their need for accountability in, and justification of, their decision-making. All principals emphasized their decisions should indicate not only to students but also to other stakeholders the principals' own level of tolerance for misbehaviour, their sanctions for misbehaviour, and the application of fairness and justice. Cesaroni and Bala (2008) contended that "deterrence theory is based on the assumption that punishment can prevent future offending and it is linked to a belief that harsher punishments will reduce levels of crime" (p. 268). While the principals did not refer to social science research that suggests knowledge of harsher consequences will not deter youth's "offending behavior" (Bala, 2011, p. 10) they generally avoided imposing harsh sanctions for student misbehaviour in most disciplinary situations. However, the principals' support of less punitive consequences was juxtaposed against a belief that certain behaviours, such as bullying or racially-motivated acts, should be denounced as conduct that was particularly intolerable, and that in those cases they could use sanctions that had a "general deterrent effect" (Bala, 2011, p. 9). It is worthwhile to note that "general deterrence is not a principle of youth

5 Charron J. of the Supreme Court of Canada defines "deterrence" in *R. v. B.W.P.* (2006) as "the imposition of a sanction for the purpose of discouraging the offender and others from engaging in criminal conduct" (para. 2). When deterrence is aimed at the particular offender, "it is called 'specific deterrence'; when aimed at others, 'general deterrence'" (para. 2). The Court goes on to note that when general deterrence is factored into a sentence, the offender is "punished more severely... because the court decides to send a message to others" (para. 2). Denunciation is described as "'a symbolic, collective statement that the offender's conduct should be punished for encroaching on our society's basic code of values'" (Public Legal Education, 2012, p. 5).

6 *Youth Criminal Justice Act*, S.C., 2002, c. 1.

sentencing under the present regime [the *YCJA*]" (*R. v. B.W.P.*, para. 4), and that judges "cannot sentence one young person with the aim of sending a message to other youth" (para. 12).

Certainly, many criminal acts committed by young people are distinct from student misbehaviour in schools, yet the principals seemed unaware of any parallels that could be drawn between their disciplinary decision-making and the underlying notions behind the principles of deterrence and denunciation in youth sentencing. The principals appeared to understand the application of certain disciplinary consequences as being necessary to send a message to students or to denounce objectionable conduct. In arguing against the addition of denunciation and deterrence as sentencing principles under proposed amendments to the *YCJA*, Bala (2011) pointed to "the fact that moral development and judgment [of youth] are not fully developed until adulthood" (pp. 9–10). The findings of my study do not clearly reveal if the principals either understood or considered the stages of moral development and judgment in children and young people.

Balancing Competing Interests to be Fair

The principals also seemed to interpret justice and fairness as finding the proper balance between competing interests. One of the principals summed up this need to balance as much as possible the conflicting rights and interests of the individual and the group, stating "For me, it is very important that I can say to myself and go to bed at night and say 'I balanced these two things'" (Findlay, 2012a, p. 261). The high level of discretion delegated to the principals might leave the achieving of justice and the balancing of interests to the "judgment of individual officials" (Vorenberg, 1976, p. 676). As one principal realized, accommodating the interests and needs of all stakeholders may not always be possible when her collaborative decision-making in an incident involving a fight among girls in her school resulted in sustained criticism and solid resistance by her staff and colleagues. In her words, "mistakes happen when all the stakeholders are not considered and perhaps circumstances have not been communicated clearly...discretion is not a biased action ... but the ability to meet the needs particularly of the child...[and] to accommodate the needs of other stakeholders" (Findlay, 2012a, p. 349).

The principals understood the exercise of discretion as enabling them to be fair in their decision-making and to balance all interests, but in their attempts to resolve disciplinary issues, they may have unwittingly assumed the values of fairness and justice were "differentiated by degree rather than by kind" (p. 152), an error Hodgkinson (1991) called a "homogenetic fallacy" (p. 151) made by administrators. Justice and fairness seemed to be absolutes for the principals as they individually interpreted them, but, as Willower (1996) suggested, absolutes often break down in practice. However, the principals appeared to be primarily concerned with being perceived as fair by students and stakeholders and also to believe that, by creating this perception, their decisions created a "climate of mutual respect and justice" (Manley-Casimir, 1979, p. 25). The need for fairness also appeared to be related to the difficulty of reconciling decisions with consequences that may include the principals being accused of being either too harsh or too lenient. While they seemed to believe their exercise of discretion in reconciling competing interests and rights usually resulted in a perception of fairness among students, staff and stakeholders, the principals also understood that the dissatisfaction of students, staff and stakeholders indicated the exercise of discretion may not have achieved the fairness they so desired in balancing those interests.

Conclusion

Sossin's (2002) description of discretionary decision-making as often based on "assumptions, value judgments, first impressions and broader personal and ideological agendas which are rarely disclosed" (p. 835) seems especially apt. The appropriate and just exercise of discretion appears to require a precarious balance, which Lipsky (1980) characterized as being between "compassion and flexibility ... and impartiality and rigid rule application" (pp. 15–16). Principals may often be accused of abusing discretion and be "criticized for being too lenient, too harsh, discriminatory, racist, [or] preferential to athletes," so school administrators are encouraged to "use their discretion wisely" (Drizin, 2001, p. 40). In their discretionary decision-making in matters of student discipline, the principals in my study seemed, at times, to be positioned between the Charybdis of wide-ranging latitude, where capriciousness and arbitrariness dwell, and the Scylla of rigidity, where restrictive policies left them little room for flexibility or for differentiation in the treatment of students. Sitch and McCoubrey (2000) advocated for discretion that "must not remain totally unrestricted because it can be abused in ways that are contrary to our democratic values" (p. 196), yet a solid case can be made for delegating "broad discretionary jurisdiction," which allows principals to "maneuver in carrying out their complex tasks" (MacKay, 2008, p. 4). A more pragmatic course may involve delegating to decision-makers different levels of discretion for different types of student behaviour, given organizational "goals and structures" (Paquette & Allison, 1997, p. 181).

My study's (Findlay, 2012a) findings have implications for school administrators' practice and offer possibilities for enhanced discretionary decision-making. School administrators could acquire additional training in honing their analytical and investigative skills (Kajs, 2006) and in developing their judgment and decision-making abilities. These objectives might be achieved through "in-basket exercises" (Campbell-Evans, 1982, p. 101), case study analysis of experiences from administrators' own practices (Campbell, 1999), professional dialogue that explores the role of discretion in decision-making, and through increased administrator self-reflection and self-awareness that aim for a deepened understanding of the various values and influences upon disciplinary decision-making.

Furthermore, carefully worded school policies, clearly-defined rules for student discipline, and rule-making that "establishes" boundaries and "confines the power" (Manley-Casimir, 1974, p. 355) of administrators can help to limit the appearance of arbitrariness and to guide administrators in their decision-making and policy implementation. Requiring principals to offer defensible reasons for decisions may serve to dispel notions of capriciousness and may also provide an additional layer of accountability for them (Manley-Casimir, 1974). Howe and Covell (2010) urged for a decision-making framework based on the principle of the "best interests of the child," which must be a "primary consideration," and is based on "the interests of the whole child, informed by the principles and rights of the child, the views of children, and evidenced in outcomes" (p. 29). In the United States, Stefkovich and O'Brien (2004) also advocated for a similar model and offered practical applications of the best interests principle in decision-making, situating it within different ethical paradigms such as the ethics of justice, care, critique, community, and the profession. By building upon this notion of best interests, principals might be encouraged to gain a greater understanding of the *Convention on the Rights of the Child*, especially Article 28, which provides for assurances that "school discipline is administered in a manner consistent with the child's human dignity and in conformity with the present Convention" (*United Nations Convention on the Rights of the Child*, 1989).

Educators and principals "hold positions of great trust, confidence and responsibility" (La Forest, 1997, p. 137). Through the wise exercise of discretion in matters of student discipline, school administrators can work to meet their obligations skilfully and professionally, ensuring the rights of students are respected in the school setting. At that point, school officials and teachers will have begun to fulfill the twin imperatives of trust and duty required of them. Our students deserve no less.

References

Arum, R. (2003). *Judging school discipline: The crisis of moral authority.* Cambridge, MA: Harvard University Press.

Axelrod, P. (2010). No longer a 'last resort': The end of corporal punishment in the schools of Toronto. *The Canadian Historical Review, 91*(2), 261-285.

Bala, N. (2011). *Bill C-10 (Part 4)—Youth Criminal Justice Act Amendments.* Paper presented to House of Commons Committee on Justice & Human Rights, October 25, 2011. Retrieved from www.schoolofpublicpolicy.sk.ca/documentsevent announcements/Presentations/Bill%20 C-10%20YCJA%20amendments%20Bala Oct%202011.pdf.

Baumgartner, M.P. (1992). The myth of discretion. In K.O. Hawkins (Ed.), *The uses of discretion* (pp. 129-162). Oxford, England: Clarendon Press.

Brien, K. (2005). Disciplinary alternative to suspension: Options and considerations of high school vice-principals. In R.C. Flynn (Ed.), *Law as an agent of change in education* (pp. 1–28). Toronto, ON: CAPSLE

Brown, A.F., & Zuker, M.A. (2007). *Education law* (4th ed.). Toronto, ON: Carswell.

Campbell, E. (1999). Ethical school leadership. In P.T. Begley (Ed.), *Values and educational leadership* (pp. 151-163). Albany, NY: SUNY Press.

Campbell-Evans, G.H. (1988). *Nature and influence of values in principal decision- making.* Unpublished doctoral dissertation, The University of Toronto. Available from ProQuest Dissertations and Theses Database.

Canadian Charter of Rights and Freedoms, Part I of the *Constitution Act, 1982,* being Schedule B to the *Canada Act 1982* (U.K.), 1982, c. 11.

Canadian Foundation for Children v. Canada, [2004] 1 S.C.R. 76.

Cesaroni, C., & Bala, N. (2008). Deterrence as a principle of youth sentencing: No effect on youth but a significant effect on judges. *Queens Law Journal, 34*(1), 447-481. Retrieved from http://heinonline.org.

Clark, F.L. (2002). *Zero-tolerance discipline: The effect of teacher discretionary removal on urban minority students.* Unpublished doctoral dissertation, University of Texas at Austin. Available from ProQuest Dissertations and Theses Database (UMI No. 3099435).

Cornell, D.G., & Mayer, M.J. (2010). Why do school order and safety matter? *Educational Researcher, 39*(1), 7-15.

Cranston, N., Ehrich, L.C., & Kimber, M. (2006). Ethical dilemmas: The "bread and butter" of educational leaders' lives. *Journal of Educational Administration, 44*(2), 106-121.

Davis, K.C. (1969). *Discretionary justice: A preliminary inquiry*. Baton Rouge, LA: Louisiana State University Press.

Drizin, S. (2001). Arturo's case. In W. Ayers, B. Dohrn, & R. Ayers (Eds.), *Zero tolerance: Resisting the drive for punishment in our schools* (pp. 31-41). New York, NY: New Press.

Education Act, 1995, S.S., c. E.2. (Saskatchewan, Canada).

Findlay, N.M. (2012a). *The problem of the penumbra: Elementary principals' exercise of discretion in student disciplinary issues*. Unpublished doctoral dissertation, The University of Western Ontario, London, ON, Canada. Available from http://ir.lib. uwo.ca/etd/689.

Findlay, N.M. (2012b). At law's end: In-schools administrators' exercise of discretion in disciplinary decision making. In M. Manley-Casimir & A.D. Moffat (Eds.), *Administrative discretion in education* (pp. 15-47). Calgary, AB: Brush Education.

Findlay, N.M. (2014). Discretion in student discipline: Insight into elementary principals' decision making. *Educational Administration Quarterly*, 5, 1-36.

French, J. (10 January 2013). Plan aims to put aboriginal students on par with others, *Leader-Post*, A5.

Frick, W.C., & Faircloth, S.C. (2007). Acting in the collective and individual "best interests of students." *Journal of Special Education Leadership*, *20*(1), 21-32.

Gall, N.K. (2010). *Alternative education students' perceptions of the overall fairness of safe school rules, punishments, and rule enforcement practices in Ontario schools*. Unpublished master's thesis, The University of Western Ontario, London, ON, Canada.

Garner, B.A. (Ed.). (2009). *Black's law dictionary* (9th ed.). St. Paul, MN: Thomson Reuters.

Gelsthorpe, L., & Padfield, N. (2003). Introduction. In L. Gelsthorpe & N. Padfield (Eds.), *Exercising discretion: Decision-making in the criminal justice system and beyond* (pp. 1-28). Portland, OR: Willan.

Gregory, A., Skiba, R.J., & Noguera, P.A. (2010). The achievement gap and the discipline gap: Two sides of the same coin? *Educational Researcher*, *39*(1), 59-68.

Hall, M.T. (1999). *Administrative discretion and youth violence in schools: An analysis*. Unpublished doctoral dissertation, Simon Fraser University, Burnaby, BC, Canada. Retrieved from ProQuest Dissertations and Theses Database.

Handler, J.F. (1986). *The conditions of discretion: Autonomy, community, bureaucracy*. New York, NY: Russell Sage Foundation.

Handler, J.F. (1992). Discretion: Power, quiescence, and trust. In K. Hawkins (Ed.), *The uses of discretion* (pp. 331–360). Oxford, England: Clarendon Press.

Hawkins, K. (1992). The use of legal discretion: Perspectives from law and social science. In K.O. Hawkins (Ed.), *The uses of discretion* (pp. 11-46). Oxford, England: Clarendon Press.

Hawkins, K. (1997). Law and discretion: Exploring collective aspects of administrative decision-making. *Education & Law Journal, 8*(2), 139-160.

Hawkins, K. (2003). Order, rationality and silence: Some reflections on criminal justice decision-making. In L. Gelsthorpe & N. Padfield (Eds.), *Exercising discretion: Decision-making in the criminal justice system and beyond* (pp. 186-219). Portland, OR: Willan.

Haynes, E.A., & Licata, J.W. (1995). Creative insubordination of school principals and the legitimacy of the justifiable. Journal of Educational Administration, 33(4), 21-35. Retrieved from: http://proquest.umi.com.

Hodgkinson, C. (1991). *Educational leadership: The moral art*. Albany, NY: SUNY.

Hodgkinson, C. (1996). *Administrative philosophy: Values and motivations in administrative life*. Oxford, England: Pergamon.

Howe, R.B., & Covell, K. (2010). Towards the best interests of the child in education. *Education & Law Journal, 20*(1), 17-34.

Kajs, L.T. (2006). Reforming the discipline management process in schools: An alternative approach to zero tolerance. *Educational Research Quarterly, 29*(4), 16-25.

La Forest, G.V. (1997). Off-duty conduct and the fiduciary obligations of teachers. *Education & Law Journal, 8*(2), 119-137.

LaRocque, L., & Coleman, P. (1985). The elusive link: School-level responses to school board policies. *Alberta Journal of Educational Research, 31*(2), 149-167.

Larsen, D.E., & Akmal, T.T. (2007). Making decisions in the dark: Disconnects between retention research and middle-level practice. *NASSP Bulletin, 91*(1), 33-56.

Lipsky, M. (1980). *Street-level bureaucracy: Dilemmas of the individual in public services*. New York, NY: Russell Sage Foundation.

MacKay, A.W. (2008). Safe and inclusive schooling-expensive...quality education- priceless. For everything else there are lawyers! *Education & Law Journal, 18*(1), 21–55.

Manley-Casimir, M.E. (1974). The law: Catalyst for educational reform? *The School Review, 82*(2), 155-157. Retrieved from http://www.jstor.org/stabl e/1084105.

Manley-Casimir, M.E. (1977–78). Discretion in school discipline. *Interchange, 8*(1-2), 84-100.

Manley-Casimir, M.E. (1979). The rights of the child at school. *Education Canada, 19*(3), 9-13, 25.

Manley-Casimir, M.E. (2003). Understanding the human side of administrative enterprise: Greenfield's legacy as research agenda. In R. Macmillan (Ed.), *Questioning leadership: The Greenfield legacy* (pp. 259-272). London, ON: Althouse.

Manley-Casimir, M.E. (2012). Preface. In M. Manley-Casimir & A.D. Moffat (Eds.), *Administrative discretion in education* (pp. 6–13). Calgary, AB: Brush Education.

Marshall, C., Patterson, J.A., Rogers, D.L., & Steele, J.R. (1996). Caring as career: An alternative perspective for educational administration. *Educational Administration Quarterly, 32*(2), 271-294.

Osher, D., Bear, G.G., Sprague, J.R., & Doyle, W. (2010). How can we improve school discipline? *Educational Researcher 39*(1), 48-58.

Paquette, J., & Allison, D. (1997). Decision-making and discretion: The agony and ecstasy of law and administration. *Education & Law Journal, 8*(2), 161-181.

Public Legal Education Association of Saskatchewan. (2012). Changing perceptions, changing realities. *The PLEA, 31*(2).

R. v. B.W.P., [2006] 1 S.C.R. 941, 2006 SCC 27.

R. v. M.R.M., [1998] 3 S.C.R. 393.

Roche, K. (1999). Moral and ethical dilemmas in Catholic school settings. In P.T. Begley, (Ed.), *Values and educational leadership* (pp. 255-272). Albany, NY: SUNY Press.

Schneider, C.E. (1992). Discretion and rules: A lawyer's view. In K.O. Hawkins (Ed.), *The uses of discretion* (pp. 47-88). Oxford, England: Clarendon Press.

Shipman, G.A. (1969). Role of the administrator—policymaking as part of the administering process. In F.J. Lyden, G.A. Shipman, & M. Kroll (Eds.), *Policies, decisions, and organization* (pp. 121-137). New York, NY: Appleton-Century-Crofts.

Sitch, G., & McCoubrey, S. (2000). Stay in your seat: The impact of judicial subordination of students' rights on effective rights education. *Education & Law Journal, 11*(2), 173–202.

Smith, W., & Foster, W. (2009). Equality in the schoolhouse: Has the *Charter* made a difference? In M. Manley-Casimir & K. Manley-Casimir (Eds.), *The courts, the Charter, and the schools* (pp. 14-38). Toronto, ON: University of Toronto Press.

Sossin, L. (2002). An intimate approach to fairness, impartiality and reasonableness in administrative law. *Queen's Law Journal, 27*(2), 809-858.

Sossin, L. (2005). From neutrality to compassion: The place of civil service values and legal norms in the exercise of administrative discretion. *University of Toronto Law Journal, LV*(3), 427-447.

Stefkovich, J., & O'Brien, G.M. (2004). Best interests of the student: An ethical model. *Journal of Educational Administration, 42*(2), 197-214.

Torres, M.S., Jr., & Chen, Y. (2006). Assessing Columbine's impact on students' fourth amendment case outcomes: Implications for administrative discretion and decision-making. *NASSP Bulletin, 90*(3), 185–206.

Vinzant, J.D., & Crothers, L. (1998). *Street-level leadership: Discretion and legitimacy in front-line public service.* Washington, DC: Georgetown University Press.

Vorenburg, J. (1976). Narrowing the discretion of criminal justice officials. *Duke Law Journal, 4,* 651–609. Retrieved from http://heinonline.org.

Walker, K. (1998). Jurisprudential and ethical perspectives on "the best interests of children." *Interchange, 29*(3), 287–308. Retrieved from http://www.springerlink.com/content/102906/?sortorder=asc&po=134.

Webb, O. (2012). Student perceptions of discretion in discipline: Seeking resolution and restoration in a punitive culture. In M. Manley-Casimir & A.D. Moffat (Eds.), *Administrative discretion in education* (pp. 97–125). Calgary, AB: Brush Education.

Willower, D.J. (1996). Inquiry in educational administration and the spirit of the times. *Educational Administration Quarterly, 32*(3), 344-365.

Young, D.C., & Meyer, M.J. (2011). The Charter and special education litigation: Implications for discretion in decision-making. *EAF Journal, 22*(1), 75-86. Available from http:proquest.com.

Youth Criminal Justice Act, S.C., 2002, c. 1.

CHAPTER 3

Teacher Misconduct in Canada

Jerome G. Delaney

Abstract

This chapter examines the state of teacher misconduct in Canada, mainly in the provinces of British Columbia and Ontario. The author presents his four categories of teacher misconduct, including their definitions, statistics and real-life examples. Finally, this chapter presents some concrete strategies for curbing teacher misconduct and briefly describes four organizations involved with Education Law.

Introduction

Much of the literature on Education/School Law that discusses teacher misconduct in Canada speaks in generalities and provides little insight into the specifics of the misconduct, or the strategies that teachers may utilize to avoid situations that can cause them a great degree of anxiety and stress, and possibly even jeopardize their future in the teaching profession. One reason for this gap in the literature may be the secrecy surrounding teacher misconduct, and the lack of transparency perpetuated by teacher unions and school boards across Canada.

The major challenge for researchers wishing to study teacher misconduct in Canada is this lack of available information. In most provinces teacher misconduct of a non-criminal nature is handled primarily by school boards, and information about it is not shared with the general public. Consequently, discussing this topic from an academic perspective is challenging.

However, Ontario and British Columbia make teacher misconduct information available by publishing it online. In Ontario, teachers are certified and regulated by the Ontario College of Teachers (OCT). Its magazine, *Professionally Speaking*, is published four times a year and includes articles on professional development and teacher misconduct: investigations, dispute resolutions, and hearings.

Until 2011 in British Columbia, a similar organization, the British Columbia College of Teachers (BCCT), also certified and regulated teachers. Due to internal conflicts, the British Columbia government "decommissioned" this organization and transferred its responsibilities to the Teacher Regulation Branch of the British Columbia Ministry of Education. The BCCT also published *TC Magazine*, which was very similar to *Professionally Speaking*; this magazine regularly published specific details of teacher misconduct cases. The Teacher Regulation Branch of the British Columbia Ministry of Education has replaced *TC Magazine* with its own magazine, titled *LEARN*, which is published three times a year. This magazine's current issue, along with back issues, is posted on the Branch website. Each issue contains the section "Discipline Case Summaries," which deals with teacher discipline and discipline decisions.

This chapter will examine what teacher misconduct means and will categorize under four headings teacher actions which have created ethical, civil, and criminal difficulties for teachers. These categories are based on the author's reading of the teacher misconduct cases that have occurred in both Ontario and British Columbia in the past several years. One caveat here is that the reader should not assume that teacher misconduct is occurring in only those two provinces. Nothing could be further from the truth. We know from sporadic newspaper accounts across Canada that teacher misconduct occurs in all provinces; however, Ontario and British Columbia are the only two provinces this author is aware of that make teacher-misconduct information available to the general public. Hence, cases from only these two provinces are discussed in this chapter.

This chapter will also suggest a number of initiatives to help curb what this author considers as the ever-increasing malaise of teacher misconduct, and will also briefly describe four agencies involved with Education Law.

Defining Teacher Misconduct

The Florida Department of Education (n.d.) in the United States uses the following definition in one of its parent information sheets:

> Misconduct occurs in various forms and ranges in severity from allegations of direct harm to students (such as physical or sexual abuse) to an act detrimental to the education profession (such as falsifying documentation of continuing education courses or cheating on a professional exam). For the most part, misconduct by educators occurs either on the school campus or with members of the school community, but can also be something that happens outside of the school environment and does not involve students.

Two main topics are apparent in this definition: behaviour which causes direct harm to students, and behaviour detrimental to the education profession in general. Moreover, a significant aspect of teacher misconduct alluded to in this definition speaks to the professional misconduct directed at teachers and other educators by their colleagues, specifically fellow teachers and school administrators. Blasé and Blasé (2002) in their ground-breaking book *Breaking the Silence: Overcoming the Problem of Mistreatment of Teachers*, expose the various forms of misconduct teachers have been subjected to across North America. A fascinating read, the book is based on findings from the first-of-its-kind study conducted by the authors, in which they interviewed primary, elementary, junior high, and secondary teachers across the United States and Canada.

Categories of Teacher Misconduct

After examining the past several years of teacher misconduct summaries documented in *Professionally Speaking, TC Magazine*, and its successor, *LEARN*, this author developed four general categories of teacher misconduct for the purpose of better understanding the various types of misbehaviour teachers in Ontario and British Columbia are involved in. These categories are (1) misconduct occurring in the classroom, the school building and school grounds, and at the school board office; (2) misconduct of a sexual nature; (3) misconduct of a commercial crime nature occurring at the school building or at the school board office; and (4) misconduct occurring in the community at large and which may/may not be of a criminal nature (Delaney, 2012). A discussion of each of these categories with statistics and real-life examples follows.

Category 1: Misconduct Occurring in the Classroom, the School Building and School Grounds, and at the School Board Office

As the title suggests, this category refers to misbehaviour conducted by teachers and directed at students or colleagues in the classroom. Examples of this misbehaviour range from verbal or physical abuse of students, or verbal abuse of colleagues in front of students, to a failure to competently teach the prescribed curriculum to students. At the school board office, misbehaviour could range from professional staff refusing to fulfill their job duties as prescribed in their job definitions, to unethical and unprofessional exchanges about and between colleagues.

Statistics

In the first of two analyses conducted by the author (Delaney, 2012, 2013), teacher misbehaviour as described in Category 1 involved teachers in the province of Ontario. The Ontario College of Teachers (OCT) received 179 complaints in this category, dismissed 46 of them, referred one to another agency, and acted upon the remaining 132. These 132 complaints represented 54.8% of the total number of complaints of teacher misconduct (241) investigated by the OCT from 2007-2012.

In the second analysis, involving teachers in the province of British Columbia, 89 complaints under Category 1 were acted upon by the British Columbia College of Teachers (BCCT) and later, the Teacher Regulation Branch (TRB) of the British Columbia Ministry of Education. These 89 complaints represented 49.4% of the total number of complaints of teacher misconduct (180) investigated by the BCCT and later the TRB from 2007-2012.

Real-Life Examples

Example # 1 involves a teacher cautioned by the Investigation Committee of the OCT (Ontario College of Teachers, March, 2007). Following notification by an employer, the registrar of the OCT initiated a complaint against the teacher. The registrar alleged that while teaching junior and senior high students, the teacher used inappropriate language and shared unacceptable personal information, and made references to other teachers and students in the school. Following the investigation, the teacher agreed to complete a course of instruction, pre-approved by the registrar, regarding appropriate boundaries with students. The teacher agreed both to provide the College registrar with written notification upon successful completion of the boundaries course and to notify the registrar of any future complaints of a similar nature made by the employer.

A British Columbia teacher found guilty of professional misconduct by the British Columbia College of Teachers (BCCT) is the subject of example # 2 (British Columbia College of Teachers, Winter, 2008, p. 21). This male teacher engaged in inappropriate and harmful behaviour towards students in his class by regularly making insulting and derogatory comments about them. He also disciplined his students inappropriately through verbal abuse, physical force, and expulsion from the classroom. The BCCT issued a reprimand to this teacher.

Example # 3 involved a teacher in Ontario accused of six allegations of professional misconduct involving the use of inappropriate force against Grade 2 students (Ontario College of Teachers, March, 2007). In an agreed-upon statement, the teacher admitted to striking a male student on the forehead by using three fingers of his right hand and, on another occasion, to dragging a disturbed student from the class by the arm. The OCT's Discipline Committee ordered that the teacher appear before the Committee to be reprimanded and that the reprimand be recorded on the College's public registry. The Committee also ordered the College's registrar to suspend the teacher's certificates of qualification and registration for six months. However, the Committee further decided that this suspension be postponed for five months and would not be imposed if the teacher in question successfully completed, at his own expense, the Additional Qualification course, Special Education, Part II. The OCT noted that although the teacher's actions were relatively minor, the use of force against a student, except in extraordinary circumstances, is inappropriate and constitutes professional misconduct.

The last example (# 4) in this category of teacher misbehaviour comes from British Columbia (British Columbia College of Teachers, Winter, 2011, p. 21). A female teacher admitted to professional misconduct. While employed as a secondary school teacher, she was absent from her class on six occasions without authorization from her employer. She informed her class that she would be taking a university course during that time and made arrangements to have her class covered by another teacher. This teacher received her regular salary while she was away and made no arrangements to repay her employer for her time away from the class. She was issued a reprimand by the British Columbia College of Teachers.

Category 2 : Misconduct of a Sexual Nature

This misbehaviour refers to sexual abuse by teachers and according to Shakeshaft (2004) may be defined as follows:

> Sexual abuse may involve a wide range of behaviors that are often grouped into the broader category of sexual misconduct. Experts in this area who refer to sexual misconduct include such behaviors as physical contact (kissing, touching, fondling, and oral, anal and vaginal penetration), verbal communication (sexually related conversations, jokes, questions, personal information, and harassment), visual communication (webcam communication, sharing pictures of a sexual nature), and possession or creation of child pornography. (p. 20)

In a seminal Canadian study on sexual offending committed by Canadian teachers (Moulden, Firestone, Kingston, & Wexler, 2010), the authors offered this profile of victims:

> The victims had a mean apparent age of 11.8 years ($SD =$ 3.18), and ages ranged from 3 to 16 years. Victims were

slightly more likely to be female (56%), although no differences existed between male (M = 12.17, SD = 2.84)
and female (M = 11.43, SD = 3.40) victims with respect
to age. Using 12-years-old as a benchmark, 60% of victims
were adolescents. At the time of the offense, most victims
were living with either both (65%) or one (11%) parent(s).
In some cases, victims were living outside of the home in
either a correctional facility (9%), with relatives (7%), or
with a roommate (1%). However, in 15% of cases victims
defined their residence as "other." (p. 411)

Moulden et al. (2010) also summarized the nature of the various
sexual misconduct actions conducted by the teachers:

The most common sexual acts perpetrated included fon-
dling or hugging the victim, masturbation, and kissing. A
large proportion of offenders used minimal physical force
(49%), and none of the victims sustained any physical injuries as a result of the offense. Last, victims were released in
93% of cases. In 5% of cases the victim escaped, and in 2%
of cases the offense was interrupted or the victim was res-
cued. (p. 411)

Statistics

Very little research on teacher sexual misconduct in Canada has
been published, and consequently statistics for the total Canadian
teacher population are, to the best of this author's knowledge, not available. However, Shakeshaft (2004) does offer some statistical insight into
the United States context:

To get a sense of the extent of the number of students who
have been targets of educator sexual misconduct, I applied
the percent of students who report experiencing educator
sexual misconduct to the population of all K-12 students.
Based on the assumption that the American Association of
University Women (AAUW) surveys accurately represent
the experiences of all K-12 students, more than 4.5 million
students are subject to sexual misconduct by an employee

of a school sometime between kindergarten and 12th grade. (p. 18)

Shakeshaft (2004) acknowledged that the numbers stated in her study may have some limitations. However, surprisingly, she suggested that these limitations may have resulted in under-estimating the actual overall statistical picture in the United States (U.S.):

> Possible limitations of the study would all suggest that the findings reported here under-estimate educator sexual misconduct in schools. The limitations which might result in under-reporting are: (a) students report on their entire school career, thus making it difficult to determine prevalence by year or grade, (b) sample includes only 8th to 11th-graders, which might miss earlier incidents not remembered later; (c) questions on educator sexual misconduct are limited; (d) analysis was broad-brushed and cursory, excluding many details of educator sexual misconduct; and (e) survey only asked about incidents that were unwanted, excluding reports of misconduct that were either welcome or that did not fall into either a welcome or unwelcome category. (p. 18)

We should not extrapolate these U.S. numbers to our Canadian situation. However, given the increasing prevalence of teachers in Canada being involved in sexual misconduct with students, as reported in the media in recent years (*TC Magazine, Professionally Speaking, LEARN*), one can conclude that sexual misconduct by teachers is indeed a problem in Canadian schools. In the teacher misconduct cases in Ontario from 2007-2012, 32.8% of the complaints acted upon by the OCT were of a sexual nature (Delaney, 2012). In British Columbia, this percentage was 40.0% (Delaney, 2013).

Real-Life Examples

The first example involved a teacher in Ontario who was alleged to have repeatedly touched a female secondary school student on the shoulders and caressed her hair and face. He was also alleged to have massaged the neck of another female secondary school student when she was feeling ill. The Investigation Committee of the OCT ratified a memorandum of agreement between the member and the College in which the member: (a) agreed to be cautioned, in writing, by the Investigation Committee; (b) agreed to complete a course of instruction, pre-approved by the Registrar, regarding maintaining appropriate boundaries with students; and (c) agreed to provide the Registrar with written confirmation of successful completion of the course (Ontario College of Teachers, March, 2007).

Example # 2 involved a British Columbia male teacher who admitted to professional misconduct. A female Grade 12 student (who was a peer tutor in one of his classes) reported that he had been sending her inappropriate text messages over a period of time. At first, the messages appeared to be harmless but eventually became increasingly suggestive: Specifically: (1) "No, I wouldn't fail you. I might fail you if you didn't date me" and (2) "I got a good smell of you this morning and could feel your body through the fabric."

Later, the teacher sent the student a lengthy sexually explicit and graphic text message describing in detail specific sexual acts that would occur if they were to meet in his classroom in the evening. He suggested that she wear a skirt because it would be easier to take it off, that he would bend her over the counter and come at her from behind, and that she could "go down on her knees" and "finish him off" (British Columbia College of Teachers, Winter, 2011, pp. 22-23). The BCCT cancelled his teaching license.

The third example in this section involved a British Columbia teacher who was reprimanded for professional misconduct. He was teaching a Grade 9 Social Studies class, and one of his female students had a large, multi-coloured lollipop. The teacher commented on at least one occasion that someone should take a picture of her, and that it would be a cute picture.

After the class, the teacher suggested that the student step outside the classroom. He used his mobile phone camera to take a photo showing the student with the lollipop in her mouth, wearing a low-cut and somewhat revealing top. At the beginning of the new school year, the teacher presented the student with a mug with the photograph on it and told her to make sure she showed it to her parents. The parents were obviously not impressed. Very upset, they complained to the British Columbia Teacher Regulation Branch, and the teacher had his teaching certificate suspended for 5 days (British Columbia Teacher Regulation Branch, Spring, 2013, p. 27).

A male teacher in Ontario who had a sexual relationship with a Grade 12 female student is our example # 4. This relationship included his spending time alone with her, displaying her photographs in his office and hugging, kissing and touching her. Charged with sexual exploitation, this teacher was ordered by the court to have no contact with the student or the student's family. The teacher ignored this court order and exchanged several emails with the student. He pleaded guilty to the charge of exploitation, was fired by his school board and sentenced to 14 days in jail and 24 months of probation. Additionally, the OCT revoked his certificates of qualification and registration (Ontario College of Teachers, December, 2011).

Category 3: Misconduct of a Commercial Crime Nature Occurring at the School Building or at the School Board Office

This category involves activity whereby a teacher, school administrator or other educator is involved in the misuse of monies entrusted to the school or school board. The most common types in this category are theft, fraud, and the misappropriation of funds.

According to Hill and Hill (2005c), "theft" is a generic term for all crimes in which a person intentionally and fraudulently takes personal property of another without permission or consent and with the intent to convert it to the taker's use (including potential sale).

"Fraud" is defined as a false representation of a matter of fact—whether by words or by conduct, by false or misleading allegations, or by concealment of what should have been disclosed—that deceives and is intended to deceive another so that the individual will act upon it to her or his legal injury (Hill & Hill, 2005a).

"Misappropriation of funds" refers to the intentional, illegal use of the funds of another person for one's own use or other unauthorized purpose, particularly by a public official, a trustee of a trust, an executor or administrator of a dead person's estate, or by any person with a responsibility to care for and protect another's assets (Hill & Hill, 2005b).

Statistics

A U.S. website estimates that schools annually raise over 1.5 billion dollars (GreatSchools Staff, n.d.). Statistics are not available for Canada, but a conservative estimate would be in the millions of dollars range. With that amount of money being handled in schools across Canada, it is reasonable to surmise that a certain amount of fraud, theft and misappropriation of funds occurs in our schools.

In this author's review of the various case summaries of teacher misconduct in Ontario investigated by the OCT from 2007-2012, 2.9 percent of those investigations involved teacher misconduct of a commercial crime nature, the lowest percentage of the 4 general categories listed earlier (Delaney, 2012).

Similarly, in the author's review of the various teacher misconduct cases investigated in British Columbia from 2007-2012, 2.2 percent of those cases were of a commercial crime nature, again the lowest percentage of the 4 general categories referred to previously (Delaney, 2013).

Although these percentages in two Canadian provinces are relatively low, it is reasonable to suggest that with the amount of money being fundraised in Canadian schools each year, a significant amount of money is involved in this category of teacher misconduct.

Real-Life Examples

Example # 1 involved a male school administrator in British Columbia. In his capacity as treasurer of a local principals'/vice principals' association, he signed cheques made payable to himself in the amount of almost $29,000.00. This administrator claimed that these monies were for professional development, but he did not support this claim with substantiating documentation. By the time of his discipline hearing with the B.C. College of Teachers, he had paid most of the money back to the association. This administrator admitted to professional misconduct, and his certificate of qualification was cancelled for a period of no less than 5 years, so that he was barred from teaching in B.C. for at least 5 years (British Columbia Teacher Regulation Branch, Winter, 2012, p. 28).

This next example (# 2) involved an Ontario teacher who faced allegations of professional misconduct related to a criminal conviction for breach of trust. According to the *Criminal Code of Canada* (Gold, 2008),

> Everyone who, being a trustee of anything for the use or benefit, whether in whole or in part, of another person, converts, with intent to defraud and in contravention of his trust, that thing or any part of it to a use that is not authorized by the trust is guilty of an indictable offence and liable to imprisonment for a term not exceeding fourteen years. (p. 456)

The OCT's Discipline Committee heard evidence that this teacher, seconded by the Simcoe County School Board to chair the Insurance Trustees Committee, which managed the life and health benefits of school board employees, illegally transferred $286,593.21 from those benefits to his own bank account. He later resigned from this position, returned to the school board, apologized for this behaviour and returned the funds plus interest. Following an investigation, he was later fired by the school board. A criminal court gave him a sentence of 12 months to be served in the community and ordered him to complete 80 hours of community service over the first 435 days of his sentence.

The OCT Discipline Committee found that this teacher was guilty of professional misconduct and ordered his teaching license and registration revoked, meaning that he was no longer allowed to teach in Ontario (Ontario College of Teachers, June, 2007).

The third example of this type of teacher misconduct comes from British Columbia. A teacher twice took relatively small amounts of money from petty cash and did not keep the required proper accounting records or inform the staff that she had taken these monies. A video camera was set up in the school office and revealed the teacher entering the school office, opening the cash drawer, and making motions with her hands before closing the drawer. Staff found $20 in the drawer, and the teacher explained that she had placed the money in the drawer to repay money she had taken earlier. The teacher admitted to professional misconduct and was reprimanded by the B.C. College of Teachers. The district transferred her to another school (British Columbia Teacher Regulation Branch, Winter, 2013, pp. 29-30).

The final example (# 4) of this type of teacher misconduct involved a female teacher in Ontario. The Discipline Committee of the OCT held a hearing into allegations of professional misconduct against this teacher related to a criminal conviction for defrauding her board. Being a superintendent at the board, she had the authority to approve third-party invoices for payment. Specifically, she submitted false invoices in the name of a defunct board program in the amount of $95,493.21. Additionally, she used $1000 in board funds to buy her family Christmas presents, acquired cash from the board for her personal benefit, and further defrauded the board for a publisher's discount on textbooks. In criminal court, she was found guilty of fraud over $5000, sentenced to 18 months in prison, and ordered to pay the school board $159,000 in restitution. The Discipline Committee found her guilty of professional misconduct, and her certificates of qualification and registration were revoked, meaning that she could no longer be employed as a teacher in Ontario (Ontario College of Teachers, December, 2008).

Category 4: Misconduct Occurring in the Community at Large Which May/May Not Be of a Criminal Nature

This category involved behaviour committed by educators, not in schools or at school board offices, but in the community at large. Such behaviour may or may not contravene the *Criminal Code of Canada* but nevertheless brings disrepute to the teaching profession. Teacher associations across Canada all have codes of ethics or codes of conduct which speak to the conduct of teachers in general.

Consider this statement in the Code of Ethics developed by the Newfoundland and Labrador Teachers' Association (NLTA): "A teacher acts in a manner which maintains the honor and dignity of the profession" (NLTA, n.d.). Similarly, the Saskatchewan Teachers' Federation (STF) in its Code of Professional Ethics states that "[Teachers are] to act at all times in a manner that brings no dishonour to the individual and the teaching profession" (STF, n.d.). The Manitoba Teachers Society (MTS) includes the following statement in its Code of Professional Practice: "A member's conduct is characterised by consideration and good faith. She or he speaks and acts with respect and dignity, and deals judiciously with others, always mindful of their rights" (MTS, n.d.). A teacher is held to a higher standard of conduct than the ordinary citizen. The British Columbia Court of Appeal articulated this thinking in a decades-old ruling when it stated:

> Teachers must not only be competent, but they are expected to lead by example. Any loss of confidence or respect will impair the system, and have an adverse effect upon those who rely upon it. That is why a teacher must maintain a standard of behaviour which most other citizens need not observe because they do not have such public responsibilities to fulfil. (Covert, 1993, p. 441)

Statistics

In the author's review of teacher-misconduct cases, 7.9% of the Ontario cases came under this Category 4 heading, so that of all the cases the OCT acted upon from 2007-2012, 7.9% involved teachers in "misconduct occurring in the community at large which may/may not be of a criminal nature" (Delaney, 2012). In British Columbia, that percentage was 8.3 % (Delaney, 2013). Unfortunately, no national statistics are available for this category of teacher misconduct Canada-wide.

Real-Life Examples

This first example involved a British Columbia teacher who admitted to conduct unbecoming a member of the BCCT. In an access-dispute hearing with his former wife regarding their two children, this teacher advised her that he had surreptitiously videotaped sex acts between the two of them and threatened to send these sex tapes to her employer unless she agreed to his demands. He was arrested and charged with extortion under the *Criminal Code of Canada*, pleaded guilty to the lesser charge of engaging in threatening conduct against another person, and was given a one-year suspended sentence. The BCCT issued the teacher a reprimand, and he agreed not to return to teaching until certain conditions were met (British Columbia College of Teachers, Winter, 2009, p. 19).

Example # 2 involved a teacher in Ontario who attacked an acquaintance in his home, struck him on the head with a ceramic decoration, punched and wrestled him and stabbed him in the throat. The teacher then followed the man to a neighbour's house and when the elderly neighbour attempted to call 911, the teacher grabbed the phone and struck her with it. The teacher then assaulted the elderly neighbour's husband. The teacher pleaded guilty to one count of attempted murder and two counts of assault with a weapon; he was found guilty and sentenced to two years less a day in provincial prison, followed by three years of probation, which included anger management and counselling sessions (Ontario College of Teachers, March, 2011). The teacher was fired by his school board, and the OCT revoked his teaching certificate. This individual is highly unlikely to ever teach again.

The third example in this category involved a male teacher in British Columbia who used his 22-calibre rifle to shoot a dog in the yard across the street from his house. That dog had previously attacked the teacher's own elderly dog. He then fired his rifle twice more, missing the animal but hitting the neighbour's house. Prior to the police arriving, the teacher told a witness not to say anything to the police. The teacher was convicted of the careless use of a firearm and wilfully causing unnecessary pain, suffering or injury to an animal, pursuant to sections 86(1) and 445.1(1)(a) of the *Criminal Code of Canada* (British Columbia Teacher Regulation Branch, Spring, 2012, p. 28). The BCCT issued the teacher a formal reprimand for his behaviour.

Example # 4 involved a male teacher in Ontario who was suspended from teaching by the OCT for a period of eight months for breaking and entering the house of a colleague and stealing school property which he then sold privately. The teacher was convicted in criminal court, given a suspended sentence, placed on probation for six months and ordered to perform 50 hours of community service work (Ontario College of Teachers, September, 2010).

Curbing Teacher Misconduct

No single strategy exists for putting an end to all teacher misconduct. Rather, on a more pragmatic level, a number of different concrete strategies can be utilized to potentially reduce the number of teacher misconduct cases happening in Canada each year.

Legal Literacy of Educators

Teachers and school administrators' knowledge of education or school law is often referred to as "legal literacy." The United States research and literature in this area is fairly substantive compared to the Canadian research and literature. However, two studies done in Canada (Peters & Montgomerie, 1998; Snelgrove & Warren, 1989) examined the extent of educators' legal literacy.

Both studies, although rather dated, are still useful. They concluded that the legal literacy of teachers and school administrators was low. Specifically, Snelgrove and Warren (1989) concluded that "Educators' knowledge of the law seems to be far short of that required to function effectively in the litigious society in which they practise today" (p. 89). The Snelgrove and Warren study was limited to educators in Newfoundland and Labrador. The other study involved educators from the four western provinces only. Peters and Montgomerie (1998) reported, "Our study . . . revealed a high level of uncertainty, already referred to as self-confessed ignorance concerning rights in educational matters based in the Charter and found in the provincial statutes" (p. 45).

Educators' level of legal literacy in the United States may be perceived to be a little higher. In a United States study of public school teachers, Schimmel and Militello (cited in Eberwein, 2008) reported that only 14.3 % had taken a school law course as part of their teacher certification; 9.2% had taken a course since they started teaching; and only 4.9% had attended an in-service training session on school law. However, 87% of the principals surveyed in that study had completed a college- or university-level law course as part of their pre-service training, 19% had taken such a course since assuming the principalship, and 58%

had participated in a comprehensive school-law workshop or in-service training (cited in Eberwein, 2008, p. 173).

It is fair to say that the level of legal literacy both in Canada and the United States needs improvement. The challenge is how to achieve it. The author's experience in the Canadian school system suggests that most teachers and school administrators have little formal training in Education Law, but Canadian data on this topic is either very limited or non-existent.

Pre-service and In-service Courses in Education/School Law

Although this author has no empirical data to support this claim, he believes that most Bachelor of Education (B.Ed.) and Master of Education (M.Ed.) programs across Canada do not require a course in Education or School Law. His own Faculty of Education at Memorial University of Newfoundland offers a course in Education Law (Education 4641 – Legal Issues in Today's Schools) as an elective in the Bachelor of Education (Intermediate/Secondary) program, but this course is not available to students in the Primary-Elementary program. At the graduate level, an elective course in Education Law (Education 6335 – Legal Foundations of Educational Administration) is available to all students doing the M.Ed. program, especially students in the Educational Leadership Studies option.

Faculties of education across Canada do not appear to perceive Education Law as a priority in the undergraduate or graduate Education curriculum. A major reason for this perception could be that the general public is largely unaware of the various acts of teacher misconduct that happen regularly in the classrooms and schools across Canada and also of the profoundly negative impact such acts can have on our students.

Granted, some teacher criminal misconduct is reported in the print and electronic media, but much teacher misconduct is not criminal in nature and hence does not make its way into the court system. This non-criminal teacher misconduct is very often cumulative, and over time can result in teachers being removed from the teaching profession. The time and effort exerted in these eviction processes can be quite lengthy and exhausting, tying up scarce administrative resources in the schools. The approaches utilized are reactive as opposed to proactive. This author strongly advocates a proactive approach.

One such approach would be to ensure that all Bachelor of Education students are required to take a course in Education Law. Unfortunately, implementing this recommendation would be easier said than done, as a degree program can only accommodate so many courses, and individual faculty members are quick to promote their own subject areas. No easy solution exists for overcoming this challenge. Moreover, in faculties of education where Education Law is part of the required curriculum, the topics covered in the course must be carefully considered. Because there is never enough time in a university course to cover everything that should be covered, an emphasis on the practical as opposed to the philosophical and theoretical is highly recommended.

Topics should include the *Charter of Rights and Freedoms*, teacher codes of ethics/conduct, the provincial education/schools act, liability and negligence, sexual assault, corporal punishment, teacher-student boundaries, duty to report, bullying, due process, school fundraising, copyright law, teacher online conduct, and workplace safety. Although this list is by no means exhaustive, the university instructor will be challenged to ensure all these topics are covered in a meaningful way. Real-life case studies of teachers and school administrators who have gotten themselves into trouble, criminal and otherwise, should be utilized. Regular reference should be made to the OCT's *Professional Speaking* magazine and the B.C. Ministry of Education's *LEARN* magazine, which are excellent resources and easily accessible online to our students. Over time, enrolment in Education Law courses and significant exposure to the real-life examples under the four categories of teacher misconduct discussed earlier in this chapter would do much to increase the legal literacy levels of our educators across the country.

In-Service Professional Development in Education Law

In this author's 30 years in the Newfoundland and Labrador school system (15 years as a high school teacher and 15 years as a high school principal in 3 principalships), he attended one principals' session on school law. Presented by a local lawyer, the session was general in nature, and no mention was made of the *Canadian Charter of Rights and Freedoms*! Obviously, this session was not helpful to educators.

As alluded to earlier in this chapter, secrecy and an obvious lack of transparency in the area of teacher misconduct exist in most provinces across Canada except, of course, Ontario and British Columbia. Hence, teachers and school administrators in general are not sufficiently aware of teacher misconduct, especially that bordering on criminality.

Teacher associations across the country appear to be silent on the importance of Education/School Law for their members. Perhaps teacher associations believe that "ignorance is bliss," but for legal issues in our classrooms and schools, nothing could be further from the truth. Ignorance is definitely not bliss in educational matters, and such lack of knowledge could have profound and devastating effects on one's teaching career.

Organizations Involved in Educational Law

A number of organizations in Canada, not overly well known, are helpful to professionals involved in Education Law. This section will briefly describe the roles and functions of four of these organizations.

Canadian Association for the Practical Study of Law in Education
This organization, commonly referred to by its acronym, CAPSLE, is an offshoot from the U.S. National Organization on Legal Problems in Education, (NOLPE), which is now known as the Education Law Association (ELA). Relatively unknown in Canada, CAPSLE explained its role as follows:

> **CAPSLE** is a national organization whose aim is to provide an open forum for the practical study of legal issues related to and affecting the education system and its stakeholders. Our members include teachers, administrators, board members, trustees, unions, school board associations, educators, academics, students, government and lawyers (www.capsle.ca).

Established in 1989, CAPSLE publishes a quarterly newsletter titled CAPSLE COMMENTS, which highlights current court cases dealing with Education Law. Its website is a treasure trove of Education Law information, including back copies of CAPSLE COMMENTS as well as the various papers presented at its annual conference, held in a different cities across Canada each year. Membership is open to anyone interested in the legal aspects of Education.

The **Canadian Legal Information Institute** (CanLII) is a non-profit organization managed by the Federation of Law Societies of Canada. CanLII's goal is to make Canadian law accessible for free on the Internet. This website (www.canlii.org) provides access to court judgments, tribunal decisions, statutes and regulations from all Canadian jurisdictions. This website is an excellent source of information for all legal matters, including Education Law material.

Ontario College of Teachers: Referenced several times in this chapter, the Ontario College of Teachers (OCT) (www.oct.ca), licenses, governs and regulates the teaching profession in Ontario. Specifically, the OCT (a) sets ethical standards and standards of practice, (b) issues teaching certificates and may suspend or revoke them, (c) accredits teacher education programs and courses, and (d) investigates and hears complaints about members (www.oct.ca).

The OCT publishes a magazine titled *Professionally Speaking* 4 times a year; back issues are available on the College's website. Each issue includes 3 sections of particular interest to those who work in the area of Education Law: investigations, dispute resolutions and hearings. In addition to these sections, articles on professional development are also included. A sampling of articles in the March, 2014 issue included the following: "Remarkable Teacher," "Transition to Teaching," and "Breaking New Ground."

British Columbia Education's Teacher Regulation Branch: On its website (www.bcteacherregulation.ca), this division of B.C. Education described its role as follows: "We assess applicants for certification, evaluate teacher education programs, issue teaching certificates, and enforce standards for certificate holders." This division took over this regulatory role after the British Columbia College of Teachers was decommissioned by the British Columbia government in 2012.

As part of its mandate, the division also publishes a magazine titled *LEARN* 3 times a year. One of the regular articles is "Discipline Case Summaries" of educators who have gotten themselves into either ethical, criminal, or civil difficulty. Other articles are on professional development. The Spring, 2014 issue included the following articles: "Dollars and Sense: BC's new Math curriculum highlights financial literacy;" "Connected BC: A new student information system for the province," and "A focus on boundaries for educators."

Concluding Comments

This chapter discussed teacher misconduct in schools across Canada. In most Canadian provinces and territories, with the exception of two, teacher misconduct is a closely kept secret from the general public. Ontario and British Columbia can be commended for their transparency with respect to teacher misconduct and also for their two respective publications, *Professionally Speaking* and *LEARN*, which regularly inform their readers about specific cases of teacher misconduct.

Teacher pre-service and in-service programs obviously need to address the concerns generated by the teacher-misconduct cases in Ontario and British Columbia. Although we do not hear about, to any significant degree, the teacher-misconduct cases in other parts of Canada, we would be naïve to assume that teacher misconduct is not happening in Canada's other provinces and territories. To continue to ignore the need for Education/School Law courses in teacher-preparation programs is tantamount to negligence of the highest order. School boards and professional teacher associations have been somewhat inactive in this area of in-service. A course in Education/School Law, pre-service or in-service, would not prevent all teacher misconduct, but it would potentially help to reduce the high level of teacher misconduct that we are currently experiencing. Our students deserve nothing less.

References

Blasé, J., & Blasé, J. (2002). *Breaking the silence: Overcoming the problem of mistreatment of teachers.* New York: Corwin.

British Columbia Teacher Regulation Branch (n.d.). Retrieved from http://www.bcteache rregulation.ca.

British Columbia College of Teachers (Winter, 2008). *TC Magazine.* Retrieved from http: //www.bcteacherregulation.ca/documents/TC/2008/TCMagazine_Winter2008.pdf

British Columbia College of Teachers (Winter, 2009). *TC Magazine.* Retrieved from http: //www.bcteacherregulation.ca/document/TC/2009/TCMagazine_Winter2009.pdf.

British Columbia College of Teachers (Winter, 2011). *TC Magazine.* Retrieved from http: //www.bcteacherregulation.ca/documents/TC/2011/TCMagazine_Winter2011.pd.

British Columbia Teacher Regulation Branch (Winter, 2012). *Learn Magazine.* Retrieved from http://www.bcteacherregulation.ca/docu-ments/Learn/2012/LearnMagazine_ Winter2012.pdf.

British Columbia Teacher Regulation Branch (Spring, 2012). *Learn Magazine.* Retrieved from http://www.bcteacherregulation.ca/documents/Learn/2012/LearnMagazine_ Spring2012.pdf.

British Columbia Teacher Regulation Branch (Winter, 2013). *Learn Magazine.* Retrieved from http://www.bcteacherregulation.ca/docu-ments/Learn/2013LearnMagazine_ Winter2013.pdf.

British Columbia Teacher Regulation Branch (Spring, 2013). *Learn Magazine.* Retrieved from http://www.bcteacherregulation.ca/documents/Learn/2013/LearnMagazine_ Spring2013.pdf.

British Columbia Teacher Regulation Branch (March, 2014). *Learn Magazine.* Retrieved from http://www.bcteacherregulation.ca/documents/Learn/2013/LearnMagazine_ Spring2013.pdf.

Canadian Association for the Practical Study of Law in Education (n.d.). Retrieved from www.capsle.ca.

Canadian Charter of Rights and Freedoms, Part I of the *Constitution Act, 1982,* being Schedule B to the *Canada Act 1982* (U.K.), 1982, c. 11.

Canadian Legal Information Institute (n.d.). Retrieved from www.canlii.org Covert, J.R. (1993). Creating a professional standard of moral conduct for Canadian teachers: A work in progress. *Canadian Journal of Education, 18*(4), 429-445.

Criminal Code, R.S.C. 1985, c. C-46.

Delaney, J.G. (2012). *Teacher misconduct in Ontario, Canada.* A presentation to the 2012 annual conference of the Canadian Association for the Practical Study of Law in Education (CAPSLE). Ottawa, ON, Canada.

Delaney, J.G. (2013). *Teacher misconduct in British Columbia, Canada.* A presentation to the 2013 annual conference of the Canadian Association for the Practical Study of Law in Education (CAPSLE). Winnipeg, Canada.

Eberwein, H.J. (2008). *Raising legal literacy in public schools, a call for principal leadership: A national study of secondary school principals' knowledge of public school law* (Unpublished doctoral dissertation, University of Massachusetts Amherst). University of Massachusetts Amherst, Amherst, MA.

Florida Department of Education (n.d.). *Misconduct.* Retrieved from http://www.fldoe.or g/edstandards/misconduct_parent_faq.asp.

Gold, A.D. (2008). *The practitioner's criminal code.* Markham, ON: LexisNexis.

GreatSchools Staff (n.d.). *Raising money for your school.* Retrieved from http://www.gre atschools.org/improvement/volunteering/13-raising-money-for-your-school.gs.

Hill, G., & Hill, K. (2005a). *Fraud.* Retrieved from http://legal-dictionary.thefreedictiona ry.com/fraud.

Hill, G., & Hill, K. (2005b). *Misappropriation.* Retrieved from http://legal-dictionary.thef reedictionary.com/misappropriation.

Hill, G., & Hill, K. (2005c). *Theft.* Retrieved from http://legal-dictionary.thefrreedictionar y.com/theft.

Jaffe, P., Straatman, A., Harris, B., Georges, A., Vink, K., & Reif, K. (2013). Emerging trends in teacher sexual misconduct in Ontario 2007-2012. *Education and Law Journal, 23*(1), 19-39.

Manitoba Teachers' Society (n.d.). *Code of professional practice.* Retrieved from http://w ww.mbteach.org/inside-mts/professionalcode.html.

Moulden, H.M., Firestone, P., Kingston, D.A., & Wexler, A.F. (2010). A description of sexual offending committed by Canadian teachers. *Journal of Child Sexual Abuse, 19*(4), 403-418.

Newfoundland and Labrador Teachers' Association (n.d.). *Code of Ethics.* Retrieved from https://www.nlta.nl.ca/files/documents/memos_posters/code_of_ethics.pdf.

Ontario College of Teachers (n.d.). Retrieved from www.canlii.org.

Ontario College of Teachers (March, 2007). *Professionally Speaking.* Retrieved from http ://professionallyspeaking.oct.ca/march_2007/.

Ontario College of Teachers (June, 2007). *Professionally Speaking.* Retrieved from http:/ /professionallyspeaking.oct.ca/june_2007/go_hearings.asp.

Ontario College of Teachers (December, 2008). *Professionally Speaking.* Retrieved from http://professionallyspeaking.oct.ca/December_2008/.

Ontario College of Teachers (September, 2010). *Professionally Speaking.* Retrieved from http://professionallyspeaking.oct.ca/september_2010/go/hearings.aspx.

Ontario College of Teachers (March, 2011). *Professionally Speaking.* Retrieved From http://professionallyspeaking.oct.ca/march_2011/go/hearings.aspx.

Ontario College of Teachers (December, 2011). *Professionally Speaking.* Retrieved from http://professionallyspeaking.oct.ca/december_2011/go/ hearings.aspx.

Ontario College of Teachers (March, 2014). *Professionally Speaking.* Retrieved from http://professionallyspeaking.oct.ca/march_20141/go/ hearings.aspx.

Peters, F., & Montgomerie, C. (1998). Educators' knowledge of rights *Canadian Journal of Education, 23*(2), 29-46.

Shakeshaft, C. (2004). *Educator sexual misconduct: A synthesis of existing literature.* Retrieved from http://www2.ed.gov/rschstat/research/pubs/ misconductreview/rep ort.pdf.

Saskatchewan Teachers' Federation (n.d.). *Code of professional ethics.* Retrieved from www.stf.sk.ca.

Snelgrove, V., & Warren, P. (1989). *Legal rights in education.* St. John's, NL: Memorial University of Newfoundland.

Legal and Policy Issues Arising from Professional Learning Communities

Ken Brien

Abstract

P rofessional learning communities (PLCs) have been widely promoted and implemented by school systems in recent years. As they represent a significant culture change from the traditional bureaucratic model of schooling, PLCs give rise to challenges to existing laws and policy in education. With reference primarily to New Brunswick legal and policy documents, this chapter examines the principles of PLCs and the legal and policy implications of their implementation at the school, district, and provincial levels of the school system.

Over the past 10 to 15 years, many school systems have promoted and adopted professional learning communities (PLCs) as a means of improving teaching and learning in their schools. Governments and governmental agencies have endorsed the implementation of PLCs (e.g., Alberta's Commission on Learning, 2003; New Brunswick Department of Education, 2007; Organisation for Economic Co-operation and Development (OECD), 2005). Schools in the 21st century are working with students and teachers in a context of dramatic and continuous change, including the continuing evolution of the knowledge society and advances in technology (Williams & Brien, 2009). As Hartle and Hobby (2003) pointed out, the growing importance of knowledge puts a premium on learning and requires that educators rethink the respective roles of teachers and learners. The growth of the knowledge society has also led to an increased emphasis on student achievement in 21st century schools (Male & Palaiologou, 2015). With improved student learning as a goal, PLCs can be seen as a means to ensuring good instructional practice (Levin, 2008).

The move towards PLCs is fundamentally a shift in the organizational culture of a school, a school district, and a provincial or national school system. Organizational culture is generally defined as the norms, values, and beliefs that develop over time within an organization (e.g., Hoy & Miskel, 2005; Owens & Valesky, 2011). In simple terms, the *norms* refer to what is the right way to do things, the *values* to what is important, and the *beliefs* to what is true—according to the people who inhabit an organization. In education, laws and policies express the formally accepted norms, values, and beliefs that exist within our school system. A transformation of the culture of an organization requires, then, that its members adapt to the influence of new norms, values, and beliefs that may clash with well-embedded and widely accepted aspects of the prevailing culture. This type of cultural change requires, according to Fullan (2005), tri-level educational reform: at school, district, and provincial or national levels of the school system. As a result, the legal and policy frameworks that govern all levels of our school system will have an influence on, and will be affected by, the implementation of PLCs in schools.

The purpose of this chapter is to summarize and to clarify our understandings of the concept of PLCs as found in academic literature and to examine selected legal and policy issues that arise with the implementation of PLCs in the public school system. I will aim to show that the adoption of authentic PLCs represents a significant challenge to existing laws and policies that often reflect the mental models of schooling from the past.

The Concept of Professional Learning Communities

Educators and educational policy makers are increasingly looking towards the concept of PLCs as a means to transform the culture of our public schools to achieve sustainable improvements in student learning. But what are PLCs? What are the key characteristics of a PLC? In this section, we will look at the concept of PLCs as represented in international academic literature in order to respond to these questions.

It is important to begin with a clear understanding of the concept of PLCs, particularly as we think about legal and policy issues that arise from their implementation. While the term PLC is commonly used in schools in Canada and elsewhere, understandings and applications of the term vary widely among users. In the context of school reform initiatives, Fullan (2005, cited by DuFour, Eaker, & DuFour, 2005) observed that *terms* travel well, but that the underlying *conceptualization* and *thinking* do not (p. 9). This applies to the idea of a PLC and the variety of related terms, meanings, and understandings used by academics, professionals, and policy makers to define and apply the concept. DuFour (2004) observed that the term PLC has been applied to every combination of individuals with an interest in education. He commented that the PLC model had reached a critical juncture in the school reform process where "initial enthusiasm gives way to confusion about the fundamental concepts driving the initiative" (p. 6). Fallon and Barnett (2009) pointed out that efforts to create learning communities based on superficial understandings of authentic community often result merely in "pseudo communities." Watson (2014) commented: "The term has become so ubiquitous it is in danger of losing all meaning" (p. 19). The predictable outcome of this confusion, based upon the fate of many other well-intentioned educational reform attempts, is a cycle of difficulty, disappointment, and disillusionment for educators and education stakeholders.

The conceptual roots of PLCs can be traced to Senge's influential 1990s work on *learning organizations* that originated in the corporate world and later addressed schools (e.g., Senge, Kleiner, Roberts, Ross, & Smith, 2000). Senge (1990/2007) built his concept of a learning organization around five disciplines: systems thinking, personal mastery, mental models, building shared vision, and team learning (pp. 6 – 10). Hill and Crévola (2003) described the concept of a learning organization to include the notion of a group of individuals committed to a collective purpose who engage in systematic, collaborative problem-solving that results in continuous improvement and transformation to adapt to external change. In contrast to the paradigms of the industrial age,

Senge's concept of learning organizations is more closely associated with today's knowledge society. Commenting on Senge's work with respect to public education, Hartle and Hobby (2003) observed that our understanding of how people learn has changed, so that old assumptions about schooling are being challenged. Sackney, Walker, and Mitchell (2005) described learning in a knowledge society as the ability to create, to solve problems, to think critically, to unlearn and relearn, to deal with the environment, and to develop a lifelong learning capacity. The technical-rational school model is a part of a greater bureaucracy that was designed to meet the training needs of a more stable industrial society. It is, however, incapable of dealing with the demands for flexibility and creativity requisite for a knowledge-based society (Hargreaves, 2003).

Mitchell and Sackney's (2001) Canadian research into *learning communities* centred on the concept of building capacity within schools. They identified three types of capacity that are necessary for schools to grow as learning communities: personal, interpersonal, and organizational. In their model, personal capacity refers to the amalgam of all embedded values, assumptions, beliefs, and practical knowledge that educators carry with them and of the professional networks and knowledge bases with which they connect. Consequently, building personal capacity entails searching one's professional networks to locate new and different ideas. Interpersonal capacity shifts the focus from the individual to the group, and emphasizes collegial relations and collective practice. Mitchell and Sackney argued that interpersonal capacity is as much about how people relate to one another as it is about the dominant normative culture in the school. They claimed that a collaborative culture that fosters professional learning is enhanced by attention to affective conditions, cognitive processes, and support for necessary phases. Organizational capacity deals with the structural conditions in which a school community operates. Mitchell and Sackney pointed out that a learning community requires a different kind of organizational structure from that found in traditional schools. In particular, their model recommended significant changes in the nature of teacher interactions with each other, professional development delivery, and power relationships between teachers and administrators.

In a meta-analysis of the literature, Mullen and Schunk (2010) analyzed PLCs using three theoretical frames: leadership, organization, and culture. In their analysis, they identified the effects of leadership practices, organizational structures, and school culture on learning. With reference to PLCs, they observed that "the concept of professional learning is not new but the practical side of developing professional communities that are reciprocal, democratic, and sustainable is more recent" (p. 200). They also advocated for collaborative mentoring as a means to build organizational capacity, generate social capital, and positively impact communities.

Stoll, Bolam, McMahon, Wallace, and Thomas (2006) conducted a review of the international literature on PLCs. Although they acknowledged that there is no universal definition of PLCs, and that there may be shades of interpretation of the concept in different contexts, they claimed that there was a broad international consensus emerging about the purpose and nature of PLCs. They summarized the literature on PLCs by highlighting five key characteristics: shared values and vision, collective responsibility, collaboration, reflective professional inquiry, and the promotion of group and individual learning. This list of features appears to capture the core concepts of PLCs as described throughout the literature. For the purposes of this chapter, I will use this list as the basis for my discussion of legal and policy implications of PLCs.

Legal and Policy Implications of Professional Learning Communities

The dominant model for many organizations in our society, including the school system, can be described as hierarchical and bureaucratic. In his classic work, Max Weber (1964/2005) described the following principles of bureaucracy: (a) there is the principle of fixed and official jurisdictional areas, generally ordered by laws or administrative regulations; (b) there are principles of hierarchy and graded authority, which mean that there is a firmly ordered system of supervision of those in lower offices by those in higher offices; (c) the management of an office is based upon written documents; and (d) the management of an office follows general rules, which are more or less stable, more or less exhaustive, and which can be learned. In Weber's view, bureaucracy represents the epitome of administrative rationality based on the assumption of a largely impersonal organization in which people's work is governed by rational rules and structures and not influenced by interpersonal considerations or external forces (Fineman, Gabriel, & Sims, 2010). Bureaucratic organizations are often described using the metaphor of a machine as a way of representing the order, stability, and predictability expected from them.

By contrast, the emergence of the knowledge society in recent decades has led to different views of organizations, particularly those that emphasize the more complex and organic nature of human behaviour and interactions within organizations. In particular, Senge's (1990/2007) work on learning organizations emphasized *systems thinking* as one of his five disciplines. Systems thinking supports the metaphor of organizations as living organisms, with interactions occurring among the people in an organization and also with forces from the external environment.

In today's school system, we can see evidence of both types of organizational thinking. We see the bureaucratic model alive and well in today's schools, districts, and provincial government departments. In every province, there are provincial statutes, regulations, and policies that set out the duties and powers of teachers, principals, superintendents, elected trustees, parents, and government officials in the public education system. These provincial documents are often supplemented by corresponding policies and regulations enacted at the district and school levels. For aspiring and beginning leaders in the school system, orientation sessions led by superiors often include emphasis on examining and learning applicable provincial and district policies as integral to their job duties. In short, the four bureaucratic principles of Weber (1964/2005) described above are clearly in evidence.

On the other hand, the pressure on school systems to deliver improved student learning outcomes has led to efforts to move schools beyond the order, stability, and predictability of bureaucracy towards a more dynamic emphasis on teaching and learning. The adoption of PLCs is result of both the desire for improved learning outcomes and the greater recognition of schools as complex, living ecosystems of children and adults working together with a focus on learning. However, in the push for improved student achievement, these two organizational models continue to compete. As pointed out by Hargreaves and Fink (2006), the standards movement in education, particularly in North America, has been driven largely by bureaucratic assumptions of teaching and learning. However, Hargreaves and Fink provided evidence that this standards approach is largely unsustainable and argued instead for school leaders to adopt more sustainable principles such as depth, length, breadth, justice, diversity, resourcefulness, and conservation, all of which are consistent with a view of schools as living systems and communities of learners. In a report on sustainable school improvement in Alberta, Foster, Wright, and McRae (2008) found that "sustainability is enhanced when schools and districts are professional learning communities" (p. 7).

Since the bureaucratic model of schooling emphasizes rules, while the tenets of PLCs focus on collaborative, collective, and learning-centred efforts, it is clear that legal and policy tensions will arise in the implementation of PLCs in the school system. In particular, areas of concern include the following: shared decision-making, collaboration, and professional learning practices. In our examination of these issues, some relevant legal and policy documents will include education legislation, teacher-employer collective agreements, and teacher association policy documents. For the purposes of this paper, I will be using New Brunswick documents as the primary source for laws and policies to allow for greater clarity and depth of analysis.

Shared Decision-Making

In their review of literature on PLCs, Stoll et al. (2006) included two characteristics that speak about shared decision-making: shared vision and values, and collective responsibility. It is certainly true that the *community* element of a professional learning community emphasizes the commonality or the shared aspects of teaching and learning in schools. According to Watson (2014), "community embodies notions of belonging and this necessarily involves consideration of identities" (p. 26). In his work on *communities of practice*, with a focus on community and social learning, Wenger (2000) identified three elements of communities of practice: joint enterprise, mutuality, and shared repertoire. The communitarian nature of PLCs emphasizes personal connections among educators and the shared nature of their professional learning and work.

Shared Vision and Values

To what extent do existing laws and policies address the development of shared vision and values in education? Schools are a microcosm of our society. With the increasing diversity within our countries, our cities, and our schools, it is not always clear what we hold in common, what we want to see in our schools, and what values we share. As Watson (2014) pointed out, questions arise about shared vision and values: "What exactly is it that is shared (and how is this sharing accomplished); which (whose) values are valued; and what is the nature of the 'and' between vision and values?" (p. 22). Using New Brunswick legislation as an illustration, let us examine the process prescribed by law for the development of vision and values at the provincial, district, and school levels. According to the New Brunswick *Education Act* (1997), the Minister of Education has the duty to set out the broad educational goals for public schools: "The Minister ... shall establish educational goals and standards and service goals and standards for public education" (s. 6(a)). The Minister is also required to provide a provincial education plan (s. 6(a.1)), which is defined by the *Act* as follows: "A detailed plan establishing priorities for the improvement of pupils' educational performance towards the achievement of prescribed learning goals" (s. 1). At the district level, there is a similar legislative requirement for the elected District Education Councils (DECs) to establish a three-year district education plan (s. 36.9(1)). The district plan is to be consistent with the provincial education plan and shall include "a vision, including a mission statement, goals and values" (s. 36.9(2)(a)). The superintendent of the district has "primary responsibility for the preparation and implementation of the district education plan" (s. 48(2)(c)). At the school level, the corresponding document is the school improvement plan and the duties of principals include "preparing, in consultation with the Parent School Support Committee and the school personnel, a school improvement plan" (s. 28(2)(a)). Each New Brunswick school is required to have a Parent School Support Committee (PSSC) (s. 32(1)), a body with six to 12 members, a majority of whom are parents of students enrolled at the school. The school improvement plan is subject to review by the DEC (s. 36.9(5)(d)).

There are several observations to be made about the development and articulation of vision and values in New Brunswick's provincial school system as prescribed by legislation. The first is that each document, whether at the provincial, district, or school level, is expected to include an articulation of some combination of goals, vision, values, and mission. Second, there is one person at each level who is given the primary responsibility for preparing this document: the Minister of Education, the superintendent, and the school principal have this responsibility at the provincial, district, and school levels respectively. While there are requirements for consultation by the principal with the PSSC and for approval by the DEC for the superintendent, it appears that the Minister is not required to consult with anyone in the development of the provincial education plan. Third, there appears to be a hierarchical structure to the development of these three plans. In particular, the district education plan must be consistent with the provincial education plan (*Education Act*, 1997, s. 36.9(2)) and, as noted above, a school improvement plan is subject to review by the DEC (s. 36.9(5)(d)). While the legislation does provide some scope for the PSSC to advise the principal on matters related to the school mission, culture, and climate in relation the school improvement plan (s. 33(1)), it is unlikely that the plan presented by the principal to the superintendent and to the DEC, particularly with respect to the vision and values of the school, would be allowed to vary greatly from the provincial or district plans.

Collective Responsibility

So what do we make of the apparent absence of any reference to *shared* vision and values in the New Brunswick legislation? What do these provisions say about collective responsibility at these three levels of the school system? Let us consider first the exercise of collective responsibility at a single school. As noted earlier, one of the key characteristics of school-based PLCs is shared decision-making. Since the educators in a school-based PLC, including teachers and administrators, share collective responsibility for the learning environment for students in their school, it follows that teachers should share in school-based decision-making. If the power of a learning organization is to be unleashed by drawing upon the collective wisdom and commitment of all educators within a school, then it makes sense for teachers to participate in important decisions that fall within the range of their expertise and responsibility (Louis, Marks, & Kruse, 1996). However, legal barriers to this aspect of PLCs can arise from the statutory duties of teachers and principals.

Under the New Brunswick *Education Act* (1997), the duties of teachers, as listed in section 27, include the delivery of the *prescribed* curriculum and *assistance* in the development and implementation of the school improvement plan. Section 27 also states that teachers are accountable to the superintendent through their principals. By contrast, according to section 28, the statutory duties of principals specify that they are the educational leaders and administrators in their schools and that they have overall responsibility for their schools and their staff. Moreover, principals are accountable to their superintendent for the performance of their duties and for the overall educational progress of their students.

These two sections of the New Brunswick *Education Act* (1997) appear to provide both barriers and opportunities for shared decision-making in schools. Clearly, the legislation indicates that principals are to be the educational leaders in their schools. While this does not mean that principals are not allowed to consult with teachers in their schools, there is certainly no requirement that they do so. Moreover, since principals are accountable to their superintendents for their performance and that of their students, they certainly cannot delegate that responsibility to their teachers. Regardless of the consultative process that principals may choose to use with their teachers, the legislation makes it clear that principals are ultimately and solely accountable to the superintendent for the educational outcomes of school decisions. Furthermore, since teachers are accountable to superintendents through their principals, and principals have overall responsibility for their teachers, this means that teacher responsibility for their individual and collective decisions is filtered through their principals. In other words, principals bear the bulk of responsibility for the decisions made by teachers, regardless of the process or motivation behind these decisions. While the legislation allows for participation in decision-making, it does not allow for collective responsibility for school decisions.

The New Brunswick *Education Act* (1997) also appears to place some limits on shared decision-making in curriculum matters. While the duties of teachers include "identifying and implementing learning and evaluation strategies that foster a positive learning environment aimed at helping each pupil achieve prescribed learning outcomes" (s. 27(1)(b)), their duties are also limited to "implementing the prescribed curriculum" (s. 27(1)(a)). This means that New Brunswick teachers may be responsible for the *how* of curriculum delivery, but the *Act* clearly indicates that the *what* of curriculum delivery is to be prescribed by others. Indeed, section 6 specifies that the Minister has the power to prescribe education programs and section 6.1 allows DECs, with the approval of the Minister, to develop instructional programs tailored to their local communities. While these provisions do not prevent teachers and principals from making shared decisions on curriculum delivery issues, they certainly place clear boundaries on the scope of such collective decision-making. Furthermore, since principals are accountable for "the overall educational progress of the pupils enrolled in the school" (s. 28(1)(b)), they may allow and encourage teachers to reach some curriculum delivery decisions collectively, but principals will still be held accountable for the outcomes of these decisions. The extent to which principals may want to engage in shared decision-making in curriculum matters will depend on their level of trust in the collective wisdom and ability of their teachers.

It is interesting that the New Brunswick *Education Act* (1997) does identify the school improvement plan as one area in which teacher participation is not only allowed, but is actually required. The duties of a New Brunswick teacher include assisting in the development and implementation of the school improvement plan (s. 27(1)(g)). Unlike curriculum matters, where teachers' duties are limited to making implementation decisions, teachers are expected to assist in the development and implementation of school improvement plans. With this statutory expectation in place, not only can principals invite teachers to participate in the decision-making process associated with the school improvement plan, but teachers would also be entitled to expect—and perhaps, when necessary, insist on—a role in the process. It is noteworthy that the school improvement plan is also subject to input from other education stakeholders, notably the PSSC and the DEC. The PSSC is required to advise the principal on the establishment, implementation, and monitoring of the school improvement plan (s. 33(1)). As noted earlier, the DEC is also required to review the school improvement plan for each of its schools (s. 36.9(5)(d)). Although the scope is strictly limited, it appears that New Brunswick legislators chose the school improvement plan as a vehicle for shared decision-making at the school level.

But what about collective responsibility of educators at the district and provincial levels? If PLCs represent a tri-level reform of the school system, as noted earlier by Fullan (2005), then to what extent is the principle of collective responsibility reflected in education laws and policies? For example, if teachers are legally required to participate in the development of school improvement plans, it would be logically analogous for principals to be similarly involved in the development of district education plans. As noted earlier, in New Brunswick the superintendent has the primary responsibility for developing this document. While there is nothing in the legislation to prevent the superintendent from inviting the participation of principals, the New Brunswick *Education Act* (1997) makes no provision for participation of principals in developing the district education plan. Indeed, section 28 of the legislation, which lists the legal duties of principals, makes no reference to any duties or expectations beyond their assigned schools. If we take the analogy of collective responsibility to the provincial level, one would expect that district superintendents would have a role in decision-making at the provincial level under the leadership of the Minister of Education and provincial department officials. However, the statutory duties of a New Brunswick superintendent include accountability to the DEC (s. 48(1)) and a list of district-related tasks and responsibilities (s. 48(2)), but, as with principals, superintendents do not appear to have any legal duties beyond the schools in their districts.

Collaboration

Stoll et al. (2006) found collaboration to be another key characteristic of PLCs in the literature. Indeed, a collaborative culture flows readily from an environment of shared values and collective responsibility. The root meaning of *collaboration* is co-labouring or working together. McGregor (2003), in a British study of three comprehensive schools, found that teachers identified the concept of collaboration as working together for a common purpose through sharing of values, knowledge, ideas, facilities, and materials. She also observed that, while there was consensus in articulating the theory of collaboration, actual descriptions of the practice varied widely among respondents. Riveros, Newton, and Burgess (2012) pointed out that current descriptions of PLCs have emphasized a shift from individual to collaborative approaches to teaching and learning. Fullan (2007) described this change as deprivatizing teaching, where teachers observe other teachers, are observed by other teachers, and participate in debate about the quality and effectiveness of their instruction. He pointed out, however, that this type of collaborative practice represents a cultural change from a deeply rooted norm of privacy and requires some risk-taking by teachers and leaders. Indeed, teacher collaboration does not always occur naturally, but requires conditions such as common planning time, supportive teacher supervision and evaluation practices, and trusting professional relationships.

Common Planning Time

If teachers are expected to collaborate, they need the time to do so with their colleagues during the workday. Consequently, Louis et al. (1996) described common planning time as an important feature of school-based PLCs. In order for teachers to work together to enhance student learning, it is necessary to structure the school day so that this can happen. In the traditional organizational structure, teachers work in isolation in their own classrooms to plan lessons for their own students. There are two main legal and policy sources that affect the assignment of common planning time for teachers. The first is the statutory and regulatory requirements concerning the school day and the allocation of instructional time within the school day. The second is the negotiated teacher-employer collective agreement provisions governing assigned duties and teacher entitlements to preparation time during the school day. In New Brunswick, the Minister of Education is required to provide from 4.0 to 5.5 hours of instructional time per day, exclusive of the noon recess, with the number varying according to the grade level of students (*School Administration Regulation*, 1997, s. 3(2)). Furthermore, school hours are defined to include all the time between the opening and closing of school for the day (s. 3(1)).

More detail concerning the school year, including hours of instruction, teacher preparation time, and other time commitments of New Brunswick teachers, is found in the teacher-employer collective agreement (*Agreement between Board of Management and the New Brunswick Teachers' Federation* (NBTF Agreement), 2012). It is noteworthy that the New Brunswick collective agreement contains the following specific provision concerning conflicts between provincial education regulations and the collective agreement: "In cases of direct conflict between provisions of the *Regulations* under the *Education Act* and any clause of this Collective Agreement, the latter shall prevail" (Article 12.01). In cases where the provincial legislature passes a law that nullifies some section of the collective agreement, the employer and the teachers' federation are to renegotiate a replacement provision, and the parties may seek arbitration if agreement cannot be reached (Article 12.02). These provisions are necessary in the New Brunswick context because the employer is defined to include the Department of Education and Early Childhood Development (Article 1.01). Clearly, if the government were empowered to override the collective agreement unilaterally through legislation, then that would seriously undermine the integrity of the negotiations process and any subsequent agreement reached.

According to the NBTF Agreement (2012), there are minimum and maximum daily hours of instruction for students in Kindergarten to Grade 2 (K – 2), Grades 3 to 8, and Grades 9 to 12 (Article 18.01). The minimums are 4.0 hours in K – 2, 5.0 hours in Grades 3 to 8, and 5.5 hours in Grades 9 to 12 and correspond to the instructional time specified in the *School Administration Regulation* (1997, s. 3(2)). At each level, the maximum hours of daily instruction are set at half an hour more than the respective minimum. Teachers are also entitled to preparation time, where local circumstances permit, of not less than 35 minutes per day or the equivalent over a longer period of time (Article 19.01). A significant aspect of this provision is that this preparation time is to occur "within the hours of instruction during which teachers are required to teach and students are required to remain in class" (Article 19.01). There are two other provisions, one in the collective agreement and one in the regulations, which are relevant to the issue of the scheduling of common planning time for teachers. According to Article 18.02, teachers recognize that their professional responsibilities may require the performance of their duties beyond the hours of instruction described in Article 18.01. In addition, according to the *School Administration Regulation* (1997), "a teacher shall ... attend all meetings called by the principal of the school or ... superintendent of the school district" (s. 25(1)(j)).

Within the legal and regulatory provisions set out for the school day and teachers' assigned working hours, there are two observations that can be made with respect to whether existing regulatory conditions support common planning time as part of the implementation of school-based PLCs. The first is that there appears to be some flexibility in the allocation of instructional time. While the regulations and the collective agreement give the times in terms of hours per day, the regulations do allow for the instructional time to be allocated in an equivalent fashion over the course of the school year (*School Administration Regulation*, 1997, s. 3(2)). Using this flexibility, the school district in Fredericton, for example, altered its school schedule many years ago to allow for students to be dismissed from elementary schools at noon on Wednesdays by adding approximately 30 minutes of instructional time to each of the other four school days each week. This arrangement permits elementary teachers to have common planning and professional development time on Wednesday afternoons on a regular basis.

The second observation is that the collective agreement appears to require that the 35 minutes of daily preparation time assigned to teachers occur during the school day while students are required to be in class (NBTF Agreement, 2012, Article 19.01). This means that a principal who wants to arrange for common planning time using teachers' preparation time needs to find a way to schedule this time for teachers and ensure that students are still being taught during this time. If, for example, the principal wanted to arrange for all the Grade 4 teachers to hold a common planning meeting during the school day, then the principal would need to find some way to provide instruction to the Grade 4 students while their teachers were attending the meeting. Some creative solutions have included large-group student activities in the gymnasium or somewhere similar supervised by school administrators or other teachers without assigned classroom duties during that time. Principals need to be cautious about ensuring that legitimate curriculum instruction is being delivered in these large-group activities and also about the assigned teaching time of those called upon to supervise the students during these times.

Teacher Supervision and Evaluation

Teacher collaboration can be affected by policies governing teacher supervision and evaluation. Principals who want to promote collaboration among their teachers would want to know if collaborative skills and behaviours can be included among the criteria used for the supervision and evaluation of their staff. Conversely, can teachers be disciplined by their employer for failing to participate in collaborative activities, either during or outside the school day? If teachers engage in a collaborative learning venture that is not successful in some way, do all these teachers share in the responsibility for the failure? What if some teachers really did not support the collaborative initiative, but were required to take part anyway? Senge (1990/2007) referred to *mental models* among the components of a learning organization. Mental models refer to the embedded ways of thinking of people in an organization. For learning and change to occur, members of an organization need to expose and then challenge their mental models. In our schools and our culture, one of the mental models is individual responsibility. In schools, for example, students expect that their academic standing and grades will be based on their individual performance, not that of others. When students participate in group assignments, there is often resentment if the performance of one or more members of a group appears to negatively affect each member's individual grade. The questions posed about teacher responsibility for collaborative ventures reflect that same mental model. Principals may similarly reflect that same mental model when they are reluctant to delegate responsibility or tasks to teachers when they know that they will be held accountable for the results.

If teachers were to be judged on their collaborative skills and participation as part of their performance evaluation, then this would need to become more widely accepted within the profession. There are efforts within the profession to promote the expectation of collaborative practice. For example, the document entitled *21st Century Standards of Practice for Beginning Teachers in New Brunswick* (n.d.) includes this expectation: "Teachers collaborate with colleagues and related professionals interdependently as a team in promoting and nurturing the academic, physical, emotional and social safety and development for all students in their classes." There is a further statement about teacher collaboration in a recent New Brunswick 10-year education plan entitled *Everyone at Their Best* (Province of New Brunswick, 2016). In reference to efforts to promote literacy among students, the document stated that school staff members are to take collaborative action: "Throughout the school day and across curricular areas, educators and support staff will identify and promote current and authentic opportunities to engage in meaningful literacy learning" (p. 2). In New Brunswick, teacher supervision and evaluation are based on a professional growth model. For example, teachers in the Anglophone West School District (2014) are required by district policy to submit professional goals to their principals in the first month of each school year. Principals could certainly promote increased collaboration as a professional goal for their teachers as part of this process, and hold them accountable for specific behaviours to meet this expectation. If collaboration required meetings to be held outside of school hours or beyond the specifically allocated preparation time, New Brunswick principals could rely on the provision in the *School Administration Regulation* (1997) noted earlier that requires teachers to attend all meetings called by the principal (s. 25(1)(j)).

The NBTF Agreement (2012) provides guidance with respect to teacher performance evaluations. Teachers are entitled to prompt notification of any concerns with their performance that have been placed in their official file: "A teacher must be informed within a reasonable period of time of any problems or difficulties observed with respect to his/her performance" (Article 55.04(b)). If teachers have corrected the performance issue, they are entitled to have any unfavourable report removed from the file within a reasonable time (Article 55.04(c)). It is important to note that teachers can be disciplined only on the basis of materials contained in their official file (Article 55.05) and that teachers are entitled to be notified of any unfavourable items placed in their file (Article 55.04(a)). If principals have concerns about teachers' performance with respect to collaboration, the collective agreement thus provides guidance for the process to be followed to ensure teacher compliance with collaborative expectations.

Like any change in prevailing norms, however, it will take time for such a change to take hold. Employers may need to provide additional resources and training to support these new expectations. In the NBTF Agreement (2012), the section on technological change, while not strictly relevant, is instructive. Article 60 refers to technological change in reference to the introduction of new equipment and "a change in the manner in which the Employer carries on its operations" in direct relation to this equipment. Under the terms of Article 60.03, the employer is required to provide training, and it shall be voluntary for teachers if this training is organized outside school hours. The tone of this section suggests that if increased teacher collaboration were to be mandated and were to significantly change the expectations placed on teachers' work, then the teachers' union may expect the employer to allocate resources to in-service and other support during the school day to help teachers meet these expectations.

Trusting Professional Relationships

Apart from structural considerations, such as common planning time and supervisory practices, the existence of trusting professional relationships is at the heart of collaborative practice among educators. In any human organization, the level of trust and respect among members is a crucial aspect to its operations. Wasonga and Murphy (2007), in a study of 25 aspiring school administrators in the United States, found that efforts to co-create leadership in schools can fail because of a lack of trust. Their study found that trust was not commonly found in schools, a situation with far reaching consequences for school governance and student outcomes. Accordingly, trust and respect have been shown to be core elements of positive school culture (Louis et al., 1996). This is especially important in a PLC because of the enhanced levels of interpersonal interaction. According to Macmillan, Meyer, and Northfield (2005), trust is a reciprocal relationship that is not automatic but is negotiated and earned. They claimed that without trust some teachers might retreat to the minimal requirements with regard to instruction, and resist becoming involved in school improvement efforts.

Teacher codes of ethics typically include provisions that govern relationships among teachers. In particular, a common requirement is that teachers refrain from unfairly undermining the confidence of others in their colleagues. For example, the *Code of Professional Conduct* of the Alberta Teachers' Association (ATA) (2004) requires that a teacher "not undermine the confidence of pupils in other teachers" (s. 12). If it is necessary for an Alberta teacher to criticize the work of a colleague, a very specific process is mandated: "The teacher criticizes the professional competence or professional reputation of another teacher only in confidence to proper officials and after the other teacher has been informed of the criticism" (s. 13). According to the *Code of Professional Conduct* of the New Brunswick Teachers' Association (NBTA) (2011), criticism of a fellow teacher is unethical under the Code of Ethics except in three situations:

> It shall be unethical for a teacher to ... criticize a fellow teacher except (i) when demanded or authorized by law or workplace policies; (ii) in response to enquiries for factual information by the administrative staff, in carrying out the normal course of their duty to the employer; or (iii) where warranted to protect the interests of the profession. (s. 2(d))

While the ATA code allows a teacher to take the initiative to criticize a colleague through a defined process, it appears from the language of the NBTA code that the New Brunswick teacher is normally expected to take a more passive role by expressing criticism of a colleague only if asked or in limited circumstances.

Teacher codes of ethics, including the provisions cited above, are relevant to the issue of teacher collaboration in PLCs. In the traditional model of schools, teachers generally work alone in their own classrooms with their own students. Any collaboration on teaching matters with colleagues would normally be voluntary and the presence of a teacher in a colleague's classroom would normally occur only by invitation. It would also be understood that a teacher would not become involved with another teacher's students except when invited or authorized to do so. This latter point is noted in the code of ethics of the Ontario Teachers' Federation (OTF) (2014): "A member shall ... avoid interfering in an unwarranted manner between other teachers and pupils" (p. 7, s. 18(1) (a)). The only teachers normally authorized to exercise some presence in another teacher's classroom would be principals, vice-principals, and, in some cases, department heads or lead teachers. The language in the OTF document reflects the cultural norm for teachers to respect the professional autonomy of their colleagues and their dealings with their students.

In a PLC, however, this norm is challenged because of the expectation that teachers would be working together much more frequently, regularly, and intensively. If teachers spend time planning lessons and units together, and perhaps co-teaching larger groups of students, it is more likely that they will have to work out differences in pedagogical philosophy, instructional methods, and overall teaching style. These differences can lead to conflict and criticism that must be addressed. When teachers work separately in their own classrooms, these differences are less likely to draw criticism from colleagues since teachers would accept that their colleagues are responsible for their own students. This new context of PLCs requires teachers to develop and practice enhanced collaborative and conflict resolution strategies with their peers. While teacher pre-service and in-service programs generally prepare teachers to work with students, including dealing with teacher-student and student-student conflict, it is now more important that pre-service and novice teachers receive training or professional development in dealing with teacher-teacher conflict as part of their preparation for working collaboratively in PLCs. Hoaglund, Birkenfeld, and Box (2014) provided a helpful and timely report on efforts to build collaborative skills in pre-service teachers in a teacher education program at their university in Alabama. Administrators, school district officials, university faculty members, and teacher association staff need to work in cooperation to reconcile the ethical implications of teacher collaboration.

There is some evidence that the time required for teachers to collaborate, and the ways in which PLCs are structured in some schools, may be eroding the quality of trusting relationships within schools and districts. Some teacher unions have been vocal about these concerns. For example, the New Brunswick Teachers' Federation (NBTF) (2010) reported on discussions between its representatives and those of the employer on the topic of the number of meetings being held after the hours of instruction (p. 6). Although there was consensus on the types of meetings that teachers must attend, there was concern that some districts were not providing sufficient guidance to schools about an acceptable number of these meetings. The NBTF urged that the number of these meetings be monitored to avoid undue burden on teachers.

A sharper rebuke of the practices of PLCs, particularly with respect to the level of authentic and voluntary collaboration, came from the Elementary Teachers' Federation of Ontario (ETFO) (2007):

> Although ETFO recognizes the potential of this new structure, it is becoming increasingly aware of situations where the Professional Learning Community is not collaborative, where shared decision-making is not the norm, where the PLC is under-resourced, and the focus is only on improving student results on EQAO tests. (p. 1)

ETFO went on to express support for PLCs under several conditions, including that teacher participation is voluntary and that sufficient resources are provided to enable teachers to meet and collaborate during the school day, exclusive of teacher preparation time and meal breaks. The NBTF (2010) expressed a similar concern about teachers being directed to meet during their preparation periods for PLC meetings, taking the position that teachers cannot be directed to meet for PLCs during their preparation time as a violation of the spirit of Article 19 of the collective agreement (NBTF Agreement, 2012). Writing on behalf of the British Columbia Teachers' Federation, Naylor (2007) observed the problematic dichotomy of some writing on PLCs: positive messages of collaboration tempered with prescription and control (p. 2). Naylor takes particular issue with the following statement by DuFour et al. (2005): "Educators must develop a deeper, shared knowledge of learning community concepts and practices, and must then demonstrate the discipline to apply those concepts and practices in their own settings if their schools are to be transformed" (pp. 9 – 10). Naylor's opposition to the prescriptive language ("educators must") in reference to PLCs was supported by Hargreaves and Fink (2006): "Professional learning communities can't be forced; they can only be facilitated and fed" (p. 129). Hargreaves and Fink also commended PLCs as a means to create focus and cohesion among a diverse community of teachers with demonstrable but differing skills and talents, provided that PLC members are not restricted to externally prescribed priorities.

Building a collaborative culture clearly requires more than a legislative or policy mandate. While it certainly requires the allocation of necessary resources, especially time for collaborative work, and the use of appropriate supervision and evaluation practices, most important is the creating and sustaining of trusting professional relationships. The responses of teacher unions to aspects of PLC implementation in some schools and districts suggest that the level of trust may be inversely proportional to the extent of recourse by teachers to laws, regulations, and collective agreement provisions. In other words, a high-trust, collaborative culture consistent with the principles of PLCs will emphasize relationships over rules, in contrast to the impersonal, rule-oriented bureaucratic culture described by Weber (1964/2005).

Professional Learning Practices

While shared decision-making and collaboration are essential components of authentic PLCs, they are not ends in themselves. Professional learning communities are fundamentally about *learning*. To this end, Stoll et al. (2006) included reflective professional inquiry and an emphasis on individual and group learning in their list of key characteristics of PLCs. These two aspects of PLCs are clearly related to the professional learning practices of educators. A manifestation of reflective professional inquiry is the growing emphasis on the use of data by educators to guide instructional decisions. This emphasis on data, particularly student learning data, has also led to increased attention to the professional learning of teachers and how this is linked to student learning. However, discussions about professional inquiry and learning raise legal and policy questions for PLCs. Who decides what teachers learn? What is the responsibility of teachers for their professional learning?

Senge (1990/2007) identified team learning as a key element of learning organizations. In an authentic PLC, the learning of educators would flow from the shared vision and values, and would take place in a collaborative culture. By contrast, in the bureaucratic model of organizations described by Weber (1964/2005), the hierarchical structure includes the expectation that superiors exercise supervision over the work of subordinates. Consequently, in the school system, this would suggest that it is the responsibility of principals, superintendents, and provincial department of education officials to direct and provide the necessary professional learning opportunities to classroom teachers. In the New Brunswick *Education Act* (1997), for example, the duties of principals include "encouraging and facilitating the professional development of teachers and other school personnel employed at the school" (s. 28(2)(e)). Provincial policy on inclusive education (New Brunswick Department of Education and Early Childhood Development, 2013), known in New Brunswick as *Policy 322*, is more explicit about the role of provincial and district officials to provide professional learning to teachers: "The Department of Education and Early Childhood Development (EECD) and districts must establish and maintain a professional learning program to ensure that educational staff have the knowledge and skills needed to provide effective instruction to a diverse student population" (s. 5.2). As noted earlier, the New Brunswick Minister of Education has the legal duty to establish educational goals (*Education Act*, 1997, s. 6(a)) and the corresponding authority to establish provincial policies (s. 6(b.2)) consistent with the Act. *Policy 322* represents the enactment of the vision of inclusive education described as "the pairing of philosophy and pedagogical practices that allows each student to feel respected, confident, and safe so he or she can participate with peers in the common learning environment" (s. 3). It is interesting that this definition of inclusive education goes on to claim that "these values and beliefs will be shared by schools and communities" (s. 3). In fact, the prescriptive tone of this document suggests that its values and beliefs would be more accurately described as *mandated* rather than shared.

New Brunswick teachers are legally recognized as professionals. For example, the New Brunswick *Family Services Act* (1980) includes principals and teachers in list of professional persons with respect to the reporting of suspected child neglect or abuse (s. 30(10)). One of the typical expectations of any professional is to maintain one's competence. Indeed, the New Brunswick *Education Act* (1997) provides that the duties of a teacher include "maintaining his or her professional competence" (s. 27(1)(f)). In today's knowledge society, teachers must engage in continuous professional learning to maintain their competence, including both pedagogical and content knowledge. Accordingly, the *21st Century Standards of Practice for Beginning Teachers in New Brunswick* (n.d.) include the following provision: "Teachers understand their role as professional educators within their profession and demonstrate their commitment to professionalism through continuing learning and improvement" (s. 3(c)).

But to what extent are teachers encouraged or allowed to direct their professional learning, either individually or within the collaborative context of PLCs? According to the NBTA (2010), building a culture of professional learning takes time, requires strong beliefs, and is a process (p. 3). The NBTA's statement of beliefs regarding professional development includes the following: "Maximum effectiveness in professional development is achieved through a balanced approach, one in which choices are available and encouraged in relation to the identified needs of both educators and the organization" (p. 3). Shirley (2015), in reference to professional development days organized by the NBTA, emphasized the importance of professional learning organized "by teachers, for teachers" (p. 24), while chiding some teachers who do not take full advantage of these days for their learning. She referred to the provisions of the provincial collective agreement that allocate days for professional development. According to the NBTF Agreement (2012), Article 36.01 allows teachers to have eight days each school year for professional development and other related activities. In particular, Article 36.02 provides that three of those days will be for subject council workshops or conferences mutually arranged by the provincial teacher associations and the Department of Education and Early Childhood Development. Article 36.04 allocates four days of professional development activities determined by district superintendents in consultation with district in-service committees. These documents, taken together, suggest that teachers' professional learning is viewed by both the teacher associations and the government as a shared responsibility.

In contrast to the apparently conciliatory language expressed by the NBTA in reference to the respective role of government and teachers in this area, policy statements by other teacher organizations are more pointed in reference to professional learning in general and PLCs in particular. For example, in a news release to its members, the Ontario Teachers' Federation (OTF) (2015), in reference to a survey conducted by the Ontario College of Teachers about teachers' views of professional learning, argued that the reason for the growth in learning opportunities and teacher capacity is "the self-driven nature of teacher learning in our province which respects teachers' time and their personal motivation and understanding of their needs in their professional learning" (p. 2). The Ontario Secondary School Teachers' Federation (OSSTF) (2016) policy manual includes similar policies on professional learning. For example: "Professional development should be an activity ... designated specifically for the personal and professional growth of members and ... initiated by, planned by, implemented by, and evaluated by members" (Policy 8.8.4, p.

75). Policy 8.26.1 in the same document specifically states that participation in a PLC should be voluntary for all members (p. 84).

Campbell (2015) reported on a study of the Teacher Learning and Leadership Project (TLLP) in Ontario. Her advice to national, provincial, or district systems included cultivating respectful partnerships with teachers and teacher unions, providing enabling conditions, and resisting being overly directive in matters of professional learning. Her advice to teachers was to identify priority areas for professional learning and to seek out ways to collaborate with colleagues to share in this learning. These comments to system leaders and teachers illustrate how the culture of PLCs challenges both the top-down bureaucratic model that seeks to direct teacher learning and the teacher union arguments for a wholly voluntary teacher-centred view of professional development.

Conclusion

The implementation of PLCs in the school system represents challenges and changes to the organizational culture within schools, districts, and provincial organizations. PLCs emphasize shared, collaborative, and learning-centred values and efforts, often in contrast to traditional bureaucratic elements that persist in education. Existing laws and policies in relation to shared decision-making, collaboration, and professional learning need to be examined by all stakeholders to ensure that they provide for the building of trusting relationships and supportive conditions so that our school systems can help students achieve the learning outcomes needed for the knowledge society of today and the future.

References

Agreement between Board of Management and the New Brunswick Teachers' Federation (NBTF Agreement) [Collective agreement]. (2012). Fredericton, NB. Retrieved from http://www2.gnb.ca/content/dam/gnb/Departments/ohr-brh/pdf/ca/201.pdf

Alberta's Commission on Learning. (2003). *Every child learns. Every child succeeds.* Edmonton, AB: Alberta Learning. Retrieved from https://open. alberta.ca/publications/0778526003

Alberta Teachers' Association (ATA). (2004). *Code of professional conduct.* Edmonton, AB: Author. Retrieved from https://www.teachers. ab.ca/About%20the%20ATA/ UpholdingProfessionalStandards/ ProfessionalConduct/Pages/CodeofProfessional Conduct.aspx.

Anglophone West School District. (2014). *Policy no. ASD-W-250-15: Appendix A: Employee growth process.* Fredericton, NB: Author. Retrieved from http://web1.n bed.nb.ca/sites/ASD-W/Policies/ Documents/200%20%20Human%20Resources/ ASD-W-250-15A%20-%20Growth%20Process%20Summary%20-%20All%20 Employees.pdf.

Campbell, C. (2015). Teachers as leaders of professional learning. *Education Canada, 55*(1) [Online edition]. Retrieved from http://www.cea-ace. ca/education-Canada/article/teachers-leaders-professional-learning.

DuFour, R. (2004). What is a "professional learning community"? *Educational Leadership, 61*(8), 6-11.

DuFour, R., Eaker, R., & DuFour, R. (2005). Recurring themes of professional learning communities and the assumptions they challenge. In R. DuFour, R. Eaker, & R. DuFour (Eds.), *On common ground: The power of professional learning communities* (pp. 7-29). Bloomington, IN: National Educational Service.

Education Act, S.N.B. 1997, c. E-1.12. Retrieved from http://laws.gnb.ca/en/ ShowTdm/cs/E-1.12/.

Elementary Teachers' Federation of Ontario (ETFO). (2007). Professional learning communities. *PRS Members Bulletin, 39*, 1-2. Toronto, ON: Author. Retrieved from http://www.etfo.ca/SupportingMembers/ Employees/PDF%20Versions/ Professional%20Learning%20 Communities.pdf.

Fallon, G., & Barnett, J. (2009). When is a learning community just a pseudo community? Towards the development of a notion of an authentic learning community. *International Studies in Educational Administration, 37*(2), 3-24.

Family Services Act, S.N.B. 1980, c. F-2.2. Retrieved from https://www.canlii.
org/en/nb/l aws/stat/snb-1980-c-f-2.2/latest/snb-1980-c-f-2.2.html.

Fineman, S., Gabriel, Y., & Sims, D. (2010). *Organizing & organizations* (4th
ed.). London, UK: Sage.

Foster, R., Wright, L., & McRae, P. (2008). *Leading and sustaining school
improvement initiatives*. Edmonton, AB: Alberta Initiative for School
Improvement.

Fullan, M. (2005). Professional learning communities writ large. In R. DuFour,
R. Eaker, & R. DuFour (Eds.), *On common ground: The power of profes-
sional learning communities* (pp. 209-223). Bloomington, IN: National
Educational Service.

Fullan, M. (2007). *Change the terms for teacher learning*. Retrieved from
http://michaelfullan.ca/wp-content/uploads/2016/06/13396074650.
pdf.

Hargreaves, A. (2003). *Teaching in the knowledge society: Education in the age
of insecurity*. New York, NY: Teachers College Press.

Hargreaves, A., & Fink, D. (2006). *Sustainable leadership*. San Francisco, CA:
Jossey-Bass.

Hartle, F., & Hobby, R. (2003). Leadership in a learning community: Your job
will never be the same again. In B. Davies & J. West-Burnham (Eds.),
Handbook of educational leadership and management (pp. 381-393).
London, UK: Pearson Education.

Hill, P., & Crévola, C. (2003). Organizational learning. In B. Davies & J.
West-Burnham (Eds.), *Handbook of educational leadership and management* (pp. 394-403). London, UK: Pearson Education.

Hoaglund, A.E., Birkenfeld, K., & Box, J.A. (2014). Professional learning
communities: Creating a foundation for collaboration skills in pre-service teachers. *Education, 134*(4), 521-528.

Hoy, W.K., & Miskel, C.G. (2005). *Educational administration: Theory,
research, and practice* (7th ed.). New York, NY: McGraw-Hill.

Levin, B. (2008). *How to change 5000 schools*. Cambridge, MA: Harvard
Education Press.

Louis, K.S., Marks, H.M., & Kruse, S. (1996). Teachers' professional community in restructuring schools. *American Educational Research Journal,
33*(4), 757-798.

Macmillan, R.B., Meyer, M.J., & Northfield, S. (2005). Principal succession and the continuum of trust in schools. In H.D. Armstrong (Ed.), *Examining the practice of school administration in Canada* (pp. 85-102). Calgary, AB: Detselig.

Male, T., & Palaiologou, I. (2015). Pedagogical leadership in the 21st century: Evidence from the field. *Educational Management, Administration, and Leadership, 43*(2), 214-231.

McGregor, J. (2003). Collaboration in communities of practice. In N. Bennett & L. Anderson (Eds.), *Rethinking educational leadership* (pp. 113-130). London, UK: Sage.

Mitchell, C., & Sackney, L. (2001). Building capacity for a learning community. *Canadian Journal of Educational Administration and Policy, 19.* Retrieved from http://www.umanitoba.ca/publications/cjeap/articles/mitchellandsackney.html.

Mullen, C.A., & Schunk, D.H. (2010). A view of professional learning communities through three frames: Leadership, organization, and culture. *McGill Journal of Education, 45*(2), 185-203. Retrieved from http://mje.mcgill.ca.

Naylor, C. (2007). *Recent literature on professional learning communities: Informing options for Canadian teacher unions?* [Research report]. Victoria, BC: British Columbia Teachers' Federation. Retrieved from http://www.bctf.ca/uploadedFiles /Publications/Research_reports/2007ei02.pdf.

New Brunswick Department of Education. (2007). *When kids come first.* Fredericton, NB: Author.

New Brunswick Department of Education and Early Childhood Development. (2013). *Policy 322: Inclusive education.* Fredericton, NB: Author. Retrieved http://www2. gnb.ca/content/dam/gnb/Departments/ed/pdf/K12/policies-politiques/e/322A.pdf.

New Brunswick Teachers' Association (NBTA). (2010). *Creating a culture of professional learning.* Fredericton, NB: Author. Retrieved from http://www.nbta.ca/profession/pd/pd_guide.pdf.

New Brunswick Teachers' Association (NBTA). (2011). *Code of professional conduct.*

Fredericton, NB: Author. Retrieved from http://www.nbta.ca/resources/code_of_ethics/Code_of_Professional_Conduct.pdf.

New Brunswick Teachers' Federation (NBTF). (2010). *NBTF annual report.* Fredericton, NB: Author. Retrieved from http://nbtffenb.ca/media/050110.pdf.

Ontario Secondary School Teachers' Federation (OSSTF). (2016). *Policies and procedures*. Toronto, ON: Author. Retrieved from http://www. osstf.on.ca/about-us/constitution-bylaws-policies.aspx.

Ontario Teachers' Federation (OTF). (2014). *We the teachers of Ontario*. Toronto, ON: Author. Retrieved from https://www.otffeo.on.ca/en/ wp-content/uploads/sites/2/2 014/09/WTT-ABOUT-OTF-AND-ITS-AFFILIATES-ENG-September-2014.pdf.

Ontario Teachers' Federation (OTF). (2015). Recent Ontario College of Teachers' membership survey: What are they really asking? *Communiqué, 19*(1), 1-2. Retrieved from https://www.otffeo.on.ca/ en/wp-content/uploads/sites/2/2015/02/ Communiqué-re-OCT-Membership-Survey.pdf.

Organisation for Economic Co-operation and Development (OECD). (2005). *Teachers matter: Attracting, developing, and retaining effective teachers*. Paris, France: Author. Retrieved from http://www.oecd.org/ edu/school/34990905.pdf.

Owen, R.G., & Valesky, T.C. (2011). *Organizational behavior in education: Leadership and school reform* (10th ed.). Upper Saddle River, NJ: Pearson Education.

Province of New Brunswick. (2016). *Everyone at their best*. Fredericton, NB: Author. Retrieved from http://www2.gnb.ca/content/dam/gnb/ Departments/ed/pdf/K12/ EveryoneAtTheirBest.pdf.

Riveros, A., Newton, P., & Burgess, D. (2012). A situated account of teacher agency and learning: Critical reflections on professional learning communities. *Canadian Journal of Education, 35*(1), 202-216. Retrieved from http://www.cje-rce.ca.

Sackney, L., Walker, K., & Mitchell, C. (2005). Building capacity for learning communities: Schools that work. *Revista Electrónica Iberoamericana sobre Calidad, Eficacia y Cambio en Educación, 3*(1), 9-16. Retrieved from http://www.ice.deusto.es/RINACE/reice/Vol3n1_e/Abs_ Sackneyetal.htm.

School Administration Regulation, N.B. Reg. 97-150. Retrieved from http:// laws.gnb.ca/e n/ShowTdm/cr/97-150/.

Senge, P.M. (2007). "Give me a lever long enough ... and single-handed I can move the world." In *The Jossey-Bass reader on educational leadership* (2nd ed.) (pp. 3–15). San Francisco, CA: John Wiley & Sons. (Reprinted from *The fifth discipline* by P.M. Senge, 1990, New York, NY: Doubleday).

Senge, P., Kleiner, A., Roberts, C., Ross, R.D., & Smith, B.J. (2000). *Schools that learn: The fifth discipline fieldbook for educators, parents, and everyone who cares about education.* New York, NY: Doubleday.

Shirley, A. (2015). NBTA Council days: Our rights and responsibilities. *NBTA News, 57*(3), 24-25. Retrieved from http://www.nbta.ca/nbta_news/archive/020115.pdf.

Stoll, L., Bolam, R., McMahon, A., Wallace, M., & Thomas, S. (2006). Professional learning communities: A review of the literature. *Journal of Educational Change, 7*(4), 221-258.

21st century standards of practice for beginning teachers in New Brunswick. (n.d.). Retrieved from http://www2.gnb.ca/content/dam/gnb/Departments/ed/pdf/K12/co mm/StandardsOfPracticeForBeginningTeachers.pdf.

Wasonga, T.A., & Murphy, J.F. (2007). Co-creating leadership dispositions. *International Studies in Educational Administration, 35*(2), 20-32.

Watson, C. (2014). Effective professional learning communities? The possibilities for teachers as agents of change in schools. *British Educational Research Journal, 40*(1), 18-29.

Weber, M. (2005). Bureaucracy (H.H. Gerth & C.W. Mills, Trans.). In J.M. Shafritz, J.S. Ott, & Y.S. Jang (Eds.), *Classics of organization theory* (6th ed.) (pp. 73-78). Belmont, CA: Thomson Wadsworth. (Reprinted from *from Max Weber: Essays in sociology* by H.H. Gerth & C.W. Mills, Eds. and Trans., 1964, New York, NY: Oxford University Press).

Wenger, E. (2000). Communities of practice and social learning systems. *Organization, 7*(2), 225-246. Retrieved from http://org.sagepub.com.

Williams, R., & Brien, K. (2009). Redefining educational leadership for the 21st century. In T.G. Ryan (Ed.), *Canadian educational leadership* (pp. 7-44). Calgary, AB: Detselig.

CHAPTER 5

How Outdoor Education Prepared Me to Teach Judges about Fetal Alcohol

David Boulding

Abstract

This paper examines the potential applicability of lessons learned through experiential outdoor education to the context of educating judges on the topic of fetal alcohol. Beginning by establishing the many ways in which the current judicial system is failing with respect to people with fetal alcohol charged with a criminal offence. The author noted the many ways in which people with fetal alcohol can be cognitively and behaviourally affected on the level of brain development, and advances the argument that the current legal and judicial system simply does not adequately compensate for people with these types of developmental difficulties. The author then goes on to describe personal success stories that applied lessons in experiential education gathered from outdoor education to teaching judges key facts about fetal alcohol and its relation to criminality.

I want to talk about the confluence of outdoor education, judicial education, and fetal alcohol. There are many difficulties associated with legal questions surrounding fetal alcohol and the judicial system, some of which throw into question the very foundations of our legal system. The paper aims first to explore the inadequacy of current legal and judicial practice with respect to people with fetal alcohol; I will then share my own success teaching judges about fetal alcohol through an outdoor education framework. In my experience, much can be learned through connecting these topics under the banner of experiential education, and this paper points towards the potential for this type of experiential education as a necessary first step towards compensating for the ways in which the judicial system is currently failing people with fetal alcohol.

To begin, written communication differs in important ways from oral communication. In relying purely on written words to communicate a message, I cannot see you, or make eye contact, or encourage you to ask questions if something I say puzzles you. There are no diagrams, illustrations, body motions, or voice inflections to help guide interpretation of the intended message. You are on your own with the text at hand, so you must rely on the sum of your experience, beliefs and assumptions to build the context necessary to create meaning. This process, in which context drives meaning, involves the same principle by which judges read scholarly papers on fetal alcohol. My experience is that scholarly papers on this subject have little positive effect on what a judge will do with a fetal alcohol case. Fetal alcohol has become a legal topic like theft or murder; however, it is not like theft or murder because we are talking about humans who have been charged with a criminal offence and whose brains are missing pieces. If we want our system to do justice to people with fetal alcohol, judges must understand the difficult truth that people with fetal alcohol simply do not think like judges think. They make mistakes where we, the complete brained, would not. We need to go deeper and find the common bond that exists between people with fetal alcohol spectrum disorder and those without such developmental disorders.

While working at Strathcona Park Lodge Outdoor Education Centre (SPL) in 1973, my job was to take on overnight hikes, canoe trips, and other outdoor activities. About 400 metres south of the SPL site was a 60-acre sphagnum moss bog. The bog and its surrounding forest had a rich sampling of various kinds of natural biological zones: several types of forests, streams, ponds, lakes, rock slides, logged-off areas, and some old growth timber. SPL designed a 3-to-4-hour program called a "bog walk." The walk meanders through different biological neighbourhoods, and the children experience a wide slice of Vancouver Island. They learn about varieties of plants by gathering leaf samples, tasting trees, and generally noticing the smaller details of the natural world around them. The Centre's mantra is as follows: "Notice small things, get better information, then you will make better decisions." In geological time, a bog is half-way between a lake and a forest. The bog was named the Sundew Bog after the insect-eating plants found in the middle of it. With the luck of location, SPL had a 10,000-acre natural history museum next door. The activity was called a "bog walk," although sometimes it was also called a "shelter-building exercise," or a "search and rescue game." In the 1970's, the outdoor leaders were measured by the creativity and joyous energy they put into their bog walks.

Leading bog walks, I learned that eye contact and encouraging questions allowed the youths to get the immersive experience they wanted; an experience that worked for them, not just the one I had prepared. I learned that each bog walk could be different depending on who was in the group and what the school principal saw as a requirement. I learned that I could cover the required material and still respond to each group differently and give the children an experience they would never forget. The point of the exercise was not about rattling off the English and Latin names for the 75-plus different bog plants, although some teachers wanted that kind of taxonomic overload. To accomplish this massive name-calling, we organized the plants in families, or neighbourhoods. I learned to make my bog walks physically challenging, owing to the principle of outdoor education that body learning differs from classroom learning in important ways. I learned that body-felt experiences from a bog walk could complement the children's classroom learning in biology, for example, much like Chinese medicine complements Western medicine.

About 25 years later, I began a career teaching, writing, and public speaking about fetal alcohol and the law. Like most first-time teachers, my initial instinct was to read my first paper to the audience directly. After some months on the fetal alcohol conference circuit, however, I realized that I had to change my lesson and try something different. Slowly, I absorbed the lessons I had learned from the great teachers in my life and the books about education that they suggested I read.[1]

Now, in 2017, I can see a consistent intellectual path, and I offer this paper to explain my success with a topic that often confounds the legal system. It tends to label "difficult people" as "mental health people," or "mental health cases." My clients have incomplete brains; therefore, the standard legal process that works well for you and me fails them, and the failure is ours. We need to design a better system, as my clients' brains do not change, nor does time in jail create new brain cells.

The disabilities of people with fetal alcohol are often described by the mnemonic ALARM.[2]

'A' stands for the adaptive behaviours people with fetal alcohol sometimes lack. Adaptive behaviours are the life lessons we absorb, as opposed to those we are actively taught. For example, when it is cold outside, an adaptive behaviour may be to put on a hat. Likewise, at a funeral, it is generally understood that one should not ask the widow about events in pop culture (the Stanley Cup playoffs, for example). Some words, including many derived from Old Anglo-Saxon, are used only in narrow and specific social circumstances, and people with fetal alcohol may lack the ability to use these words in their appropriate context.

'L' stands for the difficulties that people with fetal alcohol often exhibit with respect to language and learning. There may be blank spots in the learning of my clients, whose language often seems to be above their learning. Lawyers hear this kind of language continually. Their fetal alcohol clients overload their language with legalisms they have heard, like *mens rea*, "indictable offence," and "specific deterrence." They have no idea what the words mean, yet they know that these words are important to lawyers, so people with fetal alcohol often use them to create close relationships with their own lawyers. The problem is that the lawyers then fail to see their clients' cognitive disabilities and assume that their clients understand legal terms.

'A' stands for attention, which is a key element in any attempt to understand people with fetal alcohol. Often, people with fetal alcohol have limited attention and are easily distracted.

'R' stands for reasoning, a faculty that is impaired in individuals with fetal alcohol. These people have difficulty generalizing, abstracting and predicting, and miss many social cues. For example, for these individuals, the injunction "Do not fight in the playground!" does not necessarily get translated to "Do not fight on the way home." People with fetal alcohol often have difficulties abstracting, generalizing, or making predictions regarding social situations.

'M' stands for memory, the foundation of all cognitive skills. When elderly people are diagnosed with Alzheimer's, we expect these individuals to experience memory loss. As a society, we do not expect a 27-year-old to have similar memory difficulty. Whether short term or long term, this impairment is often devastating and creates huge legal problems. Often, either hours after an arrest or later, when in front of the judge, the offender is clear: s/he knows that an act or behaviour is wrong. However, when his new friends ask him to come behind a drugstore at 1 a.m. to help load boxes for 20 dollars, s/he might not process all the facts. S/he may focus on the delight of having new friends who want him to help them. S/he may see the invitation as a powerful statement of fact (i.e., "I do have friends") and act accordingly in order to conform to this 'fact.'

Legal professionals use this ALARM mnemonic to teach police about suspects or offenders with fetal alcohol, as a few questions in these domains can help police officers begin to assess a person and can help in identifying a brain disability. The positive qualities of people with this permanent, brain-based disability need to receive more attention. For example, most people with fetal alcohol are visual learners, and therefore may find reading and writing challenging. That said, I have had great success with fetal alcohol clients when I ask them to draw a diagram explaining where they were when the police say the crime happened.

These clients have great connective social skills; when given the opportunity, they are typically generous in their trust and able to form strong and lasting relationships. While I have found that my clients have sensitivities to touch and are slow cognitive processors, they are generally quick to smile and eager to please. I have learned to talk slowly, avoid dense legalisms, and use a light touch in engaging with them. In my experience, the one-minute handshake is the best way in, and it is important to maintain eye contact to give them physical signals that you are interested in them. I had to learn to jettison the standard legal advice lecture and, instead, face the fact that sometimes a physical experience can create a connection where words fail. After all, a simple handshake begins with permission in the form of the outreached hand. This is followed by the grip, the eye contact, and the slow movement, followed by a moment of complete focus on the other person; within a few moments of this largely physical engagement, a relationship has begun. This type of quiet physicality seems to work with my fetal alcohol clients. It was my outdoor education experience that first taught me that everyone wants to matter; years later, I now apply this experimental learning framework to the topic of teaching judges how to approach cases involving people with fetal alcohol.

This particular link between outdoor education and judicial education is a great example of complementary learning. Judges I have taught generally begin by confronting the following question with respect to people with fetal alcohol: "I would not do that in those circumstances, so what is going on in that brain?" In a sense, I have a similar choice here, in that I am writing a paper for professionals. The readers in my case are exceptional, specialized and can easily consume vast numbers of pages. These readers' intellectual skills are very high, and interest is keen. The point is that a basic feature of education, and of communication, is that it requires one to make adjustments in order for one's message to be understood. My middle sister, with her freshly earned Ph.D., insists that I cannot write a single sentence here unless I quote the relevant peer-reviewed research, properly footnoted (she would make an excellent appellate lawyer). My youngest sister, who has been practicing Traditional Chinese Medicine (TCM) for 30 years, tells me to "be personal, connect, and bring myself and my various experiences" to this paper. This paper uses the latter approach, as evidenced by the fact that there are few footnotes here; rather, it offers an "experiential" view of judicial education.

The relation of fetal alcohol to the law is a significant legal problem, owing partly to the fact that society often expects judges to help solve our social issues. In some instances, judges are made to play this role because Parliament refuses to, as the history of abortion law demonstrates. Judges not only make these important decisions, which can have profound implications for society as a whole, they must also give sound reasons for these judgments. The *Canadian Charter of Rights and Freedoms* in section 52(1) requires judges to answer the questions we send them in our legal disputes by using a constitutional legal process. This involves using a reference to the *Canadian Charter of Rights and Freedoms*. Our *Charter* is clearly one of the world's finest and most progressive constitutional documents, a gift given to the country by Pierre Elliott Trudeau. Under the *Charter*, judges have the power to decide if a law is constitutional or not. They can decide if something is a legal right or not. For example, should fetal alcohol be a mitigating or aggravating factor in a criminal sentence? Does a generally nonviolent person with brain damage require jail as a sentence for a violent crime, or does fetal alcohol require different standards of mental intention?

The following is a list of some key questions about fetal alcohol that judges should consider asking: 1) What did you intend your actions to do? 2) What were you thinking? Were you thinking? 3) When were you thinking that (i.e., before the action, after the action, or after arrest)? 4) What is thinking? What is thinking like for you? 5) What are the legal expectations Canadians have of persons charged with a criminal offence when we know that the brain of a person charged with a criminal offence is missing pieces? 6) How do we make legal rules about brains, or about thinking? 7) In what ways does the law refer to or make use of scientific knowledge? 8) How much brain science information do you need to make a helpful decision? 9) To whom would such information be help-ful? and 10) Can decisions be revisited when new information becomes available?

While this paper does not claim to contain the answers to these questions, it does, however, suggest a way to begin this perplexing dis-cussion by suggesting changes regarding how we educate judges about fetal alcohol. My argument is that judges need to see fetal alcohol from the point of view of the person with fetal alcohol. In all other cases, that is what the law does. The judge says, "I would not do that because..." and then the judge tells us his/her thinking, and s/he then gives reasons for his/her opinion. These reasons, which are known as the judgment of the court, then become part of what is called the "common law."

The common law in Canada incorporates ancient Greek and Roman law, the Canon Law of the Catholic Church, and all the Norman and old English Law, which includes all associated cases from the old English courts, from the Sheriff of Nottingham to the decisions of the House of

Lords. Common law is a massive collection of legal judgments. As such, it is not common to, or shared with, people with incomplete brains. The common law seems to be exclusively designed for people with complete brains, and such a design is not fair.

We have made curved slopes in our concrete sidewalks for people with wheelchairs. In Canadian courts, we have interpreters not only for the deaf, but for almost every other language heard in Canada. Canada offer many legal accommodations in the effort to achieve fairness. For example, Aboriginal people now receive Gladue reports, named after an aboriginal person found guilty of a criminal offence, whose case (after appeals and much legal discussion) set a precedent for important changes to criminal law in Canada. The law in Canada states that when an Aboriginal person is facing a judge in the penalty phase, at sentencing, a probation officer must prepare a report, named after Mr. Gladue, detailing his/her Aboriginal background, his/her culture, and any other relevant information that a white judge might not consider. Finally, after years of Aboriginal people overloading our jails, Gladue reports are a common everyday experience in our criminal courts. Given this history of legal accommodation in Canada, I would argue that people with fetal alcohol need similar reports detailing the many ways in which their incomplete brains can affect their treatment in Canada's judicial system.

Children get special help with screens and videos in sex assault cases, so they do not have to face the person accused of hurting them. Older people with Alzheimer's are rarely charged with crimes. Fairness is the foundation of our *Charter*, and judges are given the role of deciding what is fair in Canada. Canadians want our legal system to be fair, but the task of implementing such a principle of fairness in practice is incredibly difficult and complex. Given that judges are selected from the top one percent of a very elite profession, how can educators ensure that judges truly understand the subjective experience of those with incomplete brains, and the full implications of their mental difficulties in relation to broader questions of intentionality and legal responsibility? The rest of this paper aims to guide answers to these questions of judicial education regarding fetal alcohol through an experiential learning framework, an approach that, in my experience, can help teach judges about fetal alcohol.

My success with this experiment in experiential learning is due, in part, to what I learned from outdoor education. Before beginning an English Literature and Native Studies degree at Trent University, Peterborough, Ontario, Canada, in 1977, I spent some years hiking, climbing mountains, and kayaking at Strathcona Park Lodge and the Outdoor Education Centre (SPL) on Vancouver Island. I then completed a Master's degree in modern poetry/rhetoric before I attended law school. Since 2001, my law practice has been restricted to writing, teaching, and speaking about fetal alcohol and the law.

After I received my outdoor education at SPL, I decided that I needed to go to university to pursue a range of academic interests. In my experience, high school and law school teach students that the only learning that matters is in the head, or the brain. Under this framework, marks measure your learning, describe your success, and dictate which law firm will hire you. What is lost with this perspective on education is the fact that common knowledge, collective knowledge and experiential knowledge also have value.

Because outdoor education is fun, and usually done in a group setting, it promotes a connection to the natural world and to others. Outdoor education requires exertion, movement, and attention to small things. Outdoor education fosters healthy personal relationships and positive connections with peers, as students are engaged in the various activities primarily as members of a group. The style of outdoor education taught at SPL emphasizes creating connections with self, others, and the natural world as opposed to overcoming or conquering the natural world. The SPL program has room for a wide range of outdoor education styles. For me, one's choice of outdoor education style is not a matter of right and wrong, or good and bad, but about one's philosophy, one's view of the world. I believe that if I can give a judge a physical experience, and not just a scholarly experience, we can do more together to address the question of judicial fairness for individuals with fetal alcohol, and in doing so, find the common bond we all share.

A specific function of outdoor education is building confidence. Outward Bound (OB) is a worldwide leader in outdoor education. Beginning in 1941, every OB program over the next 50 years would have an activity on their residential sites, or camps, called the "confidence course." Now every outdoor education center in the world has such a course in their program. Sometimes the activity is called a "challenge course," sometimes it is called a "rope course." A thick rope is strung up between trees 10 to 20 feet above the ground. The participants are encouraged to walk across the rope to get to the next tree, to the next element of the challenge course. Sometimes a log replaces the rope. There is no problem when the log is on the ground. Everyone can walk the log. Hoist it up 15 feet, and everything changes. The challenge is physical, not intellectual.

The theory is that if you can walk the rope or walk the log up in the air, you will learn, in the body, to have more confidence in your life. You have had an experience in your body that you can rely on later. You will create a frame of future reference. Sometimes participants find it difficult to walk that suspended rope or log, and a skilled outdoor leader can help the students in the challenge course by working to create personal confidence. The theory is that the experience of building confidence by walking the rope or log gives the learner a successful experience, a warm feeling in the body. This experience can later be called on to create success in other areas of life. I believe the body memory of success has value, not unlike the value of knowing the multiplication tables or the value of reading.

Outdoor education is also about problem solving as a group. For example, there is the rule that when we hike in the mountains, we travel at the pace of the slowest member. Most outdoor education centers provide a series of activities stressing problem solving. Tasks might have participants confronting the following questions: Who will cook over the fire? Who checks that the canoes are tied and secure for the night? How do we all cross the river safely? Who will partner with the less physically able students? While the list of questions and obstacles is long, the benefits of having to navigate these challenges follow students for life. Social life often faces us with similar difficult problems. Sometimes, we seem to be powerless and unable to find our way towards solutions. Sometimes, there are problems we simply cannot fix.

To take an example, in outdoor education, it is typical for students to look for the easy way up steep mountains. The successful leader can show students that some mountains are too much for this group at this stage of its members' learning. Often, this speech spurs one or two students to change their lives and become dedicated lifelong mountaineers. These are the people who later climb successfully in the Himalayas, in Patagonia, and the steep mountains in the Rockies. These are the types of obstacles and challenges that we can solve; some problems we can fix. Deciding which is which, however, is difficult.

Discernment is a difficult skill to teach. It takes time to learn and considerable brain power. This high-level skill is often not available to people with fetal alcohol, but we, the complete-brained, assume discernment is present for people with fetal alcohol just as it is for most people. We need to learn that the ability to discern is something most people with fetal alcohol do not have and may never have.

Section 19 of the *Criminal Code of Canada* codifies this belief in discernment. Everyone knows this basic law because the section says ignorance of the law is no defence against a criminal charge. We, as Canadians, assume all Canadians know this fact in their bones because we share a common social stock of knowledge. We may not know the intricate aspects of trading stocks and bonds, but we do know that cheating is wrong. We know punching, kicking, and using certain chemicals in our bodies are unlawful things to do. On the one hand, these criminal rules of behaviour tend to be explicit and are discussed, displayed, and dissected in various media all the time, so a relationship exists between being able to discern and being able to remember. If your memory fails you in moments of stress, you will make mistakes. You may even forget the basics that we, as reflected in our legal and judicial system, take for granted.

Wisdom, on the other hand, is different. Wisdom is usually reflective, like hindsight. Wisdom is something we all know about. All of us can discuss wisdom. Wisdom is more than a cognitive item. Wisdom has an ineffable, timeless quality, and a relation to human potential. Literature, painting, ballet, and some of the pithy stuff your mother told you contain wisdom. You see the wisdom problem on display with people with fetal alcohol. After being arrested and sitting in a police station, or in the back of the police cruiser, sometime after an offence has happened, almost all people with fetal alcohol either confess or tell the officer what happened and can say they know that what they did was wrong. This "knowing" admission is always used against them. Later, they can say their actions were not correct, not wise. Sadly, this wisdom, this awareness, is not available at the moment they commit a criminal act. We, with our good memory machines in our complete brains, shake our heads and say: "Everyone knows..." To us, this wisdom is obvious and available to our brains, ready to be applied to each set of circumstances. We take for granted many of our cognitive operations.

Then there is legal wisdom. I am reminded of Louis Armstrong when he was asked to define jazz. His answer went something like "I know it when I hear it." Legal wisdom is often clear only years later. We need, it seems, to thrash around before we agree on what is legal wisdom. Eventually we agree. Women voting, the ban on the death penalty, and legal medical marijuana are three topics that seem obvious today, but were not so in their time. Time, then, is always an issue.

Time is up. Fetal alcohol has been good science since the early 1970's. We know the cause, and the difficulties are clearly set out. Something has to change because too many people with fetal alcohol are in jail. This situation is wrong and might upset Canadians if they knew about it.

Until recently, fetal alcohol was not conceptualized as a problem. Diane Malbin, the great fetal alcohol educator, once or twice told me that her Ph.D. supervisor had a rule about social work: No solution, no problem. Diane explained that in social work, until you can give the decision makers a solution, they do not see the problem.[3]

Fetal alcohol proves this rule. Until we can give judges a solution, fetal alcohol is not a problem they can solve. They have blunt tools: jail or no jail. The readymade solution of jail and more jail is urged on them by Crown prosecutors, since the brain damage is permanent. Prosecutors want public safety. They use jail as a cold storage facility. Jail does not create new brain cells, or raise cognitive abilities. Jail, if anything, is a good training ground for more crime, more jail. The problem is a social problem, and as such, it is one that society as a whole is implicated in. As a society, we to start with the following questions: I would not do that, so what is going on in that brain? What is it like to be alive with a brain that is missing pieces? The answer to these questions is multi-faceted and complex.

I have learned from outdoor education that passion for the material is more important than performance on exams, more important than knowing the Latin names of all the forest or bog plants. Passion is in the body. I can feel passion's excitement. I vibrate. I am hot. When you see youths complete a rope course, you can sense, often hear, and see passion. When young students stoop to watch the sundews glisten and eat bugs, they are paying attention with every cell in their bodies. That is passion. Obviously, lawyers need to know the law, and law school exams are required. That the Law Society of BC has several qualification courses and tough exams is equally a good thing.

I believe passion and learning are body-felt experiences. I believe passion and feeling propel learning. Feeling is the body expressing itself in concrete ways: you feel hot, warm to cool, or cold. You sweat or shiver. You vibrate or are still. When you see a shaking youth complete the ropes course, and he or she gives you the megawatt smile of success, you know the child has been marked for life. This child now has a body experience of success, and this feeling of success is always available to the child. The theory of outdoor education is that this experience will be used later positively in the children's lives. When teaching judges, I aim to have them remember the experience in their bodies with either a smile, or a shiver.

Some years ago, I had the pleasure of teaching some 20 senior Royal Canadian Mounted Police (RCMP) from northern British Columbia about fetal alcohol during a two-day course. One of the topics in this RCMP course was brain science. Professor K. Sulik is an embryologist from the Bowles Institute for Alcohol Studies at the University of North Carolina (Chapel Hill). She is the world leader in brain imaging. Her pictures show the damage alcohol does in utero to brains. When we showed the brain-imaging pictures of mouse brain damage from Professor Sulik, many police would tear up. It was at this point that the concept of brain damage struck home to them; one could see that these police were beginning to understand fetal alcohol. All of these police had arrived with knowledge of the bad behaviour associated with fetal alcohol. However, it was the combination of the brain science in front of them and the memory of these old cases that caused the officers to react emotionally. These men, whom society has entrusted to enforce the law, began to see fetal alcohol as a brain-based permanent physical disability. They saw the brains of people with fetal alcohol were incomplete. I believe that if we can educate, through pictures and tears, Staff Sergeants in the RCMP, judges will be relatively easy to teach.

This lesson that learning also occurs in the body, and not just between the ears, I learned at SPL in 1972. After a winter apprenticeship, I was told I was an outdoor leader. I was changed forever when a senior instructor, Marcy Wolter, gave me the slim volume entitled *Acclimatizing* by Steve Van Matre. His 134-page book synthesized everything SPL taught.[4] I learned I had to find ways to engage children, ways to bring their bodies into the learning. I had to get their feelings up and out there. When I explain fetal alcohol to judges I engage them physically using the same experiential principles I used with children during bog walks.

Steve Van Matre changed the outdoor education paradigm, putting life into the outdoor education process. He took inner-city children from Chicago and walked them chest-deep through swamps, had them tasting trees, and made them face webs with spiders, demonstrating that outdoor education could be experiential, fun, and life-changing. He prioritised the excitement of passion, experience, and learning in the body over physical skills, endurance, competition, and conquering nature.

I was dropped into the maw of judicial education in November 2000. I was a criminal lawyer in Vancouver, and Judge Carly Truman phoned to say she was organizing a fetal alcohol conference in February, and that she wanted me to participate.

In February 2001, I found myself on a panel with Mr. Justice David Vickers, Judge Carly Truman, a parole officer, a probation officer, and a woman married to an inmate with fetal alcohol, in front of 1000 to 1200 paying learners: mostly social workers, probation officers, a few doctors, and some parents.

The probation officer spoke first. Over the years, she had adopted several young people with fetal alcohol and, consequently, had already experienced the difficulty of navigating the legal system, both as a probation officer (a sort of court-appointed parent, monitoring troubled children for her local judge) and as an adoptive parent with her own children in and out of jail. Her story and her presentation were crisp, fact-based, and tearful. She emphasized that her children made the same mistakes over and over again, and the judges persisted in their expectation that these children learn from their days in jail. She was a kind woman who showed a wistful sadness at the failure of judges to see the children as she did. She knew they were different and that, in some ways, they would never be like herself.

The federal parole officer told horror stories of people trapped in the federal system for infractions like stealing chocolate bars followed by a series of "not getting it" offences. These offences usually consist of actions like failing to report to the probation officer, failing to follow court orders, failing to follow no contact and no go orders, and various breaches of other probation terms. A second set of offences I call 'having bad friends' also plagues people with fetal alcohol. It is not uncommon for fetal alcohol individuals to get continuously caught for an offence, while the instigators, the planners, and the organizers rarely do. After repeat convictions, it is customary for judges to demand compliance. Judges want people to "get it" because a judge's duty is to create and maintain public safety. Given the judicial expectation that convicted offender learn from their time in jail, sadly it is too often the case that judges eventually give those people who consistently do not "get it" federal time, which in the Canadian legal system equates to more than two years in jail. Then, while in a penitentiary, it is typical for people with fetal alcohol fail to follow prison rules (despite repeated disciplinary action), and thus get more time in jail.

Following the parole officer was a woman whose husband had fetal alcohol and was currently in a federal penitentiary. She talked about how the system did not understand that her husband's brain was different and was missing pieces.

I was next. Perhaps some context may assist. Judge Truman had a pre-conference group telephone call about a 6 or 7 weeks before the conference. Everyone on the panel, except Mr. Justice Vickers, was involved in the group phone call. Everyone was conversing about fetal alcohol in relation to their presentations, but I was silent. I had learned about fetal alcohol only a month earlier, when the head of Vancouver's probation office for sex offenders, the wonderful Bill Ellis, took time out from shovelling soup into his mouth in the courthouse café to tell me, between gulps of Greta's soup, that my client "probably has FAS."

The term "fetal alcohol syndrome" is old and outdated taxonomy. Now we use an umbrella term, "fetal alcohol spectrum disorder." Under this umbrella are four discrete diagnoses, the names of which are still changing as the science develops; by the end of 2017, it is expected that we will have a different naming system again. As in a television cartoon, the lights came on with a bang for me when Bill said 'fetal alcohol.' I had never heard the words 'fetal alcohol' before. I had been in criminal courts since 1985, but my ignorance limited my contribution during the conference call to an admission: "I do not know anything about this; it seems all I do is make mistakes."

To her credit, Judge Truman was kind to me. In that special slow voice adults use with young children, she said: "That's okay, David, you just write about your mistakes." I did just that. In 20 minutes, I wrote the paper "Mistakes I have made with FAS clients."[5] I stood up, smiled, and read my paper. About halfway, I had to stop as I was tearing up. Embarrassed, I looked up and saw that most of the people in the audience were also crying. The previous speakers had created an emotional tsunami. The effects from the previous speakers and the content of my paper were upsetting, and emotions came out. I urge you to let this reaction sink in. I was in a room with over a thousand people, most of whom were professionals connected to the legal and judicial system, and most of us were in tears. After I was done, Judge Truman gave a learned account of where the law on fetal alcohol is today and spoke of her experiences as a judge in the local provincial court.

Finally, the showstopper stood up. Typically, B.C. Supreme Court judges are to be invisible. We expect our judges to show up only while in court. Not Mr. Justice Vickers! For all his professional life, he was a wonderful, tireless advocate for mentally challenged, disadvantaged, and disabled children. He gave a blistering attack on the legal system, the political system, how we train lawyers, how we train judges, how we train police officers and corrections staff, and how little society values children. This presentation was a barn burner, and people stood and cheered when he sat down. Every word rang true with the audience. Passion can move people to emotional places. Listening to Mr. Justice David Vickers was the emotional equivalent to watching Paul Henderson score the goal that beat the Russians in the 1972 Summit Series. The B.C. Supreme Court Judge had the courage to open his heart and get personal with 1000 people. He created an emotional connection with the crowd; people cheered, as if everyone was part of a single body in that convention hall.

After his speech, I spent years brooding before the full significance of that day and all that had happened became useful to me. I now know that passion is not enough. As an educator and legal professional, I must bring myself and all my energies forward, such that I am on view and personally available for my clients. I must show who I am, and when I do so I can create a connection with others, and we can quickly get on the same page, and forge a connection. Experiential learning has an emotional affective component that is equally important to the more logical, cerebral aspects typically emphasized in judicial education.

These days, when talking about fetal alcohol with judges, I do not use the law school case study method, in which judges are given thousands of pages of Court of Appeal cases in order to 'learn the law," nor do I rely on the successful method of continuing legal education programs, in which panels of lawyers provide learned papers and present a 6-minute oral précis). These methods fail when addressing fetal alcohol because the topic collides with several sacred legal cows. Being personal is unacceptable in law courts. As lawyers, we are to be dispassionate, composed, detached, and professional. The use of emotion with respect to any factor of the legal process is forbidden by nature of the legal system itself. We are trained to avoid the word "I." We are forbidden to call someone a liar. We must suggest s/he is "mistaken," or "not fully truthful." We are required to uphold the old English traditions of the aristocracy, so we sink to euphemisms. Indeed, the use of raw language and emotion in any legal decision can be a cause for discipline by one's law society.

To properly and rigorously discuss the legal framework for fetal alcohol through a scholarly paper would require pages and pages dealing with several assumptions in law that are foundational, almost unassailable. The exercise would exhaust readers. As a result, I see a legal system today that chips away incrementally at fetal alcohol to make small changes. I would argue that this process is like sticking Band-Aids on open fractures.

By way of example, the following is a sample of some of the foundational legal problems that the current legal framework for fetal alcohol inevitably confronts. In law, there is no such thing a partial guilt; guilt is either all or nothing, as set out in the rigid *Criminal Code of Canada*. Under this foundational legal principle, "guilty" or "not guilty" are the only options available. This means that no one ever receives a verdict of "innocent." The reason for this semantic distinction is complex, but it can be distilled into the following: because the rule of law is not for an individual's benefit, it is for public safety, for order, for social stability. Law, therefore, is a blunt utilitarian tool. We sacrifice the interests of individuals for the greater good of the community and the social order itself. One implication of these foundational legal principles is that, by its very nature, the law herds some of us into pens so that the rest of us can live in peace.

Another fundamental principle of the legal system, and one with profound consequence, is that the law assumes all people to be equal in their ability to understand the law. In Canada, section 19 of the *Criminal Code* states that ignorance of the law is no excuse. However, it is also a foundational principle of modern science that human organisms essentially *are* our brains, in the sense that our brains delimit our ability to perceive, experience and interact with the world around us. If an individual has a brain that gives them an emotional age or maturity age of 12 to 14 and a chronological age of 27, how can we be surprised when that person chooses "illegal" sex partners whose chronological age is the same as their own emotional age?

The law assumes that individuals understand the consequences of our actions, and more fundamentally, that actions have consequences, the chain of cause and effect that enables us to be social actors. The question of whether an offence was a crime of passion or provocation is not an admissible part of a Canadian legal defence to a criminal charge. Every boy learns this fact when his mother tells him to not hit his sisters, even when they call him nasty names. I know this myself, on a personal level. I have four younger sisters, and one is a lawyer.

Thus, there are central, foundational aspects of our legal system that have the consequence of making it exceedingly difficult for some members of society to avoid incarceration, simply on the grounds of the limitations of their brains. For example, if you lack the social regulation skills to delay gratification (i.e., I was angry when he called me stupid, so I hit him), it is likely that you will go to jail. The same is true if you fail to know enough to walk away from trouble or if you fail to learn to manage your emotions ("Mom! David is calling me stupid again, so I hit him"). If your brain processes information slowly or comes to inappropriate conclusions, the law has difficulty processing you. We focus on behaviour, perhaps obsessively, and choose to ignore the many ways in which the brain, and the limits of some brains, influence or shape the behaviour in question.

Sadly, the law is not to be blamed entirely: the truth is that we still know very little about brains. Nonetheless, what little we know seems to be unacceptable to Parliament or to most judges. I would argue that judges need to know more brain science in order to protect against the inherent biases of the legal system, as outlined above.

Another difficulty is that Canadian law does not handle false confessions well, and people with fetal alcohol give false confessions regularly. One famous case involved a young man named Gabe Baddeley. In return for a sandwich, he gave a false confession, as he was hungry. If you are interested in reading the transcript of this false confession, the University of Washington in Seattle, a leading centre for fetal alcohol scholarship, has the complete interview on its website. While the police officer comes across as a tremendously decent chap, and despite the convincing nature of the confession, the fact is that the real culprit confessed nine months later. In this particular case, after eating and confessing to the kind policeman, the original confessor Gabe asked to go home. This request is an example of the kind of cognitive impairments that can accompany brain dysfunction such as occurs as a result of fetal alcohol. While we may be inclined to say that 'everyone' knows you do not admit to burning down a school and then expect to go home for dinner, evidently Gabe's brain had learned that it is best to please people, and that telling people what they want is the best way to make one's life easier.

Under our current legal framework, we have no way to incorporate modern brain science into law when it conflicts with the McNaughten rules we inherited from the House of Lords over 160 years ago. I relish explaining the McNaughten rules because they encapsulate the best and the worst of our legal system. McNaughten was a deeply disturbed paranoid schizophrenic. He wanted Scotland independent from English rule, and at one point, travelled to London with the aim of shooting the Prime Minister. He missed and murdered the PM's secretary instead. An English jury found him not guilty by reason of insanity. The House of Lords was not happy. On its own motion, the House of Lords reviewed the trial evidence without the messy Mr. McNaughten. Experts testified, and a report was issued. The report aimed to make sure this catastrophic wrong, this precedent for getting away with murder, never happened again; thus, they sought to clarify the law on insanity. Every democratic nation has the McNaughten rules, the law on the mental requirement for a finding of guilt, in some form as the basis for its criminal law. Lawyers call this component *mens rea*: the guilty mind.

There are, of course, profound implications of these rulings. The report was written 12 years before Sigmund Freud was born, and there were no such things as MRIs, PET scans, X- rays, or blood chemistry analysis. No brain science was introduced as evidence. Careful readers will detect that the law has an elitist tinge and changes at a glacial rate. Stripped down to their essence, the McNaughten Rules say: if you know you have done wrong, we can hang you.

This framework leaves several touchy but crucial questions unaddressed: when did you know it was wrong? How did you know it was wrong? What is thinking? What were you thinking? Thus, we are left with a set of legal rules about mental abilities, intellectual intentions, cognition, and an understanding of brains that is 175 years out of date.

We smile and are surprised when the post office gives us a letter with someone else's name and address. Using the ALARM mnemonic, consider a brain that has processing difficulties, memory problems, attention issues, and reasoning flaws. People with brains that are missing pieces will make mistakes, often the same mistakes over and over again.

In law, we do not allow for any special circumstances or exceptions. Consider the following potential explanations of causality for a criminal offence: 1) "He was overstimulated, overwrought, and reacted, instead of carefully considering his options;" 2) "He cannot see that there are others in the class;" and 3) "He just does not understand, in the moment, that he must follow the rules." Current democratic legal frameworks do not make room for any of these exceptions.

Additionally, in Canadian law, courts rely on jail and have to be prodded to use probation, parole, community supervision or service, diversion, cautions, or second, and third, and fourth chances. Many Canadians are conservative and like jail, especially for criminals, and politicians are all too willing cater to this cruel bias. Readers familiar with the struggle between Stephen Harper and the Supreme Court of Canada are aware of the retrogressive positions of the current Parliament. It is worth noting that all suggested fetal alcohol amendments to the *Criminal Code of Canada* have been defeated on party lines in committee. This situation never made the front page of the *Globe and Mail*.

In criminal court, the problem of what to do with offenders with incomplete brains is reflected in an all too common situation. A defence lawyer tells the judge that the client has fetal alcohol, and the judge immediately sees this as a brain-based, permanent physical disability with no cure. Most judges, and too many prosecutors, think the correct response is "more jail time." The result is that, in our expensive jails, we have too many people who are no danger to public safety, and many of them have fetal alcohol. Fetal alcohol is a permanent, brain-based physical disability like having one leg, or being born blind. We need to make accommodations, or, as Diane Malbin suggested, try something different, rather than simply trying harder under the same inadequate legal framework.

Fetal alcohol law is as different from all other aspects of law as studying the Schrodinger equations[6] are to a mathematician, as different as learning to build a fire in the west coast rain. To uphold the standard of fairness that guides our legal system, we need to consider the brain and not let our focus be restricted to the deviant behaviour. We need to establish different legal rules when people with incomplete brains are arrested.

This brief list of problems is intimidating. These are not small problems; indeed, they challenge the foundations of law.

Now, when I speak to judges about fetal alcohol, I use what I learned from my years in outdoor education. I have learned that seemingly trivial or small experiences that contain emotional content can produce significant changes in people's learning. Perhaps the best judicial lesson ever given on fetal alcohol and the law was administered in Edmonton on April 8 of 2008. I was seated with four judges at a round table. In the meeting room, there were about 75 lawyers, and about 10 - 15 judges. The psychologist was Karen Serrette, Ph.D. On deck was K. Sulik, Ph.D., an embryologist from University of North Carolina, the Bowles Institute for Alcohol Studies. Serrette had a team of 6 or 7 grad students to help her. The students passed out elastic neck bands that fit too tightly, paper party hats that were too big and sloppy and fell over the brow on to your nose, and those funny gag glasses where the eyeballs fall out when you move your head. We were given pencils and a piece of paper. The students then walked around the room carrying three boom boxes playing loud heavy metal music. It was at this point that the psychologist over another loud speaker gave the audience an easy ten-question test on basic Canadian geography.

Significantly, no one at my table finished all ten questions. One judge threw down his pencil at question number four. The scowling judges, all men, were infuriated and said so. They acted as if someone had dropped a high school stink bomb at their daughter's wedding. It was clear from their remarks that they were more insulted than cognitively challenged. Finally, in the silence, we were instructed to take off the neckbands, the funny hats and glasses. The psychologist said: "That is what it is like to live with fetal alcohol." This demonstration was a perfect example of Steve Van Matre's definition of the value of experiential education.

Following Serrette's talk, Dr. Sulik gave a learned lecture in pictures. For 25 years, she has been feeding pregnant mice drops of alcohol. She then slices the brains of the baby mice and takes pictures of the damaged brains. The result is that Dr. Sulik has created a day-by-day brain atlas, in the sense that she can produce, on demand, the birth defects of fetal alcohol. Her pictures are sobering. I use them every time I speak because the pictures, scientifically, show that fetal alcohol brains are missing pieces. Very few words are needed. Dr. Sulik shows you a mouse with brain damage and then shows you a picture from the files of Children's Services and the facial features of the mouse and child look nearly identical. She explained that she created this brain defect by giving the pregnant mouse a certain amount of alcohol at a certain time in the mouse's pregnancy.[7]

I can only imagine what was occurring inside the minds of those judges. None of their learned legal training was mentioned. No one mentioned any cases from the Court Of Appeal, the *Criminal Code*, or even a courtroom.

The legal education program was designed to humanize, or, as Steve Van Matre would say, "acclimatize" the judges to the reality of a world they did not know. When I speak to judges, I emphasize play, fun, and, especially, the game of follow the leader. From one perspective, outdoor education as a whole is in many ways a giant game of follow the leader.

A central tenet of outdoor education is the effort to make learning fun, to make it a game. As part of my efforts to teach judges about fetal alcohol, I ask the judges to use both their hands and put their thumbs and first fingers together making a triangle. I tell them everyone in this room has a complete brain; like a solid sandstone pyramid, 99 floors high. The triangle represents the solid pyramid, their complete brain. I make sure everyone has their fingers as a triangle. I emphasize something solid, like rock. I say, "Everyone here has a brain like a solid sandstone pyramid with an elevator that goes to each floor, and, in certain conditions, we have express elevators that rush to a preselected floor." I make sure everyone in the room uses his or her fingers to make this triangle. If someone does not play along, I cajole or use the grandfather voice and say, "Do it!" Often, I find out who is the most senior judge/lawyer and say, "Judge Smith is doing it, so play along." Peer pressure works, especially with people in hierarchical organizations like courts, prisons, the military, or paramilitary organizations like the RCMP. I then use my fingers to make two interlocking circles and have the judges follow along. I say, alcohol does two things: it both kills brain cells and also connects brain cells to the wrong brain cells. I also say at the end that I can provide the references to all the science. The judges rarely ask. The point is that fetal alcohol involves cellular misconnections and missing brain cells. Brain function is therefore reduced, and the deficiency sets up behaviour issues we call "criminal code violations." I tell the judges that people with fetal alcohol have a brain like a sandstone pyramid with skylights and that their fetal alcohol elevators stop at only even-numbered floors and never get above floor 87. Their pyramid is honeycombed, and parts are blocked off or unavailable.

By this time, I have a compliant audience.

I stress that if the judges continue to participate, they will know more about fetal alcohol than most psychiatrists, psychologists, and court-ordered experts. I then have these judges, all of them, put their hands together outstretched with palms up so they form a platform, a disc with their little fingers touching and thumbs on the outside of the flat disc created. I say that this is a model of the baby's brain, at perhaps day 15 of pregnancy, a disc about the size of a pin prick. This disc grows to a ball that is the brain you have today. I show them how to make a ball by curling the fingers into two fists side by side knuckles touching. I wiggle my two thumbs and say the thumbs represent your frontal lobes. I make this disc into a ball and wiggle my frontal lobe fingers several times and make everyone do so. I did the same when teaching the sing-song saying about tying a bowline with children. I make sure that everyone participates. Laughter is an important part of this, too; the emphasis on laughter ensures that no one falls, or no one fails. The complete participation of everyone present is the key. I challenge the judges if they refuse to play, the same way I encouraged youth to climb up a rock cliff: "You can do this Bob, Come on Karen, I know you can make the next move. Just try! You are safe on the rope. I have you connected to me!"

I promise the judges again, that if they do this next bit of silliness for the next two minutes they will know more about fetal alcohol than 99% of psychiatrists. Everyone seems to enjoy picking on psychiatrists. The lesson becomes a group exercise, a bit like cheering for Team Canada.

We practice brain development. Over and over again: from a disc to a ball several times. I tell them that is how their own brains developed. I describe the stages from snake brain, to dog brain, to chimpanzee brain, finally to human brain. To give the judges a picture of the human brain, I persuade them to take their right hands and use their four fingers, two in each eye socket, and grab their foreheads with their thumbs and hand and hang on. I ask them to hold this position for about one minute. I explain that the body part they are holding is the frontal lobe, the highest stage of brain development. There is something funny about being in a room with people holding their brains and eye sockets. The humour is infectious and helps to reduce defences; we lower our guards when we are laughing. With humour, we can take chances and be foolish in a group if everyone else is also doing silly things.

Several times I say, "From a disc to a ball, from a disc to a ball." I explain that the two fists are the two hemispheres of the neocortex, left and right, and that these two fists represent the chimpanzee brain. To represent the snake brain, I ask the judges to make a fist with their right hands and hold them up. That bump, I say, is the bump on top of the snake's spinal cord. It is the reptile brain, the brain of digestion, of elimination, of heart rate and respiration, and the basic instincts of reproduction.

To add to the bump, the bump atop the spine, I put the left hand over covering the bump like a rug. This, I tell the judges, is the dog brain, the limbic brain, the emotional brain, the brain of relationships. Here, I interject the well-known truism of fetal alcohol: all successful fetal alcohol interventions are through the limbic brain, the emotional brain, the brain of relationships. Every skilled probation officer knows relationships work best. Experienced probation officers know that relationships with their clients are the key to compliance. Brute force and threats create sullen youths in jail, waiting and angry. I point out that in terms of brain development, Rin Tin Tin and Lassie, with their dog brains, have vast improvements over the snake brain.

After the judges have made a dog brain, I have them make the two fists of the neocortex (again from a disc to a ball) and again tell them that is the chimpanzee brain. This next layer of brain is a vast improvement over dogs' brains. I wiggle my thumbs and repeat that they represent the frontal lobes. Then, when the judges are again grabbing their foreheads, I say, this is the brain of Shakespeare, the brain of the engineers who put a man on the moon, and the brain that gave you the wisdom from all the stuff that your mother told you.

Part of the exercise is to look foolish, to make the activity a game, and, crucially, to include everyone present. I make sure we are all laughing as we go along. I scan the crowd, and if someone is reluctant to play I point him or her out and heckle that person until he or she plays along, as I need everyone to play so we have a positive group identity.

When I have the normal-brain-science-by-hands demonstration complete, I go back and start again, making the disc of the baby's 15-day-old brain. Now we that are all playing, everyone makes a disc. I then say to the judges: "Take your chin and rub your chin bone around the edge of this disc you have created with your fingers that represents the baby's brain." I spend about 2 minutes here, at which point everyone rubs their chins on the tips of their fingers, over and over and over and over. Then I say, "That is alcohol on the periphery of the brain." You have now killed a few brain cells in a 15-day-old brain. They are gone, gone forever, and the cells that flow from these starter cells will never appear as the brain develops to create more complex brain structures. We then go through brain development again and we have our hands enact "from a disc to the ball." I tell the judges that alcohol kills deep core structures in the brain, and that Scientists like Ed Riley and Kathy Sulik can tell which parts are damaged.

I advise the judges that scientists can tell what parts of the brain are missing by the timing of when a pregnant mother drank alcohol. I explain again that alcohol does two things: it connects the brain cells to the wrong brain cells, and, more importantly, alcohol acts as a solvent, like nail polish remover, or paint remover. Alcohol bubbles away brain cells, with the result being that these cells are gone forever. If the audience is with me, I then do what I call the "alcohol dance." I draw a circle in front of me about 5 feet around, explaining that this circle represents one brain cell. I explain that alcohol is a slippery molecule and that alcohol slips into the cell between the parts of the cell wall. I stand on the edge of the imaginary circle and wiggle dance into the centre of the imaginary circle, the single cell. At this point, I tell the judges that alcohol is on both sides of the individual brain cell. With alcohol on both sides of the cell wall, cell death occurs. I tell the judges that Professor Ed Riley, of the University of San Diego, once told me over lunch that cell death sounds like a "pop," like the sound of a cork pulled rapidly out of a wine bottle.[8]

With enough cell death, the baby's brain stays incomplete and grows into a brain with missing pieces, wherein function is impaired and cognitive ability is reduced. Thus, people with fetal alcohol have lower cognitive skills than other people. What you take for granted as normal cognitive work for you, is not easy for them. Fetal alcohol people make mistakes, often the same mistakes, over and over again. I then repeat the process again, noting how the fetal alcohol brain has missing pieces; that is, it creates a permanent, physical, brain-based disability with reduced cognitive abilities. Repetition is as a helpful educational tool, even with judges.

Some people find this 20 minutes of play exhausting, even though all they have done is manipulated their hand and chins. Usually, no one is smiling and I have their complete attention. The emotional temperature is hot in the room. At this point I tell funny stories about things my clients have done. Everyone laughs until they realize they have seen or heard similar stories in their court rooms or their law practice. I then share with the judges an accurate way to diagnose fetal alcohol in their courtroom: when, at a first appearance or bail hearing, the prosecutor reads the police report or the set of facts that lead to the arrest, and everyone in the room laughs. This reaction indicates that everyone thinks the defendant is a first-timer. Then the crown prosecutor reads out a long criminal record, and the laughing stops. I use this example to urge the judges to focus less on deviant behaviour and focus more on the brain before them. Ask: "What is going on in that brain? I would not do that, and neither would anyone I know."

I encourage questions at any stage of this experiential learning process, telling participants to just yell them out. After doing this activity for 15 years, I have learned that, whether in Australia or Alaska, the questions are the same.

I also acknowledge that this type of activity is not a standard legal lesson, and I talk law for a moment. I refer to famous fetal alcohol cases and the foundational McNaughten Rules of Victorian England. I like to end with positives, so I offer suggestions to make the judges' courtrooms more brain-friendly. The point of funny stories and hand-dancing is to activate different parts of the brain, to use storytelling as a way to discuss difficult legal and political issues. Fetal alcohol is political because we all have this little voice in our heads that says: "They should not get away with it." We demand our pound of flesh. Irrationally, society demands that jail be used to cure missing brain cells.

This paper is not arguing against "book learning." I am simply saying that too much of our judicial education is a high-speed version of law school: strictly cognitive "book learning." What is lost under this educational framework is the point that people with fragmented brains are not like us: they need to be treated differently. This lesson of difference is not easy for judges, who are trained to treat all equally.

An important part of outdoor education is that learning can be fun. I do not humiliate the people in the class, but I do push them to an edge where they can step outside their narrow judicial conservative lives and, along with others for a few minutes, do a slightly foolish exercise. Outdoor education is complementary education. For example, both high school biology and physical education are still required to be successful. I have found that the hand games and acting allow the judges to relax and transport themselves to a different place, a cognitively less defended place. Helping judges arrive at this type of less defensive outlook is crucial to this experiential process, in part because I am challenging some basic assumptions in law.

The fact is that judges have heard enough law to choke a dinosaur; they can read. They do not need or want someone to read another scholarly paper to them. What is needed is a way to talk about brains in a few minutes and in ways that are fun. Outdoor education practices, and experiential education in general, allow people to have a body memory, a new frame of reference. My work with judges is not a replacement for scholarly papers; it is designed to be complementary with other forms of learning, and it is a gentle way to explain fetal alcohol to judges.

David Boulding
January 2017

I owe Professor Emeritus Gordon Johnston of Trent University for his hours of helping a former student, and Professor Susan Brooks of Drexel University Law School for her suggestions. All the errors are mine, and the bumpy bits too.

Endnotes

1 My high school geography teacher Carl Herman was a former lawyer. He said I might read Postman and Weingartner's *Teaching as a Subversive Activity*. Written in 1969, the book was a welcome shock. Quickly, I read all Postman and Weingartner's books. I now give the book to beginning teachers. I have three extra copies, just in case I meet a young teacher.
   While studying Native Studies at Trent University, Peterborough, Ontario, Canada, I met Professor D.N. McCaskill. He said I must read Paulo Friere's *Pedagogy of the Oppressed*. While in law school, I went back to Friere and read everything he wrote. I missed meeting Friere when he came to speak at UBC. McCaskill also said I might read Carl Roger's *Freedom to Learn*. While doing my Masters' in Poetry/ Rhetoric, I went back and read everything Carl Rogers wrote. My reading has informed my teaching.

2 This mnemonic was developed by Dr. Julianne Conry, now retired from 35 years at the University of British Columbia. She is a neurological educational psychology expert and one of the authors of the only study in the world on prevalence of fetal alcohol in jails. She now works at the Asante Centre in Maple Ridge, British Columbia, Canada, doing clinical assessments of people with fetal alcohol.

3 Diane Malbin is the author of the best book on fetal alcohol: *Trying Differently Rather than Harder*. Available at fascets.org., her book is 80 pages and costs 20 dollars: I tell people if you cannot afford the 20 dollars, then write the title on your mirror and read the words daily. The second-best book, also by Diane, is called a *Collection of Information for Professionals*. It costs 25 dollars and is a plastic-coil-bound opus of 200 hundred pages and is available at the same non-profit organization in Portland Oregon. I have had hours and hours of personal conversation with Diane, who is fond of telling this "no solution, no problem" story from her student days. Diane and I both agree we had great teachers.

4 Steve Van Matre. *Acclimatizing*, 1967, published by the American Camping Association. Now out of print. It is available at Amazon used books for one dollar and $6.49 shipping. The book is the central text of experiential education.

5 The paper is widely available, translated in several languages, on the Internet and at my website: www.davidboulding.com for free.

6 This is the most obscure important fact I can think of.

7 Professor K. Sulik can be reached by email: mouse@med.unc.edu

8 Professor Ed Riley at San Diego State University has spent his life studying the brains of people with fetal alcohol. He is a distinguished Professor of Psychology and the Director of the Center for Behavioural Teratology. Along with Professor Sulik and Professor Anne Streissguth, now retired, from Seattle, and Professor Susan Astley, also from Seattle, Ed Riley is a giant in the field. Canadian research is centered in Maple Ridge BC, where Doctor K. Asante has just retired and where Dr. Julianne Conry still toils away. Dr. Sterling Clarren M.D., formerly of Seattle, heads a Vancouver consortium of researchers from the western provinces. Brilliant people are also doing necessary work in Winnipeg and St John's Newfoundland.

CHAPTER 6

Reconceptualizing Inclusion: A Critical Exploration for Educators

Luigi Iannacci, Frank Muia, and Mauro Porco

Abstract

This chapter critically explores a variety of perspectives regarding inclusion. Misunderstandings about inclusion that have depicted it as only achievable within the confines of regular classroom are also questioned. The chapter begins by exploring legal perspectives that govern and mandate inclusion, and then explores philosophical, epistemological, organizational, practical, pedagogic, and economic perspectives to form an ethical and responsive model/understanding and operationalizing of inclusion/ inclusive practices. Throughout this critical exploration, educators are provided information that allows them to re-think what they have come to know/understand about inclusion and how to lead in ways that dynamically forward it. Dominant and under-theorized/researched misconceptions and limited notions of what is meant by inclusion are destabilized throughout this critical exploration. The chapter provides framing and information that can be applied in a variety of educational contexts such as school boards, schools and in-/pre-service teacher education. Educational leaders are provided an explicit and clear frame for critically thinking about inclusion/inclusive practices that are responsive to the various needs of students with special needs and students identified as exceptional.

Introduction

Despite its importance, "inclusion" has been and continues to be an often misunderstood term within the field of education.[1] Roth (2015) uses the expression "inclusion confusion" to refer to this lack of clarity. Misunderstandings of people with disabilities are, unfortunately, nothing new. Disability and societal responses to people with disabilities have had a troubled and troubling past, influenced by problematic dominant discourses and riddled with human rights abuses. Throughout the 16th century, for example, people with disabilities were thought of as demonic and subjected to violence in an effort to exorcise the spirits that the disabled were thought to possess (Munyi, 2012). Later, in the 19th century, the eugenics movement's treatment of them as genetically undesirable led to their isolation, sterilization and death (Black, 2012). The 20th century's dominant disability discourse, which continues to prevail in Special Education, is heavily informed by medical models and metaphors that view people with disabilities as patients with ailments in need of diagnosing, pathologizing and normalizing (Heydon & Iannacci, 2008). This essentialist model (Hosking, 2008) is a re-tooling of previous ideas, as it continues to configure disability as an innate flaw requiring interventions to "fix."

Although we are now in an era of unprecedented litigiousness that has somewhat protected the human rights of people with disabilities, the nature of disability, and how we collectively respond to people with disabilities within institutions, remains conceptually unclear and operationally problematic. Hibbert (2013) astutely captures one of the most significant issues with respect to inclusion:

> [D]uring my professional practice in a school system, we initiated the under-theorized move in the Special Education field toward 'inclusive classrooms'; a practice that saw 'exceptional' students served within their own

---

1 Inclusion within education also applies to cultural, linguistic, racial, religious, gender, sexual, socio-economic and other forms of diversity, and the ways schools have responded to them. This chapter, however, focuses on inclusion as it relates to students with disabilities.

classrooms rather than being withdrawn or assigned full-time to segregated placements. The superficial and problematic 'shift' occurred in the physical world; it was only a matter of moving bodies, scheduling resources and collaborating with classroom teachers. The necessary and complex epistemological shift has proven much more challenging. To move from a universal approach to practice that focuses on optics, to a differentiated response designed around students' needs, abilities and resources, requires a sophisticated shift in thinking. (p. 29)

Our[2] collective experiences, concerns and perspectives as teachers/educational leaders in classroom/school/school board and pre/in service and graduate education contexts are very similar to those described by Hibbert (2013). Thus, we frequently encounter reductionist misnomers that fail to address the discursive nature of disability and the subsequent complexities of inclusion and have too often observed limited and limiting collective responses toward people with disabilities. In this chapter, we attempt to address these issues by critically exploring a variety of perspectives regarding inclusion in order to problematize the limited conceptualizations and misunderstandings that have restricted people with disabilities and our responses to them. The chapter begins by exploring the nature of disability in order to destabilize dominant grand narratives that have prevented a dynamic and complex understanding and operationalizing of inclusion within education. Next, this chapter explores the legal perspectives that govern and mandate inclusion. Finally, this chapter critically discusses the philosophical, epistemological, pedagogical, organizational and economic perspectives that contribute to an ethical and responsive model/understanding/definition of inclusion/inclusive practices. This critical analysis will provide educators information that will enable them to re-think their understanding of disability and inclusion and to provide responsive and dynamic leadership for developing such a model. The dominant and under-theorized/researched misconceptions of what is meant by disability and inclusion are destabilized

---

2 Throughout this chapter, "our" or "we" refers to the writers (Luigi Iannacci, Frank Muia, and Mauro Porco).

throughout this critical exploration. The chapter therefore provides an explicit framework for critically thinking about the kind of inclusion/inclusive practices that will respond to the various needs of students with disabilities. This framework can be applied to educational contexts such as school boards, schools and in/pre service teacher education in order to clarify what inclusion is and, subsequently, to help educators make decisions that will support that.

Deconstructing Disability

In order to fully understand inclusion, it is essential to critically explore how disability has been discursively organized. This unpacking and disrupting of disability will help educators develop complex understandings of inclusion that avoid reinscribing notions of disability as a monolith or, worse, a deficit (Fraser & Shields, 2010). Critical Disability Theory (CDT) is useful for destabilizing and reconfiguring dominant notions/discourses of disability. CDT conceptualizes disability as socially constructed and socially mediated (Hosking, 2008). 'Disability' is therefore neither a fossilized, neutral "thing" nor an inherent flaw. This way of understanding disability requires an interrogation of the language used to refer to those identified as disabled in the context of dis/ability and critically questions the impact of normative discourses (e.g., able/disabled binaries) and how these binaries reproduce/evoke/draw on other discourses (e.g., developmentalism and standardization) (Pothier & Devlin, 2006). Thus, disabilities as being created by society are therefore "approached best as a cultural fabrication" (McDermott & Varenne, 1995, p. 323) rather than inherent flaws within people. Titchkovsky (2007) further explained:

> 'Disability'... is a process of meaning-making that takes place somewhere and is done by somebody. Whenever disability is perceived, spoken, or even thought about, people mean it in some way. The ways that disability comes to have meaning have something to teach us about our lifeworlds. Understanding disability as a site where meaning

is enacted not only requires conceptualizing disability as a social accomplishment, it also means developing an animated sense of that which enacts these meanings. (p. 12)

Disabilities are therefore "less the property of persons than they are moments in a cultural focus" (McDermott & Varenne, 1995, p. 323). Importantly, so much of the "disability discourse serves something other than the interests of disabled people...[as it] is made viable as a metaphor to express only that which is unwanted and that which is devastatingly inept" (Titchkovsky, 2007, p. 5). Hosking (2008) adds that disability has been conceived "as personal misfortune preferably to be prevented and definitely to be cured, privileges 'normalcy' over the 'abnormal,' presumes able-bodied norms are inevitable, and values economic productivity as an essential aspect of personhood" (p. 6). The language assigned to people with disabilities and the ways in which this language compromises their personhood and reifies their identities in relation to their defined and measured deficiencies, is therefore also a central concern of CDT because "disability" is ultimately a text that can be read and written about, and also a "prime space to reread and rewrite a culture's makings" (Titchkovsky, 2007, p. 6). Critical attention to how disability is read and written is therefore one way to participate in the disability studies project of destabilization. Such attention can lead us toward reading and writing disability differently, and "provide for the possibility of developing new relations to the cultural values that ground the various appearances and disappearances of disability in everyday life" (Titchosky, 2007, p. 5). Educators must understand and be guided by this social and critical model of disability in order to support inclusion and develop inclusive practices.

An Asset-Oriented Model of Inclusion and Ethical Praxis

In response to the social model of disability, asset-oriented understandings of and approaches to disability and people with disabilities have been and continue to be developed (Heydon & Iannacci, 2008). An asset-oriented approach recognizes people with disabilities as possessing literacies and social, cognitive, artistic, emotional, cultural, linguistic, affective, and epistemological resources. Rather than seeing students with disabilities as lacking or as being deficient, this perspective positions them as capable, and full of possibility, based on their ways of knowing and learning rather than on how well they conform to and perform taken-for-granted normative ways of producing and understanding knowledge within educational environments. This perspective rejects the terms and concepts that have compromised countless students' personhood and reified their identities in relation to limited definitions and measured "deficiencies." Asset-oriented ways of seeing and responding to people with disabilities therefore also rejects "at-risk" discourses and attempts to re-position people as "at-promise" (Swadener & Lubeck, 1995). This way of understanding disability requires a critical examination of, and also a shift in, the language embedded in the dominant understandings we have about disability. The conscious use of people-first language created to ensure that individuals are not defined solely by their disabilities and, therefore, to highlight personhood and subsequently foster a paradigm shift in our understanding of disability, is one way to accomplish this shift (Snow, 2005). Critiques of people-first language (Vaughan, 2009) contend that it is cumbersome and grammatically awkward, but many people who have a disability have advocated for and benefitted from the use of such language, while others have self-identified with, and have been empowered by, the terms and labels that they have reclaimed. Critics question whether people-first language can address macro societal inequities that marginalize people who have disabilities. Although we understand and are critically aware of these arguments, we see language as *one* of many factors contributing to the problematic ways that society has constructed, understood and responded to disability. We see the use of people-first language not as a grammar issue or a matter of political correctness, but rather as a strategy that can be used to destabilize the dominant and limiting perspectives that have undermined people with disabilities. Language matters: how we talk and think and what we do are inextricably intertwined. Thus people-first language reminds us that we cannot define a person by any single attribute, and that doing so creates an "othering" distance that perpetuates the "us/them" binary that has contributed to the unethical marginalization, diminished humanity, and, in too many cases, suffering of people who have a disability.

Essentially, fostering asset-oriented informed inclusion necessitates a focus on ethics and ethical decision making *in situ*, based on students' needs, abilities and resources, rather than on an adherence to bureaucratic and dehumanizing grand narratives. Allen (2005) considered the project of inclusion to be an ethical one, and argued for a "fundamental shift away from the deficit-oriented thinking that has for so long driven educational practices" (p. 282). Developing an ethical praxis with respect to inclusion therefore requires asking critical questions about the social construction of disability in order to deconstruct and destabilize what has come to be taken for granted as the "norm" and recognizing "the special education/general education duality as a discriminatory structure" (Heydon, 2008, p. 92). Doing so does not mean a dismantling of special education, as students can benefit from what it may offer them. Rather, what is required is a commitment to deconstructing and reconceptualizing what education and, therefore, special education are and do in order to fulfill their ethical obligation to respect diversity and respond to it by creating inclusive learning environments for all students. An asset-oriented approach is just beginning to influence the field of education, and further work to create truly inclusive spaces informed by this approach is essential given the significant number of students who either have been or will be identified as having a disability. This chapter adds to the growing body of literature that is beginning to destabilize the dominant perception of disability in educational contexts and to foster an asset-oriented model and definition of inclusion.

Legal Perspectives

Contradictory ideas about inclusion in education must be addressed by clarifying some of the related legal issues. On the one hand, we have encountered educators at various stages of their careers in a variety of contexts, including classrooms, school boards and universities, who conflate inclusion with the myriad of trends, initiatives and mandates that have come and gone throughout their careers. The ways in which these fads and directives have disappeared only to be replaced by other policies, programs, pedagogies and practices have created a culture of skepticism about the longevity of inclusion, and misunderstandings about educators' responsibilities to ensure its implementation. Therefore, educators must realize that inclusion is a matter of law rather than yet another fleeting trend/movement in education. Various national and provincial laws, policies and bills (e.g., *Canadian Charter of Rights and Freedoms*, the *Ontario Human Rights Code, Education Act*) create a legal hierarchy that guarantees and requires that exceptional students have access to public education. Parts of the *Ontario Education Act* make explicit that all school boards are to provide special education programs and services for all students regardless of their exceptionality. These Canadian national and provincial laws, policies and bills are internationally supported by *The UN Convention on the Rights of Persons with Disabilities*, which asserts that everyone has the right to an inclusive education. Importantly, Canada was among the first countries to sign the convention and continues to be accountable for implementing its overarching principles. As a result, inclusion is required by law.

In contrast, the superficial view of inclusion within education (as previously articulated by Hibbert, 2013), has often been limited to the practice of including students with disabilities in regular school classes. Again, while working in schools and with teachers and administrators in professional development situations, we have often encountered this optics-driven and problematic understanding of inclusion and have been perplexed, as no legal/policy supports or validates this model. Inclusion is not, nor should it ever be, understood as a geographic location in a school (e.g., the "regular" classroom) and such an understanding/way of operationalizing inclusion does not adhere to the legal requirements for inclusion/inclusive practice. Merely placing students in a regular classroom all day, or allowing them to use a resource room, does not ensure inclusion. We have observed students who were placed in regular classrooms all day under the guise of inclusion, but were still excluded as members of their learning communities, which were not meeting these students' needs. Inclusion does not require that every student with a disability be placed in a regular classroom all day. Such an understanding recalls integration or mainstreaming. This earlier model was unsuccessful in responding to the needs, assets and interests of all students. Accordingly, offering a range of placement options is necessary to support inclusion. Winzer (2008) clarified the two models and the central issues they raise: "Integration and mainstreaming sought to change individuals to fit the existing system; inclusion seeks to change the system so that exclusion and marginalization are avoided" (p. 43). The importance of meeting students' needs is vital to inclusion, and is often emphasized in legal/policy language. To that end, education and educators must provide students who have a disability the least restrictive environment possible by ensuring that the available placement options are safe, engaging and responsive to their needs, and do not academically, socially, psychologically or emotionally marginalize students who have a disability. Thus, placement options should depend on the students involved and be chosen based on their needs, interests and assets. Placement decisions that satisfy these criteria will reflect an ethical praxis. It's interesting that this clarification and validation of decision making still needs to occur given the fact that the placement options identified during Identification Placement Review Committee (IPRC) processes and listed on Individual Educational Plans (IEPs) (legal processes and documents in Ontario) are as follows:

- Regular class with indirect support
- Special education class with partial integration
- Regular class with resource assistance
- Regular class with withdrawal assistance
- Special education class full-time

Further, in Ontario, many full-time, self-contained special education classrooms are still meeting the needs of some students identified as exceptional. Our collective experiences as teachers, administrators and teacher educators verify the potential effectiveness of this placement option in supporting inclusion within schools.

Philosophical Perspectives

Inclusion is much more than a legal requirement, or a thoughtful consideration of placement options. The "bigger picture" of inclusion means that we embrace and are responsive to the diversity within public institutions. For schools, this response requires building welcoming communities where all students are valued, provided for, have a sense of belonging, and are actively engaged in their education. Again, this philosophy does not necessarily exclude the possibility of special education classes – inclusion can still be accomplished through a variety of placement options and participation in co-curricular activities, social events, and programs. Importantly, inclusion requires positive beliefs and attitudes about the various ways people live in and know the world, as well as how they express and demonstrate their understanding of it. Disability advocate Kunc (1992) has helped to clarify what should be the main feature of philosophical understandings of inclusion:

> The fundamental principle of inclusive education is the valuing of diversity within the human community....When inclusive education is fully embraced, we abandon the idea that children have to become "normal" in order to contribute to the world....We begin to look beyond typical ways of becoming valued members of the community, and in doing so, begin to realize the achievable goal of providing all children with an authentic sense of belonging. (pp. 38-39)

Thus, a central concern of inclusion is being critically aware of the tyranny of the norm and working to destabilize its coercive power. Doing so requires educators to see present systems that categorize, organize, and evaluate people based on their "age and stage" as problematic and deeply flawed. Developmental and standardized understandings of learning and growth are therefore questioned, as are notions of what human beings are supposed to know and do based on durations of time (e.g., "By the end of Grade___, students will;" "By the end of this course, students will:" [3]).

---

3 These directives appear throughout Ontario elementary and secondary school curriculum documents.

Learning and development are understood as being shaped by a variety of factors, and as reflecting human diversity, rather than as *things* that can be measured against established norms; and subsequently they are understood as less than, deficient and in need of fixing. Harman (2009) succinctly captures how essential this thinking is to inclusion:

> Successful models of inclusion believe that ALL children are different, and ALL children can learn. There is nothing about a child that needs to be "fixed" in order for that child to fit into a system. The school system, as a whole, is enabled to change in order to meet the individual needs of ALL learners. (p. 1, original emphasis)

In order for this model of inclusion to be implemented, we need to understand disability as part of a person's identity rather than as a deficiency. Therefore we must recognize that students have a variety of social, cognitive, artistic, emotional, cultural, linguistic, and affective assets and legacies (Delpit, 2003) that must be understood and addressed. A student's disability must therefore be conceptualized as part of who the student is and how they understand the world, and as one of the many legacies he/she carries with them that are valuable to the student's community. This community should see the various identities of its members as important and educative. The community's primary focus should not be on assimilating its members into one way of being, seeing, understanding, acting, or knowing, but, rather, on collectively benefitting from the myriad of experiences and epistemologies present within that community. The importance of recognizing, responding to, and learning from the epistemological diversity available to community members in inclusive environments is further discussed in the next section.

Epistemological Perspectives

If inclusion is to be philosophically understood, its epistemological nature needs to be made explicit. Epistemology is concerned with knowing, understanding and theorizing how we know/come to know and what we consider "knowledge." As previously mentioned, an asset-oriented model of inclusion recognizes and capitalizes on people's assets and ways of knowing. This way of conceptualizing inclusion necessitates that disability be understood as a construct that requires repositioning from a deficiency-based concept to valued knowledge. Disability must therefore be seen as making valuable contributions to the epistemological diversity that exists within schools. Inclusion is much more than a model, practice, or strategy: it is a way of being and knowing. Rather than continuing to rely on studies that repeatedly assert that students with disabilities do not negatively impact "other" students academically in inclusive classrooms, (e.g., Dessemontet & Bless, 2013), educators need to think about and explore disability as an epistemology that allows learning communities to garner insights into ways of knowing and being that they would not otherwise have. This knowledge is essential and educative, and its denial contributes to the marginalization and miseducation of students. Inclusion is therefore an ethical project, because not only is it committed to respecting and responding to people with disabilities, it also fosters understandings in students; understandings that challenge and disrupt ablest sensibilities developed in environments where disability is rendered invisible as a way of knowing and deficient as a way of being. Carlson (2010) noted how difficult developing this new perspective can be, given the challenges people with disabilities may have in *articulating* their standpoint and identity, and also given that our current understandings of epistemology are founded on a *certain kind* of knowledge. In order for this issue to be addressed so that epistemological diversity is valued within inclusive environments, we need to interrogate what is meant by *articulation* and the *certain kind of knowledge* we presently privilege. Doing so requires a critical exploration of what we have recognized as literacy, because personhood and thought have been problematically linked to narrow conceptualizations of literacy.

Pedagogical Perspectives

Kliewer, Biklen and Kasa-Hendrickson (2006) have investigated how people with disabilities have been denied personhood based on the idea that they do not possess, or are incapable of demonstrating, literacy.

These authors destabilize the problematic idea that "citizenship in the literate community is an organic impossibility for people defined as intellectually disabled" (p. 163). Through a critical exploration of various cases of historical figures, Kliewer et al. (2006) demonstrated "literate invisibility as a product of cultural dehumanization" (p. 167). Dominant discourses and ideas about the nature of literacy as a print and verbocentric endeavour have contributed to this invisibility and "cultural denial of competence" (p. 163). Traditionally, literacy has been understood as the ability to use the technology of the spoken word (print) and as such, something that is articulable or demonstrated in orthographically sanctioned ways (e.g., an alphabetic system). Understandings of literacy developed by the New London Group (1996) have disrupted these ideas and helped render visible the various kinds of literacies people possess. The shift from thinking about literacy as singular to understanding it as multiple encapsulates this dynamic redefining of literacy. The two major aspects of multiliteracies are (1) the variability of meaning making in different cultural, social or professional contexts and (2) how meaning is made in ways that are increasingly multimodal and involve interactions with a range of semiotic systems (written, visual, verbal, audio, spatial, non-verbal, e.g., silence, kinesics, proxemics) (Hornberger, 2000) and also with mediating devices (e.g., technology) (Gee, 2001). Meaning-making is then related to engagements with or the creation of texts and, in short, includes the ability to make sense of and/or produce texts by using any number of modalities (Cope & Kalantzis, 2000).

An asset-oriented model of inclusion supports the notion that literacy is not just about the knowledge, acquisition, and use of a singular code, but a culture (Iannacci, 2007). The ways language and literacy develop, are understood, and are valued are a result of their use within social contexts. Thus, how people understand, come to, and use literacy in particular social contexts and what they gain in so doing becomes a central concern for understanding what literacy is and what it does (Toohey, 2000). This perspective recognizes that texts are privileged and marginalized differently in different contexts. As culture creates what is deemed literacy, the ways in which this forming of literacy reinforces ablest sensibilities become evident, and therefore what has been sanctioned as literate behaviour is not only questioned when applied to and used against people with disabilities but is also opened up in order to reveal how people make meaning of the world with a variety of communicative options that are well beyond conventional print use or verbal utterance. Viewing literacy in this way allows us to examine the values, mores, norms, and worldviews embedded in our current understandings, and also troubles what we think we know about, and how we provide for, students deemed disabled. These perspectives allow us to be conscious of how our use of specific terms and concepts compromises countless students' personhood and how we reify their identities in relation to limited definitions and measured deficiencies. Further, these perspectives also reveal how the limited and limiting ways in which pedagogies assigned to students with disabilities based on narrow notions of literacy have supported the special education/regular education binary and processes of pathologization that result in pedagogical determinism (Iannacci, 2018) wherein students with disabilities are assigned and resigned to fragmented, rote oriented, context-reduced literacy curricula (Barone, 2002, Delpit, 2003, Iannacci, 2008). Therefore we must no longer focus on whether placement options are commensurate with inclusion, but rather think critically about the quality of instruction offered to students who may benefit from placement options that are not exclusively the regular classroom.

Any placement options deemed best for students need to be questioned in terms of what is being offered to them in these learning environments. This question is vital given the pedagogically impoverished (Iannacci, 2018) instruction we have provided to students with disabilities. Multiliteracies perspectives can forward pedagogies that are dynamic and responsive to the various ways that students with disabilities make meaning and demonstrate their knowledge and identity. As such, these perspectives are commensurate with pedagogical foundations of inclusion such as universal design (UD) and differentiated instruction (DI). Allowing all students to use a variety of communication options to demonstrate what they know is universally beneficial and reflects UD. Further, when students' particular ways of knowing require specific access to modalities that allow their knowledge to be demonstrated, instruction, assessment, and evaluation can be differentiated in order to respond to these assets. Thus, instructional, assessment, and environmental accommodations and modifications can be developed to ensure responsiveness to the learner rather than a superficial compliance to a limited understanding of inclusion.

In the Spring of 2013, the Ontario Ministry of Education released Policy/Program Memorandum 119 entitled *Developing and Implementing Equity and Inclusive Education Policies in Ontario Schools*. The memo compels school boards to develop an equity and inclusive education policy that removes barriers for students with diverse learning needs. It specifically encourages the use of differentiated instruction, to take into account, "the backgrounds and experiences of students in order to respond to their individual interests, aptitudes, and learning needs" (p. 6). A multiliteracies framework supports and allows for UD and DI to be pedagogically fostered within classrooms. This way of thinking about, fostering, and instructionally planning for literacy engagement should be the focus of our thinking about inclusion and designing of inclusive practices.

Organizational Perspectives

The above discussion has direct implications for boards of education/school structures and leadership. Inclusion requires administering, planning, preparing, and support. Ongoing professional development and collaboration among various professionals engaged in supporting inclusion is therefore vital to its success. Too many teachers we have worked with have lamented not feeling equipped to implement inclusion. In some instances, this problem has led to support staff such as Educational Resource Workers (ERWs) being left solely responsible for students with disabilities (Fraser & Shields, 2009). To be clear, ERWs are not in and of themselves either an accommodation or a signifier of inclusion, and neither are resource rooms. Accommodations must be either developed in response to students' needs by teachers, or co-developed by the members of a team supporting a student. Moreover, team members must be able to access and demonstrate knowledge of the kind of programming and curriculum that is commensurate with the student's zone of proximal development (Vygotsly, 1978). Doing so means identifying programming and/or focusing on curriculum expectations just beyond the student's independent capabilities. An educator's role is therefore pivotal in identifying and designing the curriculum and the accommodations students require to engage with and achieve these expectations. Again, inclusion involves more than merely the placement of, or personnel assigned to, a student (i.e., placing a student in a regular classroom or assigning them an ERW). Educators foster inclusion by creating a learning environment that enables a student to thrive. In order to provide such an environment, educators need to understand and respond to the student's assets, interests, and needs rather than depending on a placement or resource (human or otherwise) to deliver the illusion of inclusion.

Authentic, successful practices that foster inclusion involve teachers, parents, assigned support staff, and leadership from administrators for planning and decision making. Schools and school boards need to develop effective plans and implement the required supports and services, including on-going professional development and opportunities for conversation, consulting, and the co-creation of planning and pedagogy, in order for inclusion to occur. The previously mentioned *Ontario Ministry of Education Policy/Program Memorandum 119* (2013) now requires educators to provide opportunities and plans for stakeholder collaboration in developing and implementing inclusive education. Harpell, Andrews, and Jac (2010) have identified differentiated instruction and a team approach as essential components for educational leaders attempting to systematically plan for, and provide educators opportunities to operationalize, inclusion. These authors argue that these vital components help to create a school culture where educators feel empowered to foster inclusion/inclusive practices. Similarly, Obiakor, Harris, Mutua, Rotatori, and Algozzine (2012) argued that "inclusion for students with disabilities is most effective when teachers are collaborative and consultative" (p. 482). These authors identify various strategies that can structure this collaboration and allow it to occur. What the authors outline can enable a teacher to (1) provide instruction while another teacher provides students additional support, (2) group[4] students and have teachers work with specific groups (3) allow teachers to plan together and teach a lesson to small groups, (4) have a teacher teach while another pre-teaches and re-teaches students who need additional support, and, (5) create teaching teams that provide instruction in the same room and support students simultaneously (p. 483). This attention to professional development and collaboration demonstrates that inclusion is neither a thing or place nor is it achieved by a single person. Rather, inclusion requires a collective response to ensure a community is valued, responded to, and provided for in ways that ensure its social and academic success. To provide this response, educational leaders working at various levels in schools and school boards must purposefully and thoughtfully organize opportunities for those working with students to discuss, design, and develop inclusive practices and environments.

Economic Perspectives

Much debate has occurred about the economic costs of inclusion. Unfortunately, the discussions have created a problematic binary that unproductively focuses on whether inclusion is more or less expensive than previous models (Odom, Parrish, & Hikido, 2001). These arguments have failed to critically or consciously consider the ethics of this binary. Warnock (2010), a pioneer of the inclusion movement, has stated that inclusion was originally conceptualized on the grounds of its educational merit, rather than its costs. The *Sharing Promising Practices Resource Guide: Kindergarten to Grade Four* (2010), published by the Ontario Psychological Association, reports that in one school board:

> Potential poor readers are being identified as early as kindergarten and provided with intervention through differentiated instruction in the classroom. This model means that children do not have to be removed from the

---

4 Within inclusive learning environments, groups can be organized homogenously or heterogeneously in terms of ability but can also can be formed based on students' similar assets and interests. Groups should be created and recreated fluidly and responsively.

classroom....This model is thus cheaper to implement (after teacher in-service)....(p. 100)

In addition to the problematic practice of early intervention, our responses to learners with disabilities can no longer be organized and framed in this economic and crude manner. In order for inclusion to be managed respectfully, effectively, and as originally intended, resources need to be allocated responsively and strategically rather than based on misguided objectives and monetary misnomers. Inclusion is a social justice issue, so when discussions about its efficacy are reduced to debates about whether it is a cost-saving measure or not, students with disabilities are once again dehumanized. These debates are especially important as the economics of special education already positions students with disabilities as financially lucrative.

Arguments that support labelling/categorizing structures frequently point out that students with disabilities require resources that formal identification processes can materialize, as disability becomes officiated and subsequent institutional responses require resources be allocated to a student who has been identified as disabled. This argument, however, conceals how systems create the 'hunt for disability' (Baker, 2002), perpetuated by the lure of special education funding and the belief that resources can and will provide the necessary "treatments" to help "fix" disabled students. These resources (both human and material) benefit particular groups and organizations and need to be questioned, given that current special education systems and processes have configured pathologization as a necessary endeavour in securing these resources, thus preventing a critical consideration of the ethics of special education funding. Warnock (2010) reported that the committee she was part of that originally advocated for inclusion "never thought that ... children's supposed special needs would be exaggerated and exploited in order to attract more money for schools" (p. 1-2). We therefore need to reject pathologization and focus on ensuring that resources are sought based on students' needs rather than on attributing deficits to students in order to receive additional funding. In the current education paradigm, our accounting measures perpetuate conceptualizations of exceptional students as "less than" or "faulty" because the allocation of resources is a numbers-driven process. In Ontario, for example, the reports that secure funding are submitted thrice yearly to the Ministry of Education.[5] The problematic and imprecise standards of testing, and the subjective diagnostic descriptions and rating scales used to identify disability and to secure resources, perpetuate the hunt for disability. Further, this hunt fosters a culture in which, in order to receive these resources, administrators, special educators, psychologists and consultants may find themselves unwittingly and unintentionally complicit in ensuring that these standards/criteria are met. This type of culture can create levels of disability that do not represent students' needs and a climate where students with disabilities are "used as pawns in a financial game" (Warnock, 2010). Further, this culture inaccurately and inappropriately diagnoses and perpetuates demographics that overburden systems and therefore perpetuate the argument that inclusion is unsustainable, rather than focusing on a system that requires and rewards the patholigization of students. This issue raises critical questions about the ethics of understanding inclusion to mean only placing students with disabilities in regular classrooms in our current standardized focused educational context, after we have gone to great lengths to identify their specific needs and challenges that secure funding that is supposedly to be used to support them. All of the above requires a model of inclusion focused on to whom education and educators are ethically accountable, rather than financial pursuits and polemics.

Conclusion

The reconceptualization of inclusion we have developed throughout this chapter can be summarized as follows:

- Discourses that inform our understandings of and responses to disability and students with disabilities need to be critically interrogated in order to support inclusion and asset-oriented inclusive practices.

---

5 See for example the *Special Education Funding Guidelines: Special Incidence Portion (SIP)*, 2015-2016.

- An asset-oriented model of inclusion positions students with disabilities as possessing valuable resources.
- Inclusive language is used to ensure that personhood is the focus of thinking about, talking about, and being responsive to people with disabilities.
- Ethical praxis is vital to an asset-oriented model of inclusion and depends upon decision making that addresses the individual assets, interests, and needs of students with disabilities.
- Inclusion is a legal responsibility requiring a thoughtful consideration of placement options that respond to students' needs.
- Positive attitudes and beliefs about the various ways people experience the world are essential to foster inclusive learning communities.
- Disability is an epistemology and an important part of a person's identity. As such, disability is an asset that others can learn and benefit from. Respect, responsiveness, relationship, and reciprocity are key to fostering this way of understanding disability in inclusive environments.
- Multiliteracies perspectives recognize, understand, and capitalize on the various ways people come to understand, and demonstrate their knowledge of, the world, and how this occurs in various contexts through a variety of modalities. Multiliteracies pedagogies can therefore facilitate universal design, differentiated instruction, and the development of inclusive instruction.
- Inclusion depends upon leadership that supports consultative collaboration and provides opportunities for responsive professional development.
- Discussions and decisions about the economics of inclusion and funding for students with disabilities need to be informed by an ethical stance in order to ensure that the personhood of students with disabilities is not compromised and that legitimate resources are accessed to identify and support their needs.

What we have offered throughout this chapter is not prescriptive or complete. A reconceptualization of inclusion is by its very nature open to revision. Our aims were to provide necessary clarification and critical discussion about the questions, issues and challenges facing educators while they are attempting to support inclusion. Throughout our careers as classroom and special education teachers, teacher educators, and administrators, these issues have become evident and in need of addressing in order for inclusion to continue to be thoughtfully implemented. Continued critical discussions and planning are essential to ensure that students with disabilities are understood and provided for respectfully and responsively. We offer these perspectives in order to invite this much-needed critical conversation. Ultimately our aim is to offer an ethical and asset-oriented model of inclusion focused on improving education for students with disabilities.

References

Allan, J. (2005). Inclusion as an ethical project. In S. Tremain (Ed.), *Foucault and the government of disability* (pp. 281-298). Ann Arbor, MI: The University of Michigan Press.

Baker, B. (2002). The hunt for disability: The new eugenics and the normalization of school children. *Teachers College Record, 104*(4), 663-703.

Barone, D. (2002). Literacy teaching in two kindergarten classrooms in a school labeled at-risk. *The Elementary School Journal, 102*(5), 415-441.

Black, E. (2012). *War against the weak: Eugenics and America's campaign to create a master race.* Four Walls Eight Windows, New York.

Carlson, L. (2010). *The faces of intellectual disability: Philosophical reflections.* Bloomington, IN: Indiana University Press.

Canadian Charter of Rights and Freedoms, Part I of the *Constitution Act, 1982,* being Schedule B to the *Canada Act 1982* (U.K.), 1982, c. 11.

Cope, B., & Kalantzis, M. (Eds.) (2000). *Multiliteracies: Literacy learning and the design of social futures.* London: Routledge.

Cummins, J. (2005, April). *Diverse futures: Rethinking the image of the child in Canadian schools.* Presented at the Joan Pederson Distinguished Lecture Series. University of Western Ontario.

Delpit, L. (2003). Educators as "Seed People" growing a new future. *Educational Researcher, 32*(7), 14-21.

Dessemontet, R.S., & Bless, G. (2013). The impact of including children with intellectual disability in general education classrooms on the academic achievement of their low-, average-, and high-achieving peers. *Journal of Intellectual & Developmental Disability, 38*(1), 23-30.

Education Act, R.S.O. 1990, c. E.2.

Fraser, F.G., & Shields, C.M. (2010). Leaders' roles in disrupting dominant discourses and promoting inclusion. In A.L. Edmunds & R.B. Macmillan (Eds.), *Leadership for inclusion: A practical guide* (pp. 7-18). Rotterdam: Sense Publishers.

Gee, J.P. (2001). A sociocultural perspective of early literacy development. In S.B. Newman & D.K. Dickinson (Eds.), *Handbook of early literacy research* (pp. 30-42). New York: Guilford Press.

Harman, B. (2009). *Inclusion/Integration: Is there a difference?* Proceeding from the 10th World Down Syndrome Congress, Dublin City University, Dublin, Ireland. August 19th-22nd, 2009.

Harpell, J.V., & Andrews, J.J.W. (2010). Administrative leadership in the age of inclusion: Promoting best practices and teacher empowerment. *The Journal of Educational Thought, 44*(2), 189-210.

Heydon, R. (2008). Pathologizing within special education. In R. Heydon & L. Iannacci, *Early childhood curricula and the de-pathologizing of childhood* (pp. 82-99). Toronto, ON: University of Toronto Press.

Heydon R., & Iannacci, L. (2008). *Early childhood curricula and the de-pathologizing of childhood.* Toronto, ON: University of Toronto Press.

Hibbert, K. (2013). Finding wisdom in practice: The genesis of the Salty Chip, A Canadian multiliteracies collaborative. *Language and Literacy, 15*(1), 23-38.

Hornberger, N. (2000). Multilingual literacies, literacy practices, and the continua of biliteracy. In M. Martin-Jones & K. Jones (Eds.), *Multilingual literacies* (pp. 353-369). Amsterdam; Philadelphia: John Benjamins Pub. Co.

Hosking, D.L. (2008). Critical disability theory. *Paper presented at the 4th biennial disability studies conference.* Lancaster University, UK, Sept. 2-4, 2008.

Iannacci, L. (2007). Learning to "Do" School: Procedural display and culturally and linguistically diverse (CLD) students in Canadian early childhood education (ECE). *Journal of the Canadian Association for Curriculum Studies, 4*(2), 55-76.

Iannacci, L. (2008). The pathologizing of culturally and linguistically diverse students. In R. Heydon & L. Iannacci, *Early childhood curricula and the de-pathologizing of childhood* (pp. 46-81). Toronto, ON: University of Toronto Press.

Iannacci, L. (2018). Impoverished pedagogy: A critical examination of assumptions about poverty, teaching and cultural and linguistic diversity. In M.J. Harkins & S. Singer (Eds.), *Unmasking possibility and exploring agency: Educators explore issues of diversity, social justice and school*. Toronto, On: Canadian Scholar's Press.

Kliewer, C., Biklen, D., & Kasa-Hendrickson, C. (2006). Who may be literate? Disability and resistance to the cultural denial of competence. *American Educational Research Journal, 43*(2), 163-192.

Kunc, N. (1992). *The need to belong: rediscovering Maslow's hierarchy of needs.* Retrieved February 19, 2016, from: http://www.broadreachtraining. com/ar ticles/armaslow.htm.

McDermott, R., & Varenne, H. (1995). Culture as disability. *Anthropology and Education Quarterly, 26*(3), 324-348.

Munyi, C.W. (2012). Past and present perceptions of disability: A historical perspective. *Disability Studies Quarterly, 32*(2). 1-10.

New London Group, (1996). A pedagogy of multiliteracies: Designing social futures. *Harvard Educational Review, 66*(1), 60-92.

Obiakor, F.E., Harris, M., Mutua, K., Rotatori, A., & Algozzine, B. (2012). Making inclusion work in general education classrooms. *Education & Treatment of Children, 35*(3), 477-490.

Odom, S.L., Parrish, T.B., & Hikido, C. (2001). The costs of inclusive and traditional special education preschool services. *Journal of Special Education Leadership. 14* (1), 33-41.

Ontario Human Rights Code, R.S.O. 1990, c. H. 19.

Ontario Ministry of Education. (2013). Developing and implementing equity and inclusive education polices in Ontario. *Policy/program memorandum No. 119.* April 2, 2013.

Ontario Ministry of Education. (2015). *Special education funding guidelines: Special incidence portion (SIP) 2015-2016.*

Ontario Psychological Association. (2010). *Sharing promising practices a resource guide: Kindergarten to grade four.* Toronto, ON.

Pothier, D., & Devlin, R. (2006). Introduction: Toward a critical theory of dis-citizenship. In D. Pothier & R. Devlin (Eds.), *Critical disability theory: Essays in philosophy, politics, policy, and law*. Vancouver, BC: UBC Press.

Roth, K. (2015). Commit to inclusion confusion. *Journal of Physical Education, Recreation & Dance, 86*(3), 3-4.

Snow, K. (2005). *To ensure inclusion, freedom, and respect for all, we must use people first language*. Retrieved May 2, 2005, from http://www.disabilityisnatural.com/ peoplefirstlanguage.htm.

Swadener, B.B., & Lubeck, S. (1995). (Eds.). *Children and families "at Promise:" Deconstructing the discourse of risk*. Albany, NY: Albany State University of New York Press.

Titchosky, T. (2007). *Reading and writing disability differently*. Toronto, ON: University of Toronto Press.

Toohey, K. (2000). *Learning English at school: Identity, social relations and classroom practice*. Great Britain: Multilingual Matters Ltd.

Vaughan, C.E. (2009). People-first language: An unholy crusade. Braille Monitor. Retrieved March 16, 2011, from http://www.nfb.org/images/ nfb/publications/bm/ bm/09/bm0903/bm090309.htm.

Vygotsky, L.S. (1978). *Mind in society: The development of higher psychological processes*. Cambridge, MA: Harvard University Press.

Warnock, B.M. (September 17, 2010). The cynical betrayal of my special needs children. *The Telegraph*. UK.

Winzer, M. (2008). Children with exceptionalities in Canadian classrooms 8th (ed.). Toronto, ON: Pearson Education Canada.

CHAPTER 7

Hitting, Hugging, and High-Fiving: A Stoplight Heuristic for Thinking About Touch/No-Touch Discourse in Ontario's Schools

Blair Niblett[1]

Abstract

Inspired by a 2013 composite case study in the Ontario College of Teachers' magazine, *Professionally Speaking,* this chapter introduces a heuristic for thinking about the dynamics of touch between teachers and students, with the purpose of arguing for more clear legal direction on what kinds of touch are professionally appropriate. Using a 'stoplight' metaphor, the heuristic is developed as a continuum from red through amber to green zones. Red-zone touching is harmful, and clearly prohibited in law and policy. Amber-zone instances are contested, with little clarification offered by law and policy. Green-zone touching is, I argue, a positive and important element of teaching and learning and should be clearly condoned by law and policy in order to leverage effective pedagogies that depend on touch. The heuristic is further explained by discussing the mediating dimensions that complicate the assigning of instances of touch to fixed zones.

---

1   Special thanks to Dr. Kathy Haras for her thoughtful contributions to the green-zone categories of the stoplight heuristic.

Introduction

In the "A Matter of Investigation" column in the December 2013 issue of the Ontario College of Teachers' (OCT) magazine, *Professionally Speaking*, the editors present a composite case concerning the issue of touch between students and teachers:

> The English class was over and the student wanted to catch his bus to go home for lunch ... The teacher told him to return to his seat ... He kept walking. Contact between teacher and student occurred at the doorway. How much or how little depends on whom you spoke to. The student said the teacher grabbed his wrist, which prevented him from opening the door....The teacher denied the allegation of an assault ... She admitted she and the student reached for the door handle at the same time and there may have been incidental touching. She said she stepped aside and let him pass through, and that she reported the incident to the vice principal immediately. (OCT, 2013, p. 58)

In their commentary on this case study, the college explained that a reminder was issued to the imagined teacher to reinforce that she should avoid physical contact with students: "The panel said that even if it accepted the member's version, there were concerns that she attempted to prevent the student from leaving the classroom" (Ontario College of Teachers, 2013, p. 58). While not technically a disciplinary measure, the college's issuance of a reminder in this case of minor, possibly incidental, physical contact serves as a rallying call for a broad and open discussion about the state of the *no-touch* discourse that permeates the culture of teaching in Ontario, and in other jurisdictions. In this chapter, I contribute to this discussion by interrogating no-touch discourse. I argue that teacher/student touch issues are complex, and cannot be reduced to slogans like "no-touch." I applaud the OCT for using "A Matter of Investigation" as a forum for professional reflection, but suggest that the presentation of this investigation's outcome diminishes the complexity of teacher/student touch issues by implying that teachers and students should not have physical contact in any circumstances. In response, I describe a heuristic based on a stoplight metaphor to illustrate a broad range of appropriate and inappropriate categories for teacher/student touch, with a focus on providing greater understanding of common and appropriate touching between teacher and student.

Understanding physical contact between teachers and students in absolute terms is both impractical, and pedagogically undesirable. To explain the limitations of strict no-touch doctrines, I argue that such ways of thinking about how teachers and students should be allowed to relate in a classroom contribute to the maintenance of a professional culture of fear that hinders teachers' ability to support the OCT ethical foundations: care, respect, trust, and integrity (Ontario College of Teachers, n.d.). "Zero tolerance" approaches to teacher/student physical contact privilege the standard of integrity by assuming that any touch between student and teacher is a *prima facie* violation of professional integrity. Casting professional integrity in this way, I argue, creates a *spectre of integrity*, which makes teachers fearful of engaging in relational teaching behaviours (for instance, appropriate touching) that could engender care, respect, and trust amongst teachers, students, and the wider constituency served by public education. This overall argument is embedded within a strong vision for student wellbeing—the kind of wellbeing that is best fostered in an environment where a teacher does not have to be afraid that incidental and socially appropriate touches may endanger their professional standing.

Conceptualizing Teacher/Student Touch: A Stoplight Heuristic

The composite case described in *Professionally Speaking* focuses on teacher/student touching related to the management of classroom discipline. While the classroom is an important arena for thinking about touch, it is only one of many aspects of touch in teachers and students' educational relationship. Beyond disciplinary measures, teachers and students can have physical contact for legitimate reasons. In order to conceptualize the nuanced range of intentions that teachers can have for touching students, I offer a "stoplight" heuristic (Figure 1), which assigns red, amber, and green codes to various situations in which a teacher might touch a student. The heuristic offers three inter-permeating "zones" (red, amber, and green) that represent kinds of touch that are, respectively, prohibited, contentious, and permitted. Each zone is further subdivided into categories or contexts of touch that may exist in that zone. These categories are not exhaustive; as a newly developed thinking tool, the heuristic cannot be expected to depict every possible instance of teacher/ student touch, but rather offers a thumbnail sketch of the most common kinds of touch in teacher/student relationships. Importantly, the green zone has many more categories than either of the more cautionary zones. This difference is intentional, as my purpose is to highlight an area that is largely ignored in educational law and policy.

The Red Zone

Instances of red-zone touch are reasonably well identified by educational law and policy. A professional misconduct regulation under the *Ontario College of Teachers Act* (2016) identifies physical and sexual abuse as misconduct. The related provincial laws are supported by the *Criminal Code of Canada* (2016), which includes provisions against sexual interference, invitation to sexual touching, and sexual exploitation. Additionally, a 2004 Supreme Court of Canada[2] ruling clarified the application of section 43 of the *Criminal Code*,[3] indicating that teachers using physical force that is beyond "transitory and trifling," or that is non-corrective in nature could not use s. 43 as a defence against assault charges (This ruling and s. 43 are discussed later in this chapter).

Touch that is categorized as red-zone exploits the power imbalance in the relationship between teachers and students. Teachers who use red-zone touching should know better: making teachers aware of the vulnerability of children, of the potential for teachers to easily exploit this vulnerability, and of the consequences of such actions is the thrust of most of the educational law programming in teacher-training programs in Ontario and elsewhere (Crook & Truscott, 2015; Kitchen & Bellini, 2016; MacKay, Sutherland, & Pochini, 2013). Additionally, teacher

---

2 *Canadian Foundation for Children, Youth, & the Law v. Canada (Attorney General)*, 2004 SCC 4, 16 C.R. (6th) 203, 234 C.L.R. (4th) 257, 2004 CarswellOnt 253, 2004 CarswellOnt 252 (S.C.C.) [Canadian Foundation].

3 *Criminal Code*, R.S.C., 1985, c. C-46, s. 43.

federations allocate significant resources to informing teachers about the so-called "professional boundary" issues that are directly related to the potential for red-zone touching between teacher and student, or, perhaps more commonly, to the perception that any kind of touch might be perceived to have an exploitative intention. This fear of potential mis-perception gives rise to the amber zone of the stoplight heuristic.

Figure 1 – *A Stoplight Heuristic for Discussing Teacher/Student Touch*

Zone	Category	
Red	Exploitative, taking advantage of student vulnerability or naivety (e.g., assault, sexual assault, punitive discipline)	
Amber	Disciplinary, maintaining classroom discipline (e.g., corrective discipline of a trifling nature)	
Amber	Protective, maintaining teacher and student wellbeing (e.g., self-defence, restraint of violent or self-harming behaviour)	Mediating dimensions:
Amber	Compassionate, acting as a caring adult (e.g., public hug provided to a student in distress)	-Where on the body? (Middle body/face vs. peripheral body)
Green	Trust building touch, to secure or maintain student engagement in the classroom community (e.g., Touch on arm or shoulder)	-Setting: Classroom? Hallway? Office? Public, or private?
Green	Celebratory touch (e.g., high fives to celebrate student achievement and increase student efficacy)	-Age of the student?
Green	Pedagogical touch, to effectively teach skills (e.g., holding a baseball bat, shaping movement in dance or swimming, holding a pencil, mastering paint brush strokes, coaching wrestling).	-Intention: Caring professional adult, or otherwise?
Green	Safety touch, protecting students from injury (e.g., spotting gymnastics or climbing). -Consent/assent obtained? Who initiates?	
Green	Accidental/incidental touch, contact without intention. (e.g., bumping in the hallway, reaching for the same item).	

The Amber Zone

This zone is a contested space, characterized by a high degree of uncertainty about the permissibility of certain types of touching. For instance, touching of a disciplinary or protective nature, such as a hand slap to correct behaviour, or restraining a violent outburst, is condoned under Section 43 of the *Criminal Code of Canada*, which reads that

> Every schoolteacher, parent, or person standing in the place of a parent is justified in using force by way of correction toward a pupil or child, as the case may be, who is under his care, if the force does not exceed what is reasonable under the circumstances.

In its 2004 ruling on the constitutionality of s. 43 in *Canadian Foundation for Children, Youth, and the Law v. Canada*, Chief Justice McLachlin wrote for the majority of the Supreme Court of Canada that

> Children need to be protected from abusive treatment. They are vulnerable members of Canadian society and Parliament and the Executive act admirably when they shield children from psychological and physical harm ... Yet this is not the only need of children. Children also depend on parents and teachers for guidance and discipline, to protect them from harm and to promote their healthy development within society. A stable and secure family and school setting is essential to this growth process ... Section 43 is Parliament's attempt to accommodate both of these needs. It provides parents and teachers with the ability to carry out the reasonable education of the child without the threat of sanction by the criminal law. (para 58-59)

While the Supreme Court's upholding of s. 43 protects teachers from criminal sanction when they use reasonable force to physically discipline students, these same actions may contravene Ontario's Professional Misconduct Regulation 437/97 under the *Ontario College of Teachers Act* (2016). The regulation prohibits "abusing a student physically" (§ 1.7.1) as well as the catchall behaviour of "conduct unbecoming a member"

(§1.19). The ambiguity of many of the descriptors contained in both Ontario's Regulation 437/97 and the *Criminal Code of Canada* ("reasonable under the circumstances" [§43], "conduct unbecoming" [§1.19], respectively) leaves teachers uncertain about what constitutes professional actions in situations involving disciplinary or protective touching between teacher and student. Moreover, the standard of evidence required by the College of Teachers discipline panel ("in the opinion of the Committee" [§.30.2]) to revoke certification or otherwise discipline a teacher is much lower than the standard of reasonable doubt used in criminal proceedings, leading to much teacher anxiety and insecurity related to touch/no-touch discourse.

Touch for compassionate purposes is equally contentious. Although many teachers report that young students experiencing emotional distress, or even just having a common emotional experience (because of, for example, scraping a knee, or being called names) may actively seek out physical contact with a supportive adult, the permissibility of such contact is ambiguous. Legislation and regulations are silent about the permissibility of compassionate (caring, non-sexual) contact between teacher and student, and case law shows inconsistent outcomes, largely dependent on how the court chooses to interpret the evidence presented by the plaintiff and the defendant (MacKay et al., 2013). In the face of such uncertainty, Ontario's teacher federations offer strong advice to their members not to engage students physically, even in compassionate circumstances. In outlining professional boundaries, the Elementary Teachers Federation of Ontario (2015) cautions against initiating physical contact, including for compassionate reasons: "even contact intended to comfort an upset student should be avoided" (p.1). At the high school level, the Ontario Secondary School Teachers Federation (n.d.) noted that "members need to be sensitive to students' feelings about being touched. We can show we care by being verbally supportive; an approach to students that involves a great deal of touching or hugging is *dangerous*" (¶ 18, emphasis added). These warnings of danger contrast with teachers' day-to-day reality, especially when working with young students, who often need affirmation, and seek it out through physical contact. In my work as a teacher educator, I frequently hear anecdotes from teacher candidates and practicing teachers about young students who cling to their favourite teacher excitedly, crawl onto the teacher's lap during read-aloud times, and request care-giving in the form of buttoning buttons, zipping jackets, and tying shoes.

In my own institution, we deliver an annual "duty to report" child abuse reporting workshop to help teacher candidates to understand their legal obligation to report suspected or disclosed abuse; the presenters have often demonstrated a physical "hug deflection" maneuver to ward off physical contact from a student who may seek comfort after disclosing abuse. The presenters are well-meaning: children disclosing abuse are highly vulnerable, and physical contact by the teacher may either complicate the abuse allegations, or implicate the teacher in an investigation. Still, most teacher candidates lack the depth of experience needed to understand the nuances of this recommendation: they interpret it as a condemnation of any kind of touch between teacher and student, and then report feeling highly anxious when young students frequently reach out for contact.

Indeed, MacKay et al. (2013) aptly pointed out that "it is almost impossible to teach at the elementary level without physical contact with students. That is, however, clearly where the law is directing teachers to head" (p. 48). The authors hold out hope, however, that "the law will not prevent teachers from touching their students when such conduct is appropriate and non-sexual. The educational value may justify the risk in some cases" (p. 48). This belief connects directly to the green zone of the stoplight heuristic, and also to my thesis that educational law and policy must pay more attention to appropriate examples of touching between teachers and students.

The Green Zone

This area of the stoplight heuristic involves the kind of touching that many teachers frequently use as part of their teaching practice. However, many do so while fearing that their actions, although well-intended and pedagogically sound, may contravene their legal and professional responsibilities as teachers. The green zone is subcategorized into 5 elements: trust-building, celebratory, pedagogical, safety, and accidental/

incidental touch. Like the stoplight spectrum overall, these subcategories are permeable and dynamic to the context in which they are situated.

Trust-building touching may be characterized as gestures of caring that function to develop positive learning environments, and invite students to belong to a classroom community that includes the teacher. For instance, a teacher's gentle, affirming touch to a student's arms or shoulders may be understood as such an invitation. Indeed, neuroscientist David Linden (2015), author of *Touch: The Science of Hand, Heart, and Mind,* comments that

> It's not so much that touch is a useful tool for teaching facts and strategies—it's not as if, when you stroke a student's arm as they practice algebra, they will learn algebra better ... More than anything else, what touch conveys is 'I'm an ally, I'm not a threat. Touch puts the recipient in a trusting mental state, and anything you can do to encourage the student to trust the teacher is going to make learning better. (as cited in an interview with Lahey, 2015)

Linden's neurological perspective provides some scientific support for what many educators feel intuitively: touching can be a valuable tool for community building. Findings like Linden's may be helpful in the argument against the no-touch approach that is typical in public education discourse.

Another aspect of touch within the green zone is celebratory touch. Celebration through touch may also function as trust-building, but its defining outcome is the development of student efficacy through reinforcement of classroom achievement. For instance, a teacher may exchange "high-fives" with a whole class of students who have demonstrated an achievement worthy of celebration. This category of touch is likely the most innocuous in the stoplight spectrum heuristic, probably because celebratory touch involves two of the *mediating dimensions* shown in Figure 1. First, the high five is easily shared with a group of students together in a public setting. Second, the touching of outstretched hands constitutes peripheral body touching rather than middle body touching. Both of these mitigating factors make it unlikely that a high five could be interpreted as the kind of exploitative or potentially exploitative touching found in either the amber or red zones.

In addition to building trust and leading celebrations of student achievement, green-zone touching includes instances of touch between teacher and student for a directly pedagogical purpose. In other words, sometimes touch is a strategy for instruction, especially in areas where physical skill development is central to curriculum delivery. A physical education teacher manipulates a student's arm to improve control in a free-throw shot with a basketball. An art teacher touches a student's hand to aid in developing mastery of a stippling technique for painting. A science teacher manipulates a student's thumb to help ignite a butane lighter in order to light a Bunsen burner. A drama teacher holds hands with students while leading a circle activity. In each of these scenarios, teacher touch helps to connect a student with an important skill in the discipline being studied. Critics will argue that each of these situations could be navigated without touching, and that careful modelling or demonstration without touching could achieve the end result. These critics would not be wrong. However, teaching and learning are increasingly being understood as social endeavours, and touching is a significant part of being social (Linden, 2015).

Closely related to pedagogical touch, safety touch occurs when a teacher and student may need to touch in order for the teacher to maintain the student's safety as they engage in curricular programming. For instance, teachers instructing gymnastics or adventure-based learning activities often engage in "spotting," an injury prevention approach that can require touch. Likewise, teachers working in higher risk programs where specialized equipment is used (science labs, technology workshops, etc.) may need to physically intervene in order to prevent students from injuring themselves or others. It is difficult to imagine a teacher being found guilty of professional misconduct or assault for grasping a student's wrist to prevent them from burning themselves, or contacting a moving blade. Yet, little explicit law or policy exists to tell teachers that even this most protective touch for the sake of risk management is permissible.

Finally, the amount of time that teachers and students spend together, combined with the close quarters often found in school environments, means that teachers and students inevitably will sometimes touch accidentally. In a busy high school, bodies often touch in a crowded hallway or while moving through a doorway. Similarly, inadvertent touching may occur as teacher and student reach for the same object. The anecdote from *Professionally Speaking* shared at the beginning of this chapter involves this kind of touching in the context of a doorknob; the intentions for this particular touch may be uncertain, as the story involves aspects of classroom power and control of student behaviour, but the touching could also result from bodies grazing each other in a busy cafeteria, or an even more innocent example where a primary teacher and student inadvertently touch while reaching for the same area in a bin of disorganized crayons. Critics of my position will argue against green-lighting such accidental touching because, as professionals, teachers are responsible for foreseeing such instances and acting in ways to avoid them. I offer two responses to such reasoning. First, I remind readers that all professionals are also humans who sometimes fail to foresee innocent instances of touching that might be avoidable, particularly if the teachers are deeply engaged in a teaching activity. In the doorknob anecdote, the College of Teachers seems to recognize this potential for human error; in this hypothetical case, the College decided to issue only a reminder to the imagined teacher, rather than to pursue formal disciplinary action. Second, I suggest that the level of attention that a teacher would require to prevent any and all inadvertent touching would be likely to result in robotic teachers instead of effective classroom leaders. I do not deny the paramount importance of protecting students from touching by teachers which is harmful or otherwise not in the students' best interests. Having said that, I believe strongly that developing policy instruments that clarify green-zone instances of touching would allow teachers to feel more confident in their own professionalism and in their professional relationships with students, and that such increased confidence would lead to richer pedagogies and therefore improved learning outcomes.

Mediating Dimensions

While the stoplight heuristic presented here is a useful tool for encouraging discussion about touch/no-touch policy in schools, a heuristic cannot capture all of the complexities associated with the issue of teacher/student touch. In an attempt to add depth to the heuristic as a discussion tool, I offer some mediating dimensions that highlight how the various stoplight zones blur into each other, and illustrate the need to analyze the contextual factors in any instance of teacher/student touching. The following questions are posed to show that specific instances of touching between teacher and student may fall into different zones within the heuristic depending on contextual factors:

1. Where on the body?

   ■ Sexuality educator Cory Silverberg (2015) uses the expression "middle parts" to give children language for describing the more intimate parts of their bodies. It is useful to imagine a body zone extending from below the armpits to the mid-thigh that constitutes the middle parts, which are personal and are not appropriate for teacher/student touch, unless for safety or harm-reduction (first aid, etc.). Peripheral body zones like arms, lower legs, hands, or shoulders are less intimate and may be appropriate for touch between teacher and student within an appropriate *green-zone* context.

2. What setting does the touch occur in? (Consider both the location and the actual or potential audience).

   ■ Consider whether an instance of teacher/student touch takes place in a public space that is occupied by other people when the touch is occurring. Instances that appear to clearly fall into the *green zone* when occurring in public may not do so if the context is changed to a private interaction between a teacher and single student (Wolowitz, 2013).

3. What is the age of the student?

   ■ *Amber-zone* elements like compassionate touch and *green-zone* elements like celebratory or trust-building touch are most appropriate with younger students. Pedagogical or safety touching when teaching skills can be appropriate with older students, but seeking assent to such touching is important (e.g., "I'd like to check that your climbing harness is buckled securely, may I touch your waist loop?").

4. What is the intention of the touch, both as enacted and as perceived?

   ■ Is the teacher acting as a caring professional? Is this caring intention clear to the recipient of the touch, and to potential observers?

5. Has consent and/or assent been obtained?

   ■ Reciprocal touching like a handshake or high-five initiated by the teacher provides students with the opportunity to participate or not. Touching in which a teacher acts on a student unilaterally (touching on the shoulder) requires greater levels of trust and should be exercised carefully.

Summary and Next Steps

In this chapter, I have described a stoplight heuristic for the purpose of encouraging discussion about no-touch discourse. The heuristic outlines a variety of ways in which teachers might touch students, ranging from exploitative to positive and pedagogically supportive, including a contested middle space where there is little consensus on whether touching is appropriate in these contexts (disciplinary, protective, and compassionate touch). I hope that this model opens a space for discussion outside of the often unquestioned assumption that all touch in teacher/student relationships is exploitative (or may be perceived as such) and should be avoided at all costs. I emphasize that my stoplight heuristic is intended as a conversation starter, and not as a suggested law or policy tool. More research is required, both philosophically and empirically, to support the use of this heuristic as useful legal tool. Philosophically, I am interested in politicized care theorizing (Monchinski, 2010) as a justifying foundation for green-zone touch in education law and policy, and I plan to develop this theory further in future work. Empirically, I think educators need to open and record dialog in order to ascertain clearly what messages are taken from the dominant discourses in law, policy, and practice in regards to teacher/student touch. These responses, alongside more philosophical work, can be used to transform a stoplight heuristic for teacher/student touch into a model that may be useful for developing the kind of law and policy that could lead to safer educational environments, where teachers can feel confident and comfortable in knowing when and how physical contact with students is appropriate.

References

Criminal Code, R.S.C. 1985, c. C-46 § 43 (2016).

Crook, K., & Truscott, D. (2015). *Ethics and law for teachers* (2nd Ed.). Toronto, ON: Nelson.

Elementary Teachers Federation of Ontario. (2015). Professionalism – Advice to Members. Retrieved from: http://www.etfo.ca/AdviceForMembers/ PRSM attersBulletins/PDF%20Versions/Professionalism%20 %-20Advice%20to %20Members.pdf.

Kitchen, J., & Bellini, C. (2016). *Professionalism, law, and the Ontario educator.* St. David's, ON: Highland Press.

Lahey, J. (2015, Januard). Should teachers be allowed to touch students? *The Atlantic.* Retrieved from: http://www.theatlantic.com/education/ archive/2015/01/the-benefi ts-of-touch/384706/.

Linden, D. (2015). *Touch: The science of hand, heart, and mind.* New York, NY: Penguin [Kindle Edition].

MacKay, A.W., Sutherland, L.I., & Pochini, K.D. (2013). *Teachers and the law: Diverse roles and new challenges* (3rd ed.). Toronto, ON: Emond Montgomery Publications Limited.

Monchinski, T. (2010). *Education in hope: Critical pedagogies and the ethic of care.* New York, NY: Peter Lang.

Ontario College of Teachers. (n.d.). Ethical standards. Retrieved from: http:// www.oct.ca/ public/professional-standards/ethical-standards.

Ontario College of Teachers. (2013, December). A matter of investigation: Investigation Committee Case Study. *Professionally Speaking,* 58. Retrieved from: http://oct-oeeo.uberflip. com/i/213546-ps-december-2013.

Ontario College of Teachers Act, 1996, S. O. 1996, c. 12 § O. Reg. 437/97.

Ontario Secondary School Teachers Federation. (n.d.) Member protection–
Guidelines for members. Retrieved from: http://www.osstf.on.ca/
en-CA/resource-centre/member -protection/guidelines-for-members.
aspx.

Silverberg, C. (2015). *Sex is a funny word*. New York, NY: Seven Stories.

Wolowitz, D. (2013). Guideposts for teachers to maintain healthy relationships with students. *United Educators Perspectives*. Retrieved
from: https://www.aassa.com/ uploaded/Educational_Research/
Child_Protection/UE_Guideposts_for_Teacherst oMaintain_Healthy_
Relationships_With_Students.pdf.

Fundamental Freedoms and Charter Rights

Moving Beyond Strict Neutrality: The Supreme Court of Canada and the Loyola Decision

Paul T. Clarke

Introduction

In this chapter,[1] the author examines the recent decision of the Supreme Court of Canada (SCC) in *Loyola High School v. Quebec (Attorney General).*[2] The SCC had to reconcile the state's interest in promoting the recognition of others and pursuit of the common good, as mandated by Quebec's mandatory Ethics and Religious Culture (ERC) program for provincial schools, with a private school's religious freedom as protected under both the *Canadian Charter of Rights and Freedoms* and Quebec's *Charter of Human Rights and Freedoms*. In the first part of the chapter, the author explains the contextual background to the case. In the second part, he describes the reasons for the judgment of the majority, penned by Justice Abella,[3] along with the reasons for the partial concurrence of the minority, authored by Chief Justice McLachlin and Justice Moldaver.[4] In the third part of the chapter, the author considers the implications of this decision for those interested in education law.

---

1 In the writing of this chapter, the author wishes to acknowledge the input and critical feedback generously provided by Dr. Michael Tymchak. He helped the author think carefully about the impossibility of "neutral" worldviews and a preferred approach based on reasonableness and fairness.

2 2015 SCC 12.

3 LeBel, Cromwell and Karakatsanis JJ. concurring.

4 Rothstein J. concurring.

This consideration includes a critique of the majority's call for teachers at Loyola High School to teach ethics in an objective and neutral manner. Some final concluding remarks are offered.

Contextual Background

Loyola High School is a private, English-speaking Roman Catholic high school for boys located in Montreal, Quebec, Canada. The school is well respected, and the Jesuit Order has administered the institution since the school's founding in the 1840s. The school's mission, teaching, and characteristics are Jesuit. Most of the students at Loyola are from Catholic families.[5]

Since 2008, Quebec's Minister of Education, Recreation and Sports (Minister) has required the province's schools to teach a secular program on Ethics and Religious Culture (ERC) as part of the mandatory core curriculum. This program obliges schools to teach about the beliefs and ethics of different world religions from a neutral and objective viewpoint. The ERC program has two main objectives: the recognition of others and the pursuit of the common good. The first goal is rooted in the idea that all people possess equal value and dignity. The second objective aims to foster shared values of human rights and democracy. Quebec seeks to inculcate in all students openness to diversity and respect for others by mandating this program in its schools.[6] To attain these twin objectives, the ERC program has three components which purport to develop three competencies among students: the ability to understand religious culture, which includes the study of world religions; the ability to reflect on ethical questions; and the ability to engage in dialogue. The three competencies are supposed to support and reinforce one another.[7]

The purpose of the religious culture component "is to help students understand the main elements of religion by exploring the socio-cultural contexts in which different religions take root and develop."[8] The

---

5 Para. 7.
6 Para. 11.
7 Para. 12.
8 Para. 13.

program takes a cultural and phenomenological approach to the study of religions, and is non-doctrinal in nature. It pays special attention to Catholicism and Protestantism, in light of Quebec's history, but teachers must also discuss Judaism, Islam, Hinduism, Buddhism, and Aboriginal belief systems.[9] The reason for the ethics component is "to encourage students to critically reflect on their own ethical conduct and that of others, as well as on the values and norms that different religious and social groups adopt to guide their behaviour."[10] The dialogue component is integrated with the ethics and religious culture components. Its purpose is "to help students develop the skills to interact respectfully with people of different beliefs in a diverse society, and to understand the impact of their behaviour on the broader community."[11] The ERC program provides a framework that teachers must use to help students develop these competencies. However, teachers have considerable flexibility to develop their own lessons and structure their course to transmit this content.[12] Justice Abella explained the orientation of the program in these terms:

> The orientation of the ERC Program is strictly secular and cultural; it requires teachers to take a "professional stance" of objectivity and impartiality. That means that they are not to advance the truth of a particular belief system or attempt to influence their students' beliefs. Instead, their role is to foster awareness of diverse values, beliefs and cultures. Teachers in the program are therefore expected to act as mediators to help their students develop the critical

---

9 *Ibid.*

10 Para. 14.

11 Para. 15 As the majority explained: The major world religions are taught through themes. Students explore the elements of religious traditions, including different representations of divinity, creation stories, and religious rites, rules and duties. ... Students develop competency in ethics by exploring themes such as freedom, autonomy, and tolerance, among others. They develop competency in dialogue by learning about different forms of dialogue; strategies for developing, explaining or challenging a point of view; and processes and patterns of thought that can undermine dialogue, such as stereotyping and prejudice (para. 17-18).

12 Para. 16.

capacity to understand, articulate and question different points of view.[13]

In *S.L. v. Commission scolaire des Chênes*,[14] and in the context of the public school system, the Supreme Court of Canada (SCC) upheld the constitutional validity of the ERC program. In that case, a group of parents argued that the program would confuse their children and interfere with their religious freedom because it exposed them to information about various world religions from a secular perspective. The parents claimed that this exposure amounted to a violation of s. 2(*a*) of the *Canadian Charter of Rights and Freedoms*.[15] The SCC rejected this argument and affirmed the constitutionality of the ERC Program as a mandatory component of the curriculum in Quebec's public schools. In her reasons, Justice Deschamps declared:

> [P]arents are free to pass their personal beliefs on to their children if they so wish. However, the early exposure of children to realities that differ from those in their immediate family environment is a fact of life in society. The suggestion that exposing children to a variety of religious facts in itself infringes their religious freedom or that of their parents amounts to a rejection of the multicultural reality of Canadian society and ignores the Quebec government's obligations with regard to public education. Although such exposure can be a source of friction, it does not in itself constitute an infringement of s. 2(*a*) of the *Canadian Charter* and of s. 3 of the *Quebec Charter*.[16]

---

13 Para. 19.

14 2012 SCC 7, [2012] 1 S.C.R. 235.

15 Section 2(a) of the *Charter* states:
Everyone has the following fundamental freedoms:
freedom of conscience and religion;
Enacted as Schedule B to the *Canada Act 1982*, **1982, c. 11 (U.K.).** *Charter of Human Rights and Freedoms*, CQLR, c. C-12.

16 Above note 13 at para. 40. For a detailed review of this case, see Clarke, P.T. (2012). Religion and public schools in Quebec: The Supreme Court of Canada has spoken . . . At least for now. *Education & Law Journal, 21*(2), 167–183.

The Minister may grant private schools an exemption from the ERC program if they can demonstrate that they will offer an alternative program that the Minister deems to be *equivalent*.[17] Loyola applied in writing for an exemption. The Minister denied the request on the basis that the school's entire proposed program was to be taught from a Catholic perspective. Consequently, the Minister concluded that it was not *equivalent* to the ERC program. Loyola sought judicial review of the Minister's decision on the grounds that it interfered with the school's religious freedom as protected under s. 2(a) of the *Canadian Charter of Rights and Freedoms* and s. 3 of the Quebec *Charter of Human Rights and Freedoms*. The Quebec Superior Court sided with Loyola and ordered the Minister to grant an exemption because the court found that the school's proposed program was *equivalent*.[18] The Quebec Court of Appeal reversed this decision, holding that the Minister had properly exercised her discretion and had good reason to deny the request for an exemption.[19] On appeal, our highest court split over whether to grant a full exemption. Led by Justice Abella, four of the seven justices hearing the case granted a partial exemption. Justices McLachlin and Moldaver, writing for a block of three justices, would have granted a complete exemption.[20]

---

17 Section 22 of the *Regulation respecting the application of the Act respecting private education* states: Every institution shall be exempt from the [compulsory curriculum] provided the institution dispenses programs of studies which the Minister of Education, Recreation and Sports judges equivalent. See CQLR, c. E-9.1, r. 1.

18 See 2010 QCCS 2631.

19 See 2012 QCCA 2139.

20 Prior to the case arriving in front of the SCC, Loyola had previously claimed that the *entire* orientation of the ERC Program constituted a violation of its freedom of religion on the basis that discussing any religion through a neutral lens would be incompatible with Catholic beliefs. It took a revised position before the highest court. Loyola did not object to teaching *other* world religions objectively in the first component of the ERC program which focuses on "understanding religious culture." However, it still wanted to teach the *ethics* of other religious traditions from the Catholic perspective rather than in an objective and neutral way. Loyola continued to assert the right to teach Catholic doctrine and ethics from a Catholic perspective. The private school took no position on the perspective from which it would seek to teach the dialogue component, which would be integrated with the other two components of its proposed alternative program. Above note 1 at para. 31.

Reasons of Justice Abella

Loyola did not challenge the Minister's statutory authority to impose curricular requirements in all schools in Quebec. Rather, it objected to her discretionary decision to deny Loyola an exemption from the ERC program. Justice Abella framed her analysis in these terms:

> The reasonableness of the Minister's decision depends on whether it reflected a proportionate balance between the statutory mandate to grant exemptions only when a proposed alternative program is "equivalent" to the prescribed curriculum, based on the ERC Program's goals of promoting tolerance and respect for difference, and the religious freedom of the members of the Loyola community who seek to offer and wish to receive a Catholic education.[21]

Justice Abella acknowledged that Loyola is a non-profit corporation constituted under Quebec's *Companies Act*.[22] Loyola also argued that its own religious freedom had been violated by the Minister's decision. Justice Abella recognized that "individuals may sometimes require a legal entity in order to give effect to the constitutionally protected communal aspects of their religious beliefs and practice, such as the transmission of their faith . . . ."[23] She sidestepped the question, however, as to whether corporations enjoy religious freedom in their own right under s. 2(*a*) of the Canadian *Charter* or s. 3 of the Quebec *Charter of Human Rights and Freedoms*. Justice Abella preferred to focus her analysis on the Minister's obligation to exercise her discretion "in a way that respects the values underlying the grant of her decision-making authority, including the *Charter*-protected religious freedom of the members of the Loyola community who seek to offer and wish to receive a Catholic education."[24]

---

21 Para. 32.
22 CQLR, c. C-38.
23 Above note 1 at para. 33.
24 Para. 34.

Justice Abella chose to analyze the case by drawing upon the framework set out in *Doré v. Barreau du Québec,*[25] which applies to discretionary administrative decisions that engage the *Charter.* As she explained:

> On judicial review, the task of the reviewing court applying the *Doré* framework is to assess whether the decision is reasonable because it reflects a proportionate balance between the *Charter* protections at stake and the relevant statutory mandate: . . . Reasonableness review is a contextual inquiry: . . . In the context of decisions that implicate the *Charter*, to be defensible, a decision must accord with the fundamental values protected by the *Charter.*[26]

In essence, a two-step inquiry is necessary. First, does the discretionary administrative decision limit a *Charter* protection? Second, if yes, does the limit amount to proportional balancing? If yes, the decision is reasonable and stands. If no, the decision must be struck down.[27]

Justice Abella noted that the *Doré* analysis is a "highly contextual exercise."[28] She observed that the context before the Court was state regulation of religious schools. This requires a balancing act between robust protection of the values undergirding freedom of religion with the values

---

25 2012 SCC 12, [2012] 1 S.C.R. 395.

26 Para. 37.

27 This balancing is similar to the test adopted by the SCC in the R. v. Oakes case. See, [1986] 1 S.C.R. 103. As Justice Abella observed:
A *Doré* proportionality analysis finds analytical harmony with the final stages of the *Oakes* framework used to assess the reasonableness of a limit on a *Charter* right under s. 1: minimal impairment and balancing. Both *R. v. Oakes*, [1986] 1 S.C.R. 103, and *Doré* require that *Charter* protections are affected as little as reasonably possible in light of the state's particular objectives: . . . As such, *Doré*'s proportionality analysis is a robust one and "works the same justificatory muscles" as the *Oakes* test: . . . (para. 40).

28 Para. 41 In this regard, she noted:
Doré's approach to reviewing administrative decisions that implicate the *Charter*, including those of adjudicative tribunals, responds to the diverse set of statutory and procedural contexts in which administrative decision-makers operate, and respects the expertise that these decision-makers typically bring to the process of balancing the values and objectives at stake on the particular facts in their statutory decisions: (para. 47).

---

of a secular state. Justice Abella remarked that religious freedom must be understood in this context:

> Religious freedom must . . . be understood in the context of a secular, multicultural and democratic society with a strong interest in protecting dignity and diversity, promoting equality, and ensuring the vitality of a common belief in human rights.[29]

The state likewise has an interest in helping students to become tolerant and respectful citizens in a multicultural and multi religious democracy. As Justice Abella observed:

> The state . . . has a legitimate interest in ensuring that students in *all* schools are capable, as adults, of conducting themselves with openness and respect as they confront cultural and religious differences. A pluralist, multicultural democracy depends on the capacity of its citizens "to engage in thoughtful and inclusive forms of deliberation amidst, and enriched by," different religious worldviews and practices . . . .[30]

To interpret the meaning of "equivalent," Justice Abella considered the statutory objectives while taking into account "the words of the provision in this regulatory context, the scheme of the *Act*, the object of the *Act*, and the intention of Parliament." [31] Pursuant to s. 22 of the *Regulation respecting the application of the Act respecting private education*,[32] the Minister is required to grant exemptions from the mandatory program when a school offers an "equivalent" program. This regulatory context has as its focus "the minimum educational attainments required of students in private and public schools across Quebec."[33] More specifically, the Minister

---

29 Para. 47.
30 Para. 48. Here, Justice Abella referred to the work of Benjamin L. Berger, "Religious Diversity, Education, and the 'Crisis' in State Neutrality" (2014), 29 *C.J.L.S.* 103, at p. 115.
31 Para. 50.
32 CQLR, c. E-9.1, r.1.
33 Para. 51.

must "adopt measures that will contribute to individuals' education and development, and ensure that educational institutions offer services of sufficient quality. . ."[34] Under the *Basic school regulation for preschool, elementary and secondary education*,[35] the Minister prescribes the compulsory subjects that must be taught each year and determines the minimum requirements for the instructional hours to be accorded to each subject. The Minister has the power to establish core course objectives and content, curricula to teach these core subjects, and optional content that can be tailored to students' needs.[36] The prescribed curricula must be taught in private and public schools. Finally, the regulatory framework mandates that all private educational institutions hold a permit to operate. This allows the Minister to guarantee that all private schools comply with the general regulatory framework it has created.[37]

As Justice Abella explained, the ministerial power to grant exemptions is "part of the Minister's broader regulatory role of ensuring that basic educational standards are met by schools and students alike."[38] At the same time, she acknowledged that "there would be little point in offering an exemption if, in order to receive it, the proposed alternative program had to be identical to the mandatory program in every way."[39] She noted that "The exemption exists in a regulatory scheme that anticipates and sanctions the existence of private denominational schools."[40] Justice Abella remarked that the ERC program does not prescribe detailed lesson plans that teachers must cover. Rather, it is flexible and thematic and provides a general framework to help students develop competencies in ethics, dialogue, and religious culture, all geared towards the two key objectives of the program: the recognition of others and the common good. As Justice Abella stated:

---

34 Para. 51 See, *An Act respecting the Ministère de l'Éducation, du Loisir et du Sport*, CQLR, c. M-15, s. 2.

35 CQLR, c. I-13.3, r. 8.

36 Para. 52. See Quebec's *Education Act*, s. 461, CQLR, c. I-13.3.

37 See *Act respecting private education*, CQLR, c. E-9.1, ss. 10, 25 & 32, at para. 50-52.

38 Para. 53.

39 Para. 54.

40 *Ibid.*

Given the highly flexible nature of the ERC Program and its heavy emphasis on these two objectives, as well as the context of the regulatory scheme as a whole, it is unreasonable to interpret equivalence as requiring a strict adherence to specific course content, rather than in terms of the ERC's program objectives generally. Using the program's objectives as the marker for equivalence leaves the necessary flexibility for the possibility of acceptable differences between an alternative program and the ERC Program, including differences that can accommodate religious freedom. As long as the alternative program substantially realizes the objectives of the ERC Program, it should be considered equivalent.[41]

In this context, the Minister had to make a decision that proportionately balanced the fulfillment of the ERC program's objectives with respect for freedom of religion as protected by the *Charter*. In rejecting Loyola's request for an exemption, Justice Abella noted that the Minister's opinion was based on the notion that a program "that departs in any way from the ERC Program's posture of strict neutrality, even partially, cannot achieve the state's objectives of promoting respect for others and openness to diversity."[42]

Justice Abella then considered the impact of the Minister's decision on religious freedom. Drawing on Justice Dickson's (as he then was) seminal conceptualization of freedom of religion in *R. v. Big M Drug Mart Ltd.*,[43] she noted that this freedom "is founded on the idea that no one can be forced to adhere to or refrain from a particular set of religious beliefs."[44] She noted that the *Charter's* s. 2(a) promise includes both the individual and collective aspects of religious belief. As for the latter, she declared:

Religious freedom under the *Charter* must . . . account for the socially embedded nature of religious belief, and the deep linkages between this belief and its manifestation

---

41 Para. 56.

42 Para. 58

43 *R. v. Big M Drug Mart Ltd* [1985] 1 S.C.R. 295.

44 Above note 1 at para. 59.

through communal institutions and traditions . . . To fail to recognize this dimension of religious belief would be to "effectively denigrate those religions in which more emphasis is placed on communal worship or other communal religious activities."[45]

In *S.L.*, the analysis focused on the religious liberty of individual parents and students. The collective dimension of s. 2(a), however, was central to Loyola's claim because it is a "private religious institution created to support the collective practice of Catholicism and the transmission of the Catholic faith."[46] The Minister's decision to require Loyola to teach about Catholicism from a neutral perspective constituted a demonstrable interference in the running of the school's affairs and had a serious impact on the school's religious freedom. As Justice Abella stated:

> The Minister's decision . . . demonstrably interferes with the manner in which the members of an institution formed for the very purpose of transmitting Catholicism, can teach and learn about the Catholic faith. This engages religious freedom protected under s. 2(*a*) of the *Charter*. I agree with Loyola that the Minister's decision had a serious impact on religious freedom in this context. To tell a Catholic school how to explain its faith undermines the liberty of the members of its community who have chosen to give effect to the collective dimension of their religious beliefs by participating in a denominational school.[47]

She observed that the state requirement for Loyola teachers to take a neutral view about Catholicism means that the state is dictating to Loyola how to teach the very religion that infuses Loyola's identity: "It amounts to requiring a Catholic institution to speak about Catholicism

---

45 Here, she made reference to Victor Muñiz-Fraticelli and Lawrence David, "Whence a nexus with religion? Religious institutionalism in a Canadian context," forthcoming, at p. 2; Dieter Grimm, "Conflicts Between General Laws and Religious Norms" (2009), 30 *Cardozo L. Rev.* 2369, at p. 2373 and Dwight Newman, *Community and Collective Rights: A Theoretical Framework for Rights held by Groups* (2011), at p. 78.

46 Above note 1 at para. 61.

47 Para. 61-62.

in terms defined by the state rather than by its own understanding of Catholicism."[48] Furthermore, this demand for neutrality interfered with the parental right to transmit the Catholic faith to one's children because it forbids a "Catholic discussion of Catholicism."[49] Justice Abella concluded: "Ultimately, measures which undermine the character of lawful religious institutions and disrupt the vitality of religious communities represent a profound interference with religious freedom."[50] Moreover, Justice Abella held that there was "insufficient demonstrable benefit to the furtherance of the state's objectives in requiring Loyola's teachers to teach Catholicism from a neutral perspective."[51] The Minister simply treated teaching any part of the proposed alternative program from a Catholic perspective as running counter to the state's core objectives found in the ERC program. In so doing, the Minister accorded no value to freedom of religion and failed to balance this freedom with the statutory objectives. This failure rendered the decision unreasonable. As Justice Abella declared:

> In the Quebec context, where private denominational schools are authorized, forcing a religious school to teach its own religion from a non-religious perspective does not assist in realizing the ERC Program's basic curricular goals of encouraging among students respect for others and openness to others. The Minister's decision suggests that engagement with an individual's own religion on his or her own terms can simply be presumed to impair respect for others. This assumption runs counter to the objectives of the regulatory scheme as a whole and it has a disproportionate impact on the values underlying religious freedom

---

48 Para. 63.
49 Para. 64 Justice Abella referred to international human rights instruments which recognize the rights of parents to guide their children's upbringing. See para. 65 and in particular Article 18(4) of the *International Covenant on Civil and Political Rights*, 999 U.N.T.S. 171.
50 Para. 67.
51 Para. 68.

in this context. This necessarily renders the Minister's decision unreasonable.[52]

Justice Abella observed that the Minister's decision prohibited Loyola from teaching about Catholic ethics from a Catholic perspective. Such teaching was not possible:

> Catholic doctrine and Catholic ethics are simply too intertwined to make it possible to teach one from a religious perspective and the other neutrally. More to the point, there is no reason to distinguish between the two when it comes to religious freedom. In both cases, preventing Loyola from teaching Catholicism seriously impairs its Catholic identity.[53]

Loyola conceded that it would teach the first competency – world religions other than Catholicism – from a neutral perspective.[54] However, Loyola argued that its religious freedom prevented it from teaching about the ethics of other religions in a neutral fashion and that it should be entitled to do so from a Catholic perspective. Justice Abella rejected this argument:

> I agree with the Court of Appeal that requiring Loyola to teach about the ethics of *other* religions in a neutral, historical and phenomenological way would not interfere disproportionately with the relevant *Charter* protections implicated by the decision. Justice Deschamps's admonition that exposing children to a variety of religious facts does not, in itself, infringe on their parents' religious freedom remains compelling in a denominational school . . . I agree with her that in a multicultural society, it is not a breach of anyone's freedom of religion to be required to learn (or teach) about

---

52 Para. 69.
53 Para. 70.
54 Para. 71.

the doctrines and ethics of other world religions in a neutral and respectful way.[55]

By way of final disposition, Justice Abella set aside the Minister's decision and sent the matter back to the Minister for reconsideration in light of her reasons. She held that an exemption could not be withheld on the basis that Loyola must teach Catholicism and Catholic ethics from a neutral perspective.[56]

Reasoning of Chief Justice McLachlin & Justice Moldaver

The Chief Justice (CJ) and Justice Moldaver (JM) rejected the Attorney General (AG) of Quebec's position that Loyola, as a non-profit corporation, could not enjoy freedom of religion because it was not a natural person, but merely a legal person:[57]

> In our view, Loyola may rely on the guarantee of freedom of religion found in s. 2(a) of the *Canadian Charter*. The communal character of religion means that protecting the religious freedom of individuals requires protecting the religious freedom of religious organizations, including religious educational bodies such as Loyola. Canadian and international jurisprudence supports this conclusion.[58]

The AG also contended that religious freedom protects sincerely held beliefs, and a corporation can neither believe nor be sincere. The CJ and JM acknowledged that a business corporation cannot possess religious beliefs, but noted that a religious organization may very well have religious beliefs and rights.[59] In light of the collective aspect of religious freedom established in our jurisprudence, they held that an organization meets the "requirements for s. 2(a) protection if (1) it is constituted

---

55 *Ibid*. The reference to Justice Deschamps is to the SCC's decision in *S.L.* Above note 13.

56 Para. 81.

57 Para. 90.

58 Para. 91.

59 Para. 96.

primarily for religious purposes, and (2) its operation accords with these religious purposes."[60] The CJ and JM concluded that Loyola met this two prong test. Loyola is a non-profit religious corporation whose purpose is to offer a Jesuit education to children within Quebec's Catholic religious community. The school has been run for over 100 years according to this religious educational purpose.[61]

Like Justice Abella, the CJ and JM considered the legislative and regulatory scheme at issue in order to understand the Minister's decision. They noted that when the government inserted the ERC Program into the compulsory curriculum, this program was not excluded from the s. 22 exemption provision. Thus, Loyola could apply for an exemption from the requirement to teach the ERC program.[62] The CJ and JM noted that the Ministry's own publications support the finding that the legislative and regulatory scheme aims to operate in a way that respects the religious freedoms of individuals and groups in Quebec's school system.[63] They also stated:

> Section 22 functions to ensure the legislative and regulatory scheme's compliance with the freedom of religion guaranteed by s. 2(*a*) of the *Charter*. It guards against the possibility that, in certain situations, the mandatory imposition of a purely secular curriculum may violate the *Charter* rights of a private religious school. This safeguard is consistent with the obligations of the state in a multicultural society. As LeBel J. observed in his concurring reasons in *S.L. v. Commission scolaire des Chênes* . . . in the context of the public school system, "[u]nder the constitutional principles governing state action, the state has neither an obligation to promote religious faith nor a right to discourage religious faith in its public education system". . . . The state may not discourage religious faith in the public

---

60 Para. 100.

61 Para. 101.

62 Para. 107.

63 Para. 110.

education system; this obligation has even more resonance in the context of a private religious school.[64]

The CJ and JM then considered Loyola's proposed equivalent program in light of the world religions competency, the ethics competency, the dialogue competency, and the two core objectives (recognition of others and the pursuit of the common good) of the ERC program.[65] They concluded:

> As is apparent, Loyola's program departs from the generic ERC Program in two key respects. First, Loyola proposes to teach Catholicism from the Catholic perspective. Second, while ensuring that all ethical points are presented and encouraging students to think critically, Loyola proposes an approach that emphasizes the Catholic point of view when discussing ethical questions. In both respects, Loyola's teachers would depart from the strict neutrality required under the ERC Program.[66]

From an analytical perspective, the CJ and JM chose to examine Loyola's claims within the framework of a traditional *Charter* analysis. Section 2(a) of the *Charter* guarantees freedom of religion. The state can limit this right only if it can show that the limitation is "reasonable" and "demonstrably justified in a free and democratic society" by virtue of section 1 of the *Charter*.[67] The first issue was whether the Minister's decision infringed Loyola's freedom of religion. The second issue was whether that decision limited "Loyola's freedom of religion more than reasonably necessary to achieve the goals of the program."[68] The CJ and JM first considered the extent of religious freedom under s. 2(a) of the *Charter*. They observed that it is not limited to religious belief, worship, and the practice of religious customs. Based on the SCC's decision in *R. v. Big M*,[69] they held that the right protected under s. 2(a) includes the "right to

---

64 Para. 112.
65 Para. 116-129.
66 Para. 128.
67 Para. 113.
68 Para. 114.
69 Above, note 42.

manifest belief by teaching and dissemination." Consequently, Loyola's express wish to teach its curriculum according to Catholic beliefs fell within the ambit of s. 2(a)'s protection.[70]

They then considered whether the Minister's decision infringed Loyola's rights under s. 2(a) of the *Charter*. The CJ and JM drew on the Court's decisions in *Syndicat Northcrest v. Amselem*[71] and *Multani v. Commission scolaire Marguerite-Bourgeoys*[72] to inform their analysis. Under the traditional analysis, where an individual claims that his or her religious freedom has been infringed, the claimant must demonstrate "(1) that he or she sincerely believes in a practice or belief that has a nexus with religion, and (2) that the impugned conduct of a third party interferes, in a manner that is non-trivial or not insubstantial, with his or her ability to act in accordance with that practice or belief."[73] The CJ and JM recognized that an organizational claimant cannot demonstrate a sincere belief. However, they held that the expressed belief of an organization could be examined to ensure that "it is made in good faith and is neither a fiction nor an artifice."[74] They indicated that, as a threshold matter, "an organization seeking to assert a religious freedom claim under the *Charter* must at a minimum demonstrate that its purpose is primarily religious, and that it operates in accordance with this purpose."[75]

---

70 Para. 132.

71 2004 SCC 47, [2004] 2 S.C.R. 551.

72 2006 SCC 6, [2006] 1 S.C.R. 256.

73 Para. 134. Here the CJ and JM referred to the *Multani* decision at para. 34.

74 Para. 138.

75 *Ibid*. As the CJ and JM stated:

In evaluating this consistency between the claimed belief or practice and the organization's purpose and operation, the same non-exhaustive criteria from *Amselem* can be relied on. While an organization itself cannot testify, the credibility of officials and representatives who give testimony on the organization's behalf will form part of the assessment. Objective indicators will perhaps play a more prominent role. It is proper to assess the claimed belief or practice in light of objective facts such as the organization's other practices, policies and governing documents. The beliefs and practices of an organization may also reasonably be expected to be more static and less fluid than those of an individual. Therefore, inquiry into past practices and consistency of position would be more relevant than in the context of a claimant who is a natural person (para. 139).

The CJ and JM concluded that the two-part test from *Amselem* and *Multani* when modified and applied to an organization produced the following questions:

> (1) Is Loyola's claimed belief that it must teach ethics and its own religion from the Catholic perspective consistent with its organizational purpose and operation?; and (2) Does the Minister's decision to deny Loyola an exemption from the ERC Program interfere with Loyola's ability to act in accordance with this belief, in a manner that is more than trivial or insubstantial?[76]

Based on the application judge's strong findings of fact,[77] and under the first part of the test, the CJ and JM held that Loyola's religious beliefs are consistent with its organizational purpose and operation. Under the second part of the test, they found that the Minister's decision substantially interfered with Loyola's ability to act in accordance with its religious beliefs because the denial of an exemption had the effect of "requiring Loyola to teach its entire ethics and religion program from a neutral, secular perspective."[78] The application judge's extensive findings of fact buttressed this conclusion. In sum, the Minister's decision violated Loyola's freedom of religion under s. 2(a) of the *Charter*.

The CJ and JM then proceeded to a section 1 analysis to determine whether the Minister's decision constituted a reasonable limit on Loyola's religious freedom or "whether the Minister's insistence on a purely secular program of study to qualify for an exemption limited Loyola's right to religious freedom no more than reasonably necessary to achieve the ERC Program's goals."[79] The government bore the burden of demonstrating that its restriction on Loyola's freedom of religion was reasonable. Failure to do so would mean the Minister's decision was unconstitutional and had to be set aside. The CJ and JM noted that the Minister's decision

---

76 Para. 140.
77 These findings were based on testimony from senior officials within Loyola's organization and objective evidence which included a comparison of Loyola's classroom practices with the underlying principles of Jesuit education. Para. 142.
78 Para. 143.
79 Para. 146.

derived from a definition of "equivalent" which required all alternative approaches to be both "cultural and non-denominational." They held, however, that "there is nothing inherent in the ERC Program's objectives (recognition of others and pursuit of the common good) or competencies (world religions, ethics, and dialogue) that requires a cultural and non-denominational approach."[80] In fact, the legislative and regulatory scheme made it clear that the government's intention was "to allow religious schools to teach the ERC Program without sacrificing their own religious perspectives."[81] An overly rigid approach in a flexible legislative and regulatory scheme led to a substantial infringement of Loyola's religious freedom which could not be justified under s. 1 of the *Charter*:

> The legislative and regulatory scheme is designed to be flexible and to permit private schools to deviate from the generic ERC Program, so long as its objectives are met. The Minister's definition of equivalency casts this intended flexibility in the narrowest of terms, and limits deviation to a degree beyond that which is necessary to ensure the objectives of the ERC Program are met. This led to a substantial infringement on the religious freedom of Loyola. In short, the Minister's decision was not minimally impairing. Therefore, it cannot be justified under s. 1 of the *Charter* as a reasonable limit on Loyola's s. 2(*a*) right to religious freedom.[82]

Unlike Justice Abella, who sent the matter back to the Minister for reconsideration, the CJ and JM would have granted Loyola's application for an exemption to avoid further delaying the relief the school had been seeking for nearly seven years. The Minister would have accorded such

---

80 Para. 148.
81 Para. 148.
82 Para. 151.

an exemption in line with Loyola's proposal and guidelines outlined by the CJ and JM.[83]

Implications

The *Loyola* decision is important for three reasons. First, the SCC unanimously recognized the communal nature of freedom of religion claims under s. 2(a) of the *Charter* in the field of education. Prior decisions involving individual actors, such as *Multani* and *R. v. Jones*,[84] focused on the individual character of religious freedom. The collective role religion plays in people's lives did not figure in these decisions. In *Loyola*, Justice Abella held that freedom of religion includes both the individual and collective aspects of religious belief.[85] She noted that "the collective manifestation and transmission of Catholic beliefs through a private denominational school" constituted a "crucial part of Loyola's

---

83 Para. 165 The CJ and JM offered five guidelines to demarcate the boundaries of a s. 22 exemption in this case, while informing the Minister's assessment of future exemption applications. In particular, they noted:
Loyola's teachers must be permitted to describe and explain Catholic doctrine and ethical beliefs from the Catholic perspective, and cannot be required to adopt a neutral position.
Loyola's teachers must describe and explain the ethical beliefs and doctrines of other religions in an objective and respectful way.
Loyola's teachers must maintain a respectful tone of debate — both by conveying their own contributions in a respectful way, and by ensuring the classroom dialogue proceeds in accordance with respect, tolerance and understanding for those with different beliefs and practices.
Where the context of the classroom discussion requires it, Loyola's teachers may identify what Catholic beliefs are, why Catholics follow those beliefs, and the ways in which another specific ethical or doctrinal proposition does not accord with those beliefs, be it in the context of a particular different religion or an ethical position considered in the abstract.
Loyola's teachers cannot be expected to teach ethics or religious doctrines that are contrary to the Catholic faith in a way that portrays them as equally credible or worthy of belief. Respect, tolerance, and understanding are all properly required, and the highlighting of differences must not give rise to denigration or derision. However, ensuring that all viewpoints are regarded as equally credible or worthy of belief would require a degree of disconnect from, and suppression of, Loyola's own religious perspective that is incompatible with freedom of religion. Para. 162.
84 [1986] 2 S.C.R. 284.
85 Para. 59.

---

claim."[86] The Chief Justice and Justice Moldaver likewise highlighted the tight link between the individual and collective sides of freedom of religion:

> The individual and collective aspects of freedom of religion are indissolubly intertwined. The freedom of religion of individuals cannot flourish without freedom of religion for the organizations through which those individuals express their religious practices and through which they transmit their faith.[87]

Like Justice Abella, they held that this communal dimension to freedom of religion was central to Loyola's position.

Second, the relationship of the secular state, including its supervisory role of upholding educational standards, to both the individual and institutional religious educational actors in a multicultural and multi-religious society was clarified. Justice Abella ruled that part of secularism includes respect for religious differences. A secular state cannot support or prefer the religious practices of one group over those of another. At the same time, while respecting religious differences, a secular state does not act to eliminate those differences.[88] Justice Abella remarked that a secular state supports pluralism by allowing communities with different values and practices to co-exist peacefully.[89] This support does not mean that the state must remain indifferent to all religious differences or practices. Justice Abella made it clear that religious differences cannot trump national core values.[90] Here, she quoted the Bouchard-Taylor report:

> A democratic, liberal State cannot be indifferent to certain core values, especially basic human rights, the equality of all citizens before the law, and popular sovereignty. These

---

86 Para. 61.
87 Para. 94.
88 Para. 43.
89 Para. 45.
90 Para. 46.

are the constituent values of our political system and they provide its foundation.[91]

She noted that the state has a legitimate interest in promoting and protecting these shared values of equality, human rights, and democracy.[92] Furthermore, these values "enhance the conditions for integration and points of civic solidarity by helping connect us despite our differences...."[93]

One might envision a situation in which a religious educational actor aims to teach its students that respect for certain human rights, including gender equality is inconsistent with its own religious doctrine. In this scenario, if girls and women are viewed as inferior moral beings who must submit to men, and this perspective is being actively promoted in a private religious school, the state would arguably have grounds to intervene to place restrictions on the promotion of this view, which runs counter to core values. In the specific context of the ERC program with its core objectives of promoting the public good and respect for others, the Chief Justice and Justice Moldaver recognized that "A program of purely denominational instruction designed primarily to indoctrinate students to the correctness of certain religious precepts would not achieve the objectives of the ERC Program . . ."[94] They expressed the need for state oversight in these terms:

> There is unquestionably a role for the Minister to examine proposed programs on a case-by-case basis to ensure that they adequately further the objectives and competencies of the ERC Program. In certain cases, the result may be that the religious freedoms of private schools are subject to justifiable limitations.[95]

---

91 Above, note 1 at para. 46. See Gérard Bouchard and Charles Taylor, Commission de consultation sur les pratiques d'accommodement reliées aux différences culturelles, *Building the Future: A Time for Reconciliation* (2008), at p. 134).

92 Para. 47.

93 As McLachlin J. noted in *Adler v. Ontario*, [1996] 3 S.C.R. 609 (dissenting in part), "[a] multicultural multireligious society can only work . . . if people of all groups understand and tolerate each other:" Para. 212. Cited by Justice Abella at para. 47.

94 Para. 148.

95 Para. 150.

In sum, the state has a compelling interest in ensuring that all students, whether in public schools or private schools, are taught the core objectives of the ERC program: respect for others and pursuit of the common good.

Third, there is consensus among all seven Justices (and indeed the parties to the litigation themselves) that the core objectives of the ERC program are laudatory, including the promotion of three competencies chosen to attain these objectives: the ability to understand religious culture, the ability to reflect on ethical questions, and the ability to engage in dialogue. The divide between Justice Abella and Chief Justice McLachlin/Justice Moldaver was whether Loyola had to teach other religions' ethical frameworks from a neutral and objective perspective. At first blush, this divide creates an important conceptual chasm between the two sides. Justice Abella claimed that the case for teaching the ethical frameworks of other religions from an objective perspective was even more compelling in a faith-based school:

> My starting point is that in a religious high school, where students are learning about the precepts of one particular faith throughout their education, it is arguably even more important that they learn, in as objective a way as possible, about other belief systems and the reasons underlying those beliefs.[96]

She held that teaching other ethical frameworks through the lens of Catholic ethics and morality, even if done respectfully, would essentially transform "the ethics component of the ERC Program from a study of different ethical approaches into a class on Catholicism."[97] This outcome would create unacceptable risks and contradict the ERC's program goals:

> The resulting risk is that other religions would necessarily be seen not as differently legitimate belief systems, but as worthy of respect only to the extent that they aligned with the tenets of Catholicism. This contradicts the ERC Program's goals of ensuring respect for those whose

---

96 Para. 72.
97 Para. 75.

religious beliefs are different, a goal no less worthy in a religious school than in a public one.[98]

Justice Abella held that this requirement for objectivity and neutrality did not seriously undermine Loyola's religious freedom:

> I have difficulty seeing how this can undermine the values of religious freedom. I do not dispute that the belief systems Loyola's teachers are required to explain to their students may not reflect their personal beliefs, or Loyola's institutional allegiances. But teaching about the ethics of other religions is largely a factual exercise. It need not be a clash of values. Nor is asking Loyola's teachers to teach other religions and ethical positions as objectively as possible a requirement that they shed their own beliefs. It is, instead, a pedagogical tool utilized by good teachers for centuries — let the information, not the personal views of the teacher, guide the discussion.

Justice Abella's call for neutrality can be contrasted with that of the Chief Justice (CJ) and Justice Moldaver (JM). The CJ and JM held that requiring teachers to remain neutral on ethical questions related to other religions posed serious practical challenges while constituting a serious violation of Loyola's freedom of religion:

> Requiring Loyola's teachers to maintain a neutral posture on ethical questions poses serious practical difficulties and represents a significant infringement on how Loyola transmits an understanding of the Catholic faith. It is inevitable that ethical standards that do not comport with Catholic beliefs will be raised for discussion. Faced with a position that is fundamentally at odds with the Catholic faith, Loyola's teachers would be coerced into adopting a false and facile posture of neutrality. The net effect would be to render them mute during large portions of the ethics discussion — a discussion that is, as the ERC Program

---

98 *Ibid.*

presupposes, crucial to developing a civilized and tolerant society.[99]

To illustrate the point, the CJ and JM highlighted the discussion of pre-marital sex and how the subject is viewed by other religions. They claimed it was inconceivable that a Catholic teacher could sincerely express a neutral viewpoint on the topic. The practical effect of such an approach would be the teacher's "coerced silence."[100] This silence would of course be broken when the teacher came to discuss the same topic from a Catholic perspective when talking about his or her own religion. The CJ and JM found this to be problematic:

> This delayed ability to express honest beliefs and actively moderate the classroom discussion does not illustrate a tolerable compromise between the state's interest in fur-thering the objectives of the ERC Program and Loyola's freedom of religion. Rather, it illustrates the unsuitability and unworkability of such a framework.[101]

The CJ and JM supported Loyola's position, which offered an integrated approach whereby the school could present the moral and ethical impli-cations about premarital sex from a Catholic point of view in a general discussion about the ethical perspectives of other religions on the topic. Therefore, Loyola's teachers could engage students and acknowledge that other religions, including some versions of Christianity, do not strictly forbid sexual intimacy between unmarried individuals. Discussion would highlight the dominant secular narrative in Western society, which tol-erates and even encourages sex outside of marriage.[102] As the CJ and JM observed:

> Students would be encouraged to think critically about the different views. Teachers would clearly identify the Catholic position, and the justifications for it, while

---

99 Para. 156.
100 Para. 157.
101 *Ibid.*
102 Para. 158.

respectfully considering the other points of view. If asked
a question challenging the Catholic point of view, teachers
would be free to answer and defend that position — again,
in the context of an open-minded and respectful conversation, but one that is grounded in the inescapable reality
that Loyola is a Catholic high school whose students and
parents have voluntarily selected an education infused with
Catholic beliefs and values.[103]

The CJ and JM noted that the dialogue competency requires teachers
to be honest and to participate actively in the classroom discussion.
Enforced neutrality does not promote the objectives of the ERC program in this regard. In fact, it puts Catholic teachers in an untenable
situation. Either they can present a neutral and, consequently, insincere
perspective on an ethical question related to a precept of the Catholic
faith, or they may choose to remain silent. As the CJ and JM observed:
"Neither insincerity nor silence is conducive to the ERC Program's objectives of promoting individual deliberation and the exchange of ideas."[104]
The CJ and JM indicated that neutrality would lead to a violation of freedom of religion:

> [R]equiring a religious school to present the viewpoints of
> other religions as equally legitimate and equally credible is
> incompatible with religious freedom. Indeed, presenting
> fundamentally incompatible religious doctrines as equally
> legitimate and equally credible could imply that they are
> both equally false. Surely this cannot be a perspective that
> a religious school can be compelled to adopt.[105]

The CJ and JM noted that a strict neutrality requirement means presenting "all religious perspectives . . . as equally valid."[106] This assumption
appeared to be anchored in the Minister's belief that this approach was

---

103 *Ibid.*
104 Para. 159
105 Para. 160
106 *Ibid.*

necessary to achieve the ERC program's objectives.[107] The CJ and JM claimed that this position presents a false dichotomy:

> Loyola has strongly and repeatedly expressed that its proposed alternative program would treat other religious viewpoints with respect — going to the extent of inviting religious leaders from other faiths into the classroom to ensure students have a rich and full understanding of differing perspectives.[108]

Furthermore, this false dichotomy does not square with the ability of different religious communities to come together to promote interfaith engagement, notwithstanding deeply differing views of religious and epistemological truth. As the CJ and JM state:

> Additionally, this dichotomy does not accord with principles of interfaith cooperation and collaboration, which brings together people with deeply held commitments to their own faiths (and who therefore, by implication, have rejected other religious doctrines as "equally legitimate" or "equally credible") but who are nonetheless able to foster deep ties based on sincere mutual respect. As Loyola submitted in its letter to the Minister, [TRANSLATION] "our ethical ideal is not simply to 'tolerate' others but indeed to 'love' others, as our Christian faith teaches us."[109]

Upon closer inspection, this dichotomy between Justice Abella and the CJ/JM may not be as wide as it first appears. As Justice Abella explained:

> I quickly acknowledge that in a religious school, teaching other ethical frameworks in a neutral way may be a delicate exercise. A school like Loyola must be allowed some flexibility as it navigates these difficult moments. Catholicism's answer to ethical questions, for instance, will sometimes conflict with the approach taken by the ethics of other

---

107 *Ibid.*
108 *Ibid.*
109 Para. 161.

religions. It would be surprising if, in classes discussing other belief systems, students did not ask for comparative explanations, questions Loyola's teachers are clearly free to answer. A comparative approach that explains the Catholic ethical perspective and responds to questions about it is of course legitimate.[110]

For her, this approach means that the Catholic teacher is neither silenced nor forced to forego her own beliefs. This teacher is indeed allowed to explain the Catholic perspective and how it differs from other faiths.[111] Justice Abella recognized that the Minister's call for strict neutrality is not necessary for Loyola to achieve the state's goals related to the ERC program.

However, Justice Abella's resort to the language of neutrality and objectivity remains part of the problem. Philosophically, when it comes to belief systems and values, there is no neutral viewpoint which stands outside of the various religious and humanistic traditions and ideologies. Everything is embedded in, and infected with, a world view or position from somewhere. Pragmatically, and by her own admission, Justice Abella acknowledged that strict neutrality is simply unworkable and would place unreasonable restrictions on invaluable exchanges in the classroom. Student curiosity, spontaneity, and organic discussions must inevitably lead to comparative assessments of diverse moral and ethical perspectives. For obvious pedagogical reasons, such discussions cannot and should not be avoided if we wish to help our students think critically, constructively, and creatively. Justice Abella couched her reasoning in language which recognized the impossibility of strict neutrality. She called for "An emphasis on objective instruction insofar as possible," and stated that teaching other ethical positions while considering Loyola's own ethical framework "would necessarily be part of the discussion, but the role will be one of significant participant rather than hegemonic tutor."[112]

This relaxed standard of objectivity and neutrality should be replaced with the language of fair-mindedness and reasonableness. As a

---

110 Para. 73.
111 Para. 78.
112 Para. 76.

Roman Catholic school with a long and distinguished reputation, Loyola is historically and epistemologically committed to a social justice view of reality that is neither objective nor neutral. Loyola could not be otherwise. Equally important, and as highlighted by the Chief Justice (CJ) and Justice Moldaver (JM), Loyola has consistently maintained that its proposed alternative program would treat other religious perspectives with respect. Doing so would entail inviting religious leaders (such as rabbis and imams) from other faith communities into the classroom to meet with students and to ensure those students have a rich and better understanding of those differing perspectives.[113] At the end of the day, an authentic dialogue may lead to the ultimate conclusion that one faith community (or individual members of that community) believes the other faith community is wrong in its religious world view. Authenticity would be measured by respectful dialogue, tough questions, different opinions on fundamental questions, deep and passionate convictions, rigorous argument, and a willingness to engage in spite of different values and competing belief systems. The assumption is that this type of discussion would ensue in a civil and respectful manner and environment that would be fair-minded, reasonable, and reflect social reality. Such a discussion would require listening actively to the other and abandoning the language of strict, and even relaxed, neutrality, which is mere artifice. Replacing this requirement of neutrality with a call for fair-mindedness, reasonableness, and openness would not undermine the twin core values of the ERC program: respect for others and pursuit of the common good. In fact, an openness and willingness to engage with those whose ethical ideals conflict either partly or completely with our own in an atmosphere of trust and respect will better prepare students on a moral and human level for adulthood. The ability to engage the other on his or her own terms and to change one's own mind about ideas and convictions when there is good reason to do so is an excellent form of education we can offer our students. They will require this capacity to learn and to adapt in an increasingly complex, multicultural, and multi-religious reality in which they will live with and interact with others.

---

113 Para. 160.

Conclusion

In his book, *The wayfinders*, Wade Davis (2009) makes a compelling case for the diverse web of social life he calls the *ethnosphere*:

> Together the myriad of cultures makes up an intellectual and spiritual web of life that envelops the planet and is every bit as important to the well being of the planet as is the biological web of life that we know as the biosphere. You might think of this social web of life as an *ethnosphere*, a term perhaps best defined as the sum total of all thoughts and intuitions, myths and beliefs, ideas and inspirations brought into being by the human imagination since the dawn of consciousness. The ethnosphere is humanity's greatest legacy. It is the product of our dreams, the embodiment of our hopes, the symbol of all we are and all that we, as a wildly inquisitive and astonishingly adaptive species, have created.[114]

This marvellous social tapestry matters because, as Davis argued, "there are indeed alternatives, other ways of orienting human beings in social, spiritual, and ecological space."[115] According to Maclure and Taylor (2011), moral and religious diversity "is a structuring and, as far as we can see, permanent characteristic of democratic societies."[116] This type of diversity inevitably leads to conflict. Finding ways to cooperate and to resolve outstanding tensions stemming from divergent, and at times seemingly intractable, representations of reality and underlying values is one of the most pressing projects the human race faces. As Maclure and Taylor note:

> [C]ontemporary societies must develop the ethical and political knowledge that will allow them to fairly and consistently manage the moral, spiritual, and cultural diversity

---

114 Davis, W. (2009). *The wayfinders: Why ancient wisdom matters in the modern world*. Toronto: Anansi Press, at p. 2.

115 *Ibid*. at 217.

116 Maclure, J., & Taylor, C. (2011). *Secularism and freedom of conscience*. Translated by Jane Marie Todd. Cambridge, Mass.: Harvard University Press, at 106.

at their heart. Those who embrace worldviews such as the great historical monotheisms, the Eastern religions, spiritual eclecticism, aboriginal spiritualties, militant atheism, agnosticism, and so on must learn to coexist and, ideally to establish bonds of solidarity.[117]

The Loyola school in Montréal, as an expression of the Jesuit tradition, makes an important contribution to the religious diversity which characterizes Canada. O'Malley (2000)[118] described the evolution of Jesuit education from the founding of the first Jesuit school in Messina, Sicily, in 1548 to the Jesuit primary/secondary school as we know it today. He highlighted the value of both the scholastic and humanist traditions, and claimed that the Jesuits did not view these traditions as incommensurable:

> Unlike some of their contemporaries, they did not oppose humanistic education to scholastic (university or professional) education, as if these were two incompatible systems or cultures. They saw them, rather, as complementary. They esteemed the intellectual rigour of the scholastic system and the power of the detached analysis it provided, and they believed in its goal of training highly skilled graduates in the sciences and in the professions of law, medicine, and theology. They at the same time esteemed in the humanist system (primary and secondary education) the potential of poetry, oratory, and drama to elicit and foster noble sentiments and ideals, especially in younger boys; they believed in its potential to foster *pietas* that is, good character.[119]

117 *Ibid.* at 110.
118 O'Malley, J.W. (2000). How the first Jesuits became involved in education. The Jesuit ratio Studiorum. 400th anniversary perspectives. Https://books.google. ca/books?hl=en&lr=&id=uvFn6N2dA3YC&oi=fnd&pg=PA43&dq=Jesuit+education+primary+and+secondary&ots=16huVcXReu&sig=GNmu_Vxddz4DEU9GeM993YXMPm8#v=onepage&q=Jesuit%20education%20primary%20and%20secondary&f=true.
119 *Ibid.* at 55–56.

He further stated:

> [F]rom both these systems of education they appropriated the conviction that human culture and religion were not competitive but complementary values, each enriching and challenging the other. Both systems taught in fact that philosophical, ethical, and to some extent even religious truths were available outside Christianity, and that these truths had to be respected. They were both thus reconciliatory in their ultimate dynamism.[120]

Academic rigour, commitment and service to others, and respect for different religious or moral positions are the hallmarks of the type of education offered to students at Loyola, as highlighted by Chief Justice McLachlan and Justice Moldaver. Although the state cannot endorse, for obvious reasons, Loyola's worldviews, or those of any other religious community in a secular society, it must be careful not to stamp out legitimate and responsible expressions of religiously infused education in the name of a militant secularism. Teachers at Loyola must be trusted with the religious and moral education of their students. While they seek to pursue the twin objectives of respect for others and pursuit of the common good, those teachers must not be silenced nor required to be strictly neutral. At the same time, they must be fair-minded, reasonable, and respectful of moral and religious traditions which run counter to their own. If they model academic integrity and a deep concern for others through interfaith dialogue and exposure to humanist and secular perspectives, their students will be well served and our communities strengthened.

---

120 *Ibid.* at 56.

CHAPTER 9

Copyright in the Canadian Education Context

José R. da Costa and José L. da Costa

Abstract

The last two decades have seen sweeping changes to intellectual property rights throughout the world. In Canada this shift is seen in the 1996 *Copyright Act* and the 2012 *Copyright Modernization Act*. These acts, along with two landmark Supreme Court of Canada decisions, set the landscape for understanding copyright for educators in contemporary Canadian Schools. The first of these cases, handed down in 2004, *CCH Canadian Ltd. v. Law Society of Upper Canada,* clarified the criteria for determining fair dealing. The second case, *Alberta v. Canadian Copyright Licensing Agency* (2012) further defined fair dealing in the educational context. This chapter explores the current balance between intellectual property rights and teacher rights for use of copyrighted materials.

Introduction

Mr. Techy asked his principal for money to purchase a class set of "The Outsiders" (published in 1967 by S.E. Hinton). The principal replied that no money was left in the school's budget to purchase the book. Not to be dissuaded, Mr. Techy thought about just reading the book in class to his students, putting only some really important excerpts up on the classroom digital white board, but after thinking through this option, he decided, instead, to purchase a digital copy of the book from Amazon. ca. He downloaded the digital copy to the District computer that had been assigned to him. Next, he removed the DRM (Digital Rights Management digital lock, which took all of two minutes after he had searched the Internet for information on the process) and converted the file into a PDF, which he then posted to his English class website for his students to access freely. As a teacher, he knew the importance of ensuring that every one of his students had his or her own copy of the book.

Mr. Techy knew that the most recent revisions to Canadian Copyright Act had exemptions for educational purposes, so he was pretty sure that his actions were legal. He did read his School District's policy, which simply stated that teachers were not to break any Provincial or Federal laws.

Later the same week, one of Mr. Techy's students told his mother how wonderful Mr. Techy was because he had enabled everyone in the class to read "The Outsiders." Unfortunately for Mr. Techy, the student's mother was a sales representative for Bantam-Dell Publishing, the company publishing and distributing "The Outsiders." She relayed this story to her boss. Within a few weeks, a lawsuit was launched against Mr. Techy and his school board. The case dragged on in the court system for several years while appeals of lower court decisions were being made. Finally, a decision was rendered ....

It has been said that teachers are masterful in adapting others' work to enable them to teach in their classrooms and other learning environments. The question of copyright infringement is often not even considered, for teachers in every discipline adopt, adapt, and even copy creative works produced by other people. Many teachers, and people in general, believe that copyright law applies only when the copyright symbol (i.e., "©") is placed somewhere on the piece of work. This belief is false! Copyright exists, is in effect immediately once an author produces a work, and currently in Canada continues to be recognized for 50 years following the death of the author or creator.

Teachers need to be aware of society's elevated expectations of them as role models for their students, and young people generally. Moreover, society expects teachers to obey the law, including copyright law. Infringement of copyright can lead to either criminal charges or civil litigation, and a teacher who violates either criminal or civil law will also have violated teacher professional codes of conduct and teacher contractual obligations to his or her school board.

Copyright, the means by which intellectual property rights holders protect their work, is constantly evolving through legislative reforms that reflect current economic and political climates. Legislators have an obligation to protect rights holders while still providing enough personal freedom for content consumers to utilize intellectual property legally and fairly. The need to strike an appropriate balance between these two opposing sides has motivated governments to continue to transform copyright laws and policies. The landscape of copyright is never static. Corporate lobbyists, activists, and court rulings have created an ongoing debate, providing arguments for enhancing the power of either the copyright holder or the content consumer. Two critical Supreme Court of Canada (SCC) decisions help to clarify how copyright applies to educators. The first was decided in 2004 in *CCH Canadian Ltd. v. Law Society of Upper Canada*, which clarified the criteria for determining fair dealing. The second was handed down in 2012 in the Province of Alberta's appeal of a lower court decision in favour of the Canadian Copyright Licensing Agency (also known as "Access Copyright") (*Alberta v. Canadian Copyright Licensing Agency*, 2012). The decision, in favour of the Province of Alberta, helped define fair dealing in the context of photocopying materials for use by students. This chapter will explore where the current balance of power is currently situated in Canada, what the current balance means for educators, and what can and cannot be done under the current legislation.

The Canadian Copyright Act and the Copyright Modernization Act

The *Canadian Copyright Act* (Bill C-42, 1996) and its updated amendments as introduced by the *Copyright Modernization Act* (Bill C-11, 2012)[1] exist for a very simple reason: to protect the unique work of creators from those who would seek to take or make use of their creations without appropriately remunerating the creator. Such inappropriate actions include downloading a musical work, a film, episode of television, or an electronic copy of a book without permission from the creator or publisher. The copyright on these works exists to ensure that people are paid for their work, making it profitable for individuals to create more intellectual property in the future, and guaranteeing the survival of creative industries.

At its most basic level, the *Canadian Copyright Act* is akin to many other pieces of copyright legislation. It defines what constitutes intellectual property (Government of Canada, *Canadian Copyright Act*, section 2). It describes how copyright is broken (Government of Canada, *Canadian Copyright Act*, section 27). Finally, it lists the charges one can face for breaking copyright (Government of Canada, *Canadian Copyright Act*, section 34). Educators should be aware that the *Canadian Copyright Act* is *not* the *Digital Millennium Copyright Act* (often referred to as the *DMCA*), an American piece of legislation (United States Copyright Office, 1998). With Canadian and American culture often blurring together, the specifics of the two laws can be easily confused.

Confusion can be exacerbated because much online content is provided by American servers, which must abide by American copyright laws. For this reason, when a user searches for a music album download, for example, by using Google's search engine, the search results are filtered based on copyright infractions as defined by the *Digital Millennium Copyright Act*, rather than by legislation from other countries. It does not matter that the searcher might be using a computer connected to

---

1 *The Canadian Copyright Act* (1996) and the amendments made through the *Copyright Modernization Act* (2012) will be referred to simply as the *Canadian Copyright Act* in this chapter.

the Internet by a Canadian Internet service provider. The information being requested will still be routed through American servers operated by American Internet service providers.

Fair Dealing

Accessing information in different countries raises an interesting question: what law is applicable to me? Provided a person is physically located in Canada, Canadian law applies. The *Canadian Copyright Act* entitles content consumers located in Canada to benefit from *fair dealing,* which is essentially the relaxation of particular rules found within the *Copyright Act* and the granting of copyright exceptions for different types of activities. The nuances of fair dealing have been written about at length, but have been best summed up by Geist (2012), a lawyer and a Canada Research Chair in Internet and E-Commerce Law at the University of Ottawa. Geist (2012) explained what people residing within the borders of Canada are allowed to do with copy-written material: "Time shifting, or the recording of television shows, is now legal under Canadian copyright after years of residing in a grey area. The law also legalizes format shifting, copying for private purposes, and the creation of backup copies." Time shifting is digitally recording a program so that it can be watched at a later time, colloquially referred to as DVR (digital video recording). Private copying and creating backups makes it legal for Canadians to take purchased content like a DVD (digital video disc) or CD (compact disc) and put the content on a digital device (e.g., a laptop or iPod) (Government of Canada. *Canadian Copyright Act.* 29.21(1)). According to Geist (2012), "Canadians can make use of excerpts or other portions of copyright works without the need for permission or payment. The scope of fair dealing has been expanded with the addition of three new purposes: education, satire, and parody."

In addition to identifying the three new categories described above, this portion of the law makes it legal to reproduce content for five other reasons originally included in the *Canada Copyright Act* (1996): scholarship or research, private study, criticism, review, and news reporting. This *Act*, however, limits the amount of content that can be reproduced. An educator cannot simply duplicate an entire textbook with a photocopier and distribute the text to students.[2] The *CCH Canadian Ltd. v. Law Society of Upper Canada* (2004) SCC decision provided six criteria for assessing the extent of fair dealing: (1) "Purpose of the Dealing" (p. 372) – to be considered fair dealing, the use of a work must fall into one of the eight categories described in the *Canadian Copyright Act*, section 29 (2012); (2) "Character of the Dealing" (p. 372) – consideration of the number of copies, the number of works being copied, and the number of recipients receiving the copies; (3) "Amount of the Dealing" (p. 373) – the reasonableness of the proportion of the work being copied necessary to meet the purpose of the dealing; (4) "Alternatives to the Dealing" (pp. 373-374) – explores the question of whether non-copyrighted material is available to achieve the goals of the dealing; (5) "Nature of the Work" (p. 374) – considers the question of whether the work or works copied are necessary to achieve the purpose of the dealing (i.e., one or more of the eight categories of purpose of dealing); (6) "Effect of the Dealing on the Work" (p. 374) – interrogates the extent to which the market for artist's or content creator's work has been diminished as a result of the copies that were made and distributed.

While exploring in detail each of the six criteria for fair dealing is beyond the scope of this chapter, teachers often ask about the amount of copy-protected material that can be considered fair dealing. The *CCH Canadian Ltd. v. Law Society of Upper Canada* (2004) decision offers some insight. Specifically, it stated:

> The quantity of the work taken shall not be determinative of fairness, but it can help in the determination. It may be possible to deal fairly with a whole work. As Vaver pointed out, there may be no other way to criticize or review certain types of works such as photographs ... (SCC 13, pp. 367-368).

---

2 However, subsection 29.4(3) of the *Canadian Copyright Act* does allow for manual reproduction of work. This subsection allows teachers, for example, to create their own reproductions (i.e., not digital copies) to display on dry-erase boards, chalk boards, over-head projectors, etc.

Thus, for example, multiple short excerpts from a single work, one chapter from a book, a single article from a periodical, an entire artistic work (painting, photo, map), an entire newspaper article or page, an entire single poem or musical score, or an entry from an encyclopedia would be considered fair (Noel & Snel, 2012; University of Alberta, n.d.). Further, (Geist) 2012 noted:

> The law also includes a unique user generated content provision that establishes a legal safe harbour for creators of non-commercial user generated content such as remixed music, mashup videos, or home movies with commercial music in the background. The provision is often referred to as the "YouTube exception," though it is not limited to videos.

This portion of the legislation makes it legal for individuals to create content by using the intellectual property of others to make something unique, and has far-reaching implications for services such as library "Makerspaces," which allow patrons to edit their own videos with professional software, or even school computer classes to engage in similar activities. For example, if a patron or student created his or her own video recording and edited it to include a commercially available song, that person would not be breaking Canadian copyright law.

While guidelines regarding the amounts that may be copied regularly refer to the figure of ten percent of a work as consistent with fair dealing (e.g., Noel & Snel, 2012; University of Alberta, n.d.; Western University, 2013), the *Canada Copyright Act* does not mention such an amount, and the seminal SCC cases do not provide a precedent In fact, the SCC justices, in *Alberta v. Canadian Copyright Licensing Agency* (2012) wrote:

> The Copyright Board's approach to the "amount of dealing" factor was also flawed. Having found that teachers only copied short excerpts of each textbook, the Board was required to determine whether the proportion of each of the short excerpts in relation to the whole work was fair. This factor is not a quantitative assessment based

on aggregate use, but an examination of the proportion between the excerpted copy and the entire work. (p. 350)

Balancing the Consumer and Publisher

Fair dealing actually gives Canadian content consumers a large breadth of freedom to use materials that have a copyright on them. Consider the power that major publishers wield. Corporations such as Disney ($48.8 billion revenue), Universal Music Group ($6.5 billion revenue), or Pearson Publishing ($7.8 billion revenue) represent multi-billion dollar industries actively lobbying governments for increased copyright restrictions. Many of these organizations have proven themselves extremely eager to pursue copyright violators in massive litigations, making examples of those who have taken the organizations' intellectual property illegally and forcing copyright violators to pay for court fees and staggering, multi-million-dollar law suits.

The *Canadian Copyright Act's* provisions for consumer protection are almost astonishing, given that these corporations are so hostile to granting content consumers any control whatsoever. Trosow (2003) characterizes the attitude of publishers as tending "towards the promotion of ever more effective exclusion mechanisms" (p. 233), the bias of which, "seems to be hard-wired into the economic analysis of copyright as its driving assumption, which has constricted the full consideration of policy options" (p. 233). Essentially, the publishing industry desires continuous reform to copyright laws, with the goal of increasing industry control over users. For publishers, control is synonymous with increased revenue.

Industry pressure has ensured that the *Canadian Copyright Act* has protections in place for copyright holders. As Geist (2012) explained "The most significant new restriction involves the controversial digital lock rules prohibiting by-passing technological protections found on DVDs, software, and electronic books." Digital locks and technological protections were initially created to prevent piracy. Computer software is a good example. Anyone familiar with installing software such as versions of Microsoft's Windows from the late 1990s until the early 2000s on their computer should be familiar with the idea of a registration [CD] key.[3] The key is a string of numbers required to prove that a consumer has a genuine and unique copy of a software product. Failure to input the correct key prevents the software from functioning properly. The coding that prevents the software from working is called a digital lock. Under Canadian law, if a consumer, including anyone belonging to the teaching profession, decides to subvert the authentication process that the lock requires – using something like a software crack – he or she would be guilty of breaking a technological protection measure and would be violating the *Canadian Copyright Act*.

Copyright Violation

The most critical difference between legislation in Canada and the United States involves the punishment of violators. If the law is broken by copying more than permitted, or if an individual is caught pirating intellectual property, there are two potential outcomes: (1) If the individual has violated copyright law for his or her own private use, intellectual property holders may seek statutory damages in a "sum of not less than $100 and not more than $5,000 that the court considers just, with respect to all infringements involved in the proceedings for all works or other subject-matter, if the infringements are for non-commercial purposes" (Government of Canada. *Canadian Copyright Act*. 38.1 (1)), and (2) if the individual has resold another's intellectual property without authorization, the copyright holder may seek "a sum of not less than $500 and not more than $20,000 that the court considers just, with respect to all infringements involved in the proceedings for each work or other subject-matter" (Government of Canada. *Canadian Copyright Act*. 38.1 (1)).

The *Canadian Copyright Act* distinguishes between copyright infringement and the breaking of a technological protection measure

---

3 This example may be somewhat dated as many pieces of software require an Internet connection to work, and an actual "key" is no longer required. Microsoft currently performs its verification directly through the Internet and does not require a key. However, circumventing any type of digital lock to access and use of an unlicensed product is seen as by-passing the digital lock.

(e.g., a digital lock). Here, the law placates the desires of corporations and their lobbyists:

> Every person, except a person who is acting on behalf of a library, archive or museum or an educational institution, is guilty of an offence who knowingly and for commercial purposes contravenes section 41.1 and is liable (a) on conviction on indictment, to a fine not exceeding $1,000,000 or to imprisonment for a term not exceeding five years or to both; or (b) on summary conviction, to a fine not exceeding $25,000 or to imprisonment for a term not exceeding six months or to both. (Government of Canada. *Canadian Copyright Act*, 48(3.1))

Section 41.1 outlines the situations in which circumvention of a technological protection measure is acceptable. It is permissible to break digital locks if one is conducting encryption research; working for law enforcement or for the purpose of national security; or attempting to use a program, which was legally purchased, to function on a device for which it was not meant. Furthermore, if a legitimate copy is owned or licensed, circumventing digital protection in order to gain access to content to permit enhancing the content for use by individuals with perceptual disabilities is also legal.

In drafting the *Canadian Copyright Act*, legislators saw section 41.1 as creating copyright balance by allowing creators the right to lock their digital files with no exemptions for users, in return for the granting of many new rights for librarians and educators (Smith, 2012). Section 48 the *Canadian Copyright Act* reveals that libraries, archivists, and educational institutions seem free to do as they will, as long as section 41.1 is not contravened. The listed exceptions in Section 41.1 almost completely eradicate these public interest freedoms. Indeed, an educator may help someone with a vision disability to use a locked e-book, or a librarian may conduct research on encryption, but these exceptions are very narrow.

Business and Copyright

In the United States, the maximum fine for a single copyright infringement ranges from $100,000 to just under $1-million. Each subsequent infringement is treated as an independent action, with no maximum cumulative penalty. The potential for massive lawsuits has actually created an industry out of copyright litigation. Publishers and content owners hire external firms to seek out infringers, threaten them with massive lawsuits, and then offer them the choice to settle out of court for a fraction of the cost of their lawsuit (Balganesh, 2013). The American system has become so efficient that a simple form letter delivers all the required information, outlining the number of infringements, the total the defendant would have to pay if litigation is pursued through the court system and the defendant lost the court case, the amount expected for a settlement, and how to pay it. The presumption is that a settlement will be the preferred course of action for the defendant. With this presumption in mind, the main goal of this sort of action is to threaten a maximum number of people in hope that fear will drive at least a few of them to settle without putting up any legal fight whatsoever. This approach, referred to as "copyright trolling," generates revenue and provides a deterrent for potential content pirates.

While copyright trolling has not become pervasive within Canada, threats of lawsuits do happen. However, despite what a form letter from a trolling legal firm might say, as long as digital locks are not disabled or circumvented, the upper limit of $5000 is the absolute maximum one can currently be fined in Canada for any number of concurrent copyright infringements. Nevertheless, some companies in Canada have evidently been following the American example when pursuing infringers and telling consumers that infringement will be met with fines up to $150,000 per item, as outlined by the *Digital Millennium Copyright Act*. These companies are presuming that the people they approach will not know the difference between Canadian and American law and will settle out of court for fear of losing massive sums of money. This practice takes advantage of a loophole in the law. It does not prevent these companies from lying to infringers, but the companies' threats have no legal basis (Geist, 2015).

These lawsuits illustrate the lengths to which some companies are willing to go in order to protect their intellectual property. The practices that they employ are ethically dubious. Lobby groups, which are funded by major publishers, tend to play a key role in determining the inclusion and exclusion of specific parts of legislation. While publishing lobbyists wield more power in the United States than in Canada, Canadians are not immune from their reach. The American government is notorious for embedding copyright clauses in international trade agreements. The Trans Pacific Partnership, which was being negotiated in late 2013, had very heavy-handed copyright laws that any member nation signing onto the treaty would have had to agree to. Canada was in negotiations to join the partnership even though the copyright laws would have certainly clashed with Canadian fair dealing exceptions. The Trans Pacific Partnership was notorious for being drafted in secrecy with a significant amount of input from lobby organizations working for publishers (WikiLeaks, 2014).

The common refrain of copyright holders is that inadequate governmental protection is going to leave them destitute. Piracy is frequently blamed as the main culprit undermining the profitability of intellectual property. Thus, anyone who has accepted this claim will be surprised to learn that the creative industries are flourishing. For example, the Recording Industry Association of America (the RIAA), the group representing the record labels responsible for producing about 85% of the published music in the world, is one of the most aggressive and vocal lobby groups advocating for stronger copyright laws. The RIAA has described massive piracy as a scourge driving music publishers out of business, but their "losses" are actually projections that assume each individual illicit download is a lost sale (Arias & Ellis, 2013). Strict copyright and stricter enforcement of copyright are attempts to assert control and to eliminate an unpredictable variable from corporate quarterly earnings estimates.

However, piracy might not present such a significant hurdle for the publishing industry. Data are fairly easy to manipulate and interpret. For example, Peukert, Claussen, and Kretschmer (2013) determined that piracy was more complicated than publisher rhetoric would have one think. Essentially, they found that while movies likely do lose some revenue to pirates, they likely also gain revenue generated by word-of-mouth advertisement; not all people download content illegally, but their honesty does not stop them from taking suggestions from those who do. Probably because of the loss of word-of-mouth advertisement, smaller films actually experienced a decrease in sales after Megaupload was shutdown (Peukert et al., 2013).

The central, and critical, point raised in this section, as it pertains to consumers, and teachers in particular, is that copyright legislation is in constant flux. Even if the actual wording of legislation is not being modified, copyright holders are continually pressuring for more conservative interpretations of copyright legislation. Consumers, including teachers, should not assume that interpretation of copyright law is static. Indeed, seemingly unrelated agreements reached between Canada and other nations can lead to subtle, but extremely important, changes to how copyright legislation is interpreted. The corporate publishing world has much to gain by encouraging more restrictive interpretations of copyright law and by advocating for more restrictive copyright legislation.

Business and Fair Dealing

Piracy and self-service provide an interesting segue for exploring fair dealing, but from the perspective of publishers. Being aware of this perspective will help consumers and teachers to understand the motivations underlying publishers' goals and actions. Prior to the passing of the *Canadian Copyright Act* and its exclusion for education, many educational institutions and academic libraries were forced to pay for every work circulated to students, teachers, or faculty. Most payments were made through an organization called Access Copyright (formally known as the Canadian Copyright Licensing Agency), a non-profit organization representing many of the large publishers. This organization made scholarships available and charged academic libraries and educational institutions $26 per student for access to copyrighted materials, and $10 every time something was to be printed (Williams, 2014). As one might expect, Access Copyright generated millions in revenue. Since the passing of the 2012 SCC decision in the *Alberta v. Canadian Copyright Licensing Agency* appeal, which confirmed the expansion of fair dealing to educational institutions, that revenue has plummeted. Educational institutions simply have no more need for Access Copyright; they can access and print documents, provided they are not being used for commercial purposes, without any special permission.

Some individuals have found fair dealing to be quite damaging. Rick Wilks, the director of Annick Press, argued, "It's really hurting us, and it's really hurting creators, and its hurting Canadian content: There will be fewer books because of this, fewer voices, and authors won't be able to afford to write" as cited in (Williams, 2013, p. 30). Conversely, public institutions are no longer being forced to spend millions on copyright licensing. If copyright were enshrined in our society for the sake of fostering cultural and technological growth, allowing educational institutions to alleviate some of their budgetary burden by eliminating copyright payments would also help creators (Farries, 2014). Further, eliminating mandatory payments (e.g., per student fees regardless of whether copyrighted material is accessed or not) would make materials more widely available to those who cannot afford them. The International Federation of Library Association and Institutions (IFLA) statement on copyright strongly supports this argument:

> IFLA maintains that unless libraries and citizens are granted exceptions which allow access and use without payment for purposes which are in the public interest and in line with fair practice such as education and research, there is a danger that only those who can afford to pay will be able to take advantage of the benefits of the Information Society. This will lead to an even greater divide between the information rich and the information poor. (IFLA, 2000)

Currently, Access Copyright is fighting for its existence and "has commenced litigation, arguing that these educational institutions are not adequately compensating creators and publishers for their effort and creativity" (Farries, 2014, p. 35). In reality, this organization is in court because the business model of flat-taxing educational institutes was subverted by Canadian law. Changing the *Canadian Copyright Act* to favour the old model is Access Copyright's only hope of staying relevant and viable.

Copyright as it Applies to Teachers

Under fair dealing, many exceptions allow teachers, broadly defined as "instructors," to copy small portions of a work. Such copying "for the purpose of research, private study, education, parody or satire does not infringe copyright" (Government of Canada, *Canadian Copyright Act*, section 29). Teachers should be mindful that although copyright exemptions exist under the auspices of fair dealing, they are still responsible for ensuring breaches of plagiarism are not committed, including presenting the scholarship of others as one's own by failing to acknowledge the original author or artist or the presentation of others' ideas or concepts as one's own without acknowledging their source.

Noel and Snel (2012) explained what is considered acceptable practice for teachers within the legal constraints of the *Canadian Copyright Act*. These authors emphasize that copyright exists in our society to balance the needs of the content creators (e.g., authors, artists, composers, and singers) so that they may earn a living from their creative outputs, with the needs of the individuals who are the consumers of these outputs.[4] As such, teachers need to model behaviours which do not exploit others. In fact, most teacher Codes of Professional Conduct refer to the function teachers play as role models in society. Furthermore, the language in Codes of Professional Conduct normally explicitly directs teachers, in both their professional and private lives, not to exploit others.

Specific exemptions exist for a variety of purposes. The education exemption granted by the *Canadian Copyright Act* is of critical importance to teachers. As long as the use of copyrighted material by teachers meets the fair dealing standards, as described in the SCC decision in

---

4 We strongly recommend that both in-service and pre-service Canadian teachers download and familiarize themselves with the interpretations of the *Canadian Copyright Act* provided by Noel and Snel (2012).

the *CCH Canadian Ltd. v. Law Society of Upper Canada* (2004) appeal, then teachers are on safe ground, but they must understand that this case does not provide *carte blanche* to duplicate and distribute copyrighted material indiscriminately. The *Alberta v. Canadian Copyright Licensing Agency* (2012) decision affirmed that duplicating multiple short excerpts from the same work is reasonable in educational settings, even though the complete work is available for purchase. The application of the principles outlined in the SCC decisions are deliberately very contextual because the SCC Justices rendering the decisions wanted the test of reasonableness to be applied in a variety of contexts. For teachers, however, this principle becomes problematic because no distinct demarcation exists between what is acceptable and what is not, particularly in the "grey areas" that the SCC decisions purposefully left unspecified (e.g., "character of the dealing," "amount of the dealing," and "nature of the work"). As a result, the risk of litigation, however minimal, always exists; consequently, teachers should follow very closely and carefully their school jurisdictions' policies around copyright. As their employer, their school board is vicariously liable for most of their actions. Teachers who have complied with their school boards' policies will, generally, be protected by their employer, whereas those who have not done so can expect to be left on their own.

Given the nuances discussed above, the reader is asked to think about Mr. Techy, whose fictional story was used to introduce this chapter. Should he have just read the book to his students, displaying quotes to the class as needed? As a teacher, was he justified in providing his students with a book his school could not purchase? Would the final court decision support his actions, including the removal of a digital lock? Would his employer, the School Board, stand behind him? Or would his employment with it be terminated for breach of contract? If Mr. Techy's employer is fined, because of vicarious liability for his actions, will the School Board be in a position to seek restitution from Mr. Techy? Should Mr. Techy lose his teaching credential for breach of the Teaching Code of Professional Conduct?

References

Alberta (Education) v. Canadian Copyright Licensing Agency (Access Copyright) (2012). SCC 37.

Arias, J.J., & Ellis, C. (2013). The decreasing excludability of digital music: Implications for copyright law. *American Economist, 58*(2), 124-133.

CCH Canadian Ltd. v. Law Society of Upper Canada (2004). SCC 13.

Farries, E. (2014). Copyright law: Shifting the balance in favour of digital access. *Feliciter, 60*(5), 35-36.

Geist, M. (2012). *Michael Geist Blog.* Retrieved from: http://www.michael-geist.ca/2012/ 11/c-11-impact/.

Geist, M. (2015). *Rightscorp and BMG exploiting copyright notice-and-notice system: Citing false information in legal demands.* Michael Geist Blog; retrieved from: http://www.michaelgeist.ca/2015/01/ rightscorp-bmg-exploiting-copyright-notice-notice-system-cit-ing-false-legal-information-payment-demands/.

Government of Canada (1985). *Canadian Copyright Act (R.S.C., 1985, c C-42).* Current to May 25, 2015. Retrieved from: http://laws-lois. justice.gc.ca/eng /acts/c-42/.

International Federation of Library Associations and Institutions (2000). *The IFLA Position on Copyright in the Digital Environment.* Retrieved from: http://www.ifl a.org/publications/ the-ifla-position-on-copyright-in-the-digital-environment-2000.

Noel, W., & Snel, J. (2012). *Copyright matters! Some key questions & answers for teachers* (3rd ed.). Council of Ministers of Education; Canadian School Boards Association; Canadian Teachers' Federation. Available: http://cme c.ca/Publicatio ns/Lists/Publications/Attachments/291/ Copyright_Matters.pdf.

Peukert, C., Claussen, J., & Kretschmer, T. (2013). *Piracy and movie revenues: Evidence from megaupload a tale of the long tail.* Available: http//crem. univ-rennes1.fr/Do cuments/Docs_workshops_2013/2013-10-24_ Digital_Piracy/2013-10-24_3_Peuk ertClaussenKretschmer.pdf.

Smith, C. (2012). Copyright Bill C-11 and its implementation. *Feliciter, 58*(4), 35-37.

Trosow, S. (2003). The illusive search for justification theories: Copyright, commodification and capital. *Canadian Journal of Law and Jurisprudence, 16*(2), 217-241.

United States Copyright Office (1998). *Digital Millennium Act* (1998). Retrieved from: http://copyright.gov/onlinesp/.

University of Alberta. (n.d.). *University of Alberta copyright guidelines.* Copyright and Licensing Office. Retrieved from: http://www.copyright.ualberta.ca/UofA_FairDe aling.pdf.

Western University (2013). *Copyright @ Western: Fair dealing exception guidelines.* Author. Retrieved from: http://copyright.uwo.ca/guidelines_requirements/guidelin es/fair_dealing_exception_guidelines.html.

WikiLeaks (2014). *Press release–Updated secret trans-pacific partnershipagreement (TPP)–IP Chapter (second publication).* Retrieved from: https://wikileaks.org/tp p-ip2/pressrelease/.

Williams, L.A. (September 19, 2014) Unfair dealing? *Publishers Weekly.* Retrieved from: http://www.publishersweekly.com/pw/by-topic/international/international-book- news/article/64057-unfair-dealing-canadian-publishing.html.

CHAPTER 10

Reasonable Limits on Teachers' Freedom of Expression in the Classroom

Bruce Maxwell and Kevin McDonough

Abstract

This paper identifies five principles, derived from an analysis of United States and Canadian jurisprudence, which taken together provide the contours of permissible teacher speech in the classroom, particularly in cases involving controversial and contested curricular issues. It is argued that greater clarity about the principles in question— curricular alignment, teacher even-handedness, consistency with *Charter* principles, avoidance of foreseeable inflammatory speech, and age-appropriateness—contributes at least two important benefits for educators. First, the principles serve as guidelines for responsible teacher decision making in the classroom; and second, they serve as a potential basis for resolving disputes among various stakeholders— teachers, school administrators and other school officials, and parents— which might otherwise lead to long, costly, and protracted legal conflicts.

Introduction

Canadian public sector teachers currently work within a legal framework that allows them some discretion to use teaching material, raise topics and make statements in class that may be controversial or considered offensive by some. Crucially, the courts have asserted that, on the condition that such discretion is exercised reasonably and responsibly, teachers retain that right even if their employer opposes their pedagogical choices.

In this respect, the legal context in which Canadian teachers work differs markedly from that of their U.S. counterparts. In two recent rulings – *Mayer v. Monroe County Community School Corp.* (2007) and *Evans-Marshall v. Board of Education* (2010) – U.S. high courts have undergone a paradigm shift in the way they assess teacher free speech cases. A decades-long tradition of dealing with teacher free speech cases by seeking to establish reasonable limits on curricular speech was quickly put an end to in 2007 when judges opted to evaluate teacher free speech according to the precedent established in *Garcetti v. Ceballos* (2006), a decision dealing with public employee speech (Clark & Trask, 2006; Gee, 2009). Despite the fact that the *Garcetti* ruling expressed uncertainty about whether it should apply to public school teachers, the *Mayer* and *Evans-Marshall* courts expedited the question of whether there are circumstances in which a teacher's in-class expression deserves constitutional protection by categorizing teacher speech as the expression of a public employee "pursuant to official duties" (*Mayer v. Monroe County*, 2007). Thus, as in *Garcetti*, curricular speech is regarded as mere "hired speech" not entitled to protection by the First Amendment of the U.S. constitution (Gee, 2009, p. 439).

By contrast, Canadian superior court rulings, in particular *Morin v. Board of Trustees of Reg. Admin. Unit #3* (2002)—the case of a grade 9 language arts teacher who spent over a decade fighting his employer in the courts over his right to present a critical perspective on Christian fundamentalism in his class—and the *Chamberlain v. Surrey School District No. 36* (2002)—a case which involved an elementary school teacher whose employer attempted to block the use of picture books depicting same-sex families—continue to seek a balance between the teacher's individual right to free expression with such competing interests as the state's right to establish curriculum, the school's responsibility to protect students from inappropriate speech, and students' right to an education favourable to the development of critical and autonomous thinking. As Clark and Trask (2006) argued, the strength of this "reasonable limits" judicial paradigm lies in its appreciation of the unique and necessary role that teachers play as professionals and public employees in promoting the values and democratic ideals of truth, public participation, and personal autonomy that underlie the constitutional right to free speech. "To recognize the responsible and reasonable exercise of teachers' right to freedom of expression in the classroom," Clarke and Trask (2006) wrote, "is to support the serious educational work that teachers are called to perform" (p. 111).

Although this is good news for teacher autonomy in Canada at the level of abstract legal principles—especially in a context in which teachers' professional autonomy is widely perceived as being under constant erosion by standardized testing regimes, increasingly detailed and prescriptive curricular guidelines, and other top-down measures (see Crocco & Costigan, 2007)—it leaves open two interrelated but very difficult questions about their application. This first is precisely what it means to exercise the right to free expression in the classroom in a way that is ethically reasonable and pedagogically responsible. The second is what to do in cases where a school principal disagrees with the way a teacher has exercised the right to curricular free expression. Teaching is and should be a collaborative enterprise; but the principal, as the teacher's employer, wields a great deal of *de facto* power over the teacher. This inevitably makes it tempting for teachers to defer to the principal's judgement in cases of disagreement. Furthermore, bearing in mind that the legal recognition of teachers' right to curricular free expression has been won through protracted and sometimes acrimonious interpersonal battles at a high cost to the teachers involved in both professional and personal terms, it is hard to deny Waddington's (2011) assessment that "teachers are not going to line up to walk in Morin's shoes" (p. 7). Given the choice between making a small sacrifice to professional autonomy and creating a situation that is potentially damaging to the relationship with one's employer and which exposes one to the charge of insubordination (a form of professional misconduct), it would take an ardent defender of free speech indeed not to accede to the principal's request, even if doing so means going against one's best professional judgment as a teacher.

To avoid this dynamic, it would undoubtedly be helpful for teachers and principals to agree on a set of basic principles that define the legitimate scope and reasonable limits of curricular free speech. Teachers could appeal to them to justify their choice to deal with sensitive issues in class to parents, students, and their employers. Principals could appeal to them to defend their teachers and the educational mission of the school when faced with complaints by parents or students that a teacher has raised issues or used material in a class that they find inappropriate or offensive. Last but not least, they could operate as common ground in cases of disagreements between teachers and their employers, helping them reach a friendly settlement that is respectful of the teacher's right to curricular free expression and avoiding litigation. Drawing on Canadian and U.S. jurisprudence, and secondary writings on teachers' freedom of expression in the classroom, the aim of this chapter is to propose just such a set of principles.

Some such set of principles seems necessary if disputants, particularly teachers and school officials, hope to resolve conflicts before they deteriorate to such an extent that they require the intervention of the courts. In order to appreciate this point, it may be helpful to gain an acquaintance with the usual series of events that leads to litigation. Although each case heard by the courts is unique, the legal record reveals a typical pattern of events following the initial act of a teacher introducing sensitive content or making a controversial statement in class. First, either by way of a direct complaint from a student or by way of parents who have heard about the event from a child at home, the teacher's employer becomes aware that teacher has caused some offence. Next, in the course of relating the complaint to the teacher, often accompanied by a request to modify their practice in response to the complaint, the principal encounters opposition on the part of the teacher. This opposition can take various forms ranging from refusal to comply with the request to the reaffirmation of the teacher's pedagogical choice and their right to make it. Dismissal, suspension, or the placing of a letter of reprimand in the teachers' file is not what follows in every case. As often as not, it appears, the teacher is subject to a change in contract status, occurring after the fact and sometimes months after the fact, which the teacher perceives as a retributive decision aimed to silence them, remove them from the school, and punish them for insubordination. In such cases, teachers working on a probationary contract often face non-re-newal whereas tenured teachers find themselves confronted with measures that are allowed under the terms of their contract. Being transferred to another school in an undesirable location is one common outcome. In most cases, what follows is a challenge to the employer' decision through the courts on the grounds that it involved a violation of the teacher's legal right to free expression.

Clearly, in these cases school officials and teachers often hold different and potentially conflicting assumptions about the reasonable limits of teacher freedom of expression, which eventually precipitates a legal conflict. Furthermore, as the above summary indicates, clashes over the reasonable limits of teacher free speech are likely to impose varied and costly burdens on individuals and institutions involved. At the same time, there is an important lacuna in the process that typically takes place between originating dispute and the intervention of the courts. Specifically, what seems to be missing is a process by which disputants might engage in good faith dialogue explicitly aimed at resolving the question of the reasonable limits of teacher speech in the classroom, as opposed to an adversarial process aimed at eliminating or marginalizing the offending teacher on grounds unrelated to their purportedly objectionable conduct. The principles we discuss in this paper provide a legally informed conceptual basis for bridging this void.

The discussion that follows is divided into three sections. Section one offers a brief review of the basic procedure the Supreme Court of Canada follows when deliberating on cases involving the right to free speech. Section two turns to the interests that judges and other legal arbitrators have identified as being at stake in cases of in-class free speech. In section three, we infer from our reading of the way these interests play out in the jurisprudence, a set of five principles that, taken together, seem to define reasonable and responsible curricular free speech: curricular alignment, even-handedness, consistency with *Charter* values, foreseeable avoidance of inflammatory speech, and age appropriateness.

Section One: Three Key Questions in a Case Involving Curricular Free Speech

In the Canadian legal system, the procedure for deciding whether a teacher's right to free speech is protected under the *Canadian Charter of Rights and Freedoms* is not simply a matter of first establishing whether teachers have the right to free expression in the course of their regular instructional duties and then, if they do, asking whether it can be shown that school authorities infringed on that right. Since the *Charter* was introduced in 1982, a series of precedents have come to determine the standard steps that judges follow when deliberating about cases in which the right to free expression is central. Although we do not propose a detailed overview of the steps of so-called "Section 2(b) cases" (the right to free expression appears in Section 2(b) of the *Charter*), to elucidate what is at stake in such hearings, and especially why they typically require judges to consider whose legitimate interests are affected and how to balance these stakeholders' different interests, this section presents a series of three key questions that would typically be considered in any case adjudicating an alleged violation of a teachers' right to free expression. They are: does the teacher's speech constitute "expression" in the sense of the *Charter*? If it does, is the *Charter* applicable to the alleged attempt to restrict that liberty? If the answer to both these questions is "yes," then a third question arises that refers to a unique feature of the Canadian *Charter*: Is the infringement justifiable in a free and democratic society?

As Kindred (2007) reported, the Supreme Court of Canada has tended to interpret the notion of "expression" very liberally to encompass a wide range of activities, which has included teacher expression in classroom settings. Previous rulings have regarded such activities as exotic dancing (*R. v. Mara*, 1997), a company's advertisements (*Irwin Toy Ltd. v. Quebec*, 1989), soliciting for the purposes of prostitution (*Reference re ss. 193 and 195.1(1) of the Criminal Code (Man)*, 1990), and even the possession of child pornography (*R. v. Sharpe*, 2001) as forms of expression in the sense of the *Charter*. Landmark Canadian and U.S. Supreme Court judgements have broadly recognized teachers' right to free speech at work. In *Tinker v. Des Moines Independent Community School District* (1969), a key U.S. precedent for cases involving the issue of free speech in schools, the judgement confidently asserted that, "it can hardly be argued that either students or teachers shed their constitutional rights to freedom of speech or expression at the schoolhouse gate" (p. 506). Similarly, in *R. v. Keegstra* (1990)—the well-known case of an Alberta teacher who over several years spread anti-Semitic propaganda in his high school social studies classes—the Supreme Court of Canada not only granted that Keegstra's hate speech constituted expression in the sense of the *Charter* but also that the criminal charges laid against Keegstra violated his free-speech rights.

As underlined by the ultimate outcome of *Keegstra* (1990), however, in Canadian higher court hearings, establishing that a particular act counts as free expression in the legal sense of the term is not sufficient to guarantee that it is protected by the *Charter* (Kindred, 2007). Two further main issues must be considered.

The first is whether the *Charter* applies to the alleged attempt to stifle free expression. A common misunderstanding about the *Charter* is that it covers interactions between citizens generally. In fact, the *Charter's* more limited purpose is to regulate and limit government activity (*Charter*, Section 32(1)). The term "government," like the term "expression," has been given a very broad interpretation by the courts. Municipal governments, Crown corporations, hospitals, universities, and public schools have all been accepted as government agencies in Supreme Court judgments (Kindred, 2007). As *Keegstra* (1990) dramatically attested, not only is public school teachers' in-class speech expression in the eyes of the law but it is also *prima facie* sheltered by the *Charter*. The curricular speech of teachers in private schools, however, is unlikely to be protected. Although we are not aware of any Canadian jurisprudence that has taken a position on the applicability of the *Charter* to actions of state-funded private schools, in the U.S., the constitutional provisions on free speech as outlined in the First Amendment do not protect private school teachers, even those employed by schools that receive most or even all of their funds from public sources (Schimmel, Fischer, & Stellmann, 2007).

The second main issue that courts grapple with in free-expression cases is, even if the *Charter* is applicable, whether or not the alleged attempt to stifle freedom of expression is justifiable under Section 1 of the *Charter* which permits "reasonable limitations" on the rights and freedoms outlined in the *Charter* only if they can be shown to be "justifiable in a free and democratic society" (*Charter*, Section 1). It is at this stage of the analysis where courts have to decide whether teachers' constitutionally guaranteed "negative" right not to be prevented by the state from expressing themselves is outweighed by the legitimate competing interests of other parties affected by the teacher's exercise of that individual liberty. In Canadian Supreme Court hearings, the burden of proof falls on the respondent, normally the government body against whom the case is brought and its representatives, to provide justification that the breach is justified under Section 1 of the *Charter* (Kindred, 2007). Having said that, as Waddington (2011) noted, there is a pattern of substantial deference by the courts to government assertions of reasonable limits.

The heuristic value of this brief sketch of the steps involved in analysing Section 2(b) cases in the Canadian legal context, then, is that it pinpoints the key issue that we need to think about when considering the extent of teachers' right to free expression in a classroom teaching situation. It has been clearly affirmed in the Canadian jurisprudence on teacher free expression—as well, indeed, according to the *Tinker* line of cases on teachers' in-class speech, in the U.S. (Gee, 2009)—that the question is not whether teachers' in-class speech is entitled to constitutional protection. It is. Nor, for public sector teachers at any rate, is the question whether the *Charter* applies when school boards or principals seek to limit teachers' freedom of speech. It does. The most salient issue is how to strike a reasonable balance between teachers' right to freedom of expression as individuals and the competing rights, responsibilities, and legitimate interests of others.

Section Two: Competing Interests at Stake in Cases of Curricular Free Speech

Looking back over Canadian and U.S. jurisprudence on school teachers' curricular free speech, judges can be seen consistently returning to five key interests that are important to take into account when considering whether a restriction on a teacher's right to free expression in a classroom setting is justified. These are: the state's right to set the curriculum and make sure that it is taught in schools; the need to protect pupils from inappropriate speech in school; society's interest in using the education system as a vehicle for inculcating collective values; students' right to enjoy an institutional environment favourable to learning; and, the interest of school authorities and the teaching profession in maintaining public trust in teachers and the public education system. This section discusses the meaning of these concepts and how they have been applied to selected legal cases involving teachers' right to curricular free expression.

The State's Right to Establish the Curriculum

The responsibility for maintaining an educated population is ultimately delegated to officials like superintendents and school principals, who have the task of ensuring that teachers are following the state curriculum (Clark & Trask, 2006; Gee, 2009; Kindred, 2007). As Gee (2009) pointed out, this right has been invoked by more than one U.S. superior court in an attempt to apply the so-called *Hazelwood* standard to several cases involving the issue of teacher free speech. In *Hazelwood School District v. Kuhlmeier* (1988)—a landmark U.S. superior court decision on freedom of speech in schools which, like *Tinker* (1969), primarily concerned students' (rather than teachers') freedom of speech and the right of schools to limit it—the court confirmed the constitutionality of a principal's decision to delete from a student run high school newspaper two short but controversial articles on teen pregnancy and the experience of divorce. The grounds for the decision were that the action was, as it was stated in the judgement, "reasonably related to legitimate pedagogical concerns" (*Hazelwood School District v. Kuhlmeier*, 1988, p. 261). In the original *Hazelwood* ruling, as in subsequent applications to student and teacher free speech cases,[1] this standard was nothing if not a big tent, encompassing such disparate considerations as "the age and sophistication of students, relationship between teaching method and valid educational objectives, and context and manner of presentation"

---

1   These include *Boring v. Buncombe County Board of Education* (1998), *Webster v. New Lenox School District* (1990), *Miles v. Denver Public School* (1991), and *Ward v. Hickey* (1993). For a detailed discussion of the application of *Hazelwood* to these cases, see Gee 2009, p. 421ff.

(*Ward v. Hickey*, 1993, p. 452, quoted in Gee, 2009, p. 444), and the danger that "the views of the individual are not erroneously attributed to the school" (Clarke & Trask, 2006, p. 113). One relatively unambiguous application of the notion of "legitimate pedagogical concern" to disputes over curricular free speech is that teacher expression may be subject to limitations if it sufficiently and demonstrably deviates from education objectives the school exists to promote. According to this reasoning, just as a teacher's ungrammatical, poorly written, or incoherent speech can be legitimately restricted by their employer on pedagogical grounds, so too can teacher speech that is unrelated to or contradicts the curricular content and other publicly mandated educational objectives teachers are hired to pursue (cf. Gee, 2009, p. 449-452).

To illustrate the concept using a landmark U.S. ruling, *Webster v. New Lenox School District* (1990) involved a dispute over the decision to dismiss a teacher for teaching creationism in addition to evolution. Like Morin, Webster recognized the state's right to establish the curriculum, and the duty of their employers to ensure that the curriculum is faithfully taught in schools. In his defence, however, Webster, appealing to his "academic freedom" as a teacher, argued that he had the right to teach other topics—in this case, creationism—as long as the state curriculum was taught in his classes as well. The court would have none of it, citing the need to protect children from teachers' "idiosyncratic perspectives" (*Webster v. New Lenox School District*, 1990).

Protecting Students from "Inappropriate" Speech

A second interest that courts have identified as needing to be balanced with teacher free speech is connected to the school's responsibility to protect students from forms of expression judged to be "inappropriate." Clearly, inappropriate speech can take a wide variety of forms, ranging from hate speech (as in *Keegstra*, 1990) to the use of words considered vulgar (as in *Mailloux v. Kiley*, 1971, discussed below). The broad educational concern underlying this consideration is that pupils constitute a captive audience, in the sense that they cannot simply walk away if they find the teachers' speech offensive, upsetting or simply wrongheaded. Additionally, they are psychologically vulnerable, in the sense that pupils, more than adults presumably, are especially subject to being influenced by others' ideas and behaviour.

Not surprisingly, the issue of protecting pupils from speech that could be considered inappropriate on the part of a teacher was central to the court judgement in *Webster* (1990), presented in the last section, as it was in the ruling of the P.E.I. Court of Appeals ruling in *Morin* (2002). These, and similar cases—for example, the paradigm-shifting *Mayer* (2007) judgement in the U.S. regarding an elementary teacher whose contract was not renewed because she rather innocently insinuated in front of her Grade 6 class that she was opposed to the U.S. invasion of Iraq—show that teacher speech can be considered "inappropriate" when it appears to involve the teacher abusing their position of authority to promote their own personal standpoint on a controversial issue. According to this reasoning, which clearly draws on the above-discussed assumptions about the state's right to set and enforce the curriculum, teachers are essentially civil servants. Schools hire teachers to teach subjects prescribed by the curriculum and to follow pre-established guidelines on how to teach those subjects, and society entrusts them to do so in good faith. Particularly when one considers that pupils' presence in the class is compulsory and their apparent impressionability, it is not too much of a stretch to see how a teacher promoting their own views on sensitive issues in the classroom, especially when those views depart in significant ways from the letter and spirit of the curriculum, [2] could be seen as a breach of that trust and an abuse of authority.

The concept of "inappropriate speech" may be subject to multiple interpretations, but we suggest that any reasonable interpretation should be sensitive to certain obvious facts. In two parallel cases, for example, courts rejected attempts to justify disciplinary actions taken against teachers who used vulgar language. *Keefe v. Geanakos* (1969) and *Mailloux v. Kiley* (1971) both involved teachers who introduced variants of the word "fuck" in their classrooms but did so in ways that was clearly aligned with the curriculum. Mailloux used vulgar language (albeit while employing theatrics that the judges in this case clearly felt went beyond

---

2 *Webster v. New Lenox School District* (1990) provides another case in point here.

generally accepted standards of teacherly decorum) as an example of a taboo word in the course of teaching a unit on social taboos, a theme prescribed by state curriculum. Keefe got into trouble at work for having his grade-twelve students study an article from a reputable literary magazine containing the word "motherfucker." Unlike in *Mailloux* (1971), the judges in *Keefe* (1969) regarded the teacher's actions as pedagogically unassailable, characterizing his approach as "scholarly, thoughtful and thought-provoking." Keefe cautioned his students about the article's content and language, allowed students to opt out of the related assignments if they wished and took care to clarify the meaning and origins of the offensive term, while explaining its connections to the article's politically charged theme. In the end, the court's view in *Keefe* (1969) was as unequivocal as it was in *Webster*. The judge asserted that "we would fear for their future" if high school students need protection from exposure to a swear word that is in current use and which a teacher introduced in class "for demonstrated pedagogical purpose" (*Keefe v. Geanakos*, 1969, p. 361, quoted in Gee, 2009, p. 428).

Values Inculcation and the Public School

A third consideration that recurs in court rulings on teacher free speech cases is the interest of the state in promoting collective values through the education system. According to arguments that appeal to this consideration, a teacher's exercise of free expression must be consistent with this inculcative function of the school. That schools are meant to play some role in transmitting social values is generally recognized and, until relatively recently, it was not uncommon to see teachers' duties in this regard set out in education law. Before 1990, for example, *Ontario's Public School's Act* explicitly named "truth, justice, loyalty, love of country, humanity, benevolence, sobriety, industry, frugality, purity, [and] temperance" as the "virtues" teacher had the duty to "inculcate by precept and example" (Section 100(a)). In 1998, a U.S. superior court ruling made a dramatic appeal to the inculcative function of schools when it upheld the decision of a school district to terminate the contract of a high school English teacher who had students write and perform poetry and plays depicting oral sex and other content considered profane by certain students' parents (i.e., *Lacks v. Ferguson Reorganized School District*, 1998). Citing jurisprudence established in *Bethel School District v. Fraser* (1986)—again, a case centred on students' rather than the teacher's right to expression—the judges in *Lacks* (1998) argued that public education has the mission to "inculcate the habits and manner of civility as values in themselves conducive to happiness and indispensable to the practice of self-government and the community and nation" (*Bethel School District v. Fraser*, 1986, p. 681; quoted in Gee, 2009, p. 446).

In other cases, however, values inculcation can also cut the other way, protecting controversial expression. The state's interest in promoting collective values through the education system was raised in the Supreme Court of Canada ruling in *Chamberlain v. Surrey School District* (2002), the dispute mentioned previously between an elementary school teacher and his employer over the use of story books centred on the lives of same-sex families. The school board, his employer, directed Chamberlain not to use the books, arguing that their subject matter was inappropriate for kindergarten-aged children and contrary to the values and religious beliefs of many in the community served by the school. In this case, the court overturned the school board's decision, referencing the consistency between Chamberlain's pedagogical activities, fundamental rights and freedoms as specified in the *Charter*, and the liberal values set out in the *Charter of Rights and Freedoms*—in particular the right to freedom from discrimination.

Maintaining a School Environment Conducive to Learning

A fourth interest at stake in disputes concerning in-class teacher free speech is the school's responsibility to maintain—and pupils' right to enjoy—an institutional environment favourable to learning. The seminal judgement in this regard is *Tinker* (1969), a case centred on a school's refusal to allow two students to wear black armbands in protest against the Vietnam War. In *Tinker* (1969), the U.S. Supreme Court asserted that, in schools, the right to free speech could be limited if its exercise is shown to cause a "material and substantial" disruption to the normal operations of the school. *Tinker* (1969) contained strongly worded statements to the effect that, under certain conditions, while teacher speech too enjoys constitutional protection, it is subject to essentially the same limitations as student free speech.

However, a particular feature of the interest in maintaining a positive school environment, at least as it has tended to be handled by judges, is that it requires a fairly high standard of proof. To be considered relevant, it would have to be demonstrated that the teacher speech did in fact interfere in some significant way with the school's capacity to maintain an educational environment favourable to learning. Referring to the *Tinker* (1969) decision, Gee (2009) reported that the issue of proof of disruption was indeed crucial "because the school did not show that the armbands materially, and substantially interfered with the operation of the school or the rights of others, the Court held that the school's suspension of the students was unconstitutional" (p. 417). Insufficient evidence of school disruption was also decisive in the decision of the Ontario Labor Relations Board in a matter in which teachers' in-school free speech was at stake. In this case, as discussed in Kindred (2007), a teachers' federation contested a school board policy which forbade teachers from wearing lapel pins bearing union slogans (e.g., "Fair deal or no deal") relating to an ongoing labor dispute (pp. 223-ff). The school board's defence, which turned essentially on claiming that the aim of the policy was merely a managerial decision aimed at maintaining a classroom environment conducive to learning and free of disruption by protest activities, was rejected by the Board because, among other things, the employer could produce no evidence that the buttons caused any classroom or school disruption (Kindred, 2007, p. 224).

Public Confidence

A final interest, linked to freedom from disruption to the regular functioning of the school but requiring a significantly lower standard of evidence, is that of public confidence. Several highly publicized Canadian rulings have suggested that the *Charter* does not afford protection to teacher free expression (be it inside or outside the classroom) in cases where a teacher's conduct could be reasonably expected to entail a loss of public confidence in the teacher's ability to perform their duties, or in the public school system more broadly. One such ruling was the decision of the British Columbia Court of Appeal to uphold the charge of professional misconduct against Chris Kempling, a guidance counsellor who had in several public forums expressed his moral and religious opposition to homosexuality (*Kempling v. British Columbia College of Teachers*, 2005). Although the Court found no evidence of school disruption as a result of Kempling's conduct, it asserted that the disciplinary action taken against Kempling by the British Columbia College of Teachers (i.e., one month's suspension) was reasonable because of the potential negative effect of Kempling's private activities on the social environment of his school. It is foreseeable and very likely, the British Columbia Court of Appeal suggested, that homosexual students would feel uncomfortable or unwelcome attending a school with a teacher who regards them "perverted" and "immoral," as Kempling described homosexuals in a series of letters to the editor in a local newspaper. Another ruling bearing on the issue of public confidence was *Ross v. New Brunswick Board of Education* (1996). In perhaps the best known Canadian case of teacher speech outside the classroom, the Supreme Court of Canada upheld the dismissal of Malcolm Ross, a high-school math teacher who publicly expressed anti-Semitic views in several publications and broadcast interviews. Despite the fact that Ross, unlike Keegstra, did not use the classroom as a forum to promote these views among his students—and hence could not be accused of directly exposing his students to "inappropriate speech" or abusing his position of authority as a teacher—the Supreme Court of Canada ruled that the fact of repeatedly making anti-Semitic comments easily accessible to the public was sufficient to undermine public confidence in the teacher's ability to fulfil his role. Further, even though the Court admitted that there was "no direct evidence establishing an impact upon the school district caused by [Ross's] off-duty conduct," it nevertheless held that a causal link between the conduct itself and the establishment of a "poisoned" (i.e., intolerant or discriminatory) educational context was a "reasonable inference" (*Ross v. New Brunswick School District no. 15*, 1996, p. 830-831).

Section Three: Reasonable and Responsible Exercise of Curricular Free Speech

Although we do not pretend to have provided an exhaustive overview of the Canadian and U.S. jurisprudence relevant to the question of teachers' free expression rights when dealing with sensitive issues in class, the foregoing discussion is sufficiently comprehensive, we believe, to ground a set of criteria (or conditions) that curricular speech should meet to warrant protection under Section 2(b) of the *Charter*.

Curricular Alignment

The first criterion, which links primarily to the state's interest in prescribing the knowledge and skills taught in public schools, is that teacher speech must be clearly aligned with the curriculum. That is, it must be possible to show that the particular material or topic used, and the approach to dealing with that content in class, was intentionally chosen to further a pedagogical purpose explicitly sanctioned by the curriculum. Furthermore, it must be clear that the pedagogical choice made could be reasonably expected to be effective in the pursuit of that purpose. Adhering to this principle does not imply that the teacher cannot introduce new topics or must limit themselves to using material officially approved by local educational authorities, only that the pedagogical intent was reasonably consistent with the teaching and learning objectives teachers are supposed to achieve.

To illustrate, consider the school principal's response to the use of Harry Potter books in a language arts class. In some parts of North America, teachers who use the popular books series may face criticism from parents who see the books as promoting paganism or witchcraft.[3] Imagine a teacher who has students read excerpts from the Harry Potter books to illustrate the fantasy/action literary genre as part of an instructional unit on different categories of children's literature, a prescribed

---

3 Since the publication of the first volume in the series in 1998, the Harry Potter books have been the subject of an effective campaign led by parents and religious groups to have the book banned from schools, so effective that the series occupied top positions in the American Library Association's list of banned books for the decade of 2000-2010 (http://www.d.umn.edu/~csigler/PDF%20files/PotterChallengeList.pdf).

curricular theme. The principle of curricular alignment could, it seems, be appealed to in order to explain to skeptical parents the legitimacy of using the books and to justify the teacher's choice to use them as teaching material. Given the curricular and pedagogical context, the pedagogical purpose behind using the books is clearly a legitimate one: to encourage an understanding of the characteristics of the fantasy literary genre, of which Harry Potter books are recognized as being an outstanding example. Having said that, because the Harry Potter books contain many violent scenes, they could reasonably be considered inappropriate for younger pupils. We return to the criterion of age appropriateness in more detail below.

Even-Handedness

The second criterion that curricular expression must meet in order to be consistent with what the jurisprudence suggests about the reasonable limits on teacher free speech is that the teacher must not be seen as using their position as a teacher to promote their own personal views on contested or sensitive issues. This condition links to the importance of maintaining public trust in teachers and the public school system, and providing protection for students as a recognized captive audience. Respecting this criterion does not require teachers to avoid exposing their personal views in class and it does not mean asking teacher to feign strict pedagogical neutrality, generally regarded in the scholarly literature on teacher neutrality to be an unrealistic expectation in any case (see for example the discussion of this issue in Hess & McAvoy, 2014, pp. 189-93). What it does require is for teachers to take a reasonably even-handed approach to teaching about sensitive topics so as to avoid giving the impression that they are teaching with the intent of imposing their perspective on sensitive topics on their students. There is no simple recipe for avoiding a perception of abuse of authority in this sense, but doing so would seem to entail, among other things, encouraging students to consider several competing viewpoints, treating students who adhere to views one disagrees with respectfully, and generally conducting oneself in a way in class that models honest intellectual inquiry.

Based on our understanding of the case, Deborah Mayer's interactions with her elementary school class about the Iraq War, mentioned briefly above, would be considered a reasonable and responsible exercise of curricular free expression according to the criterion of even-handedness. Seizing on what she almost certainly saw as a teachable moment—i.e., mass public protests currently taking place about a political situation of the utmost national and international consequence—Mayer had her class read and discuss an article directly dealing with the anti-war protest, an article which was published in a recent issue of a children's magazine approved by the school. As happens to almost every teacher at one time or another, a student asked her, in front of the class, to say what she thought. In response, Mayer suggested that she supported the anti-war movement, apparently without providing her pupils with a detailed justification for her position, and then proceeded to draw parallels between the peace movement and the schools' ongoing campaign to promote peaceful conflict resolution on the playground. In the circumstances, it seems hard to characterize Mayer's response to this awkward situation as anything but even-handed. It was also consistent with the values that she, as a member of the school community, had every reason to think it was her job to promote. That is to say, in addition to meeting the criterion of even-handedness—and the criterion of curricular alignment, if we assume that the reading's intent was part of a broader pedagogical plan to pursue the state curriculum in language arts—a case could be made that it also met the criterion of values inculcation, to which we now turn.

Consistency with Charter Values

The third criteria, connected to the state's interest in promoting collective values through the education system, is that teacher expression around sensitive topics must be consistent with *Charter* values. The issue of inculcating collective social values is often fraught with controversy. Public schools are democratic institutions that serve multiple constituencies that do not always share easily compatible values systems. When a conflict arises between value systems, which should take priority? The state's? The dominant values of citizens in the school district? We saw earlier that in the *Chamberlain* (2002) ruling on same-sex relationships in children's books, there was a conflict between what the teacher considered to be *Charter* values and the religious values of pupils' parents. In this case, the ruling suggested that the community of reference should be national, not local, and referenced the *Charter* value of tolerance. Similarly, the question of whose values should be promoted in schools has been central to the protracted legal and political challenges raised against Ontario's harm-reduction oriented sex-education curriculum (see Bialystock, 2016). Here, the values of a relatively progressive provincial government have been pitted against those of local parents' groups opposed to the curriculum primarily on moral grounds. One of the main complaints of these parents is that the government has no right to impose on their children certain attitudes towards sex—as, for example, are conveyed in the curriculum's morally neutral messaging about homosexuality.

The positions of the Supreme Court and the Ontario government in both cases seem consistent with the role that Canadian society has asked teachers to take on in the *post-Charter* era. Given the *Charter's* applicability to public schools as government agencies, public education must be delivered in accordance with the rights and freedoms outlined in the *Charter*, which encompasses not only how teachers, administrators and school boards deal with students and their parents but what is taught in classrooms as well (cf. MacKay, Sutherland, & Pochini, 2013, p. 69-71).

Avoiding Foreseeably Inflammatory Speech

A fourth aspect of the legally informed conception of reasonable and responsible curricular free speech relates to the school's interest in maintaining an environment conducive to learning. What this interest seems to entail is that teachers must avoid making comments, dealing with topics, or using material that could reasonably be anticipated to cause substantive and material disruption to the normal operation of the school. Like the criterion of consistency with *Charter* values, this condition raises a difficult issue. Paradoxically, the issues that are most likely to cause a disruption in a school—namely, issues that are closest to students' lives and the ones they feel most passionately about—are the ones that may offer the richest opportunities for developing skills in critical enquiry and dialogue (Oxfam, 2009, pp.1-5). In *Morin* (2002), the P.E.I. Court of Appeal recognized that dealing with sensitive topics in class was part of the serious business of education for critical thinking in a democracy, and that teachers have a right to do so even if it means that some students and their families may be upset by it. Applying this criterion, then, cannot mean avoiding heated topics, only using one's best professional judgement to avoid situations where a teachable moment turns into an institutional crisis. In addition to requiring a certain kind of pedagogical tactfulness (which most teachers certainly possess), it also necessarily draws on local knowledge, which attunes the teacher to which topics or material cross the line between controversial and inflammatory.

One stunning example of a teacher falling short of this condition was that of a Montreal teacher who showed the notorious Jun Lin murder video to his grade 10 history and civics class (CBC News, 2012). The 11-minute long video, which depicted the stabbing to death and dismembering of the victim, was being widely discussed in the media and was easily available on the internet. Apparently wishing to seize on educational opportunities afforded by the situation, but also aware that the students might find the video upsetting, the teacher held a class vote on whether to watch it. The class unanimously voted in favor, watched it, and spent the rest of the period discussing the video. Predictably, once the word got out to parents and other members of the school community, a public relations firestorm erupted which lasted several days. This was a case of egregiously bad pedagogical judgement because, among other things, the teacher failed to anticipate the negative impact of a choice to introduce sensitive subject matter into the school environment.

Age Appropriateness

Of course, the Jun Lin murder video case also throws into relief a fifth and final criterion of responsibly exercised curricular free expression: pedagogical appropriateness. As mentioned above, the courts widely recognize that the school system has a duty to make sure that young people are not exposed to "inappropriate" content at school. The notion of "appropriate" is a notoriously imprecise term frequently used to lend an air of certitude to what is ultimately mere subjective disapproval. Nevertheless, beyond the large conceptual grey zone, most people seem to agree that, in the context of schooling, inappropriate content falls into one of two categories. The first is content that a pupil could reasonably be expected to find traumatizing given their age (like showing historical footage of corpse disposal at Nazi death camps to children in elementary school) or material that is hateful, that depicts extreme violence or graphic sexuality. The second is content that is radically opposed to the prescribed curriculum (like teaching creationism in parallel with the theory of evolution in a prescribed secular, science-based curriculum). In both these senses, exposure to inappropriate speech has repercussions and links to the issue of public confidence in the sense that it could create a situation where the public school is undermined because parents would reasonably feel uncomfortable about entrusting their children to the school and children could feel uncomfortable about attending.

Conclusion

This paper proposed a set of principles for defining the legal concept of reasonable and responsible pedagogical decision making around dealing with controversial issues in the classroom. Grounded in a reading of the interests at stake in teacher in-class free speech cases as handled in Canadian and U.S. jurisprudence, we consider that the five basic principles put forward in this paper—curricular alignment, even-handedness, consistency with *Charter* values, foreseeable avoidance of inflammatory speech, and age appropriateness—should reliably predict when and why pedagogical speech and professional choices in connection with sensitive or controversial topics would likely be afforded constitutional protection by the judicial system. By allowing teachers and their employers to better understand the scope that the law affords to curricular free expression in Canada, as well as the educational, social, and individual interests that underlie the need to challenge young people to grapple with sensitive material in school, we hope that the ideas developed in this paper will help educators find common ground in this contested area. Teachers could potentially draw on these principles when trying to make pedagogical decisions about where to draw the line between controversial and inappropriate. Principals could refer to them to defend their teachers

---

when faced with student or parental complaints about a teacher's choice of content or methods. School boards could use them as the basis for drafting controversial materials policies that are legally sound, respectful of teacher autonomy, and cognizant of the need to promote critical thinking skills in public education. The legal record is a sad commentary on just how often guess-work, parental pressure, and different parties' dubious personal intuitions about what teachers have the right to do and say in class dictate the outcomes of disputes over curricular free speech. Clearer guidelines on teacher free speech in the classroom, such as the ones this chapter has attempted to establish, have the potential to not only to reduce the chances similar disputes will erupt into a legal battle in the future but, more importantly, to prevent these messy conflicts from arising in the first place.

References

Bethel School District v. Fraser, 478 U.S. 675 (1986).

Bialystok, L. (2016, March). *"My Child, My Choice"? Justifying mandatory sex education in a liberal democracy.* Paper presented at the annual meeting of the Philosophy of Education Society of Great Britain, Oxford.

Boring v. Buncombe County Board. of Education., 136 F.3d 364 (4th Cir. 1998).

CBC News (2012, June 12). Montreal teacher suspended for showing video of Lin killing. *CBC News Montreal.* Retrieved from http://www.cbc.ca/news/canada/mo ntreal/montreal-teacher-suspended-for-showing-video-of-lin-killing-1.1171798.

Chamberlain v. Surrey School District No. 36, [2002] 4 SCR 710, 2002 SCC 86 (CanLII).

Canadian Charter of Rights and Freedoms, Part I of the *Constitution Act, 1982*, being Schedule B to the *Canada Act 1982* (U.K.), 1982, c. 11.

Clarke, P., & Trask, R. (2006). Teachers' freedom of expression: A shifting landscape- Part One-Critical political expression to parents and others. *Education and Law Journal, 22*(3), 303-326.

Criminal Code, R.S.C. 1985, c. C-46.

Crocco, M., & Castigan, A. (2007). The narrowing of curriculum and pedagogy in the age of accountability: urban educators speak out. *Urban Education, 42*(6), 512-535.

Education Act, R.S.O. 1990, c. E.2. (Ontario, Canada).

Evans-Marshall v. Board of Education (2010), 624 F. 3rd 332 (6th Cir. 2010).

Garcetti v. Ceballos 547 U.S. 410 (2006).

Gee, K. (2009). Establishing a Constitutional standard. *Journal of Law and Education, 38*(3), 409-454.

Hazelwood School District School District v. Kuhlmeier, 484 U.S. 260, 262, 264 (1988).

Hess, D.E., & McAvoy, P. (2014). *The political classroom.* New York: Routledge.

Irwin Toy Ltd. v. Quebec (Attorney general), 1 S.C.R. 927 (1989).

Keefe v. Geanakos, 418 F.2d 359 (1st Cir. 1969).

Kempling v. British Columbia College of Teachers, [2004] B.C.J. no. 173 (Q.L.) (S.C.); affirmed [2005]. C.J. no. 1288 (Q.L.) (C.A).

Kindred, K. (2006). The teacher in dissent: Freedom of expression and the classroom. *Education Law Journal, 15*(2), 207-231.

Lacks v. Ferguson Reorganized School District, 147 F3d 718 (8th Cir. 1998).

MacKay, A.W., Sutherland, L.I., & Pochini, K.D. (2013). *Teachers and the law: Diverse roles and new challenges* (3rd ed.). Toronto, ON: Emond Montgomery Publications Limited.

Mailloux v. Kiley, 323 F. Supp. 1387 (D. Mass. 1971).

Mayer v. Monroe County Community School Corp., 474 F.3d 477, 480 (7th Cir. 2007).

Miles v. Denver Public School Board (1991), 944 F. 2nd 773 (10th Cir. 1991).

Morin v. Regional Administration Unit #3 (PEI), 2002, PESCAD 9.

Oxfam (2006). *Teaching controversial issues.* London: Oxfam Education. Retrieved from http://www.oxfam.org.uk/education/teacher-support/tools-and-guides/controversi al-issues.

R. v. Keegstra, 3 S.C.R. 697 (1990).

R. v. Mara, 2 S.C.R. 630 (1997).

R. v. Sharpe, 1 S.C.R. 45 (2001).

Reference re ss. 193 and 195.1(1) of the *Criminal Code* (Man), 1 S.C.R. 1123 (1990).

Ross v. New Brunswick School District No. 15 [1996] 1 S.C.R. 825.

Schimmel, D., Fischer, L., & Stellmann, L.R. (2007). *School law: What every educator should know* (1st ed.). New York: Pearson.

Tinker v. Des Moines Independent Community School District, 393 U.S. 503, 514 (1969).

Waddington, D.I. (2011). A right to speak out: The Morin case and its implications for teachers' free expression. *Interchange, 42*(1), 59-80.

Ward v. Hickey, 996 F.2d 448, 453 (1st Cir., 1993).

Webster v. New Lenox School District, 917 F.2d 1004 (7th Cir., 1990).

CHAPTER 11

Full Recognition of Sexual and Gender Minority Youth in Canadian Schooling: Matters of Access, Adjustment, and Accommodation

André P. Grace

Abstract

The full recognition of sexual and gender minority (SGM)—including lesbian, gay, bisexual, trans-spectrum, intersexual, and queer Indigenous (or, more commonly, Two-Spirit Aboriginal)—youth in Canada is still a work in progress. In schooling, matters of access, adjustment, and accommodation continue to take educational policymaking and its implementation in ethical and caring practices into the messy intersection of the moral and the political. This chapter begins with a reflection on certain realties and consequences for SGM youth navigating education and healthcare. From this perspective, it considers the importance of synchronizing research, policy, and practice to enhance possibilities for the recognition and accommodation of SGM youth across institutions charged with their care. Next, the chapter explores the dire sexual health predicament of our nation's youth, including SGM youth, highlighting the need to have comprehensive sexual health education for all included in core curriculum and instruction. Here it reflects on Canadian guidelines while problematizing the current sexual health curriculum in Alberta's high schools. It concludes with a perspective on *Bill 10, An Act to Amend the Alberta Bill of Rights to Protect our Children,* which has advanced SGM recognition and accommodation in schooling in Alberta while paradoxically leaving schools with a key roadblock to universalizing comprehensive sexual health education for all students.

Introduction

Sexual and gender minorities compose a multivariate population that includes lesbian, gay, bisexual, trans-spectrum, intersexual, and queer Indigenous (or, more commonly, Two-Spirit Aboriginal) individuals. In Canada, as for linguistic and ethnocultural minorities, law and legislation safeguard our basic rights in keeping with protections on grounds of individual differences that the *Canadian Charter of Rights and Freedoms* guarantees (Grace, 2007, 2015; Grace & Wells, 2016; Rayside, 2008). Our diverse population—diverse in terms of the array of sexual and gender differences that characterize us collectively—is marked by variations in sexual orientations and gender identities that fall outside normative understandings of sexuality and gender, as well as outside the either/or categories of the heterosexual/homosexual and male/female binaries (Grace, 2013a, 2015). As a key constituency within this diverse group, sexual and gender minority (SGM) youth, whose complexities increase in intersections with race, ethnocultural location, class, and other relational differences, remain particularly vulnerable (Brill & Pepper, 2008; Chief Public Health Officer [CPHO], 2011; Fassinger & Arseneau, 2007; Grace, 2013a, 2013b, 2015; Grace & Wells, 2016; Saewyc, 2011; Tolman & McClelland, 2011). Their full recognition as students in Canadian high schools is still a work in progress. Matters of access, adjustment, and accommodation in schooling continue to take educational policymaking and its implementation in ethical and caring practices into the intersection of the moral and the political, where historical exclusions fuelled by stereotyping, ignorance, and fear endure. The marginalization and disenfranchisement of SGM students has consequences for their safety, security, comprehensive health, and learning. Indeed, SGM students learn early that their full citizenship is insubstantial in schools as social institutions purportedly run by caring professionals.

I begin this chapter with a reflection on certain realties and consequences for SGM youth navigating historically exclusionary caring institutions, particularly education and healthcare. From this perspective, I reflect on the importance of synchronizing research, policy, and practice to enhance possibilities for recognition and accommodation of SGM youth across institutions charged with their care. Next, I look at the dire sexual health predicament of our nation's youth, including SGM youth, highlighting the need to have comprehensive sexual health education for all included in core curriculum and instruction in Canadian schooling. Then I consider how we might go about this, drawing on Canadian guidelines and problematizing the current Career and Life Management (CALM) curriculum in Alberta's high schools. I conclude with a perspective on *Bill 10, An Act to Amend the Alberta Bill of Rights to Protect our Children,* which has advanced SGM recognition and accommodation in schooling in Alberta while leaving schools with a key roadblock to universalizing comprehensive sexual health education for all students.

Running the Institutional Gauntlet: What Sexual and Gender Minority Students Undergo

Historically in Canada, as elsewhere, SGM youth, and perhaps especially those who are also poor, youth of colour, or vulnerable in other intersections of power relationships, have generally been disposable, leaving them hurt, alienated, wounded, and even dead through suicide completion or life-ending violence perpetrated against them by others (Clements-Nolle, Marx, & Katz, 2006; Grace, 2013a, 2013b, 2015; Grossman & D'Augelli, 2007; Haas et al., 2011; Hatzenbuehler, 2011). Families, schools, healthcare, and other social institutions considered caring owe them more as human beings, persons, and citizens who ought to be able to experience the fullness of their rights to live, be healthy, learn, and associate in keeping with their ways of being, becoming, belonging, and acting in their everyday lives. Such social and cultural prosperity should be a given, rather than the social and cultural deprivation that comes with being marginalized, disenfranchised, and targeted based on individual sexual and gender differences. Acknowledging biopsychosocial and cultural complexities in shaping sexuality and gender, these identities require self-affirmation to be coupled with social recognition and institutional adjustment as bases for individuals to be happy, healthy, and hopeful (Grace, 2014, 2015). The reality, though, is that sexual and gender identities are historically caught up in a limiting politics shaped by hetero-patriarchal sociality and heteronormative culture and power. Consequently, in navigating everyday existence across institutions, SGM individuals often experience adversity and trauma that can deeply affect their comprehensive health (CPHO, 2011, 2012; Grace, 2015). To transcend this sociocultural negativity and transform conditions that delimit SGM lives in frequently disconnected family, educational, healthcare, and other institutional contexts, it is important to create social and cultural cohesion marked by access and accommodation of SGM persons across life spaces, including institutional spaces (Grace, 2013a, 2015).

The historical peripheralization of sexual and gender minorities in Canada helps explain, but does not excuse, a longstanding void in research, policymaking, and practices focused on SGM persons navigating institutional contexts, and on our issues and concerns regarding equity, justice, and social inclusion (Grace, 2015). Today, as a growing body of transdisciplinary research indicates, SGM youth remain caught up in a paradoxical struggle to be cared about in education, healthcare, and other institutions presumed caring (CPHO, 2011, 2012). Indeed, SGM youth often experience schooling and healthcare services, as well as government and legal services, as a fragmented institutional patchwork insufficient to address the stressors and risk-taking associated with living with the adversity and trauma induced by homophobia and transphobia, which are ignorance- and fear-induced responses to sexual and gender differences respectively (Bowleg, Huang, Brooks, Black, & Burkholder, 2003; CPHO, 2011, 2012; Grace, 2015; Grace & Wells, 2016). For SGM youth, key stressors can include (1) neglect by such significant adults as parents, school administrators, teachers, school counsellors, and family doctors and other healthcare professionals; and, (2) abuse and victimization through symbolic violence (such as anti-SGM name calling and graffiti) and physical violence (such as bullying that includes assault and battery) (Public Health Agency of Canada [PHAC], 2014a, 2014b; Shelley, 2008; Trotter, 2009; Wells, 2008). Key risks can include truancy, quitting school, and running away; developing alcohol and drug addictions, emotional problems, and mental illness; and suicide ideation, attempts, and completions (D'Augelli, 2006a, 2006b; Grace, 2013b, 2015; Grossman & D'Augelli, 2006, 2007; Savage & Miller, 2012). This dire state of affairs indicates the urgent need to synchronize research, policy, and practice so stakeholders in Canadian education, healthcare, and other ostensibly caring institutions can collectively help vulnerable youth to build capacity (a solutions approach), moving away from unconstructive strategies focused on stigmatizing or fixing these youth as a source of social disorder (a problems approach) (CPHO, 2011, 2012; Liebenberg & Ungar, 2008, 2009; Marshall & Leadbeater, 2008; Wells, Roberts, & Allan, 2012).

In Canada, three national research reports profoundly demonstrate the need for research focused on sexual and gender minorities, especially vulnerable SGM youth. I served as an external reviewer for two of these reports: the Chief Public Health Officer's 2011 and 2012 annual reports on the state of public health in Canada. The 2011 research report—*Youth and Young Adults: Life in Transition*—draws a disturbing conclusion: while, in general, Canadian young people constitute a healthy and resilient population, SGM individuals are disproportionately represented among those who are not thriving and who are likely to have comprehensive health problems. In terms of exposure to violence, the report indicates that SGM youth are commonly at inordinate risk of experiencing physical and electronic bullying, verbal and sexual harassment, and physical violence at home and in schools and communities. They are also more likely to ideate about, attempt, or complete suicide. In the face of these stressors and risks, SGM youth also experience more comprehensive health problems, which the report states are exacerbated by a lack of adequate and appropriate healthcare and educational policies, healthcare and social services, protective measures, and educational and community programs. Linking healthcare and education, the report accentuates the importance of school-based comprehensive health education and interventions, which need to start early and consider the histories, social and cultural attributes, and sexual and gender differences depicting SGM youth.

The 2012 research report—*Influencing Health: The Importance of Sex and Gender*—is clear regarding the ways that the comprehensive health of SGM youth is in jeopardy: with sex and gender traditionally expected to function within the parameters of heterosexuality and the male/female binary, SGM youth have problems adjusting to heteronormative boundaries and expectations associated with parenting, schooling, and healthcare provision. Not adjusting can affect their success in learning and impact their comprehensive health. Thus the report accentuates the vital need to consider sex and gender in health research, policymaking, and programming. Indeed the report states that sex and gender should be considered in all research areas. In its focus on educational research, the report stresses the need to study how both sex and gender affect the development of youth, their learning experiences and outcomes, and the kinds of policy-and-practice initiatives needed to create SGM-inclusive schools. With regard to gender minority youth, much work needs to be done. As the report highlights, "To date, little research has examined the physical, mental and sexual health needs and concerns of transgendered and transsexual youth" (p. 45).

The third report, which complements these transdisciplinary comprehensive health reports, is *Every Class in Every School: Final Report on the First National Climate Survey on Homophobia, Biphobia, and Transphobia in Canadian Schools,* which Egale Canada—our national organization committed to SGM inclusion—released in 2011 (Taylor & Peter, et al., 2011). The Egale Canada report provides evidence of significant homophobic and transphobic bullying and harassment—verbal, physical, and sexual—substantiating the vital need to address these stressors in schooling. The report also links sexual harassment to dangerous health outcomes, including mental health problems, and notes the call of SGM students for SGM-specific sexual health education. The report also notes the magnified discrimination that youth experience if they are transgender or gender-nonconforming youth. Of importance, the report points to the need for educator in-service and sex-and-gender diversity and sensitivity training. Setting directions for policymaking, the climate survey concludes: (1) generic safe school policies that do not include anti-homophobia guidelines are ineffective in providing safer climates for lesbian, gay, and bisexual youth; (2) having specific anti-homophobia policies reduces incidents of harassment and bullying based on non-heterosexual orientation; and, (3) specific anti-homophobia policies, however, do not appear to reduce harassment and bullying based on gender identity, thus signaling a need for schools to develop anti-transphobia policies to advance gender-minority inclusion.

Making a Case for Comprehensive Sexual Health Education as Core Education in Canadian Schooling

Since fall 2014 I have directed the Comprehensive Health Education Workers Project—the CHEW Project@http://chewproject.ca. This project, which started with funding from the Alberta Community HIV Policy and Funding Consortium, involves provision of health and social education coupled with intervention and outreach work with SGM youth in the greater Edmonton area. In this work, we focus on their individual development, socialization, comprehensive—physical, mental, sexual, and social—health, safety, and wellbeing in street and community contexts as well as in-care, family, school, healthcare, and other institutional contexts. The CHEW Project came about in response to alarming provincial statistics. In 2013, Alberta Health reported that age-gender-specific rates of newly diagnosed HIV cases among 15 to 29 year olds in the province were disturbingly high (2013a, 2013b). In Edmonton, consecutive 2010 to 2012 rates, as well as the 2013-annualized rate of HIV were the highest in the province. As PHAC (2010) asserts, youth need to be a primary focus since individuals aged 15 to 29 years old have accounted for 26.5 percent of all positive HIV test reports since reporting began in 1979. With sexually transmitted infections, including syphilis, gonorrhoea, and HIV, generally increasing among young people in Alberta, there are significant associated costs in social, emotional, health, and economic terms; for example, the "lifetime direct cost of one HIV infection is [at least] $750,000" (Government of Alberta, 2011, p. 2).

Drawing on results from the 2012 Canadian Community Health Survey that reviewed research on the sexual health behaviours of youth aged 15 to 24, Alberta Health Services (AHS) Calgary Zone (2013) highlights these findings pertinent to schooling: (1) 30 percent of teens aged 15-17 have had at least one experience of sexual intercourse; and, (2) 9 percent have had sexual intercourse before they were 15 years old. Referencing the 2010 Health Behaviour in School-aged Children Study, a Canadian study that J.G. Freeman and colleagues published in 2011 on the participation of Canadian Grade 9 and 10 students in sexual intercourse, AHS Calgary Zone notes "that approximately 23% of grade 9 males, 18% of grade 9 females, and 31% of grade 10 males and females have had sexual intercourse. Among the sexually active teens, 2% of girls and 6% of boys reported having their first intercourse prior to the age of 13" (p. 1). Complicating matters, the AHS Calgary Zone report points out the significant use of alcohol and binge drinking in this age group, which impacts a student's ability to engage in safer sex (e.g. forgetting to use protection like condoms) as well as the ability to say no to sexual intercourse. This can be consequential in terms of the prevalence of teen pregnancy or sexually transmitted infections. It speaks to the importance of offering comprehensive sexual health education that adequately covers these topics by emphasizing prevention, intervention, risk factors, and negative outcomes.

With so much corroborating evidence, it is vital to provide quality comprehensive sexual health education in schooling for youth. Such education has been lacking historically across Canada. As research indicates, topics should include delaying sexual activity, engaging in safer sex practices if sexually active, examining risks and consequences of unsafe sexual activity, and learning about the prevention, identification, and treatment of sexually transmitted infections (AHS Calgary Zone, 2013). Rigorous comprehensive sexual health education would help students build the knowledge, skills, capacities, understanding, personal insight, and motivation necessary to be healthy and stay healthy (Grace, 2015).

The dire scenario for Alberta's youth described in the AHS Calgary Zone report is not unique. For example, it has parallels in British Columbia. In 2007, Saewyc and researchers at the McCreary Centre Society reported results of three province-wide studies of the comprehensive health of lesbian, gay, and bisexual (LGB) youth in Grades 7 to

12 in British Columbia. With this research spanning more than a decade, they concluded that LGB youth experience greater health disparities compared to heterosexual youth. They found that LGB youth were more likely to have experienced these negative outcomes:

- To have experienced physical and sexual abuse, harassment in school, and discrimination in the community.
- To have run away from home once or more in the past year.
- To be sexually experienced, and more likely to either have ever been pregnant or have gotten someone pregnant.
- To be current smokers, to have tried alcohol, or to have used other drugs.
- To have reported emotional stress, suicidal thoughts, and suicide attempts.
- LGB youth were less likely to participate in sports and physical activity, and reported higher levels of computer time.
- LGB youth felt less cared about by parents and less connected to their families than heterosexual teens, and for lesbian and bisexual females, less connected to school.
- When bisexual youth reported high family and school connected-ness, their probability of suicide attempts was much lower than for bisexual teens with lower connectedness, even when they had strong risk factors for suicide such as a history of sexual abuse and current symptoms of emotional distress. (Saewyc, Poon, Wang, Homma, Smith, & the McCreary Centre Society, 2007, p. 6)

Compared to their heterosexual peers, Saewyc and her colleagues also found that sexually experienced LGB youth more commonly had their first experience of sexual intercourse before age 14. However, they related that this result could be linked to another finding: LGB youth experience more sexual abuse. The researchers listed early sexual experience, unprotected sexual intercourse, and use of alcohol or drugs before sexual intercourse among key risks that can lead to increased rates of teen pregnancy among LGB youth. They concluded, "Compared to heterosexual peers their same age, bisexual and gay males were more than 3 times more likely to have been involved in a pregnancy, while lesbian and bisexual females were 2 to 3 times as likely to have been pregnant than heterosexual females" (p. 22). Moreover, they noted that risks such as early sexual experience and unprotected sexual intercourse could result in increased rates of HIV among LGB youth.

This terrible predicament for many LGB youth is replicated outside of Canada, with international research reporting two major negative outcomes (1) There are greater rates of teen pregnancy among sexually active LGB youth compared to their heterosexual peers, which is impacted by such factors as stigma and discrimination, lack of supports and resources, and disconnection from family and school (Office of Adolescent Health, n.d.; Schantz, 2015; Seaman, 2015). (2) Many LGB youth have pronounced experiences of enacted stigma (bullying, discrimination, harassment, and violence in schools), substance abuse, forced sex and dating violence, sexually transmitted infections (including HIV), suicidality, and homelessness (Office of Adolescent Health, n.d.; Saewyc, 2011; Schantz, 2015). Saewyc (2011) positions homeless and street-involved LGB youth as comprising a particularly vulnerable group, with significantly higher rates of such sexual risk behaviours as unprotected sexual intercourse, survival sex, and reduced condom use. These worrisome outcomes speak to the profound need to embed comprehensive sexual health education in the core curriculum as well as in social interventions like GSAs (gay-straight or gender-sexuality alliances) where contextual factors like school culture, climate, and connectedness, all of which impact a student's comprehensive health, can be addressed (Grace, 2015; Schantz, 2015).

Creating Comprehensive Sexual Health Education: Addressing Absences, Countering Negative Outcomes

Constitutionally in Canada, schooling for youth is positioned as a provincial or territorial jurisdiction. The onus then is on ministries of education to take responsibility to ensure the development of research-informed, age-appropriate, and non-judgmental comprehensive sexual health education to improve the health and wellness of all youth, including SGM youth. Moreover, such life-enhancing education should be placed within core curriculum and instruction, requiring school districts to have every school deliver comprehensive sexual health education that enables all youth to be visible and vocal participants who engage in self-care and advocate for improvements in the health of their peers.

In its call for healthy schools and healthy communities, the Ontario Physical and Health Education Association (Ophea) (2015) highlights the need for comprehensive sexual health education that meets the needs of a multivariate student population adapting and adjusting to complex and changing surroundings. When sexual health education is holistic and sufficient to be effective, Ophea states it follows the Canadian Guidelines for Sexual Health Education. It provides students with

- a deeper understanding of themselves, their specific health needs and concerns;
- the confidence, motivation and personal insight needed to act on that knowledge;
- the skills necessary to enhance sexual health and to avoid negative sexual health outcomes; [and]
- a safe, secure and inclusive environment that is conducive to promoting optimal sexual health. (Ophea, 2015, p. 2)

As Ophea points out, motivation to adhere to these guidelines and increase sexual health literacy should be driven by the unacceptability of contemporary statistics showing high rates of sexually transmitted infections, including HIV, among Canadian young people. Ophea considers sexual health to be a core component of comprehensive health, and schools are a logical place where caring professionals can provide wide-ranging education focused on students as whole human beings who, as research indicates, are entering puberty these days between the ages of 8 and 14. This challenges ministries of education, school boards, and principals and teachers on the frontlines to accept their ethical responsibility to provide students with the necessary knowledge and skills to enable them to make informed choices about individual and community health and wellness and to understand current and long-term impacts of their choices (Ophea, 2015). These educational interest groups need to work in the intersection of research, policy, and practice, and they need to work with parents/guardians, healthcare professionals, and other significant adults in students' lives. Reflecting changes in contemporary culture and society, as well as the social inclusion mandated by Section 15 of the *Canadian Charter of Rights and Freedoms,* comprehensive sexual health education should include topics reflecting the diversity of sexual orientations, gender identities, and constructions of family.

Most Canadian provinces and territories do introduce the concepts of sexual orientation and gender identity to students in sexual health education; however, the designated grade level for presenting these concepts is inconsistent across Canada. In Alberta, for example, it is unclear when these topics would be introduced to students (Young, 2015). Still, the province specifies the timing for coverage of several key topics in sexual health education. For example, students in Grade 6 engage the topic of sexually transmitted infections and their prevention (Young, 2015). In Grade 8, students learn about two vital topics: birth control and sexual abuse (Young, 2015). In Grades 10 to 12, sexual health education is included in the provincial curriculum in the course *Career and Life Management.* Alberta Education (2016a) states:

> The aim of Career and Life Management (CALM) is to help students to make well-informed, considered decisions and choices in *all aspects of their lives* and to develop behaviours and attitudes that contribute to the well-being and respect of self and others, now and in the future. *CALM is a vital component of comprehensive school health education.* It emphasizes knowledge, attitudes, behaviours, competencies and values, and provides students with opportunities to enhance their capacities in problem solving, critical thinking and reflection. (para. 1 & 2, italics added)

Despite this positioning of CALM as life encompassing, with some emphasis on sexual health education, sexuality is listed as a "sensitive topic," with this directive: "Instruction in human sexuality education requires communication with parents about the learning outcomes, topics and resources. *All human sexuality outcomes have been boldfaced and italicized in this course to assist in identification of these outcomes*" (Alberta Education, 2016b, p. 3, bolded italics in original). The high-school program of studies lists this exemption:

> For students who are not at the age of majority or living independently, parents have the right to exempt their children from school instruction in human sexuality education by submitting a letter to the school indicating their intention to do so. Schools will provide alternative learning experiences for those students who have been exempted from human sexuality instruction at the request of their parents. Students must complete the remainder of the course in order to receive credits. (Alberta Education, 2016b, p. 4)

In essence then, with this exemption provided as a government-sanctioned choice for parents, sexual health education is not universal in schools in Alberta. Indeed, the exemption places limits on inclusion, accommodation, and opportunities for learning for students excluded by their parents. This could put these students' sexual health in peril due to lost opportunities to build knowledge and understanding of key topics like sexually transmitted infections. SGM students experience an additional kind of exclusion: Even if they are permitted to complete sexual health education as a component of CALM, it is heteronormatively framed. This means CALM fails to provide SGM students with appropriate and adequate coverage in ways that specifically address their sexual health needs and concerns.

In the end, though, sexual health education is a small component of CALM, marking a key shortcoming of the current curriculum in schooling in Alberta. It is included as part of personal choices, the first of three general outcomes constituting the CALM pedagogical framework. The other two are resource choices and career and life choices. Within personal choices, sexual health education is guided by just two specific outcomes – there are 14 specific outcomes in personal choices and 36 specific outcomes for the entire course. The first specific outcome is to "examine the relationship between commitment and intimacy in all its levels" (Alberta Education, 2016b, p. 8), which includes these five objectives:

- identify expectations and commitments in various relationships,
- examine a range of behaviours for handling sexual involvement,
- describe how personal values play a role in relationships,
- explain the role of trust and ways to establish trust in a relationship, [and]
- develop strategies for dealing with jealousy. (p. 8)

The second specific outcome is to "examine aspects of healthy sexuality and responsible sexual behaviour" (p. 9), which includes these six objectives:

- explain the ongoing responsibility for being sexually healthy,
- examine a range of behaviours and choices regarding sexual expression,
- describe sexually healthy actions and choices for one's body, including abstinence,
- analyze strategies for choosing responsible and respectful sexual expression,
- describe the ways in which personal values influence choices, [and]
- assess the consequences of being sexually active. (p. 9)

On its website, Edmonton Public Schools (2016) positions sexual health education as "a responsibility that parents, schools and the community share" (para. 1), noting it is a required component of the Alberta Education curriculum that needs to be taught using "easy-to-understand, science-based facts" that are delivered in age-appropriate ways. In its *Parents Guide to Teaching Sexual Health,* the school district makes clear reference to the parents' option to request that their child be exempt from all, or particular, components of sexual health education. This exemplifies the fact that delivery of sexual health education is neither universal nor unconditional in Alberta. As part of its listed resources, Edmonton Public Schools refers both parents and teachers to the *Teaching Sexual Health* website (2016) for information regarding how sexual health education is taught in district schools. While the resource purportedly provides material on all aspects of sexuality, both CALM

Contraception Lesson 1 and Lesson 2, for example, are presented in heteronormative terms, with no mention of sexually active SGM youth in discussing topics like teen pregnancy. Similarly, CALM Pregnancy and Parenting Lesson 1 omits any discussion of SGM teenagers in terms of pregnancy involvement and teen parenting. The five CALM lessons on relationships are also constructed heteronormatively, focusing on the male-female gender binary in discussing healthy and unhealthy relationships, dating, relationship progression, choices, relationship violence, sexual abuse, and power dynamics. These topics cannot be adequately or appropriately addressed if differences in sexual orientation and gender identity, which intersect with age and other relational differences as well as cultural and other contextual differences, are not considered. While the CALM Sexual and Gender Diversity Lesson 1 importantly considers stressors like heterosexism and homophobia, as well as language issues, it does not significantly consider gender identity, transphobia, and genderism. Moreover, the lesson is misplaced in sexual health education since it amounts to an exercise in cultural education about sexual minorities and dealing with diversity. There is no attention paid to sexual health education for sexual and gender minorities. Following this exclusionary pattern, the two CALM lessons on sexually transmitted infections (including HIV) and their transmission, effects, treatments, and prevention are generic, with no material included specific to issues and concerns affecting youth across sexual and gender differences. Similarly, the two CALM lessons on substance abuse and sexual decision-making provide no learning particular to the needs of non-heterosexual youth.

Concluding Perspective: Bill 10 Is Not Enough to Move SGM-Inclusive Schooling Forward in Alberta

Bill 10, An Act to Amend the Alberta Bill of Rights to Protect our Children, went through a prolonged and stormy process of engagement and deliberation from the time it passed first reading in the Legislative Assembly of Alberta on December 1, 2014 until it received Royal Assent on March 19, 2015. The legislation came into force on June 1,

2015 (Government of Alberta, 2014). Certainly, *Bill 10* is progressive in several ways. It amended the *School Act,* inserting an addition mandating school boards to permit the establishment of gay-straight alliances upon a request by one or more students (Government of Alberta, 2015a). It also repealed Section 11.1 of the *Alberta Human Rights Act* (see Government of Alberta, 2015b, p. 7). Section 11.1 had required school boards to notify parents concerning planned and explicit coverage of sexual orientation and, by inference, gender identity in classrooms. Furthermore, *Bill 10* revised the *Alberta Bill of Rights* to include *sexual orientation* and *gender identity or gender expression* in Section 1. However, in what can be construed as a move to placate rightists in the face of this revision, *Bill 10* added Section 1 (g): "the right of parents to make informed decisions respecting the education of their children" (Government of Alberta, 2015c, pp. 1-2). This addition, which leaves the meaning of *informed* open to interpretation, is ultimately regressive. This is because the right of students to engage in comprehensive sexual health education in school is contravened when their parents block them from engaging in such learning. Indeed, this may constitute a breach of Section 1 of the *Canadian Charter of Rights and Freedoms,* which states there can be no hierarchy of rights in our country (Grace, 2015).

While *Bill 10* enhances recognition and accommodation of SGM students in some ways in Alberta's schools, advances are neither unequivocal nor universal; exclusions and limits remain. While sexual orientation and gender identity can be discussed in classrooms, these topics still lack core curricular coverage in full and meaningful ways that are truly educative in terms of comprehensive health, human rights, and other aspects of holistic living and learning. Moreover, sexual health education should be transparent, transformative, and available to all students in meaningful and appropriate ways. In this regard, Section 1 (g) of the *Alberta Bill of Rights* presents a key roadblock to universalizing comprehensive and inclusive sexual health education across the province. Educators concerned with holistic, ethical practices in curriculum and instruction should challenge ways in which this section can be harmful. For example, no parent driven by ignorance, fear, or moralism—which means they are unable to make informed decisions—should be permitted to limit possibilities for their child to learn about comprehensive sexual health as a means to be able to make good decisions with regard to sexual behaviours. Every parent and educator should want these positive outcomes, which are enabled through universal participation in comprehensive sexual health education situated as a key component of core curriculum and instruction.

References

Alberta Health. (2013a). *Notifiable sexually transmitted infections and human* immunodeficiency virus: 2013 annual report. Edmonton, Alberta: Government of Alberta, Surveillance and Assessment Branch.

Alberta Health. (2013b). *HIV in Alberta: A brief epi update.* A PowerPoint prepared by Kimberley Simmonds, Epidemiologist, Alberta Health, Edmonton, Alberta.

Alberta Education. (2016a). Career and life management. Retrieved from https://education.albert a.ca/career-and-life-management/program-of-studies/.

Alberta Education (2016b). Program of studies for high school career and life management. Retrieved from https://education.alberta. ca/career-and-life- management/program-of-studies/everyone/program-of-studies/.

Alberta Health Services Calgary Zone. (2013). *Sexual and reproductive health– teens and trends: Get the facts on teen sexuality.* Calgary, AB: Author.

Bowleg, L., Huang, J., Brooks, K., Black, A., & Burkholder, G. (2003). Triple jeopardy and beyond: Multiple minority stress and resilience among Black lesbians. *Journal of Lesbian Studies, 7*(4), 87-108.

Brill, S., & Pepper, R. (2008). *The transgender child: A handbook for families and professionals.* San Francisco: Cleis Press.

Canadian Charter of Rights and Freedoms, Part I of the *Constitution Act, 1982*, being Schedule B to the *Canada Act 1982* (U.K.), 1982, c. 11.

Chief Public Health Officer (CPHO). (2011). *The Chief Public Health Officer's report on the state of public health in Canada 2011: Youth and young adults–life in transition.* Ottawa: Office of the CPHO. Available at http://www.phac-aspc.gc.ca/ cphorsphcrespcacsp/2012/index-eng. php.

Chief Public Health Officer (CPHO). (2012). *The Chief Public Health Officer's report on the state of public health in Canada 2012: Influencing health–the importance of sex and gender.* Ottawa: Office of the CPHO. Available at http://www.phac-aspc. gc.ca/cphorsphcrespcacsp/2012/index-eng.php.

Clements-Nolle, K., Marx, R., & Katz, M. (2006). Attempted suicide among transgender persons: The influence of gender-based discrimination and victimization. *Journal of Homosexuality, 51*(3), 53-69.

D'Augelli, A.R. (2006a). Developmental and contextual factors and mental health among lesbian, gay, and bisexual youths. In A.M. Omoto & H.S. Kurtzman (Eds.), *Sexual orientation and mental health: Examining identity and development in lesbian, gay, and bisexual people* (pp. 37-53). Washington, DC: American Psychological Association.

D'Augelli, A.R. (2006b). Stress and adaptation among families of lesbian, gay, and bisexual youth: Research challenges. In J.J. Bigner (Ed.), *An introduction to GLBT family studies* (pp. 135-157). New York: Haworth Press.

Edmonton Public Schools (EPS). (2016). Parents' guide to teaching sexual health. Retrieved from https://www.epsb.ca/ourdistrict/topics/sexualhealtheducation/.

Fassinger, R.E., & Arseneau, J.R. (2007). "I'd rather get wet than be under that umbrella:" Differentiating the experiences and identities of lesbian, gay, bisexual, and transgender people. In K.J. Bieschke, R.M. Perez, & K.A. DeBord (Eds.), *Handbook of counseling and psychotherapy with lesbian, gay, bisexual, and transgender clients* (2nd ed., pp. 19-49). Washington, DC: American Psychological Association.

Government of Alberta. (2011). *Alberta sexually transmitted infections and blood borne pathogens strategy and action plan 2011-2016.* Retrieved from http:www.health.alberta.ca/documents/STI-BBP-Plan-2011.pdf.

Government of Alberta. (2014). *Bill 10: An Act to Amend the Alberta Bill of Rights to Protect our Children.* Third Session, 28th Legislature. Edmonton, AB: The Legislative Assembly of Alberta.

Government of Alberta. (2015a, June1). *School Act: Revised Statutes of Alberta 2000, CHAPTER S-3.* Edmonton, AB: Alberta Queen's Printer.

Government of Alberta. (2015b, December 11). *Alberta Human Rights Act: Revised Statutes of Alberta 2000, Chapter A-25.5.* Edmonton, AB: Alberta Queen's Printer.

Government of Alberta. (2015c, March 19). *Alberta Bill of Rights: Revised Statutes of Alberta 2000, Chapter A-14.* Edmonton, AB: Alberta Queen's Printer.

Grace, A.P. (2007). In your care: School administrators and their ethical and professional responsibility toward students across sexual-minority differences. In W.T. Smale & K. Young (Eds.), *Approaches to educational leadership and practice* (pp. 16-40). Calgary, AB: Detselig Enterprises/Temeron Books.

Grace, A.P. (2013a). Researching sexual minority and gender variant youth and their growth into resilience. In W. Midgley, P.A. Danaher, & M. Baguley (Eds.), *The role of participants in education research: Ethics, epistemologies, and methods* (pp. 15-28). New York: Routledge.

Grace, A.P. (2013b). *Lifelong learning as critical action: International perspectives on people, politics, policy, and practice.* Toronto: Canadian Scholars' Press.

Grace, A.P. (2014). 3-H clubs for sexual and gender minority youth: Working at iSMSS to make it better now. In D. Gosse (Ed.), *Out proud: Stories of pride, courage, and social justice* (pp. 313-315). St. John's, NL: Breakwater Books & Egale Canada Human Rights Trust.

Grace, A.P., (2015). *Growing into resilience: Sexual and gender minority youth in Canada.* Part II with K. Wells. Toronto, ON: University of Toronto Press.

Grace, A.P., & Wells, K. (2016). *Sexual and gender minorities in Canadian education and society (1969-2013): A national handbook for K-12 educators.* Ottawa, ON: Canadian Teachers' Federation. (Published in English & French.) Grossman, A.H., & D'Augelli, A.R. (2006). Transgender youth: Invisible and vulnerable. *Journal of Homosexuality, 51*(1), 111-128.

Grossman, A.H., & D'Augelli, A.R. (2007). Transgender youth and life-threatening behaviors. *Suicide and Life-Threatening Behavior, 37*(5), 527-537.

Haas, A.P., Eliason, M., Mays, V.M., Mathy, R.M., Cochran, S.D., D'Augelli, A.R., Silverman, M.M., & Associates. (2011). Suicide and suicide risk in lesbian, gay, bisexual, and transgender populations: Review and recommendations. *Journal of Homosexuality, 58*(1), 10-51.

Hatzenbuehler, M.L. (2011). The social environment and suicide attempts in lesbian, gay, and bisexual youth. *Pediatrics 127*(5), 896-903.

Liebenberg, L., & Ungar, M. (2008). Introduction: Understanding youth resilience in action: The way forward. In L. Liebenberg & M. Ungar (Eds.), *Resilience in action* (pp. 3-16). Toronto, ON: University of Toronto Press.

Liebenberg, L., & Ungar, M. (2009). Introduction: The challenges in researching resilience. In L. Liebenberg & M. Ungar (Eds.), *Researching resilience* (pp. 3-25). Toronto, ON: University of Toronto Press.

Marshall, E.A., & Leadbeater, B.L. (2008). Policy responses to youth in adversity: An integrated, strengths-based approach. In L. Liebenberg & M. Ungar (Eds.), *Resilience in action* (pp. 380-399). Toronto, ON: University of Toronto Press.

Office of Adolescent Health. (n.d.). LGB youth: Challenges, risks, and protective factors. Retrieved from http://www.hhs.gov/ash/oah/oah-initiatives/teen_pregnancy/traini ng/tipsheets/lgb-youth-508.pdf.

Ophea (Ontario Physical and Health Education Association). (2015). *Sexual health education in schools across Canada.* Retrieved from https://www.ophea.net/sites/ default/files/pdfs/advocacy/ADV_SexEdReportFINAL_31MY13.pdf.

Public Health Agency of Canada. (2010, July). *HIV/AIDS epi update: HIV/AIDS among youth in Canada.* Ottawa: Author.

Public Health Agency of Canada (PHAC). (2014a). *Questions & answers: Gender identity in schools.* Ottawa, ON: Author. Available at http://www.phac-aspc.gc.ca/ std-mts/rp/gi-is/index-eng.php.

Public Health Agency of Canada (PHAC). (2014b). *Questions & answers: Sexual orientation in schools.* Ottawa, ON: Author. Available at http://www.phac-aspc.gc.ca/std-mts/rp/so-os/index-eng.php.

Rayside, D. (2008). *Queer inclusions, continental divisions: Public recognition of sexual diversity in Canada and the United States.* Toronto, ON: University of Toronto Press.

Saewyc, E.M. (2011). Research on adolescent sexual orientation: Development, health disparities, stigma, and resilience. *Journal of Research on Adolescence, 21*(1), 256-272.

Saewyc, E., Poon, C., Wang, N., Homma, Y., Smith, A., & the McCreary Centre Society. (2007). *Not yet equal: The health of lesbian, gay, & bisexual youth in BC.* Vancouver, BC: The McCreary Centre Society.

Savage, D., & Miller, T. (Eds.). (2012). *It gets better: Coming out, overcoming bullying, and creating a life worth living.* New York: A Plume Book, Penguin Group.

Schantz, K. (2015, April). Pregnancy risk among bisexual, lesbian, and gay youth: What does research tell us? *Act for Youth Center of Excellence.* Retrieved from http://www.actforyouth.net/resources/rf/rf_lgb-prg_0415.pdf.

Seaman, A.M. (2015, May 14). Pregnancies more common among lesbian, gay, bisexual youths. *Reuters Health.* Retrieved from http://www. reuters. com/article/us-pregn ancy-teen-lgbt-idUSKBN0NZ2AT20150514.

Shelley, C.A. (2008). *Transpeople: Repudiation, trauma, healing.* Toronto, ON: University of Toronto Press.

Taylor, C., & Peter, T., with McMinn, T.L., Schachter, K., Beldom, S., Ferry, A., Gross, Z., & Paquin, S. (2011). *Every class in every school: The first national climate survey on homophobia, biphobia, and transphobia in Canadian schools. Final report.* Toronto, ON: Egale Canada Human Rights Trust.

Teachingsexualhealth.ca. (2016). CALM (10-12). *Teacher portal.* Retrieved from http://teachers.teachingsexualhealth.ca/lesson-plans/calm/.

Tolman, D.L., & McClelland, S.I. (2011). Normative sexuality development in adolescence: A decade review, 2000-2009. *Journal of Research on Adolescence, 21*(1), 242-255.

Trotter, J. (2009). Ambiguities around sexuality: An approach to understanding harassment and bullying of young people in British schools. *Journal of LGBT Youth, 6*(1), 7-23.

Wells, K. (2008, Winter). *Homophobic bullying* [Fact Sheet]. Government of Alberta. Edmonton, AB.

Wells, K., Roberts, G., & Allan, C. (2012). *Supporting transsexual and transgender students in K-12 schools: A guide for educators.* Ottawa: ON: Canadian Teachers' Federation.

Young, L. (2015, February 24). Sexual education compared across Canada. *Global News.* Retrieved from http://globalnews.ca/news/1847912/sexual-education-compared- across-canada/.

CHAPTER 12

The "Shirtless Jogger" and other Important Educators: 'Thinking Otherwise' to Promote Human Rights and Social Justice

Yvette Daniel and Danielle McLaughlin

Abstract

This chapter underscores the links between critical thinking and critical pedagogy in teaching for democracy and social justice. It reports on an exploration of the challenges teacher candidates face when they try to implement strategies for critical thinking into lesson plans in their practice teaching. This chapter is the result of a collaborative initiative between the Faculty of Education, University of Windsor and the Canadian Civil Liberties Education Trust (CCLET). We introduced an assignment for our teacher candidates to implement in their practicum classrooms. One component required them to reflect upon the realities of practice. Five themes emerged from the analysis of these documents: (1) making connections and relating the activities to student's experiences; (2) showing alternative viewpoints/perspectives; (3) lack of experience and understanding of critical thinking for social justice; (4) resistance from associate/mentor teachers; and (5) teacher candidates' underestimation of students' abilities based on their concepts of age and grade level.

On Canada Day 2014, Toronto's late infamous mayor, Rob Ford, returned from a rehab facility to march in a Canada Day parade. It was a hot and humid day, and many people were dressed, or undressed, for the weather. A man jogging past the parade stopped to address the Mayor. Angry at the Mayor's refusal to answer reporters' questions, the man started to ask his own. "Why don't you answer the people's questions?" He added that as a tax-payer, he had the right to ask the Mayor questions about what he had been doing in his job. The man continued to ask questions, and the Mayor continued to ignore him. The man is a teacher. The Mayor and his brother responded that as a teacher, this man should not be allowed to express his anger or his views in public – or in the classroom. Should teachers be civically engaged? Should teachers teach for, model, and nurture critical thinking for civic engagement and human rights? If not, what are teachers for?

This chapter arises from our combined passion and many hours of discussion and debates over coffee. We explore our topic by analyzing students' assignments and critically self-reflecting about the opportunities and challenges in educating teacher candidates. We share a deep interest in nurturing and enhancing educators' critical thinking skills, especially while educators are taking their first steps into the teaching profession. As two educators from very different backgrounds, working for two different organizations, we have come together for a common purpose. Although we frequently have opposing opinions on many issues, we have been able to hold crucial conversations in which we have a free flow of ideas, understand the complexities of social issues, and refrain from either-or thinking. In this project, we work toward a common goal of educating future educators to become critical thinkers and to reflect on their own beliefs and practices. We see educators as being instrumental in the survival of democracy; people who should be able to engage in critical thinking at a deep level in order to teach *for* social justice, rather than only teaching *about* social justice. These are the people who will teach the next generation to be the kind of advocates for human rights and social justice that democracies will always require. If the price of freedom is eternal vigilance, only those who teach the young can ensure that vigilance continues.

We derive our inspiration from the precepts of Jewish pedagogy in which the question is more important than the answer and every answer should generate more questions (Block, 2007). Shapiro (2011), in a self-interview, made these comments about Jewish pedagogy:

> We prefer questions to answers, and as soon as we have answers we think it is best to question them. We see paradox as the key to understanding rather than an impediment to it. We reinvent our texts by deliberately misreading them. Having lived millennia before Gutenberg, we are not bound to the linear thinking of the printed word. We were postmodern before we were even pre-modern. We don't believe in fixed meanings. Meaning comes from the interaction of story and reader/ listener/ interpreter—the three are really one. (p. 1)

Shapiro (2011) has summarized the role that 'exegesis' plays in Judaic philosophy, in which questioning is the key. This tradition of questioning is well-known. It has been said that while most mothers greet their children after school by asking, "What did you learn in school today?" a Jewish mother will often ask: "Did you ask any good questions today?" However, in schools, in an era of standardization in which getting the 'right' answers and adhering to criteria encapsulated into rubrics rule supreme, critical thinking based on thoughtfulness and inquiry has taken a back seat (Apple, 2008).

Both of us believe that the requirement to use standard methods, curricula and rubrics has negatively influenced educators' ability to foster creativity, imagination and the willingness to think 'otherwise.' As educators are focusing on skills acquisition and test scores, we fear that they are ignoring the importance of such assertions as Maxine Green's (2009), based on a line by the poet Emily Dickinson: "the possible's slow fuse is lit by the imagination" (p. 397). Teachers need to develop in themselves and their students a sense of wonder, curiosity, mystery and questioning.

Unfortunately, these skills and aptitudes cannot be prescribed and put into a rubric format.

We also fear that critical thinking will increasingly become a skill that is available only to elite parts of society. When public school systems have to cut back to bare bones, the children of wealthy parents become the main beneficiaries of enriched education. There is little doubt that arts, music, and drama programming add to the opportunities for young people to develop their critical thinking and creativity. Nilson, Fetherston, McMurray, and Fetherston (2013) argued that the arts enable students to engage in critical thinking by enabling them to make judgments about, and to question, their world. Thus, the arts "emancipate" students by allowing their independence and vision to be integrated and established. Conservative educators who have not bothered to keep up to date with the scholarship in their field see the arts as "frills." Eisner (1999) identified the marginal position that the arts now have in schools, a position related to the belief that the arts cannot be evaluated or assessed. The absence of education in the arts undermines students' ability to achieve their full potential as human beings. When, either economically or educationally, poorer students are deprived of "privileges" like engaged, inspired, and relevant teaching, we cannot be surprised when such students meet only the lowest of expectations. Teacher educators must address this growing concern in as many ways as they can find to do so.

Working together, the two authors of this chapter studied this phenomenon and looked for ways in which to address the "theory-to-practice gap" perceived by so many of our teacher candidates. This perception is further reinforced by their experience during their placements, where they often are told that university courses focus on theories, but that real learning occurs in the field. Our counter-argument is that the theory-practice gap is a fallacy because theory drives practice, and practice informs/shapes theory. Our quest is to find ways to move educators (pre-service teacher candidates in particular) into a "discomfort" or "dissonance" zone where they can find ways to identify and to integrate the two. Gordon (2006) argued that a state of discomfort is far better than a state of complacency and hubris because discomfort often "leads to a deeper and more complex understanding of the concept or issue that is being investigated" (p. 16). We hope that teacher-candidates will choose to educate their own students about human rights and social justice and that the teacher candidates will come to understand that discomfort and dissonance fostered through a critical examination of social issues will enable them to engage in critical/question-based pedagogical practices that can make a difference.

The Ministry of Education in Ontario is very specific in stating that teaching for human rights and social justice has been mandated in all facets of schooling and professional development. The Ministry's 2009 *Equity and inclusive education in Ontario schools: Guidelines for policy development and implementation,* and subject-specific curriculum documents, emphasize the importance of multiple perspectives.

Schools are expected to give students and staff authentic and relevant opportunities to learn about diverse histories, cultures, and perspectives. Lessons, projects, and related resources should allow students to see themselves reflected in the curriculum (e.g., by providing information about women's contributions to science and technology, about Black inventors, about Indigenous beliefs and practices related to the environment and by using texts written by LGBTQ authors). Students need to feel engaged in and empowered by what they are learning, supported by the teachers and staff with whom they are learning, and welcomed in the environment in which they are learning. In order for anyone to understand multiple perspectives and the value they bring to our diverse society, we must all be given explicit permission to ask questions and to disagree with one another. Our friend, the shirtless jogger, was demonstrating a level of engagement when he chose to ask the Mayor very pointed questions and to demand accountability. Such questioning is not only a citizen's right; it is his or her responsibility.

In this chapter, we argue that understanding the precepts of critical thinking and its explicit links to democracy, where human rights and social justice take precedence, is integral to a teacher education program. Teachers must be moved into a discomfort zone, where they can 'make the familiar strange.' Teachers, among others, often fail to recognize that they are making assumptions or taking a default or cultural point of view. In order to keep pace with our constantly evolving society, educators must learn that, on most issues, their own perspective is only one among many on most issues.

The terms "critical thinking," "critical pedagogy" and other such related terms have many definitions. For this reason, we cannot provide only a single one (Phan, 2010). Given the scope of this paper, we cannot discuss these definitions–some concurring while some are contradicting. Therefore, we draw upon the pedagogy of questioning and entertaining different viewpoints as important aspects of critical thinking. Further, we include Stephanovich's (2009) and Osana and Seymour's (2004) assertions that critical thinking involves questioning/challenging assumptions, understanding the viewpoints of others, and including ethics and morals in argumentation and reasoning.

In the first section, we discuss the links between critical thinking and pedagogy for teaching for democracy and human rights. Next, we detail our efforts to instill the habits of mind for critical thinking and risk-taking with teacher candidates (TCs) in an Educational Law and Ethics course, where we foster and support critical thinking. We describe and analyze a class assignment in which teacher candidates carry out a critical-thought exercise in their classrooms during their field-placement. Based on a critical reflection on our activities, we carve a path for ourselves in order to move forward to refine our pedagogies to teach for social justice through critical thinking and questioning.

Critical Thinking, Democracy and the Charter

In this section we discuss the links between critical thinking and fostering citizenship for a democratic society, and then describe how we use the *Canadian Charter of Rights and Freedoms* (through collaboration with the Civil Liberties Education Trust) as one of our tools to engage teacher candidates in the practices of critical thinking.

Critical Thinking as a Tool for Teaching for Social Justice

We turn to educational philosopher Maxine Greene (2009), who reminded us that education has much to do with power; something students do not often experience. Therefore, teachers should create "spaces for dialogue" (p. 397) by bringing controversial and difficult issues to the forefront so that our students learn to confront social justice concerns by engaging in a pedagogy of questioning. Ten Dam and Volman (2004) argued that in schools and classrooms, students must be provided with ample opportunities to engage in questioning. Critical thinking, as a reflective and thoughtful process, moves the learner to a higher level of thinking. Phan (2010) stated that "critical thinking enables us to use analytical and evaluative processes to interpret and enhance meaningful understanding of classroom materials" (p. 286). As Phan's research (2010; 2009; 2008a; 2008b; 2007) demonstrated, critical thinking has a positive impact on student achievement levels. Ward and Beach (2007) emphasized the social context when engaging in critical thinking practices:

> The association between democracy and critical thinking is most evident in discussions of critical inquiry approaches in classrooms, where social justice and equity issues are explicit aims. Teachers who use critical pedagogy take account of critical perspectives and plan instruction that encourages students to go beyond thoughtful reading to identify social injustice and, in some cases, to act on their findings. (p. 10)

The above passage echoes Edelsky (1994), whose three-part process for educating for democracy is recognized and referenced widely. She argued that the ability to engage in critical thinking and to critique is only one aspect of this educational process, which must also be linked to hope and to action:

> The other two parts are: (1) hope – something that comes from learning about prior struggles against systems of domination, struggles that did have some effect; and (2) action – linking students and ourselves to others who are doing something, no matter how small, to end systems of domination. (p. 254)

When we consider a pedagogy imbued with hope and action, we have to pay tribute to the most renowned critical pedagogue of our time, Paulo Friere (2000). In his writings, he underscored the importance of educators becoming transformative intellectuals through partnership with students. Freire tells us that by working together using critical thinking and questioning, we harness the potential for creativity and forward-thinking in our students. He inspires educators when he states that "The teacher is no longer merely the-one-who-teaches, but one who is himself taught in dialogue with the students, who in turn while being taught also teach. They become jointly responsible for a process in which all grow" (p. 80). Learning with and from each other is a life-long reciprocal process that defies the traditional boundaries of the teacher-student divide.

Canadian Civil Liberties Education Trust: An Overview

Since the early 1990s, the Canadian Civil Liberties Education Trust (CCLET) has delivered a teacher-education program called Teaching Civil Liberties. Workshops, seminars and public speeches are given in faculties of education across Ontario and in several other provinces. Tens of thousands of teacher-candidates have had the opportunity to engage with CCLET staff members and with one another in exercises designed to model hands-on critical-thinking lessons for people of all ages.

Using an approach based on an early Supreme Court of Canada decision that created guidelines for interpreting Section 1 of the *Canadian Charter of Rights and Freedoms (R. v. Oakes, 1986),* participants are instructed to avoid consensus. Since everyone living in a democracy, particularly teachers, will encounter decisions that must be made, we must understand the nature of such decisions. Critical and real-life decisions are rarely between a good and desirable thing versus a bad and undesirable thing. The choices are far more likely to be among a multitude of positive values or, even more likely, to be among a group of negative choices, and no matter what we want, we will end up with a less-than-perfect outcome.

In workshop settings, teacher candidates are presented with case studies about school-related issues dealing with rights and freedoms. The teacher candidates are then informed that there are no right answers to the problems and are instructed to avoid consensus in their small-group discussions. When the large group reconvenes, the participants report and elaborate on the variety of questions, points of view, and decisions on the issues that they were able to produce in their smaller groups.

Like judges and politicians, teachers will not be able to avoid making a decision, even when they would prefer not to. For this reason, they must learn how to make such decisions for themselves; and learn how to help their students think critically about the choices to be made. In order for any of us to have freedom of thought and belief, permission to disagree must be specifically granted. By listening to and working toward understanding points of view that differ from our own, we expand our capacity to live in and appreciate our vibrant, diverse and relatively peaceful society.

Teacher Education: The Critical-Thought Assignment

The importance of teaching critical thinking as a tool to prepare active citizens was underscored throughout the Educational Law and Ethics course in the pre-service teacher education program. During instructional time, we made explicit connections to critical thinking by using a social constructivist approach where the class is understood as a learning community. Further, we emphasized that children are reading the world as they read the word (Vasquez, 2014). Therefore, the process of questioning answers is paramount.

We provided scenarios, case studies, and activities for teacher candidates to use for honing their skills. Below, we present the last class assignment for this course. We asked the teacher candidates to plan and integrate critical thinking activities into their lesson plans during their practice teaching field placements. We instructed the teacher candidates to implement their plans, reflect upon them and write a short reflective, critical and contemplative paper describing their doubts, fears, successes, and also obstacles to completing the assignment, if any.

Five clear themes emerged from our analysis of this exercise and its relationship to the teacher candidates, to the students, as well as to their supervisors and the school community: making connections to students' experiences; showing alternative points of view; the lack of experience and understanding about social justice and critical thinking; resistance by associate teachers; and teacher candidates' underestimation of students' abilities. In order to better demonstrate our concerns with the process of teaching critical thinking in a faculty of education, we describe and explore the emergent themes below.

Making Connections to Students' Experiences

Vasquez (2010) discussed the importance of having a critical literacy (or any other subject/topic) curriculum that connects to the reality of students: "Issues and topics of interest that capture students' interests as they participate in the world around them can and should be used as text to build a curriculum that has significance in their lives" (p. 614). In following this line of thinking, we found that in their assignments many teacher candidates discussed the importance of making connections to students' life experiences. Their discussions included text-to-self connections and other ways of applying theoretical concepts to their students' everyday lives and experiences. The teacher candidates noted the importance of allowing students to establish a meaningful connection to what was being discussed. Similarly, Darling-Hammond (2005) noted:

> Teachers need to be able to inquire sensitively and productively into children's experiences and their understanding of subject matter so that they can interpret curriculum through their students' eyes and shape lessons to connect with what students know and how they learn well. (p. 8)

The most successful teacher candidates explored this relationship in some detail. They also left space and time for their own students to discover meaningful relationships between social justice issues and their lives. Here we provide some sample quotations from their reports to illustrate the themes that emerged from their assignments. In order to protect confidentiality, we have used the initials of the teacher candidates in this discussion.

ME wrote about text-to-self connections:

> These conversations led to talk about the freedom to be
> who you are without being treated unfairly. Students made
> a strong text-to-self connection with this idea in relation to
> bullying and teasing. Many students shared with me their
> story of bullying based on: not wearing nice shoes, being
> overweight, wearing a hijab (religion), or due to their race.

ME understood that students learn best when they can relate a lesson's ideas and concepts to their own experiences. By listening to one another, the students could have developed a further understanding that "bullying" is not a simple or easily described event. However, ME's reflection suggested that she had the students relate their experiences directly to her rather than to one another. Therefore, in our analysis of her paper and several similar ones, we found that ME and some of the other teacher candidates still needed to work on critical thinking as an interpretive, constructive and socially located community process. While exposing one's unpleasant experiences may have risks, a skillful teacher can mediate this sort of discussion to help all of the students to reflect on, and question, the nature of their own encounters with bullying. Such discussions, if handled well, can empower students who have been the victims of bullying behaviours, and can also help the bullies discover other ways to deal with their own negative feelings.

KG used as a "teachable moment" an experience from the playground where a fight broke out because of students using a racial slur. He made this event the basis for a lesson on "thinking differently" about controversial issues. He stated:

> I sent my students to their desk to complete the journal
> portion of their lesson and could not believe the words that
> I saw inside them. They were filled with apologies, reasons
> they had done such acts and promises to never do it again.

KG was enthusiastic about having his students reflect on their negative behaviour, but he did not use critical thinking techniques to help them understand their actions or their effects, both negative and positive, on those involved. KG did not perceive his sending the students to their desks to write in their journals as a punishment, but the students most likely did so. The apologies and promises did not demonstrate understanding, but a desire to please the teacher. As with ME, KG also appeared to be reluctant to move away from the teacher-centred approach and to allow students the freedom to think differently. Rather than a teachable moment, the event became a preachable moment! Even when he believed that he was creating a critical thought lesson, KG denied the students any opportunity to develop their own views about the event. His students' responses were predetermined by how he chose to direct their activity. While the students certainly needed to stop and apologize to the ones they had hurt, very little learning and critical thinking took place. The analysis of the assignments revealed that KG and several other teacher candidates were having trouble "letting go" and allowing their students to think critically. If we had the opportunity to conduct a follow-up activity, we would have ME and KG deconstruct their actions and conduct a follow-up to reflect on and then refine their strategies to promote critical thinking for social justice. We understand that these teacher candidates did their best given the short time that they had with us. However, in order to develop the "habits of mind" required for critical thinking, they need to unlearn many of the habits acquired through years of teacher-centred learning.

In moving forward, we need to underscore Giroux (2009), who argued that "The content of the curriculum should affirm and critically enrich the meaning, language, and knowledge forms that students actually use to negotiate and inform their lives" (p. 17). Teachers need to provide students with a safe space and the freedom to reflect critically on their experiences.

Showing Alternative Points of View

Some teacher candidates mentioned how, through debates, discussions, and thoughtful arguments, students were able to see points of view that differed from those they might have previously taken. Thus, some students realized that issues can be understood in many different ways. The following excerpt from JD's assignment illustrates our point:

Having my students explore the laws and ethics with regards to slavery was a fitting vessel for them to begin to consider the grey areas of the law within a context that was meaningful and important to them. The law is not always morally right for each of us as individuals and now my grade 6's are even more aware of that.

JD took a bold step, and one that is important in teaching about slavery. Interrogating the laws and the actual benefits experienced by countries that practiced slavery is difficult. However, JD allowed her students to express their own views on morality and law, potentially enabling the students to understand their need to question current laws and understand the plight of people who have suffered injustice, even where that injustice is not unlawful. We found JD's assignment to be more thoughtful than some of the others. She further reported on her Grade 6 lesson on slavery:

> Not only did this exercise give these students the opportunity to express deep hurts they have experience and continue to endure, it also gave other students the opportunity to hear how hurtful their own words can be. This lesson was a chance for each student to feel valued and safe.

JD appreciated that safety can be enhanced when people are allowed to express their feelings and their different perspectives. By creating an informal lesson on injustice, JD created a safe atmosphere where her students could learn about the experiences and views of people whose lives differed from their own. Engendering respect and compassion for one another, especially in a mediated setting, is an excellent way to help students to understand and appreciate civic engagement. While this learning may not follow the students to the playground, if repeated in other circumstances, it is likely to have at least a temporarily positive effect.

We return to KG's assignment (about the racial slur incident explained in the previous section). He wrote:

> What shocked me even more however was how my students began to not only open up about the times they were

ridiculed or harassed for their religion, culture, and race but the times that they were the people who were ridiculing others. I even had students get physically upset while discussing how they had bullied others. This was an experience that I will never forget during my teaching career. To see barriers come down and students hugging each other and apologizing was literally beyond words.

KG reinforced a lesson in empathy and respect, but created more of an emotional experience than one involving critical thinking. While confession and apology have very strong effects, and expiating one's guilt may well be appropriate under certain circumstances, the educational effect here may still be less than it could have been. Indeed, only a rather experienced teacher can deal with such emotional issues without allowing the emotions to grow out of proportion. This kind of activity is risky; JD for example, dealt with a less directly personal issue, which was nonetheless highly emotional. She chose to have her students' focus cognitively on multiple perspectives rather than have the lesson become an opportunity for venting emotions. The challenge for all our teacher candidates was to manage emotions while focusing on the cognitive aspects of teaching and learning. Teacher candidates will need to learn how to achieve a balance, as both are necessary for authentic learning to occur.

Lack of Experience with and Understanding of Social Justice and Critical Thinking

In reflecting on the implementation of the lessons, some teacher candidates mentioned their lack of experience with and understanding of concepts such as social justice and critical thinking. These comments demonstrate the candidates' lack of education in recognizing and critiquing inequities. Ladson-Billings (1995) highlighted this problem among teachers more than two decades ago. In order to teach for social justice, teachers themselves need to be critically aware of the complex realities and causes of social inequities, but as Ladson-Billings (1995) reported, "Teacher educators have demonstrated that many prospective teachers not only lack these understandings but reject information regarding social inequity" (p. 477). However, Apple (2008) argued:

> Many teachers do have socially and pedagogically critical intuitions. However, they often do not have ways of putting these intuitions into practice because they cannot picture them in action in daily situations. Due to this, critical theoretical and political insights, then, have nowhere to go in terms of their embodiment in concrete pedagogical situations where the politics of curriculum and teaching must be *enacted*. (p. 250)

Our assignment to the teacher candidates had a mainly positive outcome, as they revealed that they too were learning along with their students. However, a few teacher candidates had difficulty grasping the purpose of the assignment. At times, they seemed to have missed the point that critical thinking is linked to social justice. Darling-Hammond (2005) underscored the importance for teachers to acquire the skills and sensitivity needed to be attuned to cultural, local, language, class and other factors that shape students' experiences. Teachers need these skills in order to "interpret curriculum through their students' eyes and shape lessons to connect with what students know and how they learn well" (p. 8).

One teacher candidate, DB, reported candidly on this matter in his assignment:

> Initially, this was quite the daunting task, as I was lacking confidence with the topics put before me. Being forced to examine and teach myself the topics of justice, fairness and civil liberty caused me to have a deeper admiration for the society that we live in.

DB shared his fear of walking on unfamiliar ground. His self-education appears to have increased his understanding of what democracies must do in order to work toward social justice. Of course, this kind of exploration can potentially have many different outcomes. Some people become angered by what they learn about the failures of justice in society. DB's statement about "deeper admiration" may mean that he has learned to live with these failures, or more likely, that he has not yet begun to ask the kind of probing questions that his students might not be led to ask either.

Resistance from Associate Teachers

Several teacher candidates mentioned that, at times, their associate teachers seemed to resist the idea of introducing a critical thinking lesson to the class. One teacher candidate reported that her associate teacher told her that the students in her classroom were not functioning at a high enough level to be ready for critical thinking. Unfortunately, we were unable to include the associate teachers' perspectives about critical thinking and their perceptions of our critical thinking exercise. Collaboration with those involved in mentoring these field experiences is crucial. Cochran-Smith (2001), a leading teacher educator in the United States pointed out the importance of university-school partnerships:

> Constructing pre-service programs that provide the social, organizational, and intellectual contexts for learning to teach against the grain in the company of more experienced mentors has been a daunting challenge for teacher educators. A large part of that challenge has been to clarify and wrestle with complex questions about the role the university ought to play in teacher education and the larger responsibility of teacher education to and for society.

The lack of clear connection between university courses and field placements (in the schools) could lead to misunderstanding and resistance that could pose serious questions about the manner in which critical thinking is taught and practiced in schools. First, did the associate teachers, in fact, resist or were the teacher candidates trying to avoid doing the assignment? Are teachers rigid in conducting lessons and not open to new schools of thought being integrated into the curriculum? Were the associate teachers bent on demonstrating that the "right way to teach" is teacher-centered? While only a very small number of students reported experiencing this resistance, their reports are still concerning. For example, NB reported about her associate:

Unfortunately, she was unaware of the need or relevancy of a critical thought exercise. The most difficult aspect of implementing the critical thought exercise was the associate's lack of understanding, knowledge base and enthusiasm in executing a critical thought lesson.

NB perceived resistance from her associate teacher. We cannot know whether the associate teacher does not understand the importance of critical thinking or whether other factors led her to discourage the teacher candidate. In any case, NB chose not to implement a critical thinking lesson. Since critical thinking should be a part of virtually every lesson and can readily inform practically any subject area, this associate teacher might not have understood what the critical thinking assignment actually involved. It is more likely that NB herself was reticent to attempt something that appeared to be challenging for her. As a teacher candidate, NB seems not to have wanted to challenge the *status quo* as she saw it. This kind of resistance to change is significant for understanding how and why things continue to be so slow to change. NB either could not or was not willing to "ignite the slow fuse of imagination" (Greene, 2009, p. 397).

HA also reported resistance from her associate teacher:

> She told me that only a handful of students were able to critically think about concepts and ideas while the rest of the students in the class were low-end learners. Even though I had been told that I would probably have a tough time generating a discussion where the students were expected to critically think about things I decided that I was up for the challenge.

HA encountered the fallacy of "low-level learners." The belief that somehow only people of high intelligence or sophistication have the capacity to think critically has long hampered enriched learning for people who have traditionally been marginalized. Very young children, those who have low literacy or learning disabilities, among all others, have a strong sense of fairness and of curiosity. If HA's associate teacher had been asked to give examples of where she had tried to engage her learners in critical discussions and the outcome of such attempts, she might have been surprised to find that she had been making decisions based on preconceptions, prejudice and perhaps on her own lack of engagement and courage.

As soon as children start to ask "why?" they are ready to engage in critical thinking. Most children are ready by the time they are 2 or 3 years old, well before they begin formal schooling. HA decided that she was up for the challenge and implemented her lesson, which was thoughtfully planned for her Grade 1 class. She, too, was pleasantly surprised at the wide array of responses and attempts to think critically that she was able to initiate with the six-year olds. In her lesson, HA focused on respecting differences in response to ongoing arguments and altercations at recess. In one section of her report, she wrote:

> Contrary to what my associate had told me these children were capable of thinking at a deeper level (at their age and developmental levels of course!). A few students commented during the lesson that if we all followed one single opinion then we would be like robots walking around without a purpose.

Teacher Candidates Underestimating Student Abilities

In their reflection on executing their lessons for this assignment, many teacher candidates, like some associate teachers, underestimated their students' ability to engage in critical thinking. Many declared that they were surprised to see their students engaging so well with critical thinking. Others mentioned that they did not think that a critical-thinking exercise would work well with primary-school students. One teacher candidate failed to complete the assignment during a recent practicum because she was assigned to teach kindergarten. She declared that implementing a critical thinking exercise with such young children was impossible. In contrast, Comber, Thomson, and Wells (2001) found that students in Grades Two and Three were engaging in critical thinking through writing, drawing, and making connections to everyday life.

A number of teacher candidates appeared to adopt a deficit thinking approach toward their students' abilities to engage in critical/higher level thinking. Some teacher candidates were pleasantly surprised, however, when they persisted even though they had started the assignment with the preconceived notion that students at certain grade/age levels could not handle this kind of work. Our findings pose serious questions about whether teacher candidates' prejudices are creating roadblocks to learning for social justice. Some teacher candidates were reluctant to implement critical thinking in primary grades because they held unsupported beliefs about what age, grade, or social or educational level is appropriate for critical-thinking lessons. This reluctance reinforces the age and social class divides that many have described as a significant injustice in today's school systems.

Possibilities and Future Direction

The above discussion and analysis indicate that we encountered many challenges. We ask ourselves, why does our passion and commitment to critical thinking for social justice face such challenges from our future teachers? Why are these teacher candidates so afraid of taking risks? What could we do to create an environment conducive to risk-taking? How can we help teacher candidates to recognize prejudice when they encounter it, what could we do differently, and what are the constraints on our work?

As Joordens (2010) explained, we must first create opportunities for teacher candidates to address confirmation bias: "The first step to teaching critical thought, then, is to open students' minds by opening their eyes to confirmation bias." Generally, people seek out information that confirms their assumptions and perceptions, since such information is comfortable and familiar. We need to meet our teacher candidates at their level of development in this regard. In order to do so, we need more time and an extended program where we can work with them to deconstruct their experiences in a positive manner. We believe that our teacher candidates would benefit by doing a similar exercise a second time in order to measure and evaluate their growth and change in thinking and in practice. We reiterate Apple (2008) who argued that educators must embody critical theoretical and political insights in concrete practices, and provide spaces for enacting a curriculum that includes critical thinking.

Next, we need to emphasize the importance of critical pedagogy during the entire duration of a teacher education program. Giroux (2009) stated that:

> critical pedagogy forges an expanded notion of politics and agency through a language of skepticism, possibility, and a culture of openness, debate, and engagement—all those elements now at risk because of the current and most dangerous attacks on higher education (p. 195).

In our attempt to help the teaching profession and make it relevant and accountable to those living in a technological age, we have tried to increase relevance and accountability. Curricula evolve and develop through analysis, questioning and even confrontation. Offering students the opportunity to learn to think critically risks challenging the *status quo*. Can we all be permitted this "luxury?" Teachers, administrators, and teacher educators need courage and mindfulness to teach even the youngest students to use the tools of democratic engagement, but without confronting the *status quo* and thinking "otherwise," injustice goes unchallenged.

Whether or not one admires the shirtless jogger who confronted Toronto's controversial mayor, this jogger is an engaged teacher-citizen who used his lawful right to ask hard and direct questions of a person in authority. Did his unanswered questions help to shine a light on a lack of accountability and injustice in the mayor's office? As we learned from our study, sometimes questions are of much greater value than answers ever could be.

Acknowledgement

We want to express our sincere gratitude to John Antoniw. He provided us with invaluable assistance in shaping this chapter. We also want to thank all our students who participated in our critical thinking sessions.

References

Apple, M. (2008). Can schooling contribute to a more just society? *Education, Citizenship, and Social Justice, 3*(3), 239-261.

Block, A. (2007). *Pedagogy, religion and practice: Reflections on ethics and teaching.* Palgrave: USA.

Cochran-Smith, M. (2001). Learning to teach against the (new) grain. *Journal of Teacher Education, 52*(1), 3-4.

Comber, B., Thomson, P., & Wells, M. (2001). Critical literacy find a "place:" Writing and social action in a low-income Australian grade 2/3 classroom. *The Elementary School Journal, 101*(4), 451-464.

Dam, G., & Volman, M. (2004). Critical thinking as a citizenship competence: Teaching strategies. *Learning and Instruction, 14*(4), 359-379.

Darling-Hammond, L. (2005). Educating the new educator: Teacher education and the future of democracy. *The New Educator, 1*(1), 1-18.

Edelsky, C. (1994). Education for democracy. *Language Arts, 71*(4), 252-257.

Eisner, E. (1999). Arts education for the 21st century. *Kappa Delta Pi, 35*(3), 136-137.

Freire, P. (2000). *Pedagogy of the oppressed.* Bloomsbury Academic: New York, New York.

Giroux, H. (2009). Education and the crisis of youth: Schooling and the promise of democracy. *The Educational Forum, 73*(1), 8-18.

Gordon, M. (2006). Welcoming confusion, embracing uncertainty: Educating teacher candidates in an age of certitude. *Paideusis, 15*(2), 15-25.

Greene, M. (2009). Coda: The slow fuse of change. *Harvard Educational Review, 79*(2), 396-398.

Joordens, S. (2010, October/November). You can lead students to knowledge, but how do you make them think? *Academic Matters: The Journal of Higher Education.*

Ladson-Billings, G. (1995). Toward a theory of culturally relevant pedagogy. *American Educational Research Journal, 32*(3), 465-491.

Nilson, C., Fetherston, C.M., McMurray, A., & Fetherston, T. (2013). Creative arts: An essential element in the teacher's toolkit when developing critical thinking in children. *Australian Journal of Teacher Education, 38*(7), 1-17.

Ontario Ministry of Education. (2014). *Equity and inclusive education in Ontario schools: Guidelines for policy development and implementation.* Retrieved from http://www.edu.gov.on.ca/eng/policyfunding/inclusiveguide.pdf.

Osana, H., & Seymour, J. (2004). Critical thinking in preservice teachers: A rubric for evaluating argumentation and statistical reasoning. *Educational Research and Evaluation, 10*(4-6), 473-498.

Phan, H.P. (2007). Examination of student learning approaches, reflective thinking, and self-efficacy beliefs at the University of the South Pacific: A path analysis. *Educational Psychology, 27*(6), 789-806.

Phan, H.P. (2008a). Unifying different theories of learning: Theoretical framework and empirical evidence. *Educational Psychology, 28*(3), 325-340.

Phan, H.P. (2008b). Predicting change in epistemological beliefs, reflective thinking and learning styles: A longitudinal study. *British Journal of Educational Psychology, 78,* 75-93.

Phan, H.P. (2009). Exploring students' reflective thinking practice, deep processing strategies, effort, and achievement goal orientations. *Educational Psychology, 29*(3), 297-313.

Phan, H.P. (2010). Critical thinking as a self-regulatory process component in teaching and learning. *Psicothema, 22*(2), 284-292.

R. v. Oakes. 1 S.C.R. 103 17550 (1986).

Shapiro, R. (2011, April 16). Rabbi Rami Shapiro: The TNB self-interview. *The Nervous Breakdown.* Retrieved from http://www.thenervousbreakdown.com/rshapiro/2011 /04/rabbi-rami-shapiro-thetnb-self-interview/.

Stephanovich, P. 2009). The lobster tale: An exercise in critical thinking. *Journal of Management Education, 33*(6), 725-746.

Ten Dam, G., & Volman, M. (2004). Critical thinking as a citizenship competence: Teaching strategies. *Learning and Instruction, 14*(4), 359-379.

Vasquez, V. (2010). Critical literacy isn't just for books anymore. *The Reading Teacher, 63*(7), 614-616.

Vasquez, V. (2014). *Negotiating critical literacies with young children: 10th anniversary edition.* New York, NY: Taylor and Francis.

Ward, A., & Beach, S.A. (2007). Apprenticeships in critical literacy: Conversations with preservice teachers. *Policy and Practice in Education, 13*(1/2), 8-22.

CHAPTER 13

Understanding the Impact of Quebec's Bill 56 on School Administrators' Work in Maintaining a Positive School Climate

Terry Kharyati and Benjamin Kutsyuruba

Abstract

I mplementation of new laws and policies in education often poses significant challenges for school administration. In June 2012, the province of Quebec enacted *Bill 56: An act to prevent and stop bullying and violence in schools*. This chapter details a study that examined Quebec school administrators' perceptions of the impact of Bill 56 on their work in maintaining a positive school climate. Our approach is as follows: we discuss the goals and mandates of the anti-bullying legislation *Bill 56* in the province of Quebec, both as stated in the document and as perceived by Quebec school administrators; we report on how Quebec school administrators see their responsibilities and roles changing in regards to the mandates of *Bill 56*; and describe school administrators' perceptions of challenges and supports of the anti-bullying legislation *Bill 56* in the province of Quebec.

Introduction

Recognizing the efforts from the Ministère de L'Éducation, du Loisir et du Sport (hereafter referred to as MELS) and school boards to deal with violence in schools, the Auditor General of Quebec (2005) recommended in his 2004-2005 annual report that more data be gathered to help determine the scope of this issue. As a result of that recommendation, the MELS published an action plan for all public, private, elementary, and secondary schools titled Violence in the Schools: Let's Work on it Together (Quebec Ministère de l'Éducation, du Loisir et du Sport, 2009). Based on its guidelines, all schools in Quebec have participated in mandatory surveying of students regarding bullying and violence, the results of which are reflected in each school's Ministry-mandated provincial school success plan. More recently, in June 2012, the province enacted Bill 56: *An Act to prevent and stop bullying and violence in schools*. However, although implementation of new laws and policies provided supports, the introduction of new policies often poses significant challenges for school administration.

Among other requirements, Quebec's *Bill 56* requires school administrators to be more responsible for the well-being of their staff and students and accountable for all reported incidents of bullying. The school administrator is now accountable to the MELS and the school community for the success or failure of the implementation of a comprehensive plan to deal effectively with bullying and violence. With the ever-increasing daily duties and responsibilities of principals, *Bill 56* may reduce their availability and ability to focus on other issues, thus affecting their self-efficacy and confidence to effectively manage their school. Efficacy is understood as a sense of personal empowerment that gives us the confidence to take actions, engage in appropriate risks, and transmit our confidence to others, thus making our eventual success a self-fulfilling prophecy (Reeves, 2008). In turn, the effectiveness of a school administrator has a significant impact on the efficacy levels of parents, teachers, staff, and students in school (Tschannen-Moran & Gareis, 2004). In this chapter, we will not be focusing on studying the participants' levels of self-efficacy but rather, as described in Bandura (1997, p. 382), their confidence as a presentation of their strength of belief in their abilities and its potential impact on their behaviours. For principals, the strength of belief in their abilities to work effectively with *Bill 56* and its demands and expectations may directly impact their effectiveness in implementing *Bill 56*.

This chapter details a study that examined Quebec school administrators' perceptions of the impact of *Bill 56* on their work in maintaining a positive school climate. In this chapter, we discuss the goals and mandates of the anti-bullying legislation *Bill 56* in the province of Quebec as stated in the document and perceived by Quebec school administrators; report on how Quebec school administrators see their responsibilities and roles changing in regards to the mandates of *Bill 56*; report on school administrators' perceptions of challenges and supports of the anti-bullying legislation *Bill 56* in the province of Quebec. Upon a short overview of the context, extant literature, and research methodology, we will discuss the findings as they pertain to the above themes, and offer implications for policy, practice, and further research.

Understanding Quebec's Educational Context and Bill 56

The Quebec Ministry of Education (MELS) documents defined bullying as "any repeated direct or indirect behaviour, comment, act, or gesture, whether deliberate or not, including in cyberspace, which occurs in a context where there is a power imbalance between the persons concerned and which causes distress and injures, hurts, oppresses, intimidates, or ostracizes" (Quebec Official Publishers, 2012, p. 9). The MELS defined violence "as any intentional demonstration of verbal, written, physical, psychological, or sexual force which causes distress and injures, hurts, or oppresses a person by attacking their psychological or physical integrity or well-being, or their rights or property" (*Education Act*, 2012, c. 13 s. 3). In Quebec, the MELS made its concerns clear in 2009:

> Violence is a serious and complex problem that transcends borders, commanding the attention of a number of researchers. Whatever form it takes, violence in the schools has a negative impact on young people, their academic success and their quality of life at school. Indeed, observations from researchers and testimonies from the field tend

to confirm that violence in schools creates an unhealthy atmosphere and breeds mistrust, feelings of not belonging, low self-esteem, anxiety and isolation, and increases absenteeism, academic failures, the number of drop-outs, and so on. (Quebec Ministère de l'Éducation, du Loisir et du Sport, 2009, Introduction)

Based on this statement that the safety, health, and security of students in Quebec was a serious concern, the MELS embarked on a plan to create supports in the educational system that included, but were not limited to: (1) hiring support officers for the 11 MELS regional offices and setting up regional resource groups working in the area of preventing and dealing with violence; (2) setting up regional training and support sessions; (3) creating a reference tool outlining different problems involving violence and distributing a list of existing resources; (4) ensuring there is an intervention strategy in each school; (5) ensuring there is an emergency intervention plan for each school board and school; (6) producing a semi-annual newsletter, an inventory of effective practices and programs, and a website, and holding a yearly provincial forum; (7) obtaining recurrent financial support for carrying out effective actions in schools; and (8) obtaining recurrent financial support for establishing a guidance and support service for students who have been suspended or expelled from school (Quebec Ministère de l'Éducation, du Loisir et du Sport, 2009).

The MELS action plan communicated the commitment of the Ministry to prevent and deal with violence in schools, and described the perceived state of safety in Quebec schools and the potential negative impact violence has on schooling in Quebec. The MELS concluded:

Violence in the schools affects young people, as well as their families and the school staff ... Fighting violence in the schools requires periodic intervention as well as an overall joint, structured approach that is part of a series of actions and interventions to prevent and deal with violence. In addition, the school, acting alone, cannot respond to the different manifestations of violence in the community, nor can it be expected to. Indeed, the school must establish or strengthen collaborative ties with families, various partners, and community organizations so that they can work together (Quebec Ministère de l'Éducation, du Loisir et du Sport, 2009, Conclusion).

This MELS action plan foreshadowed what was going to be the framework for *Bill 56*. The recommendations found in the MELS action plan resulted in grant monies being distributed to the schools in 2009 to be used for interventions related to anti-bullying and later, in 2012, the legislation resulting in *Bill 56* (Quebec Official Publisher, 2012).

Each school must adopt such a strategy, based on its success plan, taking into account the characteristics of its population and elements such as the following: a profile of the situation, including actions carried out to prevent and deal with violence and means to evaluate their impact in the school; a profile of the manifestations of violence occurring between fellow students, between students and adults, or involving school partners, and a description of the circumstances; safety and emergency measures; measures to assist personnel and students who are victims; the role of school stakeholders (administrators, teachers, complementary services personnel, support service staff and all partners concerned, including parents); the school code; information about rights and responsibilities; legislative frameworks; occurrence report; protection of personnel and students who are victims; dealing with complaints; and, a clearly announced school policy on violence that takes into account the characteristics of the school population, etc. (Quebec Ministère de l'Éducation, du Loisir et du Sport, 2009, article 1.1.5).

Bill 56 is an act of law in Quebec that defines the term bullying and outlines educators' duties and responsibilities to provide a healthy and secure learning environment "which allows every student to develop his or her full potential, free from any form of bullying or violence" (Quebec Official Publisher, 2012, p. 2). *Bill 56* requires every public and private educational institution to adopt and implement an anti-bullying and anti-violence plan. The plan must:

Include prevention measures to put an end to all forms of bullying and violence and measures to encourage parents to collaborate in preventing and stopping bullying and violence and in creating a healthy and secure learning environment, specify the actions to be taken and the supervisory or support measures to be offered when an act of bullying or violence is observed, determine the disciplinary sanctions applicable to bullying and violence, and specify the follow-up to be given to any report or complaint concerning an act of bullying or violence. (Quebec Official Publisher, 2012, p. 2)

The new set of legal expectations and public expectations were outlined for Quebec's population: whenever "any complaint" is made to either a school or a school board employee it must be followed-up, researched, acted upon, documented, and reported to the board and the MELS. Written into the law was the school principal's responsibility: "The principal shall see to the implementation of the anti-bullying and anti-violence plan, and shall receive and promptly deal with all reports or complaints concerning bullying or violence" (Quebec Official Publisher, 2012, p. 6). It was officially passed into law that school administrators were held responsible for the well-being of their staff and students and would be held accountable for such.

Bill 56 outlines that all school-based anti-bullying and violence-prevention plans were the responsibility of the school administration and must include:

(1) an analysis of the situation prevailing at the school with respect to bullying and violence; (2) preventative measures to put an end to all forms of bullying and violence, in particular those motivated by racism or homophobia or targeting sexual orientation, sexual identity, a handicap, or a physical characteristic; (3) measures to encourage parents to collaborate in preventing and stopping bullying and violence and in creating a healthy and secure environment; (4) procedures for reporting, or registering a complaint concerning, an act of bullying or violence and, more particularly,

procedures for reporting the use of social media or communication technologies for cyber-bullying purposes; (5) actions to be taken when a student, teacher, or other school staff member or any other person observes an act of bullying or violence; (6) measures to protect the confidentiality of any report or complaint concerning an act of bullying or violence; (7) supervisory or support measures for any student who is a victim of bullying or violence, for witnesses, and for the perpetrator; (8) specific disciplinary sanctions for acts of bullying or violence, according to their severity or repetitive nature; and (9) required follow-up on any report or complaint concerning an act of bullying or violence. (Quebec Official Publisher, 2012, p. 10)

Bill 56 theoretically had a bearing on school administrators, school communities, and school boards, as it emphasized that the actions of the adults in the educational system were fundamental if children were to be kept safe. Focusing on changing and standardizing the adults' actions in the educational system was a paradigm shift from the traditional focus on changing students' actions and standardizing students' behaviours.

Review of the Literature

Positive School Climate

Social, emotional, intellectual, and physical safeties are all fundamental human needs (Maslow, 1943, 1954). Therefore, feeling safe at school is an extension of these fundamental needs in the school context, that is if learning and a healthy development is to flourish (Devine & Cohen, 2007). Hence, safe school environments are essential for learning (Cornell & Mayer, 2010; Craig, Pepler, Murphy, & McCuaig-Edge, 2010; Greene, 2005; Karcher, 2004; Mayer & Furlong, 2010; Robinson & Espelage, 2011; Whitlock, 2006).

The National School Climate Council (2007) defined school climate as "norms, values, and expectations that support people feeling socially, emotionally, and physically safe" (p. 4). School climate can also be understood as a by-product of the quality of the interpersonal relationships among students, parents, staff, and administrators. Therefore, a positive and healthy school climate is fostered when there is a shared vision of respect and caring for all people by all people in the school. The Council further noted five key elements of school climate:

> (1) safety (e.g., rules and norms, physical security, social-emotional security); (2) teaching and learning (e.g., support for learning, social and civic learning); (3) interpersonal relationships (e.g., respect for diversity, social support from adults, social support from peers); (4) institutional environment (e.g., school connectedness, engagement, physical surroundings); and (5) staff relationships (leadership, professional relationships) (p. 1).

Similarly, Hoy and Tarter (1997) noted that an important aspect of school climate is organizational health, which includes characteristics such as: emphasis on academic achievement, friendly and collegial relationships among staff, respect for all, supportive administrator leadership, consistent discipline policies, attention to safety issues, and strong family and community involvement. Academic achievement for both students and their teachers requires equal elements of trust, compassion, patience, and perseverance. Students who have a good relationship with their teachers will work towards a common goal together, and teachers who have a good relationship with their students will work towards a common goal together. Setting the standard for the vision and mission in a school based on healthy and positive interactions with each other can be seen as the beginning to all other conversations in a school setting. In a nutshell:

> A sustainable, positive school climate fosters youth development and learning necessary for a productive, contributing, and satisfying life in a democratic society. This climate includes norms, values, and expectations that support people feeling socially, emotionally, and physically safe. People are engaged and respected. Students, families, and educators work together to develop, live, and contribute

to a shared school vision. Educators model and nurture an attitude that emphasizes the benefits of, and satisfaction from, learning. Each person contributes to the operations of the school as well as the care of the physical environment. (National School Climate Council, 2007, p. 4).

Healthy relationships are one of the keys to an interconnected positive school climate. As outlined in school effectiveness research, safety and security, coupled with healthy relationships, provide the groundwork for a successful school. Lezotte (1991) outlined the correlates of effective schools and placed a safe and orderly environment as a first priority. For Lezotte (1991), order, purposefulness, and a climate free from the threat of harm should be primary goals towards achieving learning for all, and the effective school moves beyond banning undesirable behaviour to being a school where students and staff actively seek to help and care for each other. Moving from a reactive approach to student and staff behaviour to a proactive and preventative approach allows schools to focus on the behaviours that build relationships, as opposed to focusing on behaviours that destroy relationships. The essence of an effective school is linked to the essence of a healthy and positive school climate, which is the belief that all relationships in a school are important (Hansen, 1991; Hoy & Miskel, 2005; Jimerson, Hart, & Renshaw, 2012; Loukas, 2007) and that achieving and maintaining a positive climate has an impact on both academic achievement and the prevention of violence in a school (Demaray, Malecki, Jenkins, & Westermann, 2012; Greene, 2005; Hoy & Hannum, 1997; Osher, Dwyer, Jimerson, & Brown, 2012). Research has also suggested that a school that has a goal of graduating a higher number of students and lowering its drop-out rate should begin by building strong and positive relationships among the stakeholders in the school setting.

Impact of Bullying and Violence on School Climate

There has been growing recognition in many parts of the world of the widespread pervasiveness, and the sobering and serious harmfulness, of bullying in schools (Smith et al., 1999; Rigby, 2001, 2002b).

Unfortunately, bullying and violence continue to appear to be part of the school experience (Lunenburg, 2010). Rigby (2003) concluded:

> Whenever the health of children has been related to being bullied at school, findings suggest peer victimization and health status to be significantly associated ... that peer victimization is a significant risk factor and may have a causal role in reducing the health status of school children. (p. 588)

It is important that this peer victimization be a focus for educators in a school and that the school's policies and programs focus on dealing positively and effectively with students who bully and are bullied. Olweus and Limber (2007b) contended that when a school allows bullying to continue, the entire school climate can be affected, permeating the environment with fear and disrespect and hampering the ability of students to learn: "When students don't see the adults at school acting to prevent or intervene in bullying situations, they may feel that teachers and other school staff have little control over the students and don't care what happens to them" (p. xiv).

A review of the literature reveals that most people involved in bullying situations - the bully, the victim, and the bystander - are negatively affected by their experiences (Anderson et al., 2001; Boulton, Trueman, & Murray, 2008; Connolly, Pepler, Craig, & Taradash, 2000; Josephson, 2004; Nansel et al., 2001; Olweus, 1993; Rigby & Slee, 1991; Roland, 2002; Salmivalli, Kaukiainen, Kaistaniemi, & Lagerspetz, 1999). The work of Rothon, Head, Klineberg, and Stansfeld (2011) attempted to reveal the deeper negative influences bullying has on students:

> Because bullying has a negative influence on children's health and educational outcomes it is important that healthcare workers and teachers have a good understanding of bullying and its potential consequences ... Based on the literature, the key hypotheses are as follows: (1) victims of bullying will have a greater propensity to exhibit depressive symptoms; (2) victims of bullying will be less likely to reach national achievement benchmarks; (3) social

support from friends will be more effective as a protective factor than social support from the family; and, (4) bullied students with low levels of perceived social support will exhibit poorer outcomes than bullied students with higher levels of perceived social support. (p. 581)

Similarly, Rothon et al. (2011) concluded that bullying had a strong negative effect on mental health amongst secondary school pupils, and that being bullied can have a long-term impact and contribute to poor mental health, trouble with personal relationships, and unemployment risk in adulthood.

The victims of bullying are not the only students we must concern ourselves with. As Craig et al. (2010) found, students who bully are also at risk for long-term problems as adults, such as anti-social behaviour, gang involvement, and substance abuse, and, similarly, students who are bullied are at risk for anxiety, depression, and physical symptoms. Given its substantial impact on both victims and students who bully, it seems fundamental that strategies to address the problem are developed to prevent the development of the most serious consequences such as suicide attempts (Rigby & Slee, 1991).

Research into whether students are positively impacted or not by anti-bullying programs is well documented (Beran & Shapiro, 2005; Bickmore, 2011; Ferguson, San Miguel, Kilburn, & Sanchez, 2007; Merrell, Gueldner, Ross, & Isava, 2008; Smith et al., 2005; Smith, Smith, Osborn, & Samara, 2008; Wolke & Woods, 2003). In a 2005 review of anti-bullying policy and practice conducted by the Melbourne Department of Education and Training (MDET) (2006), several effective common practices emerged from the schools that were deemed in good standing in relation to student well-being: (1) effective leadership; (2) effective whole-school behaviour management systems; (3) well-being as a school priority; (4) a whole-school anti-bullying approach; (5) school pride and high expectations; and, (6) positive student-student relations. The quality of these common practices was linked directly to the policies, focus, and priorities set by the school administrator. These six common practices need to be embodied in the practices of school leaders who aim to create a healthy and positive school culture by involving the entire school population in the process.

The Role of the School Administrator in Maintaining a Positive School Climate

School administrators have an important role in the maintenance of school climate (Bulach, Boothe, & Pickett, 1998; Loukas, 2007; Kelley, Thornton, & Daugherty, 2005; Pepper & Hamilton Thomas, 2002). Smith et al. (2005) concluded that school administrators who invested their time and effort, and allocated funds to anti-bullying initiatives, yielded valuable returns by "helping to create school environments that are safer and more peaceful for children, and, by implication, more conducive for learning and healthy development" (p. 753).

Bosworth, Ford, and Hernandez (2011) concluded that "determinants of perceived safety are two components of a school's climate: organization/discipline and caring relationships" (p. 200). These authors further explained that in a well-organized school where rules are clearly outlined, adults are caring toward the students, and, where relationships between adults are respectful, professional, and caring, people in the school feel safer. Similarly Blase, Derick, and Strathe (1986) reported that supportive principal behaviours (e.g., shared vision approach, shared decision-making approach, and a focus on forming positive relationships) affected school climate and working conditions in a positive way (e.g., by making work more rewarding, by making the work environment more positive and effective, and by reducing stress).

Furthermore, understanding a school administrator's leadership approach is important for the discussions of school climate. Leithwood and Jantzi (1991) reported that a transformational leadership approach impacted a school's planning, goals, and structures, which in turn impacted the classroom conditions such as instruction, policies, and procedures. The implications for the type of leadership that would produce high levels of trust, health, safety, and professionalism are important to consider, especially in relation to working with complex and challenging issues such as bullying and violence. A large amount of literature strongly indicates that effective school leadership, specifically school administrators (principals and vice-principals), is key to achieving success in many areas of school life (Sergiovanni, 1984, 1992, 2005; Sergiovanni & Starratt, 2002).

Transformational Leadership

Transformational leadership in schools is deemed to succeed in building trusting and healthy relationships (Avolio & Bass, 1988; Bass, 1995; Hornett, 2001; Hoy & Miskel, 2001; Leithwood, 2007; Leithwood & Jantzi, 1991; Tschannen-Moran, 2003). Transformational leadership behaviours, in particular the work of school administrators, are linked to motivating and inspiring the school community, in that they "stimulate others to view their work from new perspectives, generate an awareness of the mission and vision of the organization, [and] develop colleagues and followers to higher levels of ability and potential" (Tschannen-Moran, 2003, p. 159).

Transformational leaders create an environment where students and staff respond to community values, and where they see their actions advancing the health of the collective (Sergiovanni, 2009). As Sergiovanni (2009) stated, transformational leadership starts with "leadership by building" and transcends into "leadership by binding" as transformative leadership becomes morally centered as it raises the level of human conduct and ethical aspiration of both the leader and the led (p. 169). Barnett and McCormick (2003) concluded that transformational leaders lead by building a shared vision, which helps to bind people together and establish group ownership and where consensus and commitment to school vision are developed through leadership practices such as communication, leader credibility, and the involvement of the school community in collaborative processes (p. 68). Furthermore, transformational leaders serve as role models; are ethical in their language and their conduct; share a common mission and vision; seek first to understand; are transparent, enthusiastic, goal-oriented, committed, optimistic, creative, innovative, and courageous; and, communicate clearly and effectively. These leaders can recognize and accept individual differences in needs and values, and create learning opportunities in a supportive climate (Tschannen-Moran, 2003, 2004).

According to Tschannen-Moran (2003), one phenomenon inspired by transformational leadership was "organizational citizenship behaviour," which this author described as the willingness and effort committed by staff for the betterment of the organization. Five specific categories of behaviour were described: altruism, conscientiousness, sportsmanship, courtesy, and civic virtue performed in service of the organization (Tschannen-Moran, 2003, pp. 160–161). These five categories are integral behaviour types for school leaders to foster in their own school to help build a positive school culture. In particular, when a principal must implement a new program or new policies, the betterment of the organizational values and practices is essential for the success of the specific practices and the overall effectiveness of the school leader and school staff.

Successfully implementing new programming in schools usually requires changes in school policies and in human behaviours. This has the effect of making the change process all the more challenging and intense. These programs intend to impact something as complex and, at times, ingrained as a school's climate and health. According to the research based on the overall success rates of anti-bullying and violence prevention programs, such programs are neither easily implemented nor are they always successful (Melbourne Department of Education and Training, 2006; Rigby, 1997, 2002a; Smith & Schneider, 2004). Implementing change of this kind requires that school administrators be positive, resilient, and diligent because of the complexity of the issues and because positive results are not always evident, achieved, or quick to come.

Kotter (2012) outlined an eight-stage process of creating major change: (1) establishing a sense of urgency; (2) creating a guiding coalition; (3) developing a vision and strategy; (4) communicating the change vision; (5) empowering broad-based action; (6) generating short wins; (7) consolidating gains and producing more change; and, (8) anchoring new approaches in the culture (p. 23). Considering these eight stages, a school administrator's task of implementing challenging and complex programming may require high efficacy related to personal and professional characteristics. In reviewing success stories in the major change process, Kotter (2012) revealed two important patterns: (1) useful change tends to provide the perseverance needed to overcome challenges, and (2) the process is never effective unless it is driven by high-quality leadership and "not just excellent management" (p. 22). Therefore, the challenge for school administrators to be leaders of both organizational and pedagogical change is an intricate and important process if schools are to achieve the desired results.

Research Methodology

The setting for this study was an English school board in the province of Quebec. The board had 26 schools situated in both rural and urban settings, with a diverse socio-economic student population of approximately 6300 total students. There was a mixture of large urban high schools (Grades 7 to 11), mid-size urban elementary schools (Kindergarten to Grade 6), and small rural elementary schools. There were approximately 23 administrators in the board, which had a territorial size slightly larger than the Province of Nova Scotia; hence many school administrators worked alone, and in some cases were isolated geographically from the central office and even from other schools.

This research project was guided by a phenomenological perspective that sought to examine the perceptions of a person in a particular role or position towards a particular event. Phenomenological research follows a human science approach, which emphasizes "discovery, description, and meaning" (Osborne, 1994, p. 168). This phenomenological perspective helped to facilitate an enriched understanding of how school administrators perceived their own ability to protect students and staff within the context of their leadership positions and external legal and policy changes.

This study derived data from two qualitative methods of inquiry: document analysis and interviews. Document analysis (Creswell, 2007; Patton, 2002) is a systematic procedure for evaluating documents, both in print and electronic form. Data from the documents was examined and interpreted in order to have elicited meaning, to have gained understanding, and to have developed empirical knowledge (Bowen, 2009). In particular, the main purpose for using document analysis was to analyze *Bill 56* as a document that "can provide data on the context within which research participants operate—a case of text providing context" (Bowen, 2009, p. 29). An analysis of regulations, policies, and directives was conducted specifically as they related to school administrators' role in implementation of *Bill 56*.

Furthermore, in-depth, semi-structured interviews were conducted with six school administrators. The interview questions were designed to invite the participants to give insights on the research questions that guided this study. The interviews lasted an average of 50 minutes in length and were audio-recorded and later transcribed verbatim. Etic and emic approaches to interview data-analysis were used, providing rich descriptive themes that were meaningful, poignant, and common. The data analysis presented an opportunity to explore the divergences and convergences of the findings with the existing literature. Each interview placed an emphasis on the commitment and care with which the participants watched over their respective schools.

Research Findings

The Goals and Mandates of the Anti-Bullying Legislation *Bill 56*

In *Violence in the Schools: Let's work on it together* (Quebec Ministère de l'Éducation, du Loisir et du Sport, 2009), the MELS concluded that a mandatory plan to ensure all Quebec schools were working on developing positive school climates was needed. This document stated that schools must be committed to reducing the negative experiences with bullying and violence that students in Quebec deal with, along with improving overall student achievement. Therefore, it should be no surprise to educators that the passing of Quebec's *Bill 56* mandates that school administrators are responsible and accountable for the safety of their students. According to *Bill 56,* the school administrators' accountability for their school's climate requires the production of a plan and identification of effective resources that will be adopted by the school to combat bullying and violence. It is expected that school administrators invest time, thought, effort, and resources to create a plan that will yield valuable returns and create school environments that are safer and more peaceful for children and, by implication, more conducive for learning and healthy development.

The interview findings revealed that the participants expressed a deep understanding of both the defined and implied purposes of *Bill 56*. The participants perceived *Bill 56* to have formalized a common language and common vision for all schools, with an overall positive impact on practice. They pointed to the erroneous impression of some members of the school community that *Bill 56* implied that such environments have only been prioritized after the implementation of the bill. Although the emphasis on safety in schools had always been a priority for participants personally, they acknowledged the positive impact of having a clear and formal mission and vision with regards to bullying and violence for their own school communities. This aligns with current literature regarding effective schools (Lezotte, 1991) and the work focusing on the centrality of clarity as an antecedent to organizational health (Lencioni, 2012). Participants cited that there was a positive impact of this province-wide declaration and that it set the "serious tone" for conversations with students, staff, and parents of all levels of education as it legally formalizes the responsibilities and expectations of all school community members. Furthermore, the participants recognized that these elements assisted them in fulfilling their duties as school leaders.

Overall, participants acknowledged the positive impact of a well-defined policy document such as *Bill 56*. This perspective converged with Caldwell and Spinks (1988), who described the positive impacts of policy implementation by providing a framework for planning; fostering stability and continuity; eliminating ambiguity; and showing community members that the leaders are willing to be held accountable. Based on the interview findings, these directives were, for the participants, clear and concise in their explanation of what legal steps a principal had to take to prevent violence and bullying and to deal with incidents as they occurred. However, it was noted that *Bill 56* does not offer a set of pedagogical interventions to actively deal with bullying and violence, and that ways to achieve the goals and expectations set forth in *Bill 56* are not explicitly explained or detailed. Therefore, participants saw potential imbalance that might occur when a set of expectations was outlined without providing an explanation of how to achieve those expectations.

The document analysis findings showed that *Bill 56* has a distinctly defined set of requirements whereby schools must ensure that specific interventions, policies, and practices are in place every year, and principals are accountable for ensuring the basic requirements are met. Furthermore, every school principal has to: (1) have a written plan; (2) share that written plan; (3) have a formal reporting process that is monitored by the school boards; and, (4) have a formal data collection in the school to monitor progress. Yet, as Fullan (2010) and Reeves (2009) stated, a plan is only as effective as the person leading the implementation of change. The participants acknowledged this last point as crucial in their understanding of what it takes to be an effective leader who transcends a plan by fostering greater citizenship behaviours every day (Tschannen-Moran, 2003). Researchers (Kotter, 2012; Marzano, 2000; Marzano et al., 2005; Sergiovanni, 2009) demonstrated that principals are far more effective if they are organized and are competent leaders who have a structured and standards-based approach to school leadership.

A central concern that emerged in the interviews was related to the potential of mandates to be used by schools "as a checklist to complete and move on." Participants were concerned that while legal obligations would be fulfilled, moral obligations would not be. The literature review findings identified a difference between transactional and transformational leaders (Avolio, 1999; Bass, 1985; Hornett, 2001; Lynch, 2012; Northouse, 2007; Sergiovanni, 1990; Waldman, Bass, & Einstein, 1987). The transactional leader might theoretically make sure the checklist was completed and oversee the process, making sure its requirements were being met. On the other hand, the transformational leader might make certain the list and the processes were fulfilled and then work to create a shared sense of ownership, whereby the list was understood as the responsibility of the collective. Similarly, transformational school leaders might provide the services mandated under the law while also planning to "stimulate others to view their work from new perspectives, generate an awareness of the mission and vision of the organization, [and] develop colleagues and followers to higher levels of ability and potential" (Tschannen-Moran, 2003, p. 159).

Research suggested that the success or failure of school initiatives depends heavily on the theory and practice of the school administrator (Marzano, 2000; Marzano et al., 2005). Participants in this study showed concerns regarding the level of accountability of the principal according to *Bill 56*. The level of their commitment to the value of leadership converged with Fullan (2014), who dismissed the notion that accountability is an effective motivator for change. The interview findings revealed that the accountability aspect of *Bill 56*, for the participants, existed as a reality of the legislation but did not act as a transformational motivator in their approach to student health and safety. Although the participants acknowledged added stress, their concerns went beyond the heightened levels of accountability, and even liability as a school principal associated with *Bill 56* and focused on doing what they were mandated to do.

The participants stated that *Bill 56* created a sense of urgency within the educational system. This sense of urgency, Kotter (2008) explained, is a necessary element for change. Kotter (2008) described the need for a sense of urgency to combat complacency and to motivate leadership to embark on a path of change. This is important, as an alignment can be made between the participants' view of their own buy-in of *Bill 56* and Kotter's (2008) argument that a sense of urgency can lead to meaningful change. The interview findings revealed that the participants expressed the realization that without this sense of urgency, as Kotter (2008) described, people (although very motivated to be the best they could be) might not give the needed extra push of hard work to accomplish this very complex task of keeping schools safe.

Participants cited the benefits of an Olweus Program as an example of a whole-school anti-bullying approach. Similarly, scholars (Bauer, Lozano, & Rivara, 2007; Black & Jackson, 2007; Pagliocca et al., 2007; Smith et al., 2005; Ttofi, Farrington, & Baldry, 2008) acknowledged that Olweus programming seemed to have provided more effective positive outcomes than other anti-bullying efforts. Smith and Schneider (2004) recognized that a whole-school approach might have a significant impact on school climate, but warned that there were no guarantees that a whole-school program would have a significant and/or immediate impact on bullying issues. In 2002, Barbara Coloroso wrote to parents:

> Ask for a copy of your child's school's antibullying policy. Check to see that it has the four principles (from Olweus).... In the end, you want to know that your child's school has a strong antibullying policy that is clearly articulated, consistently enforced, and broadly communicated. Along with the policy, you will want to be sure that there are procedures and programs that back up and reinforce the policy, as well as create a safe and caring environment for students. It is one thing to have a policy; it is wholly another to make sure the policy is on the school wall or placed as an inspirational piece of writing at the beginning of the student handbook. It is the school culture and social environment that these policies, procedures, and programs create as, well as reflect. (p. 178)

Without referring to Coloroso directly in the interviews, the participants indirectly expressed agreement with this message. The participants acknowledged the effectiveness of *Bill 56* in making anti-bullying and violence a prominent public priority. They also acknowledged that they had not dealt with bullying in the ways that Coloroso described in her work in 2002, as their school board or schools did not have, on record, specific anti-bullying policies until after *Bill 56* was enacted. Yet, Coloroso's (2002) visionary work outlined exactly what *Bill 56* attempts to address.

Changes in School Administrators' Responsibilities and Roles under *Bill 56*

Overall, there were three main themes that emerged from the principals' responses. First, they recognized the renewed emphasis on principals' leadership role in the success of a school's anti-bullying undertakings. Second, they emphasized that the changes in the reporting of incident processes that existed to track and to hold principals accountable were a major change. Lastly, the participants acknowledged that there was an increase in required day-to-day interventions as a direct result of implementing *Bill 56* in their schools.

The participants acknowledged the benefits of the standardization of school plans and policies regarding bullying in schools and the renewed focus on the role of the school principal as the leader in this process. Based on the findings from the document analysis, *Bill 56* requires principals to lead the way by: (1) creating a committee; (2) developing a comprehensive plan, the impact of which can be measured; (3) creating a policy and a code of conduct that must be communicated to the school community; and, (4) reacting to all reported incidents and following-up in writing to the school board. As stated before, principals had to choose a path of developing an effective school anti-bullying programming. Yet, it can prove a difficult choice for administrators. Although there is a wealth of anti-bullying and violence prevention programs, there is no consensus in the literature on which program or approach is the most effective (Howard, Flora, & Griffin, 1999). Similarly, despite some studies that outlined programs that may have had a positive impact on students (Ferguson et al., 2007; Melbourne Department of Education and Training, 2006; Rigby, 1997, 2002a; Smith & Schneider, 2004), others question whether there can be such a definitive interpretation of the positive impact of anti-bullying programs (Beran & Shapiro, 2005; Bickmore, 2011; Ferguson et al., 2007; Merrell et al., 2008; Smith et al., 2005; Smith et al., 2008; Wolke & Woods, 2003). Regardless of the program choice, the participants expressed that, without effective leadership by the principal, initiatives of any kind would not be as effective or effective at all. This perspective aligned with a 2005 review of anti-bullying policy and practice conducted by the Melbourne Department of Education and Training (2006), through which several effective common practices emerged from the schools that were deemed to be in good standing in relation to student well-being: first on the list of the effective common practices was effective leadership. Other studies strongly indicated that effective school leadership, and specifically school administrators, are key to achieving overall success in many areas of school life (Blase et al., 1986; Bosworth et al., 2011; Leithwood & Jantzi, 1991; Sergiovanni, 1984, 1992, 2005; Sergiovanni & Starratt, 2002). Through the content- and context-oriented document analysis, it was noted that, although *Bill 56* does not explicitly use the term "whole-school approach," it does promote this approach by the sum total of its mandates, which require a whole-school approach. Terms such as "whole-school approach," "forming committees," and "creating policy documents" were all cited by the participants as parts of the work and "pressures" of transitioning from pre- to post-*Bill 56* contexts. But, it is also acknowledged that with this "pressure" comes the distinct power of principals as "school leaders" to enact real changes in the policies that govern school life. Overall, *Bill 56's* structure and focus aligned with the research about the need for effective school anti-bullying programming (MDET, 2006; Smith et al., 2005; Smith & Schneider, 2004).

The participants stated that the role of the principal changed in a legal sense with the implementation of *Bill 56* because of the added responsibilities and expectations listed in *Bill 56* encompassed by the following statement: "The principal shall see to the implementation of the anti-bullying and anti-violence plan, and shall receive and promptly deal with all reports or complaints concerning bullying or violence" (Quebec Official Publisher, 2012, p. 6). The responsibility of the principal to execute such a plan was regarded to have changed because of the public nature of the implementation of *Bill 56* and the heightened awareness of students and parents. Indeed, principals are considered to have a major impact on school culture and a safe school environment (Bulach et al., 1998; Kelley et al., 2005; Loukas, 2007; Pepper & Hamilton Thomas, 2002). Yet, participants expressed concerns about the ambiguity of the written expectations regarding the reporting by the principal of all incidents of bullying by the principal. Fullan (2010) and Reeves (2009) warned educators against over-planning on paper, as this can render "fat plans" immovable. Fat plans, according to Reeves (2009), were elaborate plans which might not have the desired impact once implemented. The participants discussed certain aspects of *Bill 56*, "...like trying to report every incident whether its bullying or not to the Ministry...can take away from my time to deal with important details" (Elias), that have the potential to take away from the primary focus of the legislation, which was keeping children safe.

The participants also acknowledged the importance of having parents, students, and staff reporting all potential issues, as it signified to the participants that attention was being paid to victims. The need to build trust among all members of the school environment has also been emphasized by researchers (Booren & Handy, 2009; Hoy & Feldman, 1987; Kutsyuruba, Walker, & Noonan, 2011; Tschannen-Moran, 2004). As a result of trust, effective interventions and strategies were emerging and stronger relationships were developing between students and adults. This understanding converges with Tschannen-Moran (2014) who noted, "studies of resilience among adolescents who have succeeded despite living in highly adverse and difficult circumstances found that they frequently credited a supportive relationship with an adult, usually a teacher, as crucial to their success" (p. 173).

The participants believed that the expectations during and after the implementation of *Bill 56* increased their workload in part because of the need to provide an increased number of interventions. Although there was a consensus that the increase in interventions was a positive outcome *of Bill 56,* respondents added that they felt the pressure of ensuring there was adequate time to investigate and intervene, of being competent enough to effectively deal with situations, and of providing appropriate and timely resources for support and follow-up for both victims and perpetrators. These functions required considerable effort and time in addition to accomplishing their other daily tasks and responsibilities. Fullan (2014) noted that principals' responsibilities have increased enormously over the past two decades: "They are expected to run a smooth school; manage health, safety, and the building; innovate without upsetting anyone; connect with students and teachers; be responsive to parents and the community; answer to their districts; and, above all, deliver results" (p. 6).

Challenges of the Anti-Bullying Legislation *Bill 56*

The participants shared comments related to the following challenges: (1) the challenge of the multifariousness and complexity of bullying situations; (2) the challenge of "getting it right;" (3) the challenge of "buy-in;" and, (4) the challenge of building trust.

The principals in this study recognized that bullying situations are complex and that it may be much more challenging to resolve them than it would seem at a first glance. Olweus and Limber (2007a) maintained that bullying is a complex issue that needs to be addressed at all levels of a student's experience, and explained that the entire school climate is impacted when adults at a school allow bullying situations to continue. Most people involved in bullying situations: the bully, the victim, and the bystander, are negatively affected by their experiences (Anderson et al., 2001; Connolly et al., 2000; Josephson, 2004; Nansel et al., 2001; Roland, 2002; Salmivalli et al., 1999). Participants acknowledged that dealing with emotional and intricate social phenomena can be a considerable challenge. Coloroso (2002) described the multi-layered process of stopping violence:

> Breaking the cycle of violence involves more than merely identifying and stopping the bully. It requires that we examine why and how a child becomes a bully or a target of a bully (and sometimes both) as well as the role bystanders play in perpetuating the cycle. (p. xvi)

Principals commended *Bill 56*'s focus on educating the school community on the negative effects of bullying, and requiring that all school community members speak up to deal with the phenomenon of violence in schools. They also felt the intensity of the pressure of effectively dealing with both victims and potential perpetrators. This pressure does not seem to be generated by the number of situations to be dealt with, but more by the confidence and competence of the staff who work with bullying situations where children are involved.

As noted before, principals considered that *Bill 56* has heightened the awareness and understanding of the seriousness of the issues surrounding bullying and its impact on children. Social, emotional, intellectual, and physical safeties are all fundamental human needs (Maslow, 1943, 1954). Feeling safe at school is an extension of these fundamental needs in the school context, if learning and healthy development are to flourish (Cornell & Mayer, 2010; Craig et al., 2010; Devine & Cohen, 2007; Greene, 2005; Karcher, 2004; Whitlock, 2006). Therefore, damages done by a negative, threatening, and hurtful school climate can rob students of their spirit; their educational, physical, and mental health; and, sadly, sometimes their lives (Wessler & Preble, 2003). Because of the ever-present pressure of keeping children safe, school administrators experienced the overwhelming challenge, and associated stress, of "getting it right" or else students would suffer. As Hoy and Miskel (1978) explained, "too often administrators define problems quickly and narrowly and, in so doing, restrict their options and treat only the symptoms of the problems" (p. 270). Similarly, "bullying, forms of discrimination, harassment, and others may fall under the radar of an unobservant school leader who is focusing exclusively on management rather than what is happening in the climate of the school" (Blanchfield & Ladd, 2013, p. 4). Although *Bill 56* outlines the responsibilities of principals with regards to responding to all reported incidents of bullying and violence in their schools, the participants worried that some students would never come forward and they would never have the whole picture of the situation. The challenge of "getting it right" was seen as a persistent and startlingly real pressure as they began to gather the data through polls and surveys of their students and staff. What was promising is that principals showed leadership in dealing with this hard and stressful issue in their schools, and actually preferred that the responsibility to "get it right" was on their shoulders. As Kotter (2012) noted, the change process is never effective unless it is driven by high-quality leadership and "not just excellent management" (p. 22).

In order to be successful in their efforts, principals emphasized the importance of getting staff, students, and parents to "buy in" and actively support the idea that schools need to be bullying-free and violence-free. Although it seemed natural that the participants expect this from everyone, they acknowledged that bullying was a multifarious phenomenon and admitted that not all members of their school community were on board with the processes they were trying to put in place. This reality shows that the challenge for school administrators to be leaders of both organizational and pedagogical change is an intricate and important process if schools are to achieve desired results in all areas of school life. Kotter (2012) explained that school administrators' task of implementing change processes and policies requires high confidence and competence related to personal and professional characteristics. Although it may be argued that *Bill 56* does not require any collective buy-in in a literal sense, the participants noted that for it to be effective legislation, members of the school community must go beyond just abiding by the rules and policies. The participants recognized that if the expectations are to be fulfilled, and the ultimate goal of a safe school is to be achieved, much more complex interactions must take place. The discussions with the participants revealed that effective buy-in, in the context of *Bill 56*, could be defined simply as the voluntary acceptance of an idea as worthwhile, and recognition that adults must keep kids safe. According to Kotter and Whitehead (2010), effective leaders help others understand the necessity of a desired change, help others accept a common vision and mission, and inspire them to take action to achieve the desired outcome.

Finally, participants noted the challenge process of developing trusting relationships in a school. Based on the information gleaned from surveying the students as part of *Bill 56*-related initiatives, some participants learned about the lack of faith and trust some students had in the adults in their own school. As they pointed out, whether in the context of *Bill 56* or in a general sense, when trust does not exist in a school, people do not feel safe. A lack of trust, the participants stated, could lead to: less reporting of incidents, a possible increase of incidents as a result, a resentment building in students towards schooling, feelings of lack of safety among staff and students, and a host of other negative possibilities. This challenging perspective was described by Tschannen-Moran (2014):

> Principals and other school leaders need to earn the trust of the stakeholders in their school community if they are to be successful. They need to understand how trust is built and how it is lost. Getting smarter about trust will help school leaders foster more successful schools (p. 8).

A necessary element to enacting the spirit of *Bill 56*, and giving meaning to the legislation is establishing trust with the students so that they trust the adults to report issues and they trustfully respond to adult interventions. Fullan (2014) noted, "Spreading trust entails mastering directness and honesty about performance expectations; following through with actions on commitments made; ensuring clear understanding of key communications; and being comfortable in dealing with conflict" (p. 130). Similarly, Lencioni (2012) posited that a leader is responsible for establishing an environment of transparent trust where people are completely comfortable, honest, and vulnerable with one another. Furthermore, principals expressed how challenging it is for school leaders to cultivate trust, and then maintain it once established. It was encouraging to see trust being described by respondents as essential if their schools were going to achieve the requirements of *Bill 56*. Therefore, they vowed that their schools were going to become safe, positive, and healthy environments, and that as role-models they were committed to this promise to follow the written expectations set forth in *Bill 56*. As Tschannen-Moran (2014) wrote, "being a positive model is never more necessary than when it comes to cultivating a culture of trust. Discontinuity between word and deed will quickly erode a principal's ability to lead" (p. 256). Similarly, principals in Kutsyuruba et al. (2011) believed that trust restoration efforts are to be undertaken despite considerable amounts of effort and time dedication and all the hurdles and disappointments.

Supports of the Anti-Bullying Legislation *Bill 56*

Participants regarded the following as supports brought on by *Bill 56*: (1) the support of the school board in challenging cases; (2) the support derived from developing an effective anti-bullying team and program; (3) the support through personal reflection on their practice and learning together with other principals; and, (4) the legislation's framework support as a change agent.

The support from the board office provided participants with more confidence when making difficult decisions in the context of handling future bullying cases. Of particular value was the support they received from their director of education after complaints were made about school-level decisions; it gave them the feeling of validation in the work they were doing. Tschannen-Moran and Gareis (2005) cited district support as a significant contributor to principal self-efficacy. In particular, their study revealed that the support afforded to principals from the superintendent had significant impact.

The participants appreciated the Olweus Program training afforded to the schools and principals of the entire school board. The school board mandated that all its principals be trained in the Olweus Program, in recognition of one of the leading international authorities on bullying. They credited this opportunity for providing principals with a practical framework from which they could draw ideas, interventions, and policies. Participants noted that *Bill 56* attempted to mandate schools to include in their approach key principles that are parallel to those in the Olweus Program (Olweus, 1993; Olweus & Limber, 2007a): (1) positive and involved adults; (2) firm limits on unacceptable behaviour; (3) fair, clear, and consistent discipline and consequences vs. punishment; and, (4) behaviour by adults that does not lead to authoritative adult-child interactions. The participants appreciated that one of the strengths of having had to work with Olweus was the fact that the directives for adults were strictly laid out. As found by Tschannen and Gareis (2005), district-level support with regards to resources shared with principals contributed to principals' self-efficacy and confidence.

Interview findings indicated that participants gave considerable praise to the teams that have formed in their own schools and the impact these committees have had on the culture of the school. This is congruent with the findings of Tschannen-Moran and Gareis (2005), who explained that the most "strongly related support variable in principals' self-efficacy ... was the perceived support from constituent populations at the building level" (p. 107). The authors stated that this "bottom-up" support from teachers and students mattered the most to their participants. The principals in this study mentioned the importance of school board support of their work as important, but repeatedly referred to the importance of teamwork from the school community to make *Bill 56* work.

The participants were a closely-knit group of principals, as their school board was a small one with a culture of positive principal collegiality. This finding linked to what the participants considered as an important factor contributing to their support system. The participants' experiences of working together to share plans and discuss best practices was congruent with Fullan's (2014) claims and the concept that principals must be open to working with each other for the betterment of all the schools in the board. Fullan (2014) argued that being a "district team player" is key to that principal's effectiveness. Finally, the participants revealed that the process of being interviewed about *Bill 56* and reflecting on their own personal leadership practices were very positive experiences that affected their understanding and practice, and consequently their resiliency towards the challenges.

Through the context-oriented document analysis, it could be inferred that *Bill 56* is a change agent in the educational scene in Quebec. As such, *Bill 56* brought to principals the requirement that a team be formed and the intent, one could concur, was to legislate a team-oriented approach. It was clear that supervising and managing the actions of students was one component of the expectations laid out in *Bill 56*; however, it could also be inferred that the emphasis of *Bill 56* was mainly on the actions of adults. Participants realized that they could not put in place structures and interventions by themselves, and that the teaching staff was important in evolving a school's culture by role-modelling desired behaviours and implementing the essence of the plan by reporting potential issues. This belief in the importance of staff buy-in converged with the work on distributed leadership (Harris, 2012, 2013a, 2013b), a model that is focused on collaborative work of administrators, teachers, support staff, and students as leaders. Hargreaves (2007) described distributed leadership as central to system reconfiguration and organizational redesign that necessitates lateral, flatter decision-making processes. Although it is not without its risks, for those "genuinely seeking transformation and self-renewal, this is a risk well worth taking" (Harris & Spillane, 2008, p. 33).

Overall, *Bill 56*'s policy framework support is evident in the intent to create a long-term positive and healthy school climate. Well-written and disseminated policies, Caldwell and Spinks (1988) stated, provide clarity, stability, continuity, consistency, and an overall feeling that decisions will be made according to a standard policy. Moreover, school administrators are positioned as key leaders in the process of successful policy implementation (Sergiovanni, 1984, 1992, 2005; Sergiovanni & Starratt, 2002). The *Bill 56* framework's scaffolding is intended to fulfil this role by requiring principals to invest time, efforts, and funds and to maintain cooperative relationships and teamwork in order to create school environments that are safe and conducive for learning and healthy development (Smith et al., 2005; Yukl, 1994).

Conclusions and Implications

In sum, the findings suggest that *Bill 56* had a positive impact on school culture. Although the implementation of *Bill 56* presented some challenges to the participants, the overall consensus was that *Bill 56* positively impacted the work lives of principals. Participants acknowledged that creating and maintaining a healthy school climate by being transformative leaders was one of their main goals, and that *Bill 56* has provided the framework to achieve that goal. We conclude this chapter with some research implications for practice, policy, and further research.

As Hoy and Miskel (1978) stated, principals must approach complex school problems as decision makers, and "decision makers need relevant facts" (p. 272). The primary responsibility to lead the way is on the principal. The following list of potential implications for practice of principals, students, school anti-bullying committees, school staff, and schools boards is based upon the data from the participants and *Bill 56* itself. Participants advocated that school administrators should use *Bill 56* to their advantage, making certain that everyone in the school is well-informed and that a common language is shared among all. There should be a clear understanding of the step-by-step process that will take place should they choose to report an incident. It was emphasized that how adults approach each incident reported by students is a central aspect in building individual and collective trust, as well as the overall success of the intervention. School leadership would benefit by focussing its attention on the effectiveness of staff implementation of a written plan, and would benefit from school boards' standardized training. School board interventions could include specific, standard, province-wide professional development and resources, along with a standardized data collection process that could be recognized province-wide for the purpose of evaluating the implementation of *Bill 56*. School leadership would benefit from a deeper understanding that principals require time in their schools to develop the trusting relationships needed to create positive school climates.

In terms of implications for policy, this study facilitated an enriched understanding of how school principals perceived their own ability to address bullying and violence in a school setting. School leaders, school board personnel, and provincial level personnel can collaboratively play a role in developing and implementing anti-bullying legislation effectively. Principals and school anti-bullying committees would benefit from a provincially standardized data collection system focussed on the effectiveness of their anti-bullying and violence prevention programming. *Bill 56*'s requirement that there be a formal reporting of incidents of bullying to the board by the principal must be more clearly outlined, helping to define what exactly must be reported to the school board and what mechanism principals use to report incidents. Participants recommended that succession planning policies allow principals to remain in schools "longer than five years when improvement efforts are doing well" (Hargreaves, 2005, p. 172). The implementation of *Bill 56* came with little overall training from the Ministry of Education in Quebec (although, as noted by the participants, some training was provided by their school boards). Therefore, it is important that effective, relevant, ongoing training by committed staff be made possible to allow for opportunities to implement their training, reflect upon the implementation, and consistently improve the way schools intervene in bullying situations. Students would benefit from standard and consistent follow-ups when students are bullied, and evidence collected as to whether staff and interventions are having the desired results is also important.

Finally, we conclude with implications for further research. This study used a phenomenological perspective that sought to examine the insights of principals within the context of their experiences dealing with the phenomenon of bullying in Quebec schools. This phenomenological research project followed and focused on *Bill 56*, the challenges it presented the participants, the participants' perceptions, and the impact on the confidence of principals in Quebec schools. This methodology also invited the participants to reflect upon their lived experiences and encouraged them to share their reflections in their own way (van Manen, 1990). Further study using different approaches to methodology (quantitative and mixed methods) would enhance our understanding of the school safety issues that principals and their students experience. Using data collection that mixes anecdotal, quantitative, and qualitative methods may lead a school or school board to a more in-depth understanding of the level of safety their students feel. Furthermore, more studies are needed to link the impact of the importance of the pedagogical approach to anti-bullying initiatives in schools (e.g., classroom and school-wide lessons). Similarly, a further study would do well to explore the link between leadership approaches and the effective implementation of anti-bullying initiatives in school settings, especially around the issue of how trust is built, maintained, and sustained by principals in the context of addressing school safety, violence, and anti-bullying issues.

References

Anderson, M., Kaufman, J., Simon, T.R., Barrios, L., Paulozzi, L., Ryan, G. ... School-Associated Violent Deaths Study Group. (2001). School-associated violent deaths in the United States, 1994-1999. *Journal of the American Medical Association, 286*(21), 2695–2702.

Auditor General of Quebec. (2005). *Report to the national assembly for 2004-2005, Volume 1.* Retrieved from http://www.vgq.gouv.qc.ca/en/en_publications/en_rap port-annuel/en_fichiers/en_Rapport2004-2005-T1.pdf.

Avolio, B.J. (1999). *Full leadership development: Building the vital forces in organizations.* Thousand Oaks, CA: Sage Publications.

Avolio, B.J., & Bass, B. (1988). Transformational leadership, charisma, and beyond. In J.G. Hunt, B.R. Baliga, H.P. Dachter, & C.A. Schriessheim (Eds.), *Emerging leadership vistas* (pp. 29–50). Lexington, MA: Lexington Books.

Bandura, A. (1997). *Self-efficacy: The exercise of control.* New York, NY: W.H. reeman Company.

Barnett, K., & McCormick, J. (2003). Vision, relationships and teacher motivation: A case study. *Journal of Educational Administration, 41*(1), 55–73.

Bass, B.M. (1985). *Leadership and performance beyond expectations.* New York, NY: Free Press.

Bass, B.M. (1995). Theory of transformational leadership redux. *The Leadership Quarterly, 6*(4), 463–478.

Bauer, N., Lozano, P., & Rivara, F.P. (2007). The effectiveness of the Olweus Bullying Prevention Program in public middle schools: A controlled trial. *Journal of Adolescent Health, 40*(3), 266–274.

Beran, T., & Shapiro, B. (2005). Evaluation of an anti-bullying program: Student reports of knowledge and confidence to manage bullying. *Canadian Journal of Education, 28*(4), 700–717.

Bickmore, K. (2011). Policies and programming for safer schools: Are "anti-bullying" approaches impeding education for peacebuilding? *Educational Policy, 25*(4), 648–687.

Black, S.A., & Jackson, E. (2007). Using bullying incident density to evaluate the Olweus Bullying Prevention Programme. *School Psychology International, 28*(5), 623–638.

Blanchfield, K., & Ladd, P. (2013). *Leadership, violence, and school climate: Case studies in creating non-violent schools.* New York, NY: R & L Education.

Blase, J.J., Derick, C., & Strathe, M. (1986). Leadership behavior of school principals in relation to teacher stress, satisfaction, and performance. *Journal of Humanistic Counseling, Education, and Development, 24*(4), 159–171.

Booren, L.M., & Handy, D.J. (2009). Students' perceptions of the importance of school safety strategies: An introduction to the IPSS Survey. *Journal of School Violence, 8*(3), 233–250.

Bosworth, K., Ford, L., & Hernandaz, D. (2011). School climate factors contributing to student and faulty perceptions of safety in select Arizona schools. *Journal of School Health, 81*(4), 194–200.

Boulton, M.J., Trueman, M., & Murray, L. (2008). Associations between peer victimization, fear of future victimization and disrupted concentration on class work among junior school pupils. *British Journal of Educational Psychology, 78,* 473–489.

Bowen, G. (2009). Document analysis as a qualitative research method. *Qualitative Research Journal, 9*(2), 27–40.

Bulach, C., Boothe, D., & Pickett, W. (1998). "Should nots" for school principals: Teachers share their views. *Journal of School Research and Information, 16*(1), 16–20.

Caldwell, B.J., & Spinks, J.M. (1988). *The self-managing school.* London, ON: Falmer Press.

Coloroso, B. (2002). *The bully, the bullied, and the bystander: From pre-school to high school: How parents and teachers can help break the cycle of violence.* Toronto, ON: Harper Collins.

Connolly, J., Pepler, D., Craig, W., & Taradash, A. (2000). Dating experiences of bullies in early adolescence. *Child Maltreatment, 5*(4), 299–310.

Cornell, D., & Mayer, M. (2010). Why do school order and safety matter? *Educational Researcher, 39*(1), 7–15.

Craig, W.M., Pepler, D.J., Murphy, A., & McCauig-Edge, H. (2010). What works in bullying prevention? In E. Vernberg & B. Biggs (Eds.), *Preventing and treating bullying and victimization* (pp. 215–242). London, UK: Oxford Press.

Creswell, J.W. (2007). *Qualitative inquiry and research design: Choosing among five approaches.* Thousand Oaks, CA: Sage.

Demaray, M.K., Malecki, C.K., Jenkins, L.N., & Westermann, L.D. (2012). Social support in the lives of students involved in aggressive and bullying behaviors. In S. Jimerson, A. Nickerson, M.J. Mayer, & M.J. Furlong (Eds.), *Handbook of school violence and school safety: International research and practice* (2nd ed., pp. 57–67). New York, NY: Taylor and Francis Group.

Devine, J., & Cohen, J. (2007). *Making our school safe: Strategies to protect children and promote learning.* New York, NY: Teachers College Press.

Education Act, 2012, c. 13 s. 3 (Quebec).

Ferguson, C.J., San Miguel, C., Kilburn, J.C., & Sanchez, P. (2007). The effectiveness of school-based anti-bullying programs: A meta-analytic review. *Criminal Justice Review, 32*(4), 40–414.

Fullan, M. (2010). *Motion leadership: The skinny on becoming change savvy.* Thousand Oaks, CA: Corwin.

Fullan, M. (2014). *The principal: Three keys to maximizing impact.* San Francisco, CA: Jossey-Bass.

Greene, M.B. (2005). Reducing violence and aggression in schools. *Trauma, Violence, & Abuse, 6*(3), 236–253.

Hansen, E.M. (1991). *Educational administration and organizational behavior.* Boston, MA: Allyn & Bacon.

Hargreaves, A. (2005). Leadership successions. *The Educational Forum, 69*(2), 163–173.

Hargreaves, A. (2007). *System re-design – 1: The road to transformation.* London: SSAT.

Harris, A. (2012). Distributed leadership: Implications for the role of the principal. *Journal of Management Development, 31*(1), 20–32.

Harris, A. (2013a). Distributed leadership: Friend or foe? *Educational Management and Administration, 41*(5), 545–554.

Harris, A. (2013b). *Distributed leadership matters: Perspectives, practicalities, and potential.* New York, NY: Corwin Press.

Harris, A., & Spillane, J. (2008). Distributed leadership through the looking glass. *Management in Education, 22*(1), 31–34.

Hornett, M. (2001). Transformational leadership in the health promoting school. *Orbit, 31*(2), 13–15.

Howard, K.A., Flora, J., & Griffin, M. (1999). Violence-prevention programs in schools: State of the science and implications for future research. *Applied and Preventative Psychology, 8*(3), 197–215.

Hoy, W.K., & Feldman, J.A. (1987). Organizational health: The concept and its measure. *Journal of Research and Development in Education*, *20*(4), 30–38.

Hoy, W.K., & Hannum, J.W. (1997). An empirical assessment of organizational health and student achievement. *Educational Administration Quarterly*, *33*(3), 290–311.

Hoy, W.K., & Miskel, C.G. (1978). *Educational administration: Theory, research, and practice*. New York, NY: Random House.

Hoy, W.K., & Miskel, C.G. (2001). *Educational administration: Theory, research and practice* (6th ed.). Boston, MA: McGraw-Hill.

Hoy, W.K., & Miskel, C.G. (2005). *Education administration: Theory, research, and practice* (7th ed.). New York, NY: McGraw-Hill.

Hoy, W.K., & Tarter, C.J. (1997). *The road to open and healthy schools: A handbook for change, elementary edition*. Thousand Oaks, CA: Corwin.

Jimerson, S.R., Hart, S.R., & Renshaw, T.L. (2012). Conceptual foundations for understanding youth engaged in antisocial and aggressive behaviors. In S. Jimerson, A. Nickerson, M. Mayer, & M. Furlong (Eds.), *Handbook of school violence and school safety: International research and practice* (2nd ed., pp. 3-14), New York, NY: Taylor and Francis Group.

Josephson, G. (2004). *A model of depressive symptoms in gay men* (Unpublished doctoral dissertation). University of Ottawa, Ottawa, ON.

Karcher, M.J. (2004). Connectedness and school violence: A framework for developmental interventions. In E.R. Gerler (Ed.), *Handbook of school violence* (pp. 7–40). Binghamton, NY: Haworth Press.

Kelley, R.C., Thornton, B., & Daugherty, R. (2005). Relationships between measures of leadership and school climate. *Education*, *126*(1), 17–25.

Kotter, J. (2008). *A sense of urgency*. Boston, MA: Harvard Press.

Kotter, J., Whitehead, L.A. (2010). *Buy-in: Saving a good idea from being shot down*. Boston, MA: Harvard Press.

Kotter, J. (2012). *Leading change*. Boston, MA: Harvard Press.

Kutsyuruba, B., Walker, K., & Noonan, B. (2011). Restoring broken trust in the work of school principals. *International Studies in Educational Administration*, *39*(2), 81–95.

Leithwood, K. (2007). What we know about educational leadership. In J. Burger, C. Webber, & P. Klinck (Eds.), *Intelligent leadership: Constructs for thinking educational leaders* (Vol. 6, pp. 41–66). Dordrecht, The Netherlands: Springer.

Leithwood, K., & Jantzi, D. (1991). Transformational leadership: How principals can help reform school cultures. *School Effectiveness and School Improvement, 1*(4), 249–281.

Lencioni, P. (2012). *The advantage: Why organizational health trumps everything else in business.* San Francisco, CA: Jossey-Bass.

Lezotte, L. (1991). *Correlates of effective schools: The first and second generation.* Okemos, MI: Effective school Products.

Loukas, A. (2007). What is school climate? High-quality school climate is advantageous for all students and may be particularly beneficial for at-risk students. *Leadership Compass, 5*(1), 1–3.

Lunenburg, F.C. (2010). School violence in America's schools. *Focus on Colleges, Universities, and Schools, 4*(1), 1–6.

Lynch, M. (2012). *A guide to effective school leadership theories.* New York, NY: Routledge.

Marzano, R.J. (2000). *A new era of school reform: Going where the research takes us.* Aurora, CO: Mid-Continent Research for Educational Learning.

Marzano, R.J., Waters, T., & McNulty, B.A. (2005). *School leadership that works: From research to results.* Alexandria, VA: ASCD.

Maslow, A.H. (1943). A theory of human motivation. *Psychological Review, 50*(4), 370–96.

Maslow, A.H. (1954). *Motivation and personality.* New York, NY: Harper.

Mayer, M., & Furlong, M. (2010). How safe are our schools? *Educational Researcher, 39*(1), 16-26.

Melbourne Department of Education and Training (MDET). (2006). *Safe schools are effective schools.* East Melbourne, Victoria: S. R. Frankland.

Merrell, K.W., Gueldner, B.A., Ross, S.W., & Isava, D.M. (2008). How effective are school bullying intervention programs? A meta-analysis of intervention research. *School Psychology Quarterly, 23*(1), 26–42.

Nansel, T.R., Overpeck, M., Pilla, R.S., Ruan, W.J., Simons-Morton, B., & Scheidt, P. (2001). Bullying behaviors among US youth: Prevalence and association with psychological adjustment. *Journal of the American Medical Association, 285*(16), 2094–2100.

National School Climate Council. (2007). *The school climate challenge: Narrowing the gap between school climate research and school climate policy, practice guidelines and teacher education policy.*

Northouse, P.G. (2007). *Leadership: Theory and practice.* Thousand Oaks, CA: Sage Publications.

Olweus, D. (1993). *Bullying at school: What we know and what we can do.* Blackwell, MA: Malden.

Olweus, D., & Limber, S.P. (2007a). *Olweus bullying prevention program: teacher's guide.* Center City, MN: Hazelden.

Olweus, D., & Limber, S.P. (2007b). *Olweus bullying prevention program: schoolwide guide.* Center City, MN: Hazelden.

Osborne, J.W. (1994). Some similarities and differences among phenomeno-logical and other research methods of psychological qualitative research. *Canadian Psychology, 35*(2), 167–189.

Osher, D., Dwyer, K., Jimerson, S.R., & Brown, J.A. (2012). Developing safe, supportive, and effective schools: Facilitating student success to reduce school violence. In S. Jimerson, A. Nickerson, M. Mayer, & M. Furlong (Eds.), *Handbook of school violence and school safety: International research and practice* (2nd ed., pp. 27-44). New York, NY: Taylor and Francis Group.

Pagliocca, P.M., Limber, S.P., & Hashima, P. (2007). *Evaluation report for the Chula Vista Olweus bullying prevention program.* Unpublished report prepared for the Chula Vista (CA) Police Department.

Patton, M.Q. (2002). *Qualitative research and evaluation methods* (3rd ed.). Thousand Oaks, CA: Sage.

Pepper, K., & Hamilton T.L. (2002). Making a change: The effects of the leadership role on school climate. *Learning Environments Research, 5,* 155–166.

Quebec Ministère de l'Éducation, du Loisir et du Sport. (2009). *Violence in the schools: Let's work on it together.* Quebec: Gouvernement du Québec.

Quebec Official Publisher. (2012). *Bill 56: An Act to prevent and stop bullying and violence in school.* Retrieved from http://www2.publications-duquebec.gouv.qc.ca/ dynamicSearch/telecharge.php?type=5&-file=2012C19A.PDF.

Reeves, D.B. (2008). *Reframing teacher leadership to improve your school.* Alexandria, VA: ASCD.

Reeves, D.B. (2009). *Leading change in your school: How to conquer myths, build commitment, and get results.* Alexandria, VA: Association for School Development.

Rigby, K. (1997). What children tell us about bullying in schools. *Children Australia, 22*(2), 28–34.

Rigby, K. (2001). Health consequences of bullying and its prevention in schools. In J. Juvonen & S. Graham (Eds.), *Peer harassment in school*. New York, NY: Guilford Press.

Rigby, K. (2002a). *A meta-evaluation of methods and approaches to reducing bullying in pre-schools and early primary school in Australia*. Canberra, Australia: Australian Attorney-General's Department.

Rigby, K. (2002b). *New perspectives on bullying*. Melbourne, Australia: Astam Books.

Rigby, K. (2003). Consequences of bullying in schools. *Canadian Journal of Psychiatry, 48*(9), 583–588.

Rigby, K., & Slee, P.T. (1991). Bullying among Australian school children: Reported behavior and attitudes toward victims. *Journal of Social Psychology, 131*(5), 615–627.

Robinson, J.P., & Espelage, D.L. (2011). Inequities in educational and psychological outcomes between LGBTQ and straight students in middle and high school. *Educational Researcher, 40*(7), 315–330.

Roland, E. (2002). Bullying, depressive symptoms and suicidal thoughts. *Educational Research, 44*(1), 55–67.

Rothon, C., Head, J., Klineberg, E., & Stansfeld, S. (2011). Can social support protect bullied adolescents from adverse outcomes? A prospective study on the effects of bullying on the educational achievement and mental health of adolescents at secondary schools in East London. *Journal of Adolescence, 34*(3), 579–588.

Salmivalli, C., Kaukiainen, A., Kaistaniemi, L., & Lagerspetz, K.M. (1999). Self- evaluated self-esteem, peer evaluated self-esteem, and defensive egotism as predictors of adolescents' participation in bullying situations. *Personality and Social Psychology Bulletin, 25*(10), 1268–1278.

Sergiovanni, T.J. (1984). Leadership and excellence in schools. *Educational Leadership, 41*(5), 4–13.

Sergiovanni, T.J. (1990). Adding value to leadership gets extraordinary results. *Educational Leadership, 47*(8), 23–27.

Sergiovanni, T.J. (1992). *Moral leadership: Getting to the heart of school improvement*. San Francisco, CA: Jossey-Bass.

Sergiovanni, T.J. (2005). *The lifeworld of leadership: Creating culture, community, and personal meaning in our schools*. San Francisco, CA: Jossey-Bass.

Sergiovanni, T.J. (2009). *The principalship: A reflective practice perspective* (6th ed.). Boston, MA: Pearson.

Sergiovanni, T.J., & Starratt, R. (2002). *Supervision: A redefinition.* New York, NY: McGraw-Hill.

Smith, J.D., Cousins, J.B., & Stewart, R. (2005). Anti-bullying interventions in schools: Ingredients of effective programs. *Canadian Journal of Education, 28*(4), 739–762.

Smith, J.D., & Schneider, B.H. (2004). The effectiveness of whole-school antibullying programs: A synthesis of evaluation research. *School Psychology Review, 33*(4), 547–560.

Smith, P.K., Morita, J., Junger-Tas, D., Olweus, D., Catalano, R., & Slee, P.T. (1999). *The nature of school bullying: A cross-national perspective.* Routledge: London.

Smith, P.K., Smith, C., Osborn, R., & Samara, M. (2008). A content analysis of school anti-bullying policies: Progress and limitations. *Educational Psychology in Practice, 24*(1), 1–12.

Tschannen-Moran, M. (2003). Fostering organizational citizenship in schools: Transformational leadership. In W. Hoy & C. Miskel (Eds.), *Studies in leading and organizing schools* (pp. 157-179). Greenwich, CT: Information Age Publishing Inc.

Tschannen-Moran, M. (2004). *Trust matters: Leadership for successful schools.* San Francisco, CA: Jossey-Bass.

Tschannen-Moran, M. (2014). *Trust matters: Leadership for successful schools* (2nd ed.). San Francisco, CA: Jossey-Bass.

Tschannen-Moran, M., & Gareis, C.R. (2004). Principals' sense of efficacy: Assessing a promising construct. *Journal of Educational Administration, 42*(5), 573–585.

Tschannen-Moran, M., & Gareis, C.R. (2005, November). *Cultivating principals' sense of efficacy: Supports that matter.* Paper presented at the Annual Meeting of the University Council for Educational Administration, Nashville, TN.

Ttofi, M.M., Farrington, D.P., & Baldry, A.C. (2008). *Effectiveness of programmes to reduce school bullying.* Swedish National Council for Crime Prevention.

Van Manen, M. (1990). *Researching the lived experiences: Human science for an action sensitive pedagogy.* London, ON: Althouse Press.

Waldman, D.A., Bass, B.M., & Einstein, W.O. (1987). Leadership and outcomes of performance appraisal processes. *Journal of Occupational Psychology, 60*(3), 177–186.

Wessler, S., & Preble, W. (2003). *The respectful school: How educators and students can conquer hate and harassment.* Alexandria, VA: Association for Supervision and Curriculum Development.

Whitlock, J.L. (2006). Youth perceptions of life at school: Contextual correlates of school connectedness in adolescence. *Applied Developmental Science, 10*(1), 13–29.

Wolke, S., & Woods, D. (2003). Does the content of anti-bullying policies inform us about the prevalence of direct and relational bullying behaviour in primary schools? *Educational Psychology, 23*(4), 381–401.

Yukl, G. (1994). *Leadership in organizations* (3rd ed.). Englewood Cliffs, NJ: Prentice.

SECTION THREE

Higher Education and the Law

CHAPTER 14

Clarifying Institutional Legal Responsibilities to Address Sexual Violence as University Contexts Expand Beyond Campus Borders to the Online Realm

Shaheen Shariff[1]

Abstract

This chapter addresses policy dilemmas confronted by University Administrators as they attempt to balance free expression, safety and protection, accountability, and regulation with due process and discipline when incidents of sexual violence occur in the "university context." The chapter unpacks the notion of what a "university context" means if the definition of rape culture is taken to include the online context and the continuum of sexual violence that include sexist and misogynist online comments, threats, non-consensual distribution of intimate images, peer rating of female or LGBTQ classmates, and sexist jokes about disabled or international students. The chapter addresses the policy vacuum and the increasingly blurred lines regarding institutional responsibilities to address off-campus and/or on-line sexual violence, and will discuss legal accountability through case law analysis and analysis of media reported incidents of sexual violence on Canadian campuses, as well as and

---

1   I would like to acknowledge my Research Assistants, Nazampal Jaswal, Chloe Garcia, Sarah Lewington, Alastair Hibberd, Emil Briones, Shannon Hutchison, Anna Goldfinch, and Esther Dionnes Desbiens, for their research contributions that inform this chapter and Chris Dietzel for his help with editing.

---

the subsequent university responses or lack thereof. It concludes by recommending a multi-sector partnership approach to reclaiming the role of universities in developing educational responses that will help reestablish their role as educators of society on issues such as sexual violence and civil responsibility.

Introduction and Context

The issue of sexual violence at universities across Canada and abroad has surfaced as an urgent public policy concern over the last three to four years (Backhouse, McRae, & Iyer, 2015; MacKay, 2013; Swain, 2015). This is not a new phenomenon. In the late 1980s and 90s, there was a wave of concerns about violence against women and other minorities on Canadian campuses (Hutchison, 2010), illustrating the enduring nature of the problem yet there is a dearth of evidence-based research on the extent and nature of the problem. Without evidence-based disciplinary policies, University responses may continue to have undesirable effects. University administrators confront unprecedented policy dilemmas because sexual violence is no longer limited to physical campuses; it also occurs among members of university communities on-line, off-campus and outside of classroom hours. This expansion of "university context" has blurred the lines of administrative responsibilities, accountability, appropriate regulation, and legal liability. Policy and decision-makers at post-secondary institutions often grapple with protecting students, faculty members, and staff who are targeted or become victims of sexual violence and survive to report the incidents ("survivors"). Administrators confront the need to balance protection of survivors, who are often justifiably shocked, afraid and angry, with the due process rights of "alleged perpetrators" on- and offline. This is especially important in universities because, ultimately, the ability of victims and perpetrators to continue with their studies, and even their future careers are at stake. Moreover, their physical and emotional health is often significantly affected (Hinduja & Patchin, 2010). Cyberbullying research confirms that perpetrators are often victims of violence themselves, which perpetuates the complexity and the need for fairness (Hinduja & Patchin, 2010). Add to this two other challenges: 1) The insistence by some university public-relations offices that public acknowledgement of such problems and additional media publicity could negatively affect their university's reputation (Lalonde, 2014); and 2) The stance, adopted by several in-house legal departments, that university students are adults – and therefore any forms of sexual violence that occur online or physically off-campus are not within the purview of university administrative obligations. In order to unravel and clarify the issues and responsibilities, the discussion in this chapter is framed around three key considerations:

1. Universities do not function within a social or cultural bubble. How do social sectors such as the legal justice system, popular culture, and media (news and social media), tacitly condone, normalize, and sustain a culture of sexual violence within and outside universities that influence the university context. To what extent are these embedded in what is sometimes described as "rape culture?"[2]

2. What do we mean by "university context," and what are the boundaries of legal responsibility and liability of universities to protect victims and survivors of sexual violence, prevent tacit condoning of sexual violence, and keep campus contexts free of barriers to safety, protection, due process and worry-free learning when it occurs online, outside of the physical campus and operating teaching hours and on-line?

3. What approaches can universities undertake to develop sustainable policy and educational responses to sexual violence and "rape culture" in an online contemporary society that would help reclaim their

---

2 "Rape culture" is a controversial definition. I explain the controversy later in the chapter. Feminist theories recognize rape culture as the way in which sexist societal attitudes and language tacitly condone, minimize and/or normalize sexual violence, mostly against women, but also against other genders through institutions, communities, and individuals. Rooted in discrimination, rape culture surfaces along a continuum of intersecting, sexist behaviours, which include jokes, harassment, non-consensual distribution of intimate images, and rape (Buchwald, Fletcher, & Roth, 2005; Kelly, 2013; Williams, 2007). These intersecting forces reinforce its presence in universities. The definition used in this chapter draws on that definition, but expands it to include the online context such as social media and the continuum of sexual violence that include sexist and misogynist on- and offline comments, threats, non-consensual online distribution of intimate images, peer rating of female or LGBTQ and trans-gender classmates, and online sexist jokes about disabled or international students. It also includes sexist comedy, intersecting forms of racism, sexism, homophobia, religion, and ableism.

---

fundamental role as central institutions of higher education, a role which, ultimately, is to educate and inform greater society?

To begin addressing these concerns, I provide examples of recent, highly publicized incidents of sexual violence at Canadian universities. Next I present the main critiques of university and public policy approaches in Canada and the United States within the framework of the three key concerns noted above, and draw on court decisions that clarify university legal obligations to address sexual violence that takes place off-campus or online. These obligations are discussed within definitions of "rape culture" as it might be informed, influenced, and/or prevented by the legal justice system, arts and popular culture, and news media and social media. The objective of the discussion framed in this way is to provide university administrators with a clearer appreciation of the parameters of their legal responsibilities, specifically in a "university context" that fluctuates between social and learning environments that include an inseparable overlap between on and off-campus and on- and offline spaces. Educational institutions, especially when there is a nexus to the university between perpetrators and victims/survivors, an obligation to act responsibly, and with accountability.

As part of a solution to the policy vacuum on sexual violence in universities, I argue that a multi-sectored, partnered approach shows greater promise than reactive policy development that fails to protect either victim or alleged perpetrator, especially when incidents are censored or over-regulated. To that end, my chapter concludes with an overview of a 7-year federally funded research project of which I am the Principal Investigator and Project Director (IMPACT: Collaborations to Address Sexual Violence on Campus, www.mcgill.ca/definetheline).[3] The project examines the roles and influence of three public sectors on university contexts and cultures: A) the role of law; B) the role of arts and popular culture; and C) the role of news media and social media. All three tacitly

3 IMPACTS: Collaborations to address sexual violence on campus. Social Sciences and Humanities Research Council of Canada Partnership Grant Number: 895-2016-1026. Project Director, Shaheen Shariff, PhD. McGill University (referenced here as the "IMPACTS Project"). Some information available at www. mcgill.ca/definetheline which is currently under reconstruction with updates for the new project.

condone or sustain rape culture, but also have the power to mobilize awareness and implement sustainable prevention of sexual violence. Our partnership involves 12 university partners, 24 academics, 15 community partners, 14 collaborators and over 50 graduate researchers.

This collaborative approach reclaims the role of universities to educate students and society as a whole, while meeting the institutional legal obligations defined by the Supreme Courts - in both Canada and the United States - as they relate to sexual violence and cyber-sexual-violence, or cyberbullying of a sexual nature. This is especially true with regards to fostering a safe climate that is free of sexual discrimination and harassment, and which is conducive to learning. Our student-sector partnered approach overcomes the silo effect by bringing universities together to research, develop, and implement policies and programs together. The project is expected to provide a sustainable strategic model for Canadian universities as they navigate and attempt to balance the complex dilemmas presented in this chapter. Consider several highly publicized incidents which occurred over the last few years.

Sexual Violence at Canadian Universities

Media Publicized Incidents: In 2014, three critical events dominated Canadian news headlines: (1) Three male students at the University of Ottawa published "jokes" online about raping their female student union president (Ormiston, 2014); (2) Male and female students endorsed non-consensual sex through chants at St. Mary's University during freshmen orientation (CBC News, 2013a; CBC News, 2013b)— St. Mary's appointed Co-Applicant MacKay as Chair of a task force to investigate the incident; and (3) A group of male dentistry students at Dalhousie University made jokes in a Facebook group about drugging classmates with chloroform and sexually assaulting female students (Backhouse et al., 2015). Their comments and jokes raised particularly important concerns about how these male dental students would behave in a professional environment, and as to whether female patients would also be at risk.

Disciplinary Processes, Accountability and Student Activism: Traditional methods of punishment, such as expulsion or suspension, have proven to be inadequate to address the complex forces that enable rape culture at universities. As far back as the late 1980s and 90s, there was an earlier wave of concerns about violence against women and other minorities on Canadian campuses (Hutchison, 2010), illustrating the enduring nature of the problem. Meanwhile, without evidence-based disciplinary policies, hastily thrown together university responses may have undesirable effects. Our preliminary research discloses that thirty-two universities across Canada have implemented sexual violence policies (Define the Line Project, Draft White Paper, 2016). The extent to which these policies are transparent, consultative, and include the concerns of the university community and particular survivors, is yet to be determined under the Define the Line Project. This will be done through in depth analysis of all thirty-two policies and evaluation of related implementation approaches.

In the absence of a coherent sexual violence policy and subsequent to the dental school incident, Dalhousie University chose to engage in a restorative justice process with the dentistry students whereby the perpetrating male students and their targeted female classmates could meet in the presence of others. The Backhouse et al. (2015) Task Force observed, however, that this process placed undue pressure on one female complainant and ostracized the male whistleblower. The same report also highlighted a lack of communication between central administration and faculty administrators and staff as to what processes needed to be followed once the matter was reported. The report suggests clear and consistent reporting directions, safe spaces, and access to information and remedies at universities.

Need for Evidence-Based Research: Several news media features have drawn attention to the need for comprehensive, long-term academic studies on sexual violence in universities (Surman, 2014; Swain, 2014). Feminist scholars support this view and explain that implementing sexual assault, sexual harassment or sexual violence policies is not enough. They argue that "rape culture" in universities will not be diminished unless the roots of sexual violence that reside in wider society are addressed (Bailey

& Hanna, 2011; Shariff, 2015; Steeves, 2014). Furthermore, student advocacy groups and politicians have mobilized their anger and frustration into organized activism to hold universities to account when they have failed to address the issues in ways that support survivors – or worse, where university leaders have refused to acknowledge the seriousness of the problem (Porter, 2016). One example is the angry student, public, and political outcry and vigils that took place in Quebec City subsequent to Laval University's lack of immediate response to sexual assaults in the female student residences. A perpetrator broke into female dormitories and assaulted female students in the middle of the night. It took three days of protests before the university President came out and addressed students to say that something would be done (Porter, 2016).

Informed and Transparent Policies Take Time to Implement: When considered from a university administration perspective, decision-makers are often caught between a rock and a hard place. The recent attention to sexual violence has, on one hand, resulted in a rush to develop sexual violence policies and hire qualified staff members to receive and handle reports through clearly delineated processes. On the other hand, activists and scholars note that simply having a sexual violence, sexual assault, or sexual harassment policy in place (or all of these) is not enough (Desai, 2017; Lalonde, 2014). If the content of those policies has not been developed through a transparent process, taking into consideration the experiences and perspectives of all stakeholders, especially survivors, such policies simply add to the bureaucracy that has resulted in so much anger from activists. The reality is that consultative and transparent processes take time – sometimes at least one or two years to develop and implement effectively. In the meantime, despite well-intentioned administrative initiatives (e.g., new or updated sexual violence policies or Ad Hoc committees to engage in qualitative research to give all university stakeholders a voice), those administrations continue to be publicly called out by student activists for their perceived lack of action or slow progress in improving their responses satisfactorily.

Bypassing Official Reporting Processes and Turning to the Online Realm: This distrust by student activists and advocacy groups of their administrators (although sometimes justified), can impede progress even when university leaders are genuinely committed to improvement and change. For example, encouraged by the success of #rapedbutnever-reported (Montgomery, 2014), a hashtag that went viral online during former CBC celebrity talk show host Jian Ghomeshi's criminal trial, students at some universities disclosed their experiences with sexual violence on student union or related organizational social media pages (Desai, 2017), despite (or due to) the fact that these pages are highly public.

Although social media is a powerful medium through which to mobilize public awareness, in a university context disclosing sexual violence online limits students' legal options. Once they disclose on social media they close the door to accessing official university reporting processes (and to subsequent disciplinary and/or legal options). This places claimants and alleged perpetrators (students, faculty members, administrators, or staff) at significant risk of losing out on potential due process and legal remedies.

Moreover, when university administrators first hear about sexual violence incidents involving students, faculty, or other members of their campus communities through social media platforms easily accessed by media outlets, their options to take disciplinary or legal action are limited. Social media accusations against alleged perpetrators can also have devastating results: Alleged perpetrators are vulnerable and subject to trial in the court of public opinion.

Accordingly, it is essential that advocacy groups and university administrators are clear on their legal obligations and the limits of those obligations, vis-à-vis due process and protecting the human rights of both survivors and alleged perpetrators.[4] Although the pendulum needs to swing towards increased support of survivors, which I illustrate later in this chapter as shamefully lacking in the criminal justice system, it is imperative that universities as public institutions navigate realistic balances between free expression, safety, privacy, protection,

---

4 Elsewhere, I have made similar arguments for school administrators and
   their need to understand their legal parameters when dealing with cyberbullying,
   sexting, and the non-consensual distribution of intimate images online (see Shariff,
   2015, Sexting and Cyberbullying, Cambridge University Press).

regulation, and accountability—both on campus and online. Bringing the pendulum to the middle can be a very difficult task. Survivor disclosures on social media can also impact university reputations – a concern that might result in attempts to censor or cover up the issues (Bailey & Telford, 2008; boyd, 2014; Danay, 2010; Eltis, 2011; Lalonde, 2014, Shariff, Case, & Manley-Casimir, 2000), thus setting off a vicious cycle of accusations by advocates that the only options they have are to go public on social media.

Clearly, these nuanced challenges require an analysis of the extent to which universities are legally required to act in cases of sexual violence, the boundaries of their intervention and responsibilities, their fundamental obligations to members of their community, and, more pragmatically, the role of universities in society to model and educate sustainable prevention of sexual violence through their curricula and commitment to change. The incidents described above also raise issues about the need for strong leadership and clarity regarding reporting processes, as well as concerted efforts to balance free expression and equality rights. If university leaders respond to sexual violence with hastily developed policies and vague or disjointed processes, they risk legal challenges for breach of students' and others' constitutional or human rights. First and foremost it is essential that they understand their own context and culture thoroughly. If they are to successfully navigate these dilemmas, they need to address the considerations I raised at the outset, namely:

1. *Universities do not function within a social or cultural bubble. How do social sectors such as the legal justice system, popular culture, and media (news and social media), tacitly condone, normalize, and sustain a culture of sexual violence within and without universities that influence the university context. To what extent are these embedded in what is sometimes described as "rape culture?"*[5]

---

5 The definition used in this chapter includes the online context, such as social media and the continuum of sexual violence that include sexist and misogynist on- and offline comments, threats, non-consensual online distribution of intimate images, peer rating of female or LGBTQ and trans-gender classmates, and sexist jokes about disabled or international students, which encompasses comedy, hyperbole, intersecting forms of racism, sexism, homophobia, religion, and ableism.

Rape Culture as Consumed and Internalized within University Communities: In an earlier footnote I mention that "rape culture" is a controversial term and that I would expand on my use of the term in this paper. The term, as I see it, is better understood if we first consider key societal influences on the way university students in contemporary society internalize and live their world, with very few divisions between on- and offline social and/or ethical norms.

Influence of Media: University students as millennials are prolific consumers of social media, online news, and entertainment (Junco, Heiberger, & Loken, 2011; Mihailidis, 2014; Rosengard, Tucker-McLaughlin, & Brown, 2014). High-profile "Task Force Reports" (Backhouse et al., 2015; MacKay, 2013) observed that although rape culture in broader society is mirrored within universities, few studies focus on the influence of law, media, and popular culture on university communities.

Feminist theories recognize rape culture as the way in which sexist societal attitudes and language tacitly condone, minimize, and/or normalize sexual violence, mostly against women, but also against other genders, through institutions, communities, and individuals, including popular culture such as comedy, sitcoms, music lyrics, advertisements, and language, all of which sexualize and objectify women and members of the LGBTQ, ethnic minority, and disabled communities. Rooted in discrimination, rape culture surfaces along a continuum of intersecting, sexist behaviours, which include jokes, harassment, non-consensual distribution of intimate images and rape (Buchwald et al., 2005; Kelly, 2013; Williams, 2007). These intersecting forces reinforce its presence in universities. For example, a Quebec-based study, spearheaded by researchers at UQUAM (Bergeron, et al, 2016), found that attention to international students and students with disabilities is often overlooked in university policies and responses. International students tend to be "exoticized" by supervisors or student peers (Lee & Rice, 2007), making them more vulnerable to sexual violence and much less likely to come forward to report it.

Celebrities, Politicians and a Justice System that Tacitly Condones Rape Culture: Rape culture can also be modelled by celebrities, many of who operate with impunity or have the financial and systemic means to avoid accountability. In the United States, one of the world's most powerful politicians (a former reality show celebrity) engages in almost daily perpetration and modelling of rape culture, misogyny and cyberbullying against women, especially female reporters, often through his Twitter feed.[6] Another highly publicized example was, while campaigning, his famous "grab them by the pussy" comments that were caught on tape (YouTube, 2016). Other celebrities such as Bill Cosby and Jian Ghomeshi were charged with criminal sexual offences but largely escaped unscathed because of an adversarial legal justice system that is unduly harsh on complainants of sexual violence (Globe & Mail, 2017; Puente, 2017).

Increasingly blurred definitions and judicial applications of the legal notion of "consent," and loopholes that allow for large out of court settlements, reinforce the fact that survivors who come forward have minimal chance of success and a high expectation of their own backgrounds and reputations being maligned (METRAC, 2014; Patel, 2014; Surman, 2014; Swain, 2015). The high profile criminal trial of CBC celebrity talk show host Jian Ghomeshi (Boesveld, 2014; Donovan & Brown, 2014) highlighted that when survivors are unsure or uninformed as to the boundaries of consent they risk losing their case. Three of the nine women who came forward to report sexual violence by Ghomeshi testified in court. His highly proficient defence lawyer, Marie Heinan discredited their testimony with ease. Angry survivor advocates accused her of supporting rape culture. However, in an exclusive CBC interview with National News host Peter Mansbridge, Heinan explained she was simply doing her job within the confines of the existing criminal justice system (CBC, Mansbridge Interview with Marie Heinan, March 30, 2016); a system that needs to adapt to become more supportive of survivors of sexual violence. This perspective is supported by a YWCA infographic that illustrates that out of every 1,000 sexual assaults occurring in Canada each year, only 12 offenders are charged, and only 3 are convicted (Patel, 2014). Research also suggests that alleged perpetrators from racial

---

6 http://www.nbcnews.com/politics/politics-news/trump-twitter-attack-morning-joe-hosts-n778081.

minorities receive harsher treatment, less due process in universities, and longer jail sentences (Gerson & Suk, 2016). Two factors are responsible:

1. *An Adversarial and Out-dated Criminal Justice System:* Our criminal justice system is adversarial and is set up for one party to win. Defence counsel for alleged perpetrators are free to expose complainants past sexual histories, the way they dress, past relationships, and often their confused notions of consent, to establish reasonable doubt regarding their claims of sexual assault (Boesveld, 2014; Donovan & Brown, 2014). The process often involves slut-shaming and victim-blaming, tactics which are accepted and normalized within a justice system that is especially unsympathetic to female survivors of sexual assault (Shariff, 2015).

2. *Deeply embedded rape culture and need for sensitivity training:* There is an urgent need to sensitize the judiciary, prosecutors, and defence counsel to the realities of sexual violence in contemporary, racially and culturally diverse, on- and offline social contexts. The judiciary, prosecutors, police, and defence counsel need to become aware of the shifting and intersecting social norms that allow a higher threshold for misogynistic, racist, sexist, and homophobic jokes, slurs, online comments, non-consensual distribution of intimate images, and cyberbullying among millennials (Eltis, 2011; Shariff, 2015; Ybarra, Mitchell, Wolak, & Finkelor, 2006). Through their own insensitive, and highly offensive and misogynist comments about, and to, female complainants of sexual violence, the behaviour of a few Canadian male judges certainly contributed to and reflected rape culture attitudes. For example, comments by Canadian Federal Court Justice Camp that a homeless female victim of sexual violence "should have sat further back in the sink and kept her knees together..." while being raped, were highly inappropriate and also portrayed an economic bias against homelessness. Camp fought to keep his place on the bench but finally resigned as the House of Commons called for his dismissal. On March 8, 2017, The Canadian Judicial Council's report to Parliament (Canadian Judicial Council, 2017) noted that his conduct was "So manifestly and profoundly destructive of the concept of impartiality,

integrity and independence of the judicial role, that public confidence was sufficiently undermined (paragraph 11).

The result of these - and similar - responses by insensitive judges has resulted in significant pressure on universities to better educate their law students, but even more so on the Federal Government to legislate sensitivity training for judges to correct the imbalance. Legislation proposed by former opposition leader Rhona Ambrose is to be considered by the Senate at some point in the Fall of 2017 (Smith, 2017).

Rape Culture as a Controversial Term: For those of us who are familiar with constitutional protections under Section 15(2) of the Canadian Charter of Rights and Freedoms, as well as an understanding of Human Rights laws that fundamentally protect against discrimination and violence of any kind based on any form of difference, it is not a stretch to understand the notion of rape culture within the feminist perspective that I present. However, there are scholars both in Canada and the United States who vehemently dispute the fact that rape culture exists. McElroy (2016) argues that context or culture have nothing to do with sexual violence and that the accountability rests with individuals, their morals and behaviour, rather than social norms or systemic barriers. She then contradicts herself by stating that rape culture only exists in countries such as Afghanistan and Pakistan where women are systemically oppressed. With these blanket racialized assumptions, she effectively erases her own argument that sexual violence is an individual and not a cultural or systemic phenomenon. Others, such as Karian (2009) make a more complex and coherent argument that calls for consideration of feminist agency. She also argues that common perspectives on rape culture and resulting sexual violence policies ought to take into consideration Queer theories, individual agency, and evolving sexual norms; otherwise they unsuccessfully continue to address sexuality as viewed through traditional lenses which no longer apply in a contemporary society.

Ultimately, it is essential that university administrators understand the range of perspectives on rape culture so that their policies, processes, and curricular development are more relevant to the realities of their university communities' individual agency. As James Wertsch (1998) would argue, individuals internalize, afford, or resist information that they encounter and process every day. Thus it is important to examine the degree to which the law, arts and popular culture, and news and social media might be internalized, afforded, resisted or normalized in social relationships, and how this in turn might play out as offensive sexual behaviours or sexual violence in physical and virtual university environments. University administrators need to define and clarify the parameters of their own "university context" - which takes us to the second key consideration in our framework of discussion:

2. **What do we mean by "university context" and what are the boundaries of legal responsibility and liability of universities to protect victims and survivors of sexual violence, prevent tacit condoning of sexual violence, and keep campus contexts free of barriers to safety, protection, due process, and worry-free learning when it occurs outside of the physical campus and operating teaching hours and online?**

American Public Policy Context: American scholarship, statutory, and case law are informative in this regard, and provide a starting point for Canadian universities to assess whether they want to be bound by similar obligations. American and Canadian courts have handed down similar decisions when it comes to on- and off-campus speech or behaviours, especially when there is a nexus (or relationship) to the institution. The common law in both countries, at least to date, is also similar when it comes to the need to foster discriminatory-free and safe learning environments. Whether this will change with the Trump government and conservative Supreme Court appointees is yet to be determined. In the meantime, consider the current U.S. legal context as it relates to sexual violence:

Publicized Sexual Violence at American Campuses: Universities in the U.S. have also had their share of controversial incidents of sexual violence. One particular high profile case at Stanford University in California raised several important legal issues for consideration. Alleged perpetrator Brock Turner, was an Ivy League son of a rich family who was on the

Olympic swim team. He was accused of raping a female student who had drunk too much at a party and was unconscious during the rape. Two male students found and helped get her to the hospital. Stark differences emerged between the survivor's horrifying experience in giving police statements and telling her story in court, as a victim of rape, compared to Turner's experience as an alleged perpetrator at Stanford. His status as an Olympic team swimmer and son of a rich donor to the university; his social class and status within the institution clearly offered him significant protection. His father denied that his son could commit such a crime – publicizing his clean shaven Ivy League photograph. His father blamed the survivor and argued for reduced sentence given that his son's career and future would be ruined. Turner was released from jail after 3 months. By contrast, a young black student accused of a similar crime was jailed for 10 years without bail, illustrating the racial differences and the privileged role that class can play in such cases (Buncombe, 2016). These incidents, and how universities and the justice system handle them, not only raise thorny issues of equality and due process, but also draw attention to the learning environment and "culture" in universities, especially as to society's social norms in dealing with sexual violence based on ethnicity, race, and socio-economic class of the survivor or alleged perpetrator.

American Legal Response to Sexual Violence in Public Educational Institutions:

It is important at this juncture to highlight the American response to sexual violence over the last few years. Although the survivor was subjected to the same humiliating treatment in court as many of the Canadian survivors, the official response to sexual violence in American universities appears to have swung from a lack of support for survivors to overregulation of sexual behaviour on campuses in attempts to protect survivors.

In 2001, the U.S. Department of Education's Office of Civil Rights ("OCR") published a document entitled "Questions and Answers about Title IX and Sexual Violence," intended to clarify campuses' legal requirements regarding tying non-compliance to funding hold-backs if universities don't have in place sexual violence policies. This is in addition to earlier legislation, the *Clery Act* (2011), that prohibited institutions from sex discrimination by requiring universities to report any crimes on campus. Harvard scholars Gerson and Suk (2016) argue this has resulted in a "sex bureaucracy" on university campuses, where government appointed sexual violence officers create so much bureaucracy that they in effect regulate "sex." This is especially true when they conduct workshops about the meaning of "consent" and describe it as "enthusiastic" or tie it to the influence of alcohol.

This bureaucratic approach largely ignores the fact that so much sexual violence among classmates and members of university communities are perpetrated online – where there is no option for consent. My own research (Shariff, 2015) on sexting among millennials between ages 8 to 25 disclosed that non-consensual distribution of intimate images begins as early as age 8. We provided students who participated in our survey with two hypothetical scenarios that compared non-consensual online distribution of two separate photographs. The first featured "Angie" while drunk. The second featured Dana, who had sent her boy-friend an intimate sexual photograph of herself in confidence. We asked students to decide whether Angie or Dana were justified in being angry about the distribution of their photographs online. In Angie's case, 98% of the participants agreed she was right to be angry about non-consensual distribution of her photograph while she was drunk, because it would get her into trouble with her parents. Only 49% believed that Dana had a right to complain about her boyfriend's breach of trust and distribution of her nude photograph online without her permission. The notion of "enthusiastic" consent as described by Gearson and Suk (2016) becomes moot when sexually demeaning behaviour becomes so normalized among millennials. Dana, like her real life counterparts -- Rehteah Parsons and Amanda Todd had minimal opportunities to consent to distribution of her photograph. None of them had a say in the increasingly sexist, misogynist and life-threatening comments that continued to plague them online in their private time and on-campus when they returned to school.

Given these research findings, it is imperative that university administrators act when there is a "nexus" or connection through the university, between the individual who is humiliated, threatened and demeaned online and her/his perpetrator(s). The fact that this occurs online makes it even more important for universities to intervene because online sexual violence allows the wider public, and therefore numerous additional perpetrators to sexually harass, demean and threaten members of their own university community. Online sexual violence facilitates opportunities for entire classrooms or dormitories or athletic teams to engage in group cyberbullying such as the perpetration of sexual violence, sexist jokes, insults, demeaning comments and distribution of embarrassing photographs. Students or staff who become targets of such abuse have no options but to face their perpetrators *within the physical university context. They cannot escape them online either*. Surely this is not the type of behaviour or attitudes universities seek to foster within their communities. It creates a chilled or poisoned environment and as courts have noted, there are obligations on public institutions to ensure environments free of discrimination and harassment and conducive to learning.

The American College of Trial Lawyers in March, 2017 wrote a White Paper on Campus Sexual Assault Investigations that supports Geerson and Suk (2016). They argue that tying the reporting process to funding has the impact of reducing procedural due process and impartial investigations. They recommend that universities pay special attention to these as well as to the right to counsel, access to evidence, and notice of allegations for alleged perpetrators.

In Canada, universities and provincial governments are less inclined to get involved in regulating sexual violence, and have thus avoided regulating sex. Education is under provincial jurisdiction, and individual provinces have recently begun to introduce new legislation with similar requirements to those in the U.S. Currently, 32 universities have developed stand-alone sexual violence policies, mainly focused on health and safety, counselling, and academic support for survivors, including educating the campus community on consent and training designated staff to address complaints (Define the Line, 2016). The highly publicized case of Rehteah Parsons rape and suicide in Nova Scotia resulted in the *Protecting Canadians from Online Crime Act* (2014) and the Nova Scotia *Cyber Safety Act* (2013). The *Cyber-Safety Act* was struck down as unconstitutional in December, 2016.

Policy Makers Often Overlook Online Sexual Violence

Our preliminary review of sexual violence policies indicate that despite the fact that most young people spend the majority of their time online, few university policies mention online sexual violence or clearly address the increasingly blurred lines of responsibility, privacy, and accountability (IMPACT Project, 2016). A significant percentage of sexual harassment and offensive forms of sexual violence such as non-consensual distribution of intimate images or rape filmed and posted online, as in the Stuebenville case in the U.S. and two teen suicide cases in Canada (Rehteah Parsons and Amanda Todd, see Shariff, 2015), involved online sexual violence. Ironically many women posted sexist slurs and offensive posts of a violent nature on the social media pages of the student who had been drugged, raped, filmed and the videos posted to social media online.

Not Our Responsibility Off-Campus

University administrators, especially Boards of Governors, legal departments, and communications officers, often argue that if sexual violence occurs outside of school hours and off-campus, it is not their responsibility to address it. This is not the case. The courts in both Canada and the United States have established legal obligations on public educational institutions to address sexual violence, cyberbullying, and related forms of harassment and discrimination.

As early as 1987, a Canadian landmark Supreme Court of Canada case involving the responsibility of public institutions (*Robichaud v. Canada (Treasury Board)*, 1987) established that if the recipient of that behaviour has to face her/his perpetrator within the institutional environment, regardless of whether offensive behaviour takes place outside the institution, the administration is responsible for correcting the problem. In this case equal opportunity to work or learn was at issue; *Robichaud* was continuously harassed outside the workplace but had to face her perpetrator at work. The high court explained that in order to meet the broader objectives of human rights law (namely, to eradicate antisocial conditions in society), human rights law must be consistent with *Charter* principles, especially Section 15(2). Administrators must ensure that individuals have equal opportunities to learn and work without fear of harassment. This was supported in several landmark decisions that focused on learning and working environments, placing an obligation on public institutions to, *inter alia*:

- Avoid creating or fostering a "deliberately dangerous environment" (*Davis v. Munroe, 1999, U.S.*);
- Avoid creating, supporting or fostering a "poisoned environment" (*Ross v. New Brunswick School District, 1996, Canada*);
- Provide an "environment free of discrimination or harassment that is conducive to learning" (*Jubran v. North Vancouver School District et al.,* 2002, Canada).
- Ensure that if there is a nexus at the university such that the victim has to face their perpetrator within the institutional context, the university must meet their obligation to act to protect the victim/survivor. This is especially true if the sexual violence or related form of harassment "materially or substantially affects learning" and "interferes with the educational mission" (*Morse v. Frederick,* 2009, *Tinker vs. Des Moines Independent Community School District,* 1969, *U.S.A. v. Baker,* 1995).

The dissenting opinion in the landmark U.S. Supreme 5:4 decision in *Davis v. Munroe* (1999) was worried that the majority decision would build a "fence made of small sticks" and unleash the floodgates to litigation relating to sexual violence in public institutions. Courts in Canada have ruled that "perceived harm" from an online threat that results in suicide amounts to "actual harm" (*R. v. D.W.H,* 2001), which again places an onus on the institution to ensure they take online threats seriously.

Marin's (2015) analysis of *Pridgen v. University of Calgary* (2012) highlights the importance of a "nexus" to the university community. The case involved two brothers who made negative comments about their female professor on social media. He explains that although universities may legitimately discipline students for online misconduct, it requires that student comments amount to harassment of members of the university community or threaten the learning environment. He also observed that social media raises the stakes for accused students and victims, arguing for broader and more extensive procedural fairness, such as the kind advocated by the American College of Trial Lawyers (2017).

These court decisions suggest that whether the sexual violence takes place physically off-campus and/or online, university administrators need to be vigilant and respond to ensure that if there is a nexus that ties perpetrator and victim to the university context, they properly respond to their obligation to act. Once again, these obligations speak to a fine balance between free expression and equality rights, safety, privacy, protection, accountability, and regulation. The sooner universities learn how to navigate this complex maze, the less legal and publicity challenges they will have on their hands.

Universities cannot accomplish this alone, in silos, or without evidence-based research. As I noted at the outset of this paper, they need support from public and community sectors – especially those such as the legal justice system whose decisions can greatly impact careers and futures, as well as arts and media sectors whose products are widely consumed by university students, especially millennials. This brings us to the final consideration within the framework of discussion.

3. **CONCLUSION AND RECOMMENDATIONS:** *What approaches can universities undertake to develop sustainable policy and educational responses to sexual violence and "rape culture" in an online contemporary society that would help reclaim their fundamental role as central institutions of higher education and help re-establish their role as educators of society?*

Two years ago, as I grappled with these issues, it occurred to me that we have significant opportunities to engage in academic and sector partnerships to address these complex issues. In the absence of evidence-based research on how sexual violence is currently playing itself out, all we have are highly publicized media reports. Most of the time, reputable media outlets and journalists report these stories fairly, and the media community joins academics in calling for evidence-based research to help inform policies (Swain, 2015). Policies on their own simply pay lip-service to the need to address sexual violence. If universities are to succeed in navigating the complex challenges of making a sustainable dent in preventing or reducing sexual violence they need to better understand the university context, the culture within their institutions, and their ultimate legal obligations. The most important element, however, is that they need to hear and embed the voice of their students and other members of the university community to inform any initiatives to address sexual violence.

Moreover, many research projects and universities have centered their research on the notion of consent. I would argue that although consent is an important factor, it is not the only aspect involved in protecting survivors. By engaging both public and private sectors that sometime fail to protect victims of sexual violence, such as law, entertainment arts and ads that tacitly condone sexual violence through objectification or slut-shaming of women, news and social media, universities would benefit from dialogue with experts from those sectors (the "Influencing Sectors"). It would also help key members of these influential sectors reconsider the issues and better understand the impact their products and approaches might have on millennials. I believe it is essential to include experts from those sectors to work closely with students and faculty to develop and inform through mentorships and internships and critical and evidence-based curriculum initiatives that can be integrated into every educational program on campus. We anticipate that when partner representatives from our project return to their sectors, they will take with them fresh critical perspectives from the students they meet. Furthermore, it is important for sector partners to also engage with students in professional and science-based programs. Given the aftermath of the Dalhousie dentistry incident it is clear that such partnerships should not be limited to the social sciences and humanities. Thus, it made sense for my colleagues and I to apply for research funding to the Social Sciences and Humanities Research Council of Canada (SSHRC), which funded our Letter of Intent in 2015 and our final SSHRC Partnership Grant in 2016 (Define the Line, 2016[7]).

In April, 2016, we received funding to implement our detailed strategic plan with a view to providing Canadian and international universities with a strategic and sustainable model on how to prevent sexual violence in the long term. To address the key areas and the complexities illustrated earlier in this chapter, our overarching goal in our 7 years study is to reclaim of the role of universities as central educational agents in society. The central role of universities is to effect transformational change in society through intellectual debate, critical and scholarly teaching, evidence-based research, and publications concerning issues of public policy (METRAC, 2014; Shariff, 2015). Our SSHRC Partnership will take up the challenge to lead universities across Canada and abroad to address the policy vacuum as follows:

1. *Reclaim university research mandates for safer learning environments*: Although news media and isolated institutional surveys have been undertaken (Surman, 2014; Swain, 2015), few long-term academic research studies address this phenomenon. Despite Canadian universities' commitment to evidence-based scholarship, as noted earlier, when it comes to addressing sexual violence, the tendency of administrators is to implement reactive rather than preventative policies (Backhouse et al., 2015; MacKay, 2013). Our 7-year, multidisciplinary partnership fills this gap, providing opportunities for in-depth evaluation, reflection, research, and Knowledge Mobilization (KM) of study outcomes. As diverse members within their own University Communities, our 24 Co-Applicants expect to fulfill a collective responsibility to engage in long-term, evidence-based research to unveil and dismantle biases and barriers that sustain unsafe learning environments.

---

7 Social Sciences and Humanities Research Council of Canada Partnership Grant Number: 895-2016-1026. Project Director, Shaheen Shariff, PhD. McGill University, 2016.

2. *Reclaim university educational mandate for safer learning environments*: Our Partnership will facilitate the creation of safe dialogic spaces that combine research with critical and participatory action theories detailed later. Through curricula as taught by partners, we will develop capacity for critically informed media, arts, and legal literacy among students and faculty, enabling opportunities to rethink social norms and recognize the insidious nature of rape culture. Our unique strategy to bring key partners from Influencing Sectors to inform research, policy, and curricula will: (a) educate society at large, as community partners learn from partnered research and engagement with students, disseminating knowledge gained to their own sectors; and (b) educate students who will graduate and go on to lead society with informed insights on rape culture as we have defined it, thus reducing its societal impact.

3. *Build student capacity through safe spaces*: Our research is expected to empower students to contribute to safer on- and offline societies. We will create safe social media platforms and physical learning spaces that include classrooms but extend to theatres, art galleries, and conferences. In turn, these spaces will bring students and the public together in critical but safe dialogues.

4. *Connect partners reducing the "silo effect:"* Some might argue our work is done, as several universities are already implementing strategic plans to address sexual violence. While admirable, these initiatives operate in isolation and are, thus, incomplete. Task Force Reports, for example, may not always be grounded in empirical research, or deeply consider how external sectors like media and the arts specifically perpetuate rape culture within universities. Our long-term, multi-sector research partnership seeks to critique and build on the frameworks established by university responses in order to uncover the complexities of rape culture that they fail to capture. The diversity of our partnership, we hope, will allow us to put research into action to have significant impact nationally and internationally.

Specific Objectives: We are engaging 3 partnered research teams (Project Teams A–C), in 3 separate but integrated projects (Projects A–C), to clarify complex policy, legal and educational questions that contribute to the current confusion surrounding the roots of rape culture.

Project A-Role of Universities

- *Objective A1: Systemic Barriers Sustaining Rape Culture:* How might universities tacitly condone and sustain rape culture through policies, curriculum, and official responses (University Responses) to sexual violence and how can empirical research with students, faculty, staff and administrators (University Communities) disclose inadequacies in University Responses?

- *Objective A2: Intersections between Education and Human Rights Law:* (i) What legal frameworks govern, impact or intersect with university administrative processes and provide human rights remedies against discrimination and sexual violence?; and (ii) To what extent are these acknowledged, reflected and applied in University Responses?

- *Objective A3: Legal Literacy among University Communities:* To what extent are Universities aware of their legal responsibility in providing effective University Responses and to what extent do students understand the legal remedies available to them following incidents of sexual violence?

- *Objective A4: Case Law and Academic Literature:* What case law, legal-academic literature and legal literacy programs might provide University Communities with insight as they grapple with balancing free expression, privacy, protection and the regulation of sexual violence?

- *Objective A5: Gaps in Social Awareness in Professional Ethics Programs:* Using the McGill Faculty of Dentistry as a case study, we will address concerns on student norms as identified by the Dalhousie Task Force Report (Backhouse et al., 2015) and drawing on research findings, improve McGill Dentistry's policies and curriculum on social awareness and ethics to address rape culture.

- *Objective A6: Educational Potential of Universities:* What role can universities play through multidisciplinary programs to engender a deeper understanding of rape culture, and how can they create safe spaces for reporting and legally defensible University Responses?

Project B-Role of Arts and Popular Culture

- *Objective B1: Sustaining Influence:* What is the nature and extent to which this Influencing Sector fosters, tacitly condones, perpetuates, and sustains rape culture through content, policy, and popular culture norms and how are these messages interpreted within University Communities?
- *Objective B2: Educational Role and Influence:* How can Arts Partners work With University Communities to facilitate on- and offline dialogic spaces, innovative educational resources, critical literacies and counter-narratives to address rape culture in universities - and ultimately greater society?

Project C-Role of News and Social Media

- *Objective C1: Sustaining Influence:* What is the nature and extent to which this Influencing Sector fosters, tacitly condones, perpetuates, and sustains rape culture through content, policy, and communications norms, and how are these messages interpreted within University Communities?
- *Objective C2: Educational Role and Influence:* How can Media Partners work with University Communities to facilitate on- and offline dialogic spaces, innovative educational resources, critical literacies and counter-narratives to address rape culture in universities - and ultimately greater society?

Role of Multi-Sector Partners in Engaging Students:

Engaging Partners from the fields of law, arts and entertainment, and news media and social media in sub-research projects will include training and mentoring activities. These activities will provide Sector Partners with an appreciation of how university aged students consume, experience, and reflect their media or arts content. Institutional Partners will: (a) gain insight on how their University Responses unintentionally create systemic barriers that sustain rape culture; (b) understand legal risks and remedies; (c) connect with Influencing Sector and Advocacy Partners to develop informed curricula through student engagement; and (d) expand their multidisciplinary networks.

Methodologies as Informed by Theoretical Perspectives:

Given the complex nature of this insidious phenomenon, our Partnership also integrates diverse theoretical perspectives to inform our methodologies, outcomes, and knowledge mobilization to address rape culture.

1. *Feminist Socio-linguistic* & *Post-Structuralist Theories on Rape Culture (FRC Theories):* As cultural practices support conditions leading to sexual violence, it is clear that we have a collective responsibility to respond to its proliferation (May & Strikwerda, 1994). In rape culture, violence is presented as "sexy" and so, women face a continuum of sexual violence that manifests itself in leers, sexual remarks, and jokes about rape, which can lead to unsafe working and learning conditions (Marcus, 1992). News, social media, and popular culture condone this milieu by utilizing a "language of rape," a vocabulary "that portrays women as sexual, subhuman, or childlike temptresses [perpetuating] the idea of women as legitimate sexual prey" (Benedict, 1993, p. 103). Yet, the term has been contested for being defined as a heterosexual crime, excluding sexual violence among same sex or trans individuals (Malinen, 2013).

2. *Knowledge Transfer (KT) Conceptual Framework:* The KT conceptual framework will help us investigate systemic policy, procedural, educational, and legal barriers that directly or indirectly sustain rape culture in universities. Through it we will examine how experiential knowledge can influence how information is transferred and policies are informed and implemented depending on change within organizations (Adhikari, 2010; Dalkir, 2011; Jonsson, 2008). These may include: lack of transparency or adequate policies, inconsistent

communications, minimal access to equitable processes, and lack of legal literacy (Van Praagh, 2006). Knowledge transfer is a complex and 'sticky' (e.g., difficult to imitate, change, or sell) phenomenon (Szulanski, 1996). Nonetheless, the KT framework will help us to analyze a university culture and structure, in which frequent changes in leadership and support staff can lead to "corporate amnesia" (Kransdorf, 1998), resulting in inconsistent policy implementation. University Communities are transient populations, making interpretation of disciplinary guidelines more complex. Still, policymakers have a crucial role in implementing and sustaining safe learning environments.

3. *Moving Beyond a Threshold Approach (TA):* This conceptual framework was developed to examine policy application to co-worker violence in professional organizations; nonetheless, it raises critical questions about the efficacy of current prevention efforts. Modern workplace violence prevention policies commonly direct organizations to adopt a "threshold approach" (TA) in assessing and addressing co-worker violence claims by predetermining specific behavioural baselines for policy application (NIOSH, 2006; OSHA, 2004). Behaviours falling short of these thresholds do not activate official policy responses. For example, some universities may not recognize sexual innuendoes as harassment. One can argue, however, that behaviours above and below these thresholds are inseparable, as mild behaviours can escalate (Andersson & Pearson, 1999) and negative behaviours can stem from the same underlying causes (Neumann & Baron, 1998; Willness, Steel, & Lee, 2007). This framework may demonstrate how daily sexist behaviour can be ignored by university policies and procedures.

4. *Human Rights and Legal Pluralism (HRLP) Frameworks:* Legal pluralism illustrates the difficulty of addressing rape culture in strictly legal terms. "Legal pluralism" refers to a society with multiple legal orders (Griffiths, 1986) governed by formal and informal norms and rules (Tamanaha, 2008). Often, there is tension between these norms and difficulty deciphering which norms apply in a particular circumstance (Sheppard, 2010). For example, criminal law approaches to

rape culture are potentially damaging as students can receive criminal records for "jokes" made online. However, in a civil lawsuit, the Supreme Court of Canada (SCC) ruled in favour of a young victim's right to privacy in suing her perpetrator anonymously (Supreme Court of Canada, 2012). The court balanced free expression with privacy in granting media the right to publish details of the case but not her name. Meanwhile, a landmark U.S. case, *Davis v. Munroe County Board of Education* (1999) set the civil rights standard for institutional rape culture when it urged schools to avoid creating "deliberately dangerous learning environments" when students experience sexual harassment. Human rights frameworks can thus help facilitate proactive change and safe spaces within institutional cultures.

5. *Critical Theory (CT); Sense-Making (SM); Participatory Action (PA); Social Learning (SL)*: Four theoretical frameworks will inform Project B's (Arts) methodologies:

- **Critical theory** analyzes existing conditions and potential liberation from oppressive systemic structures. Case studies and qualitative research methodologies are appropriate for this project they allow us to address "what" ideological patterns are strategically represented through popular culture to perpetuate rape culture and "how" university students experience these representations "How" and "what" are the ways that artistic research practices in various media contribute to pedagogical counter-narratives and social change (Stake, 1995; Yin, 2003).

- **Sense-making** (Dervin, Foreman-Wernet, & Lauterbach, 2003) is a user-centric communication framework that aims to improve the quality of information sharing by factoring in the importance of individual perceptions and experiences increasing information effectiveness by tailoring it as much as feasible to the specific situation and for the specific person. This framework will thus guide the production of more effective messages or counter-narratives.

- **Participatory action:** The project is also guided by research methodologies merging socially engaged art practice and pedagogy, (Leavy, 2009; Sullivan, 2010) that are flexible, reflexive, and serve as pathways of imaginative and critical inquiry. These dialogues will provide opportunities for collaborative knowledge and experience exchange between students, faculty, and administrators. The arts engage participants as **cultural producers** to create active spaces for social change (Buckingham & Sefton-Green, 1994; Schratz & Walker, 1995). They evoke emotional and imaginative responses to societal and personal concerns (Beare, 2015; Fels & Belliveau, 2008) and prompt reflection (Eisner, 2002). Participants will be invited to create visualizations and stories from situated perspectives (Haraway, 1988), along with those of the researchers, guest artists, and students.

- *Social learning* occurs when the students feel respected (Palmer, 2007). Creating a sense of community within classrooms involves "dialogical exchange in which our ignorance can be aired...and our knowledge expanded" (p. 76). Differing perceptions are discussed openly to build a communal voice that challenges ill-informed views.

6. *Risk-Based Analysis (RBA); Critical Media Literacy (CML); and Participatory Bonded Design (PBD):* The theoretical frameworks relevant to Project C include the following: *Risk-based analysis* (Appadurai, 2013; Hoechsmann & Poyntz, 2012) examines the relationships between young people and news, entertainment, and social media. Scholars observe that in addition to socioeconomic, family, and health factors, media significantly shapes student attitudes. Research suggests that while sustained media engagement does not make young people violent, it has *degrees of effect* in perpetuating violence in their lives (Kline, 2005; von Felitzen, 2009). Project Team C will thus develop a risk-based analysis to account for the role of media in perpetuating practices that sustain rape culture. *Critical media literacy* (Alvermann, Moon, & Hagood, 1999; Kellner & Share, 2005) is an inquiry-based pedagogical tool, which questions assumptions, messages, and consequences of a given form of media. It involves: analyzing a piece of media and questioning the presence of some messages and the absence of others in the text; observing the colours, editing, and appearances of people in the media; comparing media portrayals

in one's surroundings to reality; and questioning who produced the given media text. Finally, *participatory bonded design* theory (Large, Nesset, Beheshti, & Bowler, 2006) engages students in the creation of digital storytelling projects. It will help us draw out the ways media condones or challenges rape culture.

Last year, in Year 1, we began to set up a Partnership website and a detailed work plan for the 7-year term, prepared ethics applications, and held a well-attended project launch meeting in November, 2016 to establish strategies, roles and responsibilities, and create a yearly evaluation plan. We want to ensure these outcomes are seamlessly integrated into the research process throughout the term. Some of the activities and timelines have changed slightly, but by and large these are the methods we plan to use to integrate research and initiatives that fully engage students, faculty members, and partners.

Qualitative Research: We are currently at the stage of obtaining university ethics approvals for qualitative research (surveys, interviews, and focus groups) that we plan to undertake in each of our 12 university partners. This will allow us to proceed without issues of concern.

Critically Informing Curriculum and Policies, and Engaging Student-Multi-Sector Dialogues: Drawing on the foregoing theoretical perspectives and qualitative research, we propose to develop evidence-based policies and curriculum that is student-partner developed. This will be accomplished through qualitative research analysis and dialogues, creative expression (with the help of arts and popular culture experts), drama, advocacy and activism, and critical analysis of the framing of news media reports; the intended outcome being developing critical legal literacy among students as they analyze case law relating to sexual violence in universities and beyond. We are also beginning to collect archived art materials to examine the extent to which the arts have depicted sexuality and sexual violence and compare this with contemporary society's easy access and vulnerability to news media and social media communications.

Our projects are expected to develop White Papers for University administrators, and policy briefs for House of Commons and Senate committees that could lead to potential new law on mandatory sensitization of judges to sexual violence issues.

Training and Mentoring Students: Student training and mentoring are integral objectives of our Partnership. Three groups of students will benefit from engagement in the project:

1. At least 25 Graduate students will receive stipends under the SSHRC budget for the duration of their PhD or Master's programs in their disciplines. We anticipate that 3 cohorts of PhD students and 4 cohorts of Master's students from participating university faculties will complete approximately 12 PhD dissertations and 13 Master's Theses informed by research they will directly undertake, resulting in academic publications, conference papers, policy briefs, and curricula that integrate research findings. Students will be trained and mentored by junior and senior academic Co-Applicants and Partners through our Student Mentorship Committee.

2. Approximately 20-25 Graduate and undergraduate Research Assistants (RAs) will also be hired under the SSHRC budget to assist with the research. With the student mentorship structure and supervisory contributions of 24 academics we anticipate undertaking numerous conference presentations and cross-disciplinary publications in journals and books. The project will develop workshops for each sector, drawing on the Partner and academic expertise available to us. These products and resources are anticipated to enhance public, academic, and multi-sector dialogue over 7 years, with a ripple effect through the three sectors, to raise awareness. As each graduate student defends and publishes a thesis or dissertation, or creates film, video, fine arts or dramatic creations, and as each student receives compulsory social justice education (as in McGill's dentistry faculty), we anticipate that they will be more careful in their student and professional lives. Our Data Repository will capture, organize, and provide public access to the publications through McGill's libraries.

Opportunities to Network for Change: We anticipate our project will build lasting networks and relationships through student involvement in sector-based participatory research, student internships and hands-on training with advocacy and professional regulatory organizations, innovative curriculum development, and the extension of research into national and international on- and offline public communities through our Arts and Media Partners. Through teaching, research, and communication, we will raise public awareness of rape culture and invigorate debate across Canada and abroad. We will enhance a network of students, community scholars, and practitioners who will enhance our multidisciplinary academic networks with Influencing Sector Partners, resulting in job creation and opportunities for students. These new researchers will develop their own novel approaches to address complex issues that transcend the capacities of any one scholar, institution, or discipline.

In this Chapter I have highlighted the complex legal, educational, social, and professional dilemmas that confront university administrations as they attempt to navigate a balance between free expression, safety, protection, privacy, equality, accountability, and regulation. I have explained the need for the pendulum in Canada to swing away from subjecting survivors of sexual violence to disproportionate scrutiny towards a more balanced and equitable starting point through which to resolve the issues. I have argued that universities cannot handle this alone, and that working in silos or in isolation will make it more difficult to reduce institutional censorship and concerns over reputation. In my earlier research on the impact of censorship within public educational institutions I have argued that attempts to ignore issues and silence stakeholders who raise or report problems often backfire. The conflicts, disagreements or issues that institutions sometimes attempt to cover-up inevitably bubble to the surface in more widely publicized controversies that can significantly impact the reputations of censoring institutions or their administrators (Shariff & Manley-Casimir, 1999; Shariff et al., 2000). My recommendations on how to address the issues in a sustainable, equitable and preventative way are embedded in the core structure of a strategic research plan overseeing three individual, but integrated, sub-projects that examine the influence of the law, arts and popular culture, and news media and social media on the perpetration or prevention on sexual violence in universities.[8] I have provided an explanation of how and why we need to engage a multi-sector approach so that multi-directional exchange will result and sow the roots of sustained social change. As Partners and students exchange ideas and challenge the status quo to dismantle rape culture on university campuses, and within broader society, university policies will have to incorporate student voices. Curriculum programs across faculties will need to be better integrated and collaborative to reflect and include the perspectives of their students. These can successfully be achieved when student graduate research assistants work closely with multi-sector partners to engage in creative and critical dialogues on rape culture and sexual violence. We anticipate that this ambitious and pragmatic, but realistically feasible, project will put Canada on the map as a leader of sustainable university models to address sexual violence.

---

8 Thank you to the Social Sciences and Humanities Research Council of Canada for funding this long-term Partnership grant, and for your support of my research career over the last 14 years at McGill University. This support has helped to provide Canadian researchers, academics, policy makers, and legislators with invaluable evidence-based knowledge, which is essential in ultimately fostering inclusive change that moves closer to significantly reducing sexual violence through an improved understanding of its nuanced complexities.

Bibliography, References, & Jurisprudence

Adhikari, D.R. (2010). Knowledge management in academic institutions. *International Journal of Educational Management, 24*(2), 94-104.

Alvermann, D.E., Moon, J.S., & Hagood, M.C. (1999). *Popular culture in the classroom: Teaching and researching critical media literacy.* Literacy Studies Series. Newark, DE: International Reading Association.

Andersson, L., & Pearson, C. (1999). Tit for tat? The spiraling effect of incivility in the workplace. *Academy of Management Review, 24*(3), 452–471.

Appadurai, A. (2013). *The future as cultural fact: Essays on the global condition.* London: Verso.

Backhouse, C., McRae, D., & Iyer, N. (2015). Report of the task force on misogyny, sexism, homophobia in Dalhousie University Faculty of Dentistry. Retrieved from: http://www.dal.ca/content/dam/dalhousie/pdf/cultureofrespect/Dalhousie Dentistry-TaskForceReport-June2015.pdf.

Bailey, J., & Hanna, M. (2011). The gendered dimensions of sexting: Assessing the applicability of Canada's child pornography provision. *Canadian Journal of Women and the Law, 23*(2), 405–441.

Bailey, J., & Telford, A. (2008). What's So "Cyber" About It? Reflections on cyber feminism's contributions to legal studies. *Canadian Journal of Women and Laws, 19*(2), 243-271.

Beare, D. (2015). Theatre is a social art: A five-stage social art development model for secondary theatre education. In M. Carter, M. Prendergaast, & G. Belliveau (Eds.), *Drama, theatre and performance education in Canada: Classroom and community contexts* (pp. 86-96). Ottawa, ON: Canadian Association for Teacher Education.

Benedict, H. (1993). The language of rape. In E. Buchwald, P.R. Fletcher, & M. Roth (Eds.), *Transforming a rape culture* (pp. 101–105). Minneapolis, MN: Milkweed Editions.

Bergeron, M., Hebert, M., Ricci, S., Goyer, M., Duhamel, N., & Kurtzman, L., (2016). Violences Sexualles en milieu Universite au Quebec: Rapport de Reschereche de l'enguete ESSIMU. Retrieved from: http://salledepresse.uqam.ca/fichier/documen t/PDF/Rapport_ESSIMU_FMINAL.pdf

Boesveld, S. (2014, October 31). Jian Ghomeshi scandal becoming a tipping point for anger over mistreatment of women. *National Post*. Retrieved from http://nationalpost.com/g00/news/canada/jian-ghomeshi-scandal-becoming-a-tipping-point-for-anger-over-mistreatment-of-women/wcm/9fbf2a2e-a1fd-4cde-9182-d7de2108070a?i10c.referrer=https%3A%2F%2Fwww.google.ca%2F.

Boyd, d. (2014). *Its Complicated: The social lives of networked teens*. Connecticut. Yale University Press.

Buchwald, E., Fletcher, P.R., & Roth, M. (Eds.). (2005). *Transforming a rape culture*. Minneapolis, MN: Milkweed Editions.

Buckingham, D., & Sefton-Green, J. (1994). *Cultural studies goes to school: Reading and teaching popular media*. London: Taylor & Francis.

Buncombe, A. (2016, September 2). Stanford rape case: Read the impact statement of Brock Turner's victim. Retrieved from http://www.independent.co.uk/news/people/stand.

Buzzfeed (2016) https://www.buzzfeed.com/katiejmbaker/heres-the-powerful-letter-the-stanford-victim-read-to-her-ra?utmterm=.sfkANoqdNd#.pr0eX2ZOXO.

Calanan, J. (July 10, 2015). Dalhousie students disciplined for misogynist Facebook group finding dentistry work, lawyer says. The Canadian Press. Retrieved from https://www.theglobeandmail.com/news/national/dalhousie-students-disciplined-for-misogynistic-facebook-group-finding-dentistry-worklawyersays/article254098 31/.

Canadian Judicial Council. (2017). Retrieved from https://www.cjcccm.gc.ca/cmslib/gen.

Cantor, D., Fisher, B., Chibnall, S. H., Bruce, C., Townsend, R., Thomas, G., & Lee, H. (2015, September 21). *Report on the AAU campus climate survey on sexual assault and sexual misconduct*. Retrieved from http://sexualassaulttaskforce.harva rd.edu/files/taskforce/files/final_report_harvard_9.21.15.pdf.

CBC News. (2013a, September 7). UBC investigates frosh students' pro-rape chant: Chant condoned non-consensual sex with underage girls. *CBC News*, British Columbia. Retrieved from www.cbc.ca/news/canada/british-columbia/ubc-investigates-frosh-students-pro-rape-chant-1.1699589.

CBC News. (2013b, December 19). Saint Mary's pro-rape chant sparks 20 new recommendations. *CBC News*. Retrieved from http://www.cbc.ca/news/canada/no va-scotia/saint-mary-s-pro-rape-chant-sparks-20-new-recommendations-1.2469851.cc-csc/en/item/10007/index.do?r=AAAAAQAFeW91dGgB567.

CBA National News (2016). Dalhousie suspends 13 dentistry students from clinic amid Facebook scandal. http://www.cbc.ca/news/canada/nova-scotia/dalhousie-suspends-13-dentistry-students-from-clinic-amid-facebook-scandal-1.2889635.

CNBC (2017): http://www.cnbc.com/2017/06/29/trump-attacks-morning-joe-anchors-in-personal-tweets.html.

Dalkir, K. (2011). *Knowledge management in theory and practice*. Boston, MA: Institute of Technology Press.

Danay, R. (2010). The medium is not the message: Reconciling reputation and free expression in cases of Internet defamation. *McGill Law Journal*, 56(1), 1-37.

Dervin, B., Foreman-Wernet, L., & Lauterbach, E. (2003). *Sense-making methodology reader: Selected writings of Brenda Dervin*. Cresskill, NJ: Hampton Press.

Desai, S. (February 22, 2017). News/SSMU VP External resigns amid allegations of sexual violence: Community Disclosure Network releases statement condemning David Aird's "history of sexualized and gendered violence." *The McGill Daily*.

Dick, B. (December 21, 2016) Dalhousie's dentistry scandal: A costly lesson in communications. *CTV Atlantic*. http://atlantic.ctvnews.ca/dalhousie-s-dentistry-scandal-a-costly-lesson-in-communications-1.3212800. Retrieved July 24, 2015.

Donovan, K., & Brown, J. (2014, October 26). CBC fires Jian Ghomeshi over sex allegations. *The Star*. Retrieved from http://www.thestar.com/news/canada/2014/1 0/26/cbc_fires_jian_ghomeshi_over_sex_allegations.html.

Eisner, E. (2002). *The arts and the creation of the mind*. New Haven, CT: Yale University Press.

Eltis, K. (2011). The judicial system in the digital age: Revisiting the relationship between privacy and accessibility in the cyber context. *McGill Law Journal*. 56(2), 289-316.

Fels, L., & Belliveau, G. (2008). *Exploring curriculum*. Vancouver, BC: Pacific Educational Press.

Garcia, A. [Alex Garcia]. (2016, October 7). *Trump gets caught saying "Grab her by the pussy"* [Video file]. Retrieved from https://www.youtube.com/watch?v=o21fXqguD7U.

Gersen, J., & Suk, J. (2016). The sex bureaucracy. *California Law Review*, 104(4), 881- 948.

Globe & Mail (2017, January 5). Ghomeshi acquitted: Read the verdict and catch up on what you missed. *Globe & Mail*. Retrieved from https://www.theglobeandmail.co m/news/national/jian-ghomeshi/ article28476713/.

Griffiths, J. (1986). What is legal pluralism? *The Journal of Legal Pluralism and Unofficial Law, 18*(24), 1-55.

Haraway, D. (1988). Situated knowledges: The science question in feminism and the privilege of partial perspective. *Feminist Studies, 14*(3), 575-599.

Hinduja, S., & Patchin, J.W. (2010). Bullying, cyberbullying, and suicide. *Archives of Suicide Research, 14*(3), 206-121.

Hoechsmann, M., & Poyntz, S.R. (2012). *Media literacies: A critical introduction*. Toronto, ON: Wiley-Blackwell.

Hutchison, P. (2010, January/February). When we were feminists. *Briarpatch Magazine*. Retrieved from http://briarpatchmagazine.com/articles/ view/when-we-were-feminists.

IMPACT Project White Paper (in progress*). IMPACT: Collaborations to Address Sexual Violence on Campus. Social Sciences and Humanities Research Council of Canada Partnership Grant Number: 895-2016-1026. Project Director, Shaheen Shariff, PhD. McGill University* (referenced here as the "IMPACTS Project").

Jonsson, A. (2008). A transnational perspective on knowledge sharing: Lessons learned from IKEA's entry into Russia, China and Japan. *The International Review of Retail, Distribution and Consumer Research, 18*(1), 17-44.

Junco, R., Heiberger, G., & Loken, E. (2011). The effect of Twitter on college student engagement and grades. *Journal of Computer Assisted Learning, 27*(2), 119–132.

Karaian, L. (2009). The troubled relationship of feminist and queer legal theory to strategic essentialism: Theory/praxis, queer porn, and Canadian anti-discrimination law. In M.A. Fineman, J.E. Jackson, & A.P. Romero (Eds.) *Feminist and queer legal theory: Intimate encounters, uncomfortable conversations* (pp. 375-394). New York: Routledge.

Kellner, D., & Share, J. (2005). Toward critical media literacy: Core concepts, debates, organizations and policy. *Discourse: Studies in the Cultural Politics of Education, 26*(3), 369–386.

Kelly, L. (2013). *Surviving sexual violence*. New York: John Wiley & Sons.

Kline, S. (2005). Countering children's sedentary lifestyles: An evaluative study of a media-risk education approach. *Childhood, 12*(2), 239-258.

Kransdorf, A. (1998). Corporate amnesia. *European Business Review, 98*(6), iv-viii.

Lalonde, J.S. (2014, December). *From reacting to preventing: Addressing sexual violence on campus by engaging community partners.* Retrieved from https://www.uottawa.ca/president/sites/www.uottawa.ca.president/files/task-force-report-appendix-1-from-reacting-to-preventing.pdf

Large, A., Nesset, V., Beheshti, J., & Bowler, L. (2006). "Bonded design:" A novel approach to intergenerational information technology design. *Library & Information Science Research, 28*(1), 64-82.

Leavy, P. (2009). *Method meets art: Arts-based research practice.* New York: Guilford Press.

Lee, J., & Rice, C. (2007). Welcome to America? International student perceptions of discrimination. *Higher Education, 53*(3), 381-409. Retrieved from http://www.jstor.org.proxy3.library.mcgill.ca/stable/29735060.

MacKay, A.W. (2013, December 15). *Promoting a culture of safety, respect and consent at Saint Mary's University and beyond.* Retrieved from http://www.smu.ca/webfiles/PresidentsCouncilReport-2013.pdf.

Malinen, K. (2013). Woman-to-woman rape: A critique of Marcus' 'Theory and politics of rape prevention.' *Sexuality & Culture, 17*(1), 360-376.

Mansbridge P. (2016, March 29). Marie Henein, Jian Ghomeshi's lawyer, denies she has betrayed women. *CBC News.* Retrieved from http://www.cbc.ca/news/jian-ghomeshi-marie-henein-lawyer-interview-1.3510762.

Marcus, S. (1992). Fighting bodies, fighting words: A theory and politics of rape prevention. In J. Butler & J. Scott (Eds.), *Feminists theorize the political* (pp. 385-403). New York: Routledge.

Marin, M. (2015). University discipline in the age of social media. *Education & Law Journal, 25*(1), 31-63.

May, L., & Strikwerda, R. (1994). Men in groups: Collective responsibility for rape. *Hypatia, 9*(2), 134-151.

McElroy, W. (2016). Rape culture hysteria: Fixing the damage done to men. Kindle Edition. USA: Vulgus Press.

METRAC (2014). *Campus safety audit services: Creating safer campuses for everybody.* Retrieved from http://www.metrac.org/wp-content/uploads/2014/11/campus.safet y.audits.12nov141.pdf.

Mihailidis, P. (2014). The civic-social media disconnect: Exploring perceptions of social media for engagement in the daily life of college students. *Information, Communication & Society, 17*(9), 1059-1071.

Montgomery, S (2014). Been raped but never reported. Retrieved from https://storify.com /Purnatalukder/ beenrapedbutneverreported-573a12130de4c5bd2070d683.

Neuman, J.H., & Baron, R.A. (1998). Workplace violence and workplace aggression: Evidence concerning specific forms, potential causes, and preferred targets. *Journal of Management, 24*(3), 391-419.

NIOSH (2006). *Workplace violence prevention strategies and research needs*. Retrieved from: http://www.cdc.gov/niosh/docs/2006-144/ pdfs/2006-144.pdf.

Office for Civil Rights (2014): Questions and Answers about Title IX and Sexual Violence. U.S. Dept. of Education (April 29, 2014). Retrieved from: http://www2.ed.gov/about/offices/list/oct/docs/ qa-201404-title-ix-pdf.

Ormiston, S. (2014, September 29). University of Ottawa's hockey scandal raises questions about rape culture on campuses. *CBC News.* Retrieved from http://www.cbc.ca/player/Shows/Shows/The%20National/ About%20the%20Show/Susan%20Ormiston/ID/2536086548/.

OSHA (2004). *Guidelines for preventing workplace violence for health care & social service workers*. Retrieved from: http://www.osha.gov/ Publications/osha3148.pdf.

Palfrey (2009). Hearing on cyberbullying and other online safety issues for children (United States House of Representatives, Committee on the Judiciary, Subcommittee on Crime, Terrorism and Homeland Security). Retrieved from http://judiciary.house.gov/_files/hearings/pdf/ Palfrey090930.pdf.

Palmer, P. (2007). *The courage to teach*. San Francisco, CA: John Wiley & Sons.

Patel, A. (2014, October 30). 460,000 sexual assaults in Canada every year: YWCA Canada. *The Huffington Post Canada*. Retrieved from http://www.huffingtonpost.ca/2014/10/30/sexual-assault-can-ada_n_6074994.html.

Porter, I. (2016, October 31). La reaction des tetes dirigeantes est primordiales selon une chercheuse. *Le Devoir.* Retrieved from http://www.ledevoir.com/societe/educatio n/482902/ la-reaction-des-tetes-dirigeantes-est-primordiale-selon-une-chercheuse.

Puente, M. (2017, June 17). Bill Cosby trial: How did a mistrial happen? And what comes next? *USA Today.* Retrieved from https://www.usatoday. com/story/life/peo ple/2017/06/17/bill-cosby-trial-how-did-mistrial-happen-and-what-comes-next/10 2812764/.

Rosengard, D., Tucker-McLaughlin, M., & Brown, T. (2014). Students and social news: How college students share news through social media. *Electronic News, 8*(2), 120-137.

SCC 46, [2012] 2 S.C.R. 567). Retrieved from http://scc-csc.lexum.com/scc-csc/s Schratz, M., & Walker, R. (1995). *Research as social change: New opportunities for qualitative research.* London: Routledge.

Servance, R. (2003). Cyber-bullying, cyber-harassment and the conflict between schools and the First Amendment, (6), 1213-15.

Shariff, S. (2009). *Confronting cyberbullying: What schools need to know to control misconduct and avoid legal consequences.* New York: Cambridge University Press.

Shariff, S. (2015). *Sexting and cyberbullying: Defining the line on digitally empowered kids.* New York: Cambridge University Press.

Shariff, S., Case, R., & Manley-Casimir, M.E. (2000). Balancing rights in education: Surrey school board's book ban. *Education & Law Journal, 10*(1), 47-105.

Shariff, S., & Churchill, A. (Eds.) (2009). *Truths and myths of cyber-bullying: International perspectives on stakeholder responsibility and children safety.* New York: Peter Lang.

Shariff, S., & DeMartini, A. (2016). Defining the legal lines in sexting and cyberbullying among university students. In H. Cowie and C. Myers (Eds.), *Bullying among university students.* London: Routledge Press.

Shariff, S., Wiseman, A., & Crestohl, L. (2012). Defining the lines between children's vulnerability to cyberbullying and the open court principle: Implications of AB (Litigation Guardian of) v. Bragg Communications Inc. *Education Law Journal, 22*(1), 1.

Sheppard, C. (2010). *Inclusive equality: The relational dimensions of systemic discrimination in Canada.* Montreal: McGill-Queen's Press-MQUP.

Smith, J. (2017, May 15). Rona Ambrose's bill on training for would-be judges wins liberal support. *The Canadian Press.* Retrieved from http://www.huffingtonpost.c a/2017/05/15/liberals-to-support-ambrose-s-bill-on-training-for-would-be-judges_ n_16626582.html.

Stake, R.E. (1995). *The art of case study research.* Thousand Oaks, CA: Sage.

Steeves, V. (2014). Young Canadians in a wired world, phase III: Sexuality and romantic relationships in the digital age. *Media Smarts.* Retrieved from http://mediasmarts. ca/ sites /mediasmarts/files/pdfs/publication-report/full/YCWWIII_Sexuality_Ro mantic_ Relationships_Digital_ Age_FullReport.pdf.

Sullivan, G. (Ed.). (2010). *Art practice as research: Inquiry in visual arts.* Thousand Oaks, CA: Sage.

Surman, R. (2014, November 27). Ryerson University to review sexual assault policies. *The Ryersonian.* Retrieved from http://ryersonian.ca/ryerson-university-to-review-sexual-assault-policies/.

Swain, D. (2015, February 9). Sexual assault on campus. *CBC News.* Retrieved from http://www.cbc.ca/player/News/TV%20Shows/The%20National/Canada/ID/2652 946187/.

Szulanski, G. (1996) Exploring internal stickiness: Impediments to the transfer of best practice within the firm. *Strategic Management Journal, 17*(2), 27-43.

Tamanaha, B.Z. (2008). Understanding legal pluralism: Past to present, local to global. *Sydney Law Review, 30,* 375-411.

The American College of Trial Lawyers (2017). White Paper on Campus Sexual Assault Investigations. Task Force on the Response of Universities and Colleges to Allegations of Sexual Violence. Approved by the Board of Regents, March 2017. https://www.actl.com.

Van Praagh, S. (2006, January). Rethinking what and how we teach: Curriculum reform at McGill's Faculty of Law. *Canadian Association of Law Teachers Bulletin,* 13-14.

Vanhorn, T. (2001, September 28). Tori Amos says Eminem's fictional dead wife talked to her. *MTV News.* Retrieved from http://www.mtv.com/news/1449422/tori-amos-says-eminems-fictional-dead-wife-spoke-to-her/.

Vincent, A. (2014, December 30). How feminism conquered pop culture: Alice Vincent explains how 2014 was the year it became cool to use the F-word. *The Telegraph.* Retrieved from http://www.telegraph.co.uk/culture/culturenews/11310119/femini sm-pop-culture-2014.html.

Von Feilitzen, C. (2009). *Influences of mediated violence: A brief research summary.* Goteborg, SW: International Clearinghouse on Children, Youth and Media at Nordicom, University of Gothenburg.

Warner, A. (2013, June 24). Misogyny makes a comeback: Kanye, Robin Thicke and degrading women. *CBC Music.* Retrieved from http://www.cbcmusic.ca/posts/112 05/misogyny-makes-a-comeback-kanye-robin-thicke-and-d.

Warner, A. (2014, February 26). Lilith Fair, Riot grrrls, and Kurt Cobain: WTF happened to '90s feminism in music? *CBC Music.* Retrieved from: http://www.cbcmusic.ca/ posts/11201/riot-grrrls-kurt-cobain-and-lilith-fair-wtf-happen.

Webster, A. (2015, March 6). How League of Legends could make the internet a better place. *The Verge Magazine*. Retrieved from https://www.theverge.com/2015/3/6/8 161955/league-of-legends-online-happy-place.

Wertsch, J.V. (1998). Mind as action. New York: Oxford University Press.

Williams, J.E. (2007). Rape culture. In G. Ritzer (Ed.), *The Blackwell encyclopedia of sociology* (pp. 3783–3787). Malden: Blackwell Publishing.

Willness, C.R., Steel, P., & Lee, K. (2007). A meta-analysis of the antecedents and consequences of workplace sexual harassment. *Personnel Psychology, 60*(1), 127- 162.

Woolf, N. (2014, December 16). The Bill Cosby sexual abuse claims – accusation by accusation. *The Guardian*. Retrieved from https://www. theguardian.com/world/20 14 /nov/24/ the-bill-cosby-sexual-abuse-claims-accusation-by-accusation.

Ybarra, M.L., Mitchell, K.J., Wolak, J. & Finkelor, D. (2006). Examining characteristics and associated distress related to Internet harassment: Findings from the Second Youth Internet Safety Survey. *Pediatrics, 118*(4), 1169-1177.

Yin, R.K. (2003). *Case study research: Design and methods*. Thousand Oaks, CA: Sage.

Jurisprudence Referenced or Reviewed

A.B. v. Bragg Communications Inc., 2012 SCC 46, [2012] 2 S.C.R. 567. A.B., by her Litigation Guardian, C.D. Appellant. v. Bragg ...September 27, 2012.

Davis v. Munroe County Bd. Of Ed., 526 U.S. 629 (1999).

Eldridge v. British Columbia (Attorney General), 1997.

Jubran v. School District No. 44 (North Vancouver), 2005.

Mahmoodi v. Dutton and University of British Columbia, 1998.

Morse v. Frederick, 2009.

Mpega v. Université de Moncton, 2001.

Nova Scotia (Public Safety) v. Lee, 2015.

Pacheco v. Dalhousie University, 2005.

Pappajohn v. The Queen, [1980] 2 S.C.R. 120.

Pridgen v. University of Calgary, 2012.

R. v. D.W.H, 2001.

R. v. Elliott, 2016 ONCJ 35.

R. v. Ewanchuk, [1999] 1 S.C.R. 330.

R. v. Ghomeshi, 2016 ONCJ 155.

R. v. Mabior, 2012 SCC 47, [2012] 2 S.C.R. 584.

R. v. O'Brien, 2013 SCC 2, [2013] 1 S.C.R. 7.

R. v. Seaboyer, [1991] 2 S.C.R. 577.

R. v. Sillipp, 1997 ABCA 346.

Robichaud v. Canada (Treasury Board), 1987.

Ross v. New Brunswick School District No. 15, 1996.

Sansregret v. The Queen, [1985] 1 S.C.R. 570.

Tinker v. Des Moines Independent Community School District, 1969.

U.S.A. v. Baker, 1995.

Zhang v. The University of Western Ontario, 2010.

Statutes

Nova Scotia Cyber Safety Act (Revoked) http://nslegislature.ca/legc/ bills/61st_5th/1st_read/b061.htm

Protecting Canadians from Online Crime Act (S.C. 2014, c. 31).

CHAPTER 15

Defining Policy and Principles: Professional Practice and Mental Health Accommodations for Teacher Candidates

Fiona Blaikie, Dawn Buzza, Jackie Muldoon, and Carole Richardson

Abstract

I n this chapter, we offer a common set of defining principles and a policy that focus on mental health in relation to our expectations of teacher candidates and their professional practices. In the context of the Ontario Human Rights Commission policy (2014) on preventing discrimination based on mental health disabilities and addictions, all accommodations must provide equitable opportunities to teacher candidates with human rights protected needs. Needs cannot impede the teacher candidate's ability to meet standards of professionalism and competency which are required to graduate, given that faculties of education, school boards and other agents are not at liberty to modify policy defining standards and ethics of professional practice. Issues include the need to uphold the ethics of the teaching profession; mutual respect, dignity and reasonableness; the importance of collaboration with stakeholders; the duty to accommodate; the limits of accommodations; the need for teacher candidates to declare a limitation/disability (professional discernment suggests a duty to disclose and an ability to discern if, when, and how to disclose), and the duty to educate teacher candidates on the ethics of practice beyond the curriculum and classroom management.

Introduction

In June of 2014, the Ontario Association of Deans of Education (OADE) held a retreat to explore the important and pressing issue of accommodation for teacher candidates with mental health disabilities. At this retreat we considered this issue within the context of individual university policies, the Ontario College of Teachers' (OCT) *Ethical Standards for the Teaching Profession and Standards of Practice for the Teaching Profession*, and the Ontario Teachers' Federation's *Teaching Profession Act*. Along with invited stakeholders from government, OCT, the teaching profession, human resource professionals and legal counsel, OADE considered teacher candidates' various mental health accommodation needs and discussed numerous case studies.

In this chapter, we posit that the rights of teacher candidates must be considered within the context of their emerging professional identities and responsibilities as teacher candidates, and in the context of the right to a safe and productive environment for teacher candidates, students, staff and others in schools and alternative placement settings in Ontario and beyond. While the term "accommodation" includes making adjustments for physical, learning and mental health disabilities, we focus specifically on mental health. The duty to accommodate teacher candidates with mental health disabilities cannot be less or more than the duty to accommodate teacher candidates with physical and/or learning disabilities. OADE identified the need to create a set of overarching general principles for accommodating teacher candidates with mental health challenges. Our purpose in writing this chapter is to work towards achieving this goal.

During the June 27th 2014 retreat, OADE created the following working definition of general principles for accommodating teacher candidates with mental health challenges:

> Accommodations provide equitable opportunities to students with human rights protected needs, to the point of undue hardship, where those needs do not interfere with the students' ability to meet the OCT standards of

professionalism and competency required to graduate, without modifying those standards. (OADE retreat, June 27, 2014)

In order to meet the challenges of accommodating teacher candidates with mental health disabilities, we identified three guiding questions: (1) How do we fulfill our responsibility to ensure that our teacher candidates have attained competencies and demonstrated the ability to work within the *Standards of Practice* as specified by our certifying body, the Ontario College of Teachers? (2) How do we balance the duty to accommodate our teacher candidates with the rights of others in the schools in which our teacher candidates are placed? (3) How do we ensure that our teacher candidates have every opportunity to be successful within the constraints of these various policies and requirements, but still allow for the possibility that some will not complete the program successfully?

Ontario Human Rights Commission: New Policy on Mental Health Disabilities and Addictions

The *Ontario Human Rights Commission* (OHRC) employs a "social approach" that recognizes that what constitutes a "disability" evolves as social attitudes and perceptions change over time.

In her review of the features of the OHRC's new policy on mental disabilities and addictions, Peters (2014) noted that the policy "emphasizes that 'Organizations and individuals must assess risk based on a person's individual circumstances, using objective evidence or criteria, and not on blanket assumptions or speculations based on a person's diagnosis or perceived mental health issue'" (p. 2). This policy's recognition that responding to "the actual behaviour of individuals with mental health disabilities that causes risk" (Peters, 2014, p. 2) is not discriminatory is of great importance to our discussion.

When considering this issue, the differences between socially regulated behaviours/attitudes and legally protected human rights must be identified and clearly addressed. This distinction provides a framework for what does (and does not) fall within and beyond the somewhat porous boundaries of accommodation. Accommodation must be considered through the lens of skills and behaviours, rather than looking at a diagnosis and the assumptions and speculations related to it. Therefore, the case studies discussed here focus on behaviour and not on mental health diagnoses because behaviour can be weighed against the core competencies as recognized by the teaching profession and the OCT's *Standards of Practice*.

The OCT's *Ethical Standards for the Teaching Profession, Standards of Practice for the Teaching Profession* and *Professional Learning Framework for the Teaching Profession* outline the principles of ethical behaviour, professional practice and ongoing learning for the teaching profession in Ontario. More specifically, *Ethical Standards for the Teaching Profession* describes the professional beliefs and values that must guide the decision-making and professional actions of Ontario teachers in their professional roles and relationships. *Standards of Practice for the Teaching Profession* describes the continuum of knowledge, skills and professional practices of teachers in Ontario. The full description of these standards can be found at http://www.oct.ca/public/professional-standards.

The OCT *Standards of Practice* and *Ethical Standards* must be enacted and observed in the day-to-day actions of every OCT certified teacher. Similarly, our teacher candidates are individually accountable for upholding the OCT *Standards of Practice* and *Ethical Standards* during their teaching practica and while on campus. As well, teacher candidates fall under the jurisdiction of policies created by the Ontario Teachers' Federation (OTF) and the *Teaching Profession Act* (OTF, 2015). We refer to Article 4 of the latter:

> 4. (2) The following students are associate members of the Federation: (a) Every student in a college for the professional education of teachers established under clause 14 (1) (a) of the *Education Act*. (b) Every student in a school or faculty of education that provides for the professional education of teachers pursuant to clause 14. (1) (b) of the *Education Act*.

For further information, please see http://www.otffeo.on.ca/en/ wp-content/uploads/sites/2/2015/09/WTT-TPA-Sept-REG-2015.pdf.

A key element of our vision for accommodating teacher candidates with mental health disabilities is that of shared responsibility. All agents, including the university, the host school and the teacher candidate, must engage in information sharing; responsive and responsible decision-making around process, policies and protocols; and consideration of potential solutions. The OHRC (2014) lists the responsibilities for accommodation as follows: The person with a disability is required to (a) identify the need for accommodation; (b) provide information about relevant restrictions and limitations, including information from health care professionals to establish needs; (c) participate in discussions about possible accommodations; (d) co-operate in the accommodation process; (e) work with the accommodation provider on an ongoing basis; (f) meet agreed-upon job competencies, standards of practice and related expectations; and (g) discuss the disability with only those who need to know.

The accommodation provider is required to (a) be cognizant that individuals may need accommodation, even if a request has not been made; (b) accept the request in good faith and review each case on its own merit; (c) obtain only necessary and relevant information about the nature of the limitation or restriction; (d) take an active role in identifying possible options for accommodation and alternative solutions; (e) take adequate steps to accommodate needs and keep a record of requests and accommodations; (f) maintain confidentiality, and (g) provide reasonable accommodations of needs to the point of undue hardship.

We discuss four case studies to provide clarity in our discussion. We focus on issues related to practicum placements because conflicts around accommodations are more likely to occur when teacher candidates are placed in schools than when on the university campus. These case studies illustrate four areas of concern that have arisen in situations where teacher candidates experienced mental health challenges, and these challenges impeded the progress of a practicum. Please note that no one case represents any specific situation or individual, but rather, the cases are synthesized to best and most effectively illustrate four defined areas of concern: (1) capacity to perform duties (competency), (2) failure to disclose, (3) confidentiality, and (4) professionalism encompassing the OCT standards of practice and ethical standards.

We refer to university-based faculty members working to support teacher candidates during practica as *faculty advisors*. We refer to teachers in schools who host teacher candidates as *associate teachers*.

CASE A: Competency

This scenario is designed to illustrate why a more proactive response may be necessary to support teacher candidates when their behaviour appears to be unprofessional and prevents them from demonstrating the competencies required for graduation and certification.

Three weeks into the first term of a Bachelor of Education consecutive program, an instructor in a curriculum methods course contacted the Dean's Office, concerned that a teacher candidate had worn an inappropriate dress-up costume in class. The costume consisted of an inner tube around the teacher candidate's waist, swim aids on her arms, a bathing cap, swim goggles and a snorkel. When the instructor asked the teacher candidate why she was dressed in this way, she responded, "I was in the mood." She did not repeat this behaviour during the remainder of the course. On the first day of her practicum placement, the teacher candidate was dressed in a professional manner; however, on the following day, she arrived at school dressed in a different and equally inappropriate (unprofessional) dress-up costume including a multi-coloured clown wig, clown make-up and large clown shoes. The costume was not part of a theme day, and it alarmed and frightened the students in the Grade 3 class. The school immediately called the university faculty advisor to express concern. The teacher candidate was told not to wear a wig or dress-up costume again. The faculty advisor visited the next day to observe the teacher candidate and did not express any concerns about either her dress or performance.

In the third week of school practicum, the teacher candidate arrived 40 minutes late to teach. When the principal asked her to explain her lateness, she replied that she was late because of ethereal and ghostly events at her home. When she repeated the same behaviour on the following day, the teacher candidate was suspended from her practicum, and the placement was deemed a failure. When called in to meet the dean to discuss the issues, the teacher candidate stated, "I felt I was not able to leave my house because there were spirits present who wanted me to stay in the house." At the meeting with the dean, the teacher candidate was wearing a metal clamp on her nose. When asked why she was wearing this item, she explained that it helped her to centre her thoughts. It was suggested at the meeting that she seek support from counselling services at the university. She was also informed that she would have one final opportunity to complete a successful practicum.

On the first day of the new and final school placement, she arrived 90 minutes late. When she was unable to provide a satisfactory explanation for her lateness, she was suspended from practicum, and the placement was deemed a failure. As she had failed practicum twice, she was withdrawn from the program. She continued to lobby to be readmitted into the Bachelor of Education (B.Ed.) program, but she was not readmitted because the policy stated that failure in two practica results in automatic withdrawal from the program.

The teacher candidate did not disclose any mental health disabilities to the university. If she had done so, additional supports could have been provided to her. The teacher candidate did not make appropriate judgements about suitable dress and professional behaviour in the classroom and school setting. She arrived late on several occasions. Ultimately, this teacher candidate failed practicum because of unprofessional behaviour which resulted from an apparently limited capacity to understand or take responsibility for meeting the requirements of the teacher education program, OCT standards of practice and ethics, the need for her to be accountable, responsive and responsible as an emergent professional, as well as grasping the host school, university and community expectations of her as a teacher candidate in a classroom.

CASE B: Failure to Disclose and Capacity to Perform Duties

This scenario demonstrates how situations escalate when a teacher candidate does not disclose mental health concerns and/or does not request accommodation.

In this case, the teacher candidate was not registered with student accessibility services, nor did she indicate any need for accommodation. She had taught internationally and in a private school in Canada, but had only limited experience with the school systems in Ontario.

Both before and during her first school practicum block, the teacher candidate experienced some challenges, and she was given considerable support with pedagogy and practice. Initially, she appeared respectful and accepting of feedback, but despite considerable support and guidance from the associate teacher and faculty advisor, the first practicum was unsuccessful. The support provided included an action plan outlining areas and concrete strategies for improvement with formative assessments to help improve classroom management and student engagement, additional resources, and further instructions on modelling best practices by the associate teachers. Despite this extra help, the teacher candidate was not able to demonstrate clear competency in classroom management, differentiated instruction, and assessment. Hence, the final result was that the practicum was a failure. After failing, the teacher candidate claimed that the result was unfair, that the claims that she was unable to meet the core competencies were untrue, and that this result was discriminatory. Blaming the associate teacher, the teacher candidate formally appealed the failed placement; however, the failure was upheld.

Despite receiving considerable support, the teacher candidate again struggled in the second practicum. Both the faculty advisor and the associate teacher met with her to outline an action plan and to provide support. Near the end of this practicum and before the final evaluation, the teacher candidate appeared at the university, asking if the evaluation had been submitted. The teacher candidate became very agitated and asked what would happen if she did not pass the practicum. The dean and faculty representatives explained the policies related to repeating a practicum and making an appeal. The teacher candidate began crying and rejected the appeal processes as unfair.

At this point she collapsed, crying and repeating accusations of unfair treatment, including charging the associate teacher with lying. University security was called and remained to ensure the teacher candidate was safe. She refused any attention and continued to cry and accuse her associate teacher of being unfair. As the dean continued to try to calm her by explaining that decisions about her progress in the program had not yet been made, she continually interrupted and accused others. At one point, she violently hit herself in the head. She insisted on leaving, even though she was encouraged to stay due to concern for her safety. After walking down the hall, she returned and began knocking on the dean's door, becoming increasingly agitated. The police were called. It was reported that the teacher candidate spent the weekend in hospital.

The teacher candidate returned to the program, providing an assessment by a mental health professional as requested by the university, indicating that she was well enough to return to campus and "assume the responsibilities of a teacher." At this point, the faculty advisor suggested concrete strategies and support for managing stress. It was determined that she could return to class and continue in the B.Ed. program. After barely passing two subsequent practica with different faculty advisors and associate teachers, she struggled again in her final classroom practicum. At the mid-point, a meeting was held to develop an action plan for the student. She responded defensively and emotionally. When her progress with regard to the action plan was reviewed a week later, given her ongoing failure to perform, the faculty advisor and a university counsellor were present to provide support for her. The teacher candidate was emotional and accusatory, and left yelling and threatening to hurt herself. The student was withdrawn from the program.

CASE C: Confidentiality

This scenario demonstrates the need to protect confidentiality. Even when teacher candidates do disclose a mental health disability, universities are not permitted to communicate this information to schools without the permission of the teacher candidate.

In this case, the teacher candidate registered with the office on campus that provides services to students with disabilities (referred to here as *Student Services*) and disclosed an undiagnosed condition that would require a detailed safety plan to be put in place for her classes. The safety plan, written by the teacher candidate, outlined situations wherein her behaviour could range from staring into space for long periods of time to lapsing into unconsciousness. Upon receiving the plan, faculty members stated that they did not feel equipped to deal with the situations described, especially when the teacher candidate lost consciousness.

The teacher candidate reworked the plan with Student Services and the university practicum office to ensure that the plan would be suitable for both on-campus classes and a school-placement classroom. After the first practicum, it was discovered that the plan had not been shared with the associate teacher, although the teacher candidate had hinted to the associate teacher about potential difficulties during the practicum. The practicum office was not permitted to share the safety plan with any of the school staff. The teacher candidate continued to refer to her illness and her need for a safety plan while on placement. The associate teacher became frustrated when the practicum office would not supply further information about the teacher candidate's disability. As a result, the school questioned the university's policies about privacy and the potential safety issues for the teacher candidate, the teacher, and students as a result of the need to protect the teacher candidate's confidentiality with regard to her disclosure. Further, the teacher candidate maintained her right to confidentiality with regard to her disability and the safety plan developed with Student Services at the university. In the opinion of the Faculty of Education, as a result of this situation, the relationship with the school was significantly compromised. Ultimately, the teacher candidate did not experience any difficulties related to the safety plan and successfully graduated from the program.

CASE D: Professionalism Encompassing the OCT Standards of Practice and Ethical Standards

This scenario demonstrates the necessity of balancing the needs of teacher candidates with the need to ensure that professional competencies and standards of practice are met.

In this case, the teacher candidate self-identified with university accessibility services as a student with a learning disability. Accommodations were made specific to the teacher candidate's diagnosed learning disability and to her coursework. She did not disclose any other disabilities.

In this teacher education program, teacher candidates were required to exhibit competencies in three separate school placement blocks. The teacher candidate met the expectations for successful teaching practice in the first and second placement blocks despite both associate teachers expressing concern over the teacher candidate's apparent inability to accept critical feedback, or to entertain ideas that varied from her own. As a result, in her third placement, she was asked to focus on a number of very important competency-related issues with regard to classroom management strategies, assessment and evaluation, ensuring plans and resources were prepared ahead of time with time for review, use of a variety of teaching strategies, and her ability to respond to the individual needs of the students.

The teacher candidate attended the first day of her third placement block. On the second day of placement, she failed to appear at school and did not notify anyone of the reason for her failure or for subsequent absences. After being absent for a considerable period of time, she indicated that she was ready to return to placement and had health-related documentation indicating that she was ready to return. In order to facilitate her success, a meeting was held to discuss the university's expectations of her with regard to teaching competency across all variables while in her final placement, as well as to discuss her own stress management, and strategies that could be put in place in case of future episodes. The associate teacher offered specific support, and the teacher candidate was also encouraged to help the associate teacher better understand the candidate's particular needs in order to support her optimally. In response to these suggestions, the teacher candidate was resistant and non-committal.

Just prior to the beginning of the classroom placement, the teacher candidate cancelled the rescheduled third and last placement block, indicating mental health-related stress issues. Nevertheless, she continued to pursue the idea of completing the third and final placement. In response, the university requested further documentation to support her fitness and ability to complete the program, and another meeting was held to review strategies that could assist her. At the meeting, concern was expressed as to whether teaching was a good match for this teacher candidate. Again, she was asked to suggest how the university and the associate teacher could support her optimally. Again, the candidate resisted these requests.

A third placement block was rescheduled. Despite extensive support, again the teacher candidate struggled in the placement with competency-related challenges: classroom management, time management, curriculum, resources, use of varied teaching strategies, assessment and evaluation, and response to individual students. She expressed that she felt overwhelmed, and that the associate teacher was expecting too much of her. She indicated that she was experiencing panic attacks and unsettled sleep and eating habits. In turn, the associate teacher became increasingly concerned about the teacher candidate's inability to accept feedback, as well as her disrespectful behaviour. For example, she told the associate teacher that all feedback offered by her was a waste of time.

As the placement continued, the principal of the school hosting the rescheduled placement requested that the teacher candidate be withdrawn. The school found that this placement was compromising student learning and causing significant stress to the associate teacher. The school expressed concern about the teacher candidate's mental health and her apparent anxiety. As the teacher candidate was withdrawn from the placement, it was recorded as a failed practicum placement. In this teacher education program, two failed placements usually result in immediate withdrawal from the B.Ed. program. However, despite two failed placements, the program allowed a third attempt. In providing another opportunity, it was determined that should the teacher candidate leave her placement, or if her competency issues were not addressed successfully, she would need to withdraw from the teacher education program.

On this final placement attempt, it was determined that the teacher candidate did not demonstrate the competencies required for successful teaching in the Ontario school system. Although the faculty had done its best to support her, she struggled in many areas and resisted the help that had been offered. Her placement overwhelmed her, and she could not meet the expectations for competency as a teacher candidate.

Issues and Related Questions

With regard to Case A focusing on competency, we wonder whether the university should have been more proactive in providing support to this teacher candidate when her behaviour appeared to be contrary to professional expectations. Is it within the purview of the university to require the student to seek professional mental health support before returning to practicum placement?

With regard to Case B, we believe that failure to disclose could be premised on the extent to which the teacher candidate was aware of her mental health issues or whether she was aware that her (and other) mental health issues would and should require accommodation. We also wonder about the fear of discrimination that could result from disclosure. Further, the candidate might not have experienced any previous mental health issues, and the stress of being a teacher candidate might have caused them. Regardless of the reason for non-disclosure, if our goal is to provide all possible opportunities for teacher candidates to succeed, we need to consider what can be done to prevent escalation in this kind of situation. For instance, timing may be an issue in responding effectively to a teacher candidate's needs, even if she does not ask for support. Were there red flags that went unnoticed or institutional supports that could have been provided? As part of all performance or evaluation-related meetings with teacher candidates, support protocols could be developed that would remind the candidates that support services were available.

Nonetheless, even with such supports in place, nothing guarantees that a similar situation will not unfold and escalate.

In Case C, confidentiality was raised as an issue. We question whether withholding information from schools, especially when the teacher candidate's behaviour might pose a risk to him/herself and others, is an ethical violation of confidentiality. Further, the ability to share information with regard to the teacher candidate's mental health disabilities is critical, especially when a safety plan is required, and although doing so with the knowledge and consent of the teacher candidate is preferable, the importance of such sharing is not diminished when such consent is withheld. We question whether withholding information with the potential to affect the outcome of a practicum is reasonable and in the best interest of all stakeholders, especially teacher candidates.

In her summary of the *Ontario Human Rights Commission* policy on mental disabilities and addictions, Peters (2014, p. 4) stated, "the policy defines the 'most appropriate accommodation' as the one that most: (a) respects dignity (including autonomy, comfort and confidentiality), (b) responds to a person's individualized needs, and (c) allows for integration and full participation."

Confidentiality continues to be a grey area when working with teacher candidates as they move into classrooms with children whose human rights must also be upheld. In some instances, confidentiality puts universities in positions where, without student permission, important information cannot be communicated to schools or other placement locales in which our teacher candidates are placed. Ongoing discussion reveals different practices and understandings with regard to these issues of confidentiality. Some universities maintain that once students disclose to the university, the university has both the responsibility and the right to ensure that this information is also shared with schools. The issue can then become one of whose rights take precedence – the rights of teacher candidates, or those of the students and staff at the school placement site?

In Case D, professionalism was raised as an issue. The definition of "most appropriate accommodation" also applies here. In this case study, the Faculty of Education's actions appeared to be reactive. Could the faculty have been more proactive, by removing barriers to achieve integration and full participation by the teacher candidate? Ongoing tension occurred between ensuring appropriate accommodations and attempts to accommodate the teacher candidate's needs and enforcing the professional competencies and standards of practice identified by the Ontario College of Teachers (OCT). The teacher candidate appeared to be unable to meet the academic standards and competencies required for licensing of a teacher. We believe this teacher candidate could have been more successful had she disclosed fully her mental health disabilities. Perhaps if subsequent placement schools had been informed about the teacher candidate's behaviour during a mental health event, better accommodations might have been available.

Accommodations must be based on an understanding of where a school and faculty's duty to accommodate ends. At what point can we determine that a teacher candidate cannot fulfill the teaching competency requirements and obligations of a teacher candidate, despite accommodation strategies having been put in place? Finally, do health care providers understand the required competencies of teachers and teacher candidates sufficiently to be able to determine and direct appropriate accommodations? Further, how does a healthcare provider determine that a teacher candidate is able to assume or resume his/her responsibilities? And finally, how do we balance conflicting rights in circumstances such as these?

Pressing Issues

a. How do we identify the appropriate point at which to intervene?

b. What should we do when a teacher candidate is not willing to disclose that s/he requires accommodation and/or support, or is not aware that s/he must disclose, and that supports are available?

c. We cannot modify professional standards. What, then, is the middle ground between standards and accommodations? What happens if accommodation leads to modification of professional standards?

d. What resources should we call upon within the university and/or school boards, and at what point?

e. Does the role of certification undermine inclusive practices?

f. How do we ensure that the added dimension of the school practicum (placement outside the university) is considered in accommodation policies and practices?

g. How can we best provide information and offer support to incoming students, in the event that they experience mental health issues/challenges?

h. What type of information and support can be provided to teacher candidates and faculty?

Conclusion

We offer an emergent set of principles based on the following assumptions: Responding to mental health disability is a joint responsibility for all stakeholders. The teacher candidate has a duty to disclose, if he/she is aware of a personal mental health issue. If not, the school and the university have a duty to bring problematic behaviour to the attention of the teacher candidate. The ability to accommodate teacher candidates might be limited under circumstances where the rights (e.g., to safety) of other stakeholders must be preserved. Further, we have a duty to maintain a safe and productive learning environment in schools and other practicum settings. Policies guiding professional behaviour and professionalism are in place in educational environments. For example, in Ontario the *Standards of Practice and Ethics* as outlined by the Ontario College of Teachers (OCT) would apply. In addition, individual Faculty of Education policies define expectations for teacher candidates. Further, teacher candidates are expected to exhibit the essential skills required of students entering Bachelor of Education (B.Ed.) programs. When problems arise, typically these problems can be identified within the context of policy issues or performance in relation to expected competency levels. The following is a basic framework around which policy and protocol measures might be considered. (1) Identify and describe a range of mental health challenges. This information is important for distribution to school partners, teacher candidates, university support personnel, faculty, and associate teachers. (2) Explain to teacher candidates their duty to disclose any mental health disability of which they are aware. Also, explain any limits to confidentiality that will be in place to protect the interests of school stakeholders. (3) Study the professional standards that are in place in relation to accommodation (for example, the OCT standards in Ontario), and consider policy, protocols and implementation with regard to the following: (a) university teacher education policy, (b) disclosure materials, (c) professional standards of practice and ethical standards, (d) behaviour issues during courses in class on campus, and (e) behaviour issues during teaching practica. (4) Identify the most appropriate timing for any intervention. (5) Identify the protocols for intervention. (6) Identify resources to support teacher candidates, associate teachers, faculty advisors, and principals. (7) Identify policy and protocols for termination of teaching practica.

When behaviour is identified that is anomalous, extreme, repetitive and non-compliant with any applicable policies or with the required essential skills and dispositions, the student and faculty must be notified of the issue in question and advised of possible supports.

We also recommend that teacher candidates be given opportunities to practice receiving and responding constructively to both positive and negative feedback (e.g., through role-playing). This kind of preparation may help to "normalize" the experience of receiving feedback and reduce defensiveness, since it communicates that all new teachers can learn and improve their practices by receiving feedback.

Finally, we do recognize that some teacher candidates are unsuccessful. At times, unsuccessful candidates may be those we cannot accommodate, as the scope for accommodation is limited, given the need to protect all parties, including teacher candidates, university faculty, school students, and staff in schools. There must be a point at which faculties of education can and must make the difficult decision to require a teacher candidate to withdraw from the program even if she does not accept that decision. Simply providing more opportunities to repeat unsuccessful practica after reasonable supports have been provided will not serve the interests of the teacher candidate, the university, or the profession. In all likelihood, more opportunities will not alleviate inevitable failure. Overall, the need for disclosure, as well as sound policies and protocols to ensure confidentiality, and making accommodations based on joint responsibility and the need for professionalism offer a way forward.

References

Ontario Associate of Deans of Education (2014). *Retreat*. Toronto, Ontario.

Ontario College of Teachers (2015). *The Standards of Practice*. Available at http//www.o http://www.oct.ca/public/professional-standards/standards-of-practice.

Ontario College of Teachers (2015). *The Ethical Standards*. Available at http://www.oct. ca/public/professional-standards/ethical-standards.

Ontario College of Teachers (2015*). Poster.* Available at https://www.oct.ca/-/media/PDF /Standards%20Poster/standards_flyer_e.pdf.

Ontario Human Rights Commission (2014). *Policy on preventing discrimination based on mental health disabilities and addictions.* Available at http://www.ohrc.on.ca/e n/policy-preventing-discrimination-based-mental-health-disabilities-and-addictions.

Ontario Teachers' Federation (2014). *The Teaching Profession Act*. Available at http://www.otffeo.on.ca/en/wp-content/uploads/sites/2/2015/09/WTT-TPA-REG- Sept-2015.pdf.

Peters, C.L. (2014). Ontario Human Rights Commission Releases new policy on mental disabilities and addictions. *Canadian Corporate Counsel, 23*(7), 97-100.

CHAPTER 16

Mental Health Accommodation for Graduate Students

Tatiana Gounko

Abstract

The purpose of this chapter is to discuss the existing institutional strategies related to the accommodation of graduate students with mental health issues in order to understand their complexity and associated challenges. The author examines academic accommodation, institutional strategies, and challenges faced by graduate students with mental health disabilities. As no specific federal or provincial governmental standards exist in Canada, policies and procedures for accessing accommodations vary across universities, as do the staffing and budgets for disability services and the level of understanding among administrators and faculty. Universities are still trying to develop best practices while dealing with declining public resources and increasing demands for student services. This task is exceptionally complex, and requires the entire university community to participate in implementing the student mental health strategy in order to create an inclusive and accessible learning environment.

Introduction

The issue of academic accommodation and institutional support for students with mental health disabilities is currently on the agenda of colleges and universities across Canada. Mental health disabilities are sometimes called "invisible" disabilities because, unlike physical and learning disabilities, they may not be obvious and can occur episodically. In the past decade, general attitudes toward, and acceptance of, people with mental illnesses have changed significantly. Students who previously were not able to attend universities and colleges are now pursuing post-secondary and graduate education due to better services, medication, and changes in social perceptions. Accommodating these students is a relatively new practice for educational institutions. Most Canadian universities have a policy or strategy that specifically addresses student mental health and provides a framework and resources for the entire campus community. However, faculty members generally do not feel adequately prepared to meet the needs of these students, especially at the graduate level.

According to the National Educational Association of Disabled Students (NEADS) (2016), Canadian institutions are drafting policy and practice guidelines based on limited, anecdotal and local experience without research and information about the issues faced by graduate students with disabilities. This critical lack of research leads me to explore some of the important questions regarding institutional policies, support, and resources available to faculty who are directly involved in providing academic accommodation to graduate students with mental health conditions.

The purpose of this chapter is to discuss the existing institutional strategies related to the accommodation of graduate students with mental health issues in order to understand their complexity and associated challenges, and to review research addressing these students' needs and the approaches that faculty members can use to deal with such issues.

Student Mental Health: A Concern Growing

A report published by Queen's University, which, from 2010 to 2012, saw a series of suicides on its campus, offered several reasons for why students might struggle with mental health problems, including the stress of moving away from home, academic demands, financial constraints, time management issues, social pressures, parents' expectations, and the competitive job market:

More students than ever are entering university with a pre-existing diagnosis of mental illness, and there's less stigma attached to getting help. This partly explains the flood that counsellors are seeing. But there's something else going on, too. Some wonder if today's students are having difficulty coping with the rapidly changing world around them, a world where they can't unplug, can't relax, and believe they must stay at the top of their class, no matter what. (Lunau, 2012)

All the above described pressures make students susceptible to mental health problems, which affects their academic performance, overall health and quality of life. Today, experts agree that mental health issues will become the leading cause of disability at Canadian universities by 2020 (CASA, 2014). As a result, post-secondary institutions will be expected to implement comprehensive programs and specific services to promote mental health among all students.

Legal Obligation to Accommodate

With the advances in medical and social sciences and changes in human rights legislation, more students with disabilities are pursuing post-secondary and graduate education in Canada. Currently, the legal obligations to accommodate students with disabilities, including mental health disabilities, are grounded in Section 15 of the *Canadian Charter of Rights and Freedoms*, as well as the *Canadian Human Rights Act*, and provincial human rights legislation. Efforts to provide better services for students with mental health disabilities are also driven by the need to be responsive to new and evolving federal policies such as the Canadian Mental Health Strategy (2012), which stated that one of its priorities is to "increase comprehensive school health and post-secondary mental health initiatives that promote mental health for all students and include targeted prevention efforts for those at risk" (p. 20). According to the National Educational Association of Disabled Students (NEADS) (2016), the growing number of graduate students with disabilities will require universities, disability service providers, students themselves, graduate departments, deans, and student services directors to develop new strategies to facilitate student success and promote mental health.

Mental Health and University Policies

The Mental Health Commission of Canada (2012) stated that mental health differs from the absence of mental illness. Rather, mental health is an integral part of human overall health and wellbeing; it is "a state of well-being in which the individual realizes his or her own potential, can cope with the normal stresses of life, can work productively and fruitfully, and is able to make a contribution to her or his own community" (p. 11). Good mental health helps us cope with the daily and serious stressors in our lives. Mental health problems and illnesses range from common conditions such as anxiety and depression to less common problems and illnesses such as schizophrenia and bipolar disorder.

Today, Canadian universities are grappling with the challenge of provide safe learning environments for a diverse student body. As mental health issues typically begin to emerge during the age when young people pursue post-secondary education, universities must change their traditional approaches and services and adopt more comprehensive strategies and better coordinated programs (University of Alberta, 2015). Doing so is especially important as students with mental health disabilities often require both academic accommodation and medical or therapeutic treatment. Although most campuses offer a variety of services to students, including counselling and disability support, and some universities have designated specialists working with students with mental health conditions, student services are organized "along the traditional stand-alone structures of independent service units that are loosely affiliated at best" (p. 11). Universities must continue to work on improving access to these services.

Olding and Yip (2014) suggest that Canadian post-secondary mental health policies reflect two broad categories that have implications for student mental wellbeing. First, institutions are implementing policies that specifically support individual students experiencing mental health concerns. These policies ensure accessibility and accommodation, medical leave and re-entry procedures, access to information and protection of privacy, procedures for supporting a student in distress or crisis, and response to "at-risk" behaviour. The second set of policies was established to promote positive systemic mental health by creating fair and flexible processes for grading and conflict resolution, providing clear directions for navigating institutional processes and systems, or limiting barriers within these systems, promoting inclusive curriculum and pedagogy (academic policies), and institutionalizing an anti-discriminatory and anti-stigma perspective.

Academic Accommodation

Canadian universities are required to provide access to education and services to students with disabilities, and to offer reasonable accommodation in order to minimize barriers to equal participation in post-secondary education. Students with disabilities are protected by the *Canadian Charter of Rights and Freedoms* and provincial statutes. In recent years, in addition to existing policies on academic accommodation and access to students with disabilities, most universities have also adopted specific strategies related to student mental health. However, no specific federal or provincial governmental standards exist across Canada, so that policies and procedures vary by university, as do budgets for disability services and available programs. As a result, Canadian universities are still determining what the best practices are and how to implement them (Gulli, 2016).

An "academic accommodation" is defined as an individualized modification of environments, materials or requirements which provides the student with an alternative means of meeting essential course or program requirements. This modification is based on the legal concept of "reasonable accommodation," which refers to reasonable efforts to modify requirements so that people with disabilities are able to participate in a process or perform an essential function (University of Victoria, 2011). Accommodations are based on documented need, and students are eligible only for accommodations that address the challenges caused by their disability. The goal of academic accommodation is to provide students with the support they need while helping them to be as independent as possible (CMHA, 2016).

Canadian universities are responsible for ensuring that facilities, procedures, teaching and learning materials, and methods of assessment are accessible to all students. University policies expect all members of the university community to: share the responsibility to promote equality; remove barriers including physical, curricular, attitudinal, and informational barriers; and create a respectful and inclusive learning environment. However, appropriate academic accommodation requires shared responsibilities between students, university faculty and staff.

Students with mental health disabilities have a right to receive academic accommodation if required. All universities have disabilities services offices, which are intended to assist students seeking academic accommodation. The first step is to contact the office. Although requirements may vary from university to university, students are generally asked to provide a detailed letter from a psychologist, psychiatrist, family doctor, or registered clinical social worker familiar with the case. The letter must be based on a recent evaluation and should include the relevant medical history, a description of how the student's condition might affect her/his academic performance, current medication and its possible effects on academic performance, and the specific accommodations required. The letter and documentation represent confidential medical information that is kept on file in the Disability Services Office and used by the office staff only. This information is not shared with instructors or anyone else in the university without student permission. The Disability Services Office is essential in finding appropriate accommodation for students as, in some cases, students with mental health problems may not know what type of accommodation they need. The office staff employs specialists who help a student understand how her/his disability affects learning and what strategies and accommodations are required. Given that each university designs its specific policies and has a variety of academic programs, available accommodations can vary and may not be available at every university and for every course. For example, the University of Victoria Resource Centre for Students with Disability stated that a diagnosis of disability alone does not guarantee academic accommodations. While students do not need to self-declare a disability when they are applying or being admitted to the University, they do need medical and/or psychological documentation if they choose to register with the Disability Office. The Office will then work with students to decide what accommodations will be most helpful.

Accommodations can extend to the classroom, as well as to assignments and exams. The Canadian Mental Health Association (CMHA) (2016) lists several examples of these accommodations. If, due to illness or medication, a student has difficulty with concentrating, keeping focused, processing information and organizing thoughts, possible classroom accommodation may include a formal peer note-taker, who can help reduce anxiety and allow better participation in class. Taping lectures and note-taking technology as well as preferential seating that reduces audio and visual distraction can also be helpful for some students.

Assignment accommodation for such students may involve an academic coach or tutor to help with projects and edit student essays for organization, clarity and spelling. Arrangements can be also made for students to receive course materials in advance to allow extra time to read them. During exams, students who have difficulty concentrating due to illness or medication will benefit from preferential seating or a quiet or separate room. All of these accommodations are commonly offered by student services and faculty.

The Issue of Disclosure of Mental Condition

The Canadian Mental Health Association (2016) maintains that in order to be eligible for academic accommodation, a student needs to disclose her or his disability and provide appropriate documentation to the Disability Services Office, the only place where a student has to provide such information. A student does not have to discuss a disability with anybody else on campus, including the instructors who need to know that a student has a documented disability for which academic accommodation is required. Generally, instructors are aware of the university policies and very cooperative about accommodating students with disabilities.

For many students with a mental health disability, approaching instructors can be especially uncomfortable. The Canadian Mental Health Association (2016) provided the following advice on how to approach instructors. Communication between a student and instructor is critical; students need to approach their instructor at the beginning of the semester and give the instructor the letter from the Disability Services Office. Explaining how the student's disability affects his or her learning and what accommodations or strategies are needed in specific situations will help the instructor understand the student's needs. If the instructor cannot meet a student's request due to the nature of the course or for some objective reason, alternatives need to be discussed. Both the student and instructor must clearly understand what accommodations can be provided with help from the Disability Services Office. If an instructor has not understood the student's explanation, or does not agree that the student should receive certain accommodations, the student needs to talk with the Disability Services Office as soon as possible so that it can help resolve the issue.

Currently, university policies promote and communicate mental health strategies through academic offices, including the Faculty of Graduate Studies, university calendars, and syllabi. For example, the University of Victoria encourages all instructors to add the following accessibility statement to course outlines:

> Students with diverse learning styles and needs are welcome in this course. In particular, if you have a disability/health consideration that may require accommodations, please feel free to approach me and/or the Resource Centre for Students with a Disability (RCSD) as soon as possible. The RCSD staff are available by appointment to assess specific needs, provide referrals and arrange appropriate accommodations (http://rcsd.uvic.ca/). The sooner you let us know your needs the quicker we can assist you in achieving your learning goals in this course. (University of Victoria, 2016)

Faculties and departments play an integral role in implementing these strategies. This role may imply that the existing policies, legal obligations of universities, and desire to improve how institutions deal with students with mental health issues make academic accommodation a well-defined process, but many challenges still persist. According to the CAUSS-CMHA (2013), interrelated physical, cultural, spiritual, political, socio-economic, and organizational contextual factors significantly affect student learning experience and wellbeing.

Graduate Programs and Institutional Challenges

In graduate programs, students are expected to be independent in their academic work and to take responsibility in decision making. While, generally, graduate programs are more flexible than undergraduate programs, the former also have higher expectations, which can cause additional stress and contribute to the existing mental health problems. Some students in graduate programs also have added responsibilities and pressures including financial, family, and work obligations. Experts (e.g., Hyun, Quinn, Madon, & Lustig, 2006, 2007) have discussed a variety of stressors that contribute to the mental health problems of graduate students. The top stressors for many graduate students are poor advisor relationships, social isolation, and precarious finances and career prospects. In addition, the organization and structure of existing graduate programs present specific challenges for students. After completing required coursework, many students find themselves isolated without necessary support. As finishing one's thesis or dissertation may take several years, graduate students often become disengaged from the campus, so that their mental health and stress levels may be negatively affected. Graduate students also have multiple roles besides being students, such as working as instructors and researchers on university campuses.

Many studies have highlighted additional stressors that graduate students grapple with during their studies. According to the Canadian Federation of Students – Ontario (2016), graduate students experience pressures such as high workloads and expectations, as well as constant competition with peers for resources and funding. This competition can strain the relationships graduate students have with other members of the campus community. Graduate students are "particularly vulnerable to pressures related to conducting research and teaching, publishing, and finding employment, in addition to stress from the often ambiguous expectations of advisors" (Hyun et al., 2006). The 2016 Canadian Mental Health Association survey of graduate students also found that some students were dealing with time-to-completion anxiety, a perceived lack of support from their academic institution, and anxiety about seeking and/or affording mental health support. The fear of being stigmatized and discriminated against due to the intense competition for admission, and the competitive environment within the program may not provide conditions conducive to support and academic accommodation. Stigma, lack of understanding among family and friends, and limited knowledge of how to access student services can influence a student's ability to seek institutional support (Wyatte & Oswalt, 2013).

Some researchers (Tseng & Newton, 2002; Hyun et al., 2007; Wenhua & Zhe, 2013) have discussed international students' additional challenges, which may contribute to either pre-existing or new mental health issues. These challenges are (1) general living adjustment, such as becoming accustomed to life in a foreign context with new housing, environment, food, and transportation; (2) academic adjustment to a new university system requiring different skills for academic success; (3) sociocultural adjustment to different cultural norms and behaviours; and (4) personal psychological adjustment including dealing with homesickness, loneliness, or feelings of isolation and even lost identity. The difficulty of coping with these challenges may be compounded by limited financial resources and immigration policies in relation to student visas and employment. International students are also less likely to seek support from health services due to an unawareness of mental health issues and the cultural stigma around mental health problems. According to Hyun et al., (2007), an unmet mental health need exists among international graduate students. Special mental health outreach efforts should be directed at international graduate students, with particular attention to the relationship between students and their advisors, and to adequate financial support.

The above described challenges, experienced by all graduate students, can be compounded by the institutional structure of a university.

Universities are complex organizations that employ thousands of people to fulfill their teaching, research, and service mandates and to deliver a variety of services. University structure, strategic goals, policies, and practices affect the effectiveness of institutional services, including mental health initiatives. Faculties and departments are bound by deadlines related to instruction, program completion, research, and funding, which, at times, can be seen as contradicting mental health principles such as equity, accessibility, and flexibility. In some cases, faculties and departments cannot provide flexibility, as they themselves, and universities also, are bound by external policies and deadlines. For example, universities cannot change deadlines set by either Canadian or international funding agencies (e.g., SSHRC; NSERC; Fulbright). Regardless, universities often have internal procedures for allowing students with disabilities enough time to complete their programs. This objective can be achieved through so-called academic concessions, or accommodations made for students unable to fulfill course requirements due to extenuating circumstances, including mental health conditions. Academic concessions are often used in graduate programs.

At the University of Victoria, the Faculty of Graduate Studies works with students with disabilities to consider reasonable accommodation with respect to deadlines and time-limited regulations. Students who are affected by illness, accident or family affliction may apply for a deferral of a course grade, withdrawal from the course due to extenuating circumstances, a drop of course(s) without academic and/or fee penalty after the published withdrawal deadline, or a leave of absence from the program due to illness, accident, or family affliction. Students are advised to immediately consult with Counselling Services, University Health Services or another health professional. Applications for leaves of absence from the program must be accompanied by supporting documentation.

Students can also request directly from the course instructor a deferral or substitution of work which is due during the term. Such arrangements must be made between the student and the instructor. If the instructor denies a request for deferral or substitution of term work, the student may appeal this decision in accordance with the university's appeals procedures.

The organization and coordination of the various campus services is essential as students are dealing with serious mental health disabilities such as schizophrenia, post-traumatic stress disorder, eating disorders or self-injury that require a holistic and long-term approach (NEADS, 2016). While many students suffer from anxiety, stress, and depression and may require short-term counselling support, others may require extended medical and psychological therapy and academic accommodation. The National Educational Association of Disabled Students (NEADS) (2016) stresses the importance of establishing a stand-alone Mental Health Disabilities Office to handle the accommodation and support of such students, especially in institutions with larger populations of students with mental health disabilities. Because these students will undoubtedly have varied needs with no "one size fits all" solution, universities will need staff knowledgeable about relevant disorders, treatments, and appropriate accommodations. Some universities are already hiring disability service staff with specialized knowledge and experience, and having them deal exclusively with students with mental health disabilities. These personnel include qualified counsellors, psychologists and psychiatrists. For example, at the University of Alberta, Counselling and Clinical Services (CCS) adopted a new philosophy regarding how to provide effective and efficient services to students on the main campus by amalgamating the psychiatrists in the University Health Centre into the Mental Health Centre. This integration was intended to facilitate consultation, collaboration, and seamless service provision. In addition, a psychiatric nurse was hired to bridge the gap between psychological and psychiatric services by providing clinical support to students with psychiatric illnesses (University of Alberta, 2015).

There is no doubt that Canadian universities are taking student mental health and well-being seriously, connecting these factors to student retention and academic success. However, despite the available services, many students with mental health issues often experience difficulty accessing services and accommodations that suit their needs. In this context, the stigma surrounding mental health disabilities and the disclosure requirement are the main obstacles for these students. If a student elects not to disclose his or her disability, the University cannot ensure the appropriate evaluation or implementation of any necessary academic accommodation (UVIC, 2016). However, the requirement to disclose one's disability in order to qualify for academic accommodation was challenged in 2016. York University graduate student Navi Dhanota filed an application with the provincial human rights tribunal after the university denied her academic accommodations. After months of mediation, the Ontario Human Rights Commission unveiled a precedent-setting resolution: while students must still provide medical documentation indicating they have a disability and its limitations, they no longer have to disclose their specific diagnosis (Gulli, 2016, p. 1). This decision reflects an ever-evolving balancing act in higher education between disclosure, eliminating barriers posed by disability, and maintaining the integrity and quality of academic work. This decision also means that new accommodation requests and justifications will inevitably arise, and universities will need to develop policies to address emerging issues that were unrecognized even a few years ago (Lee, 2014).

Implications for Faculty and Universities

As increasing numbers of students are either arriving at university with mental health conditions or developing these conditions during their studies, institutions will have to broaden their services and increase their education for students, staff, and faculty. Despite the considerable changes in the student body, and the greater involvement of student services in providing accommodation to students with mental health disabilities, education on how to support students with these types of disabilities is currently limited.

Although the student mental health strategies of all universities emphasize the importance of involving faculty in promoting student mental health on campus, many faculty members are still unsure what to do when they encounter a student experiencing mental health issues. During my study leave, I received the following email from one of my international graduate students:

I am quite sorry that I have [not had] the courage to contact you until now. In the past half year I suffered from negative emotions and low confidence because of some issues about personal relationship, so I isolated myself from friends and did not log in Yahoo email for a long time.

This graduate student clearly needed help to deal with mental health issues, and perhaps should have accessed student services to help her cope with what appeared to be the isolation and depression experienced by many in graduate schools. Long before this email arrived, I suspected that the student was having some difficulties. I did ask her about her well-being and life outside the university to learn if she was having some mental health issues. As the student was not willing to share her concerns, I was not sure what to do. This situation is far from unique. Every week, I see graduate students dealing with various personal, professional, and academic issues.

Research suggests that many graduate students, especially international students, rely more on academic advisors and peers than on the campus support services. Due to this primary institutional connection, faculty and supervisors become an important factor both in the emotional wellbeing of students while in graduate programs and in directing students to appropriate services on campus:

Advisors play a pivotal role in the academic life of graduate students. The relationship between graduate student and advisor is closer in some disciplines than in others, but, regardless of area of study, graduate students rely on their advisors to facilitate advancement through the program, professional development, funding for research and other activities, as well as cooperation with other faculty and staff. (Hyun et al., 2007, p. 117)

Considering the significance of student-supervisor relationships in graduate programs, universities need to pay particular attention to the education of, and support for, faculty who work directly with graduate students. Professional development for faculty is key in implementing university policies. I found that all universities have education and training of faculty and staff listed in their mental health policies. For example, the University of Victoria in its Student Mental Health Strategy 2014-2017 wants to develop a UVic specific faculty and staff training program on student mental health, continue communicating with and educating faculty and staff on academic accommodation procedures and the duty to accommodate students with mental health issues, and encourage the adoption of universal design principles to enhance accessibility for all students (University of Victoria, 2014, p. 12). The university is looking for ways to better support at-risk students by providing "learning opportunities and resources for students, faculty, and staff to recognize early warning signs that a student may be experiencing difficulty, how to reach out to the student, and how to help connect the student to the resources and supports they need, including referral to mental health services when required" and "consultative services and enhanced support to faculty and staff when they are aware of a student experiencing challenges who may need additional support" (p. 17). The University of Toronto is also planning to develop programming and training that supports faculty, graduate supervisors, and teaching assistants in creating learning environments that encourage students to seek help without fear of judgment or repercussions. Similarly, the 2013 CACUSS-CMHA report recommended that universities should consider in-depth training/education programs for front-line faculty and academic advisors about early indicators of mental health problems, resources, roles, and boundaries in facilitating early identification and outreach. Universities need to make faculty and staff aware of the types of situations and circumstances that require crisis management, as well as knowledge of the protocols and faculty and staff roles.

The issues related to student mental health should also be addressed at the faculty of graduate studies level. The university strategy and mental health issues should be discussed through various venues including graduate student orientations, student handbooks, and meetings with advisors. At the same time, academic advisors should receive training on preventing, recognizing, and addressing mental health issues in their students, as most Canadian academics receive little training in supervising and mentoring students. Many do not feel adequately prepared to offer support in non-academic matters, including psychological support, guidance, and assistance to students who are often working through some of the most difficult periods in their lives, both personally and professionally. Academic advisors should make a point of discussing openly with their students the particular challenges of the program, and what types of assistance are available. These advisors should at least know how to recognize problems and be aware of the resources to which they can direct students (Hyun et al., 2007; Turley, 2013).

The calls for faculty education are often expressed in general statements in university strategies. No specific details are provided in terms of supporting students in distress or crisis and creating fair and flexible procedures for grading and accommodation and conflict resolution. However, the importance of education and support for faculty cannot be emphasized enough, as faculty consistently stress that they need more education and a better understanding of their role in student mental health promotion (Gulli, 2016).

Conclusion

The *Canadian Charter of Rights and Freedoms* and provincial statutes require all post-secondary institutions to be accessible to students with disabilities. As no specific federal or provincial governmental standards exist in Canada, policies and procedures for accessing accommodations vary by institutions, as do the staffing and budgets for disability services, and the level of understanding among administrators and faculty (Gulli, 2016). This variation applies to the implementation of mental health strategies across Canadian university campuses. Universities are still trying to develop best practices while dealing with declining public resources and increasing demands for student services. This task is exceptionally complex and requires the entire university community to participate in implementing the student mental health strategy in order to create an inclusive and accessible learning environment.

References

American College Health (2013). Association. American College Health Association- National College Health Assessment II: British Columbia Province Reference Group Data Report Spring 2013. Hanover, MD: Author.

Canadian Association of College & University Student Services and Canadian Mental Health Association (CACUSS-CMHA). (2013). *Post-secondary student mental health: Guide to a systemic approach.* Vancouver, BC: Author.

CASA. (2014). A roadmap for federal action on student mental health. CASA: Ottawa.

CMHA (Canadian Mental Health Association). (2016). Academic accommodations. Retrieved from http://www.cmha.ca/youreducation/accomodations.html#sub2.

Gulli C. (2016). Making accommodations. *Maclean's 129*(7), 58-60.

Hyun, J., Quinn, B., Madon, T., & Lustig, S. (2006). Graduate student mental health: Needs assessment and utilization of counseling services. *Journal of College Student Development 47*(3), 247-266.

Hyun, J., Quinn, B., Madon, T., & Lustig, S. (2007). Mental health need, awareness, and use of counseling services among international graduate students. *Journal of American College Health, 56*(2), 109-118.

Lee, B. (2014). Students with disabilities. Opportunities and challenges for colleges and universities. *Change, 1-2,* 40-45.

Lunau, K. (2012, September). The mental health crisis on campus. *Maclean's Magazine.* Retrieved from http://www.macleans.ca/education/uniand-college/the-mental-healt h-crisis-on-campus/.

NEADS. (2016). http://www.neads.ca/en/about/media/index.php?id=388#sthash.jawgw8j a.dpuf.

Mental Health Commission of Canada. (2012). *Changing directions, changing lives: The mental health strategy for Canada.* Calgary, AB: Author.

Olding, M., & Yip, A. (2014). Policy approaches to post-secondary student mental health. *OCAD University & Ryerson University Campus Mental Health. Partnership Project.* Retrieved from: http://campusmental-health.ca/wp-content/up loads/2014/05/Policy-Approaches-to-PS-student-MH.FINAL_April15-2014.pdf.

Tseng, W., & Newton, F.B. (2002). International students' strategies for well-being. *College Student Journal, 36*(4), 591-597.

Turley, N. (2013, October 7). Mental health issues among graduate students. *Inside Higher Education*. Retrieved from https://www.insidehighered. com/blogs/gradhac er/mental-health-issues-among-graduate-students.

Wenhua, H., & Zhe, Z. (2013). International students' adjustment problems at university: A critical literature review. *Academic Research International*, *4*(2), 400-406.

Wyatt, T., & Oswalt, S. (2013). Comparing mental health issues among undergraduate and graduate students. *American Journal of Health Education*, *44*(2), 96-107.

CHAPTER 17

Legal Issues in Canadian Higher Education

Kelly Clement and William T. Smale

Abstract

This chapter explores the question of bias and procedural unfairness in the admissions process for the post-secondary education system. Specifically, the chapter examines the extent to which universities' discretionary decision-making regarding admissions can be construed as being biased or unfair. Through a review of relevant case law, the authors examine factors involving faculty research funding requirements and conditional admission offers. The chapter also considers the legal implications of case law regarding the contractual nature of educational institutions' requirements to use factual and accurate information regarding their programs. The authors emphasize the importance of the legal distinction between academic issues, which are typically decided internally by the university, and contractual issues, which are subject to intervention by the courts. The authors further consider the requirement to provide due process and procedural fairness. Finally, the chapter looks at students' right to freedom of expression as defined in the *Canadian Charter of Rights and Freedoms*, and the definition of these rights in cases where students are thought to be violating the university code of conduct.

Admission Considerations

Universities are afforded some discretionary decision-making in regard to admission decisions; for example, applicants meeting the qualifications for admission may be declined admission for reasons unrelated to academic standards. In the case of *Mulligan v. Laurentian University* (2008), three applicants[1] to the two-year Master of Science graduate program in Biology (M.Sc. Biology) met the academic requirements and were recommended for admission. The applications were then reviewed by the Master of Science Oversight Committee and denied admission because of a new departmental policy (i.e., the Guaranteed Minimum Stipend) requiring the research supervisor to provide students with a fixed level of funding from a faculty member's research grants, if funding were not available from external scholarships or bursaries. The following excerpts from a letter written to the students' proposed thesis supervisor explain the funding policy:

> The Oversight Committee noted that the requirements of the Departmental policy on funding M.Sc. students were not met. The regulation of the Department of Biology stipulates that each student without a scholarship is to receive a Teaching Assistantship, a summer supplement in the first year, and contributions from research grants held by the supervisor in the amount of $6000.00 in the first year and $8000.00 in the second year....Since the departmental regulations were not met, the three students cannot be recommended for acceptance into the Biology M.Sc. program.... (Court of Appeal for Ontario, 2008, para. 6)

As the faculty supervisor was unable to provide the necessary funding to the students, admission was denied. However, the students did not require funding from the faculty member, so they decided to challenge the decision, ultimately ending up in court. Apparently, the students had other funding mechanisms in place, including family support and possible scholarships (Court of Appeal for Ontario, 2008, para. 9). In their

---

1 Bryce Mulligan, Mathew Hunter, and Hsia-Pai Patrick Wu.

complaint, the students alleged bias and procedural unfairness in the admission process, and "sought to overturn the Guaranteed Minimum Stipend policy implemented by Laurentian University's Biology Department" (Ontario Superior Court of Justice, 2007, para. 1).

On August 17, 2007, the Ontario Superior Court upheld the decision of Laurentian University, indicating that the faculty research funding requirements were part of the admission policy and involved the "core function of a university" (Ontario Superior Court of Justice, 2007, para. 2). The Court also cited the case of *Baxter v. Memorial University of Newfoundland* (1998) and noted that the courts should intervene in the academic function of a university only when the "applicants demonstrate that there has been a flagrant violation of the rules of natural justice" (Ontario Superior Court of Justice, 2007, para. 2).

The Ontario Superior Court's (2007) decision that the admission process was not biased or unfair was supported unanimously by the Court of Appeal for Ontario (2008), which stated that it saw "no lack of procedural fairness or denial of natural justice in which the University dealt with the appellants' application for admission" (Court of Appeal for Ontario, 2008, para. 6). As well, the Court of Appeal observed that the Divisional Court had been correct in concluding that no denial of "natural justice, 'flagrant' or otherwise," had occurred (Court of Appeal for Ontario, 2008, para. 22). With respect to the legal costs associated with the case, the Court of Appeal upheld the decision of the Lower Court, indicating that the student litigants should not receive any special considerations. The Court affirmed that "the fact that the appellants are students does not insulate them from the cost consequences of their decision to litigate" (Court of Appeal for Ontario, 2008, para. 26).

As universities are ranked on the basis of research, the decision of the Court in *Mulligan v. Laurentian University* (2008) is important. In the decision, the Court indicated that the ability to provide funding to students was directly related to ensuring that they would receive a high-quality academic experience. Although the applicants in *Mulligan v. Laurentian University* were apparently self-funded, the costs to the institution for accommodating the students' research programs would have totaled approximately $60,000 per student annually (R. Tyler, personal communication, June 4, 2013). As university funds are secured from numerous sources, a university must exercise due diligence in ensuring that all funds are being used for their intended purpose.

As it had done in the *Mulligan* case, the Court agreed to hear the case of *Nazik Amdiss v. the University of Ottawa* (2010) to consider a potential breach of policy/ contract. In the *Amdiss* case, the student, who was in the final year of her Honours BA psychology program, had been offered conditional admission into the French language medical program at the University of Ottawa. At that time, Amdiss had an exemplary weighted grade point average (WGPA) of 3.73. In the student's final year, she received a D on one course and a D+ on another, which reduced her WGPA to a 3.35 (Ontario Superior Court of Justice, 2010, para. 9). The student was subsequently provided additional information from the university relevant to her admission. When the Faculty of Medicine obtained the student's final grade information, her offer of conditional admission was revoked because her academic standing did not satisfy the admission criteria of the medical program. The student claimed that the admission information provided to her had led her to understand that she had been admitted to the program, and that she was not aware that her admission was contingent upon her maintaining an acceptable WGPA of 3.60.

In the deliberations of this case, it was indicated that the requirement to maintain an acceptable WGPA was not obvious to the student and that denying the student admission to the program would cause harm to her. At para. 27, the Court affirmed that the university was acting in good faith in implementing admission criteria that it believed it had in place, even though it had not clearly "communicated the continuing WGPA requirement" (Ontario Superior Court of Justice, 2010). The Court also indicated that considering the program's limited spaces and high academic standards, requiring the University of Ottawa to grant admission to the student would be unjust. According to Justice Hackland (2010), "the importance of academic excellence in the recruitment of students in medical faculties is a self-evident proposition." He concluded that, "I am also heavily influenced by my conclusion that the medical school was acting in this instance in good faith in enforcing the standards they believe they had in place, and which they followed, communication issues aside" (Ontario Superior Court of Justice, 2010, para. 31).

This case is very interesting because it allows for the possibility that the court might have ordered the University of Ottawa to admit the student if she had applied to a different program. In administration it is common to hear, "We are dealing with paper, not human lives." As a medical program does deal with human lives, this fact might have influenced the decision of the Court.

Service Obligation

Post-secondary institutions must ensure that information provided to applicants and students is factual and accurate, especially if the information could be deemed contractual. Contractual information could be information provided in the institution's academic program catalogue (alternatively referred to as an "academic course calendar"), website, student guide, letter of offer of admission, or other written documents. A post-secondary institute admitting a student to a program has a duty to provide the student with the services associated with the program. This requirement includes matters such as ensuring that required courses are offered, course materials can be obtained, and program outcomes can be achieved – essentially, institutions have a duty to ensure that their published information is factual and accurate.

In the case of *Hickey-Button and Potter v. Loyalist College of Applied Arts and Technology* (2003), Loyalist College admitted students into an advertised fast-track nursing program, referred to as the "Queen's" option.[2] The College's academic course calendar and other promotional materials indicated that the program was delivered in partnership with Queen's University, and enabled students to earn a four-year nursing degree on-site at the Loyalist College campus located in Belleville, Ontario. The students would take two years of courses offered by Loyalist College followed by a further two years of courses offered by Queen's University.

---

2 "Queen's" option: Students had the option of graduating with a four-year nursing degree from Queen's University.

Shortly after Hickey-Button began the nursing program in the fall of 1997, the Loyalist administration informed her that the "Queen's" option was currently not in place but that negotiations between the two institutions were on-going. In 1999, Hickey-Button was advised that discussions had broken down, thus ending the relationship between Loyalist College and Queen's University (Court of Appeal for Ontario, 2006, para. 13). Consequently, the students would now have to finish their "three years at Loyalist and then attend Queen's or some other university for an additional two years in order to obtain what Loyalist was supposed to have delivered, that is, a baccalaureate degree in four years, all on the site of Loyalist [College]" (Ontario Superior Court of Justice, 2003, para. 3).

Jill Hickey-Button and Bonnie Potter filed a single multi-million dollar class-action lawsuit on behalf of all the students who had entered the nursing program in 1997 and 1998, respectively. The plaintiffs alleged that the cause of action was a breach of contact for negligent misrepresentation, based on the fact that the students had paid their tuition but the College had not provided the "Queen's" option as promised. Hickey-Button also argued that the materials sent to her and the other students had falsely represented the facts (Court of Appeal for Ontario, 2006, para. 16). Loyalist's defence was that the students entering the nursing program in 1997 and 1998 were not provided any "false, misleading, or inaccurate" material concerning the "Queen's" option. Loyalist also insisted that the program material sent to the students indicated that the "Queen's" option was only in the developmental stage and therefore could not be classified as a contract (Court of Appeal for Ontario, 2006, para. 19).

The motion judge dismissed the action, finding that the claim was a verbal contract, which was not suitable for a class action lawsuit (Court of Appeal for Ontario, 2006, para. 33). The motion judge held that the verbal contract would have varied from student to student, depending on the information that Loyalist provided to each student "prior to the student enrolling in the nursing diploma course" (Court of Appeal for Ontario, 2006, para. 30). The motion judge further reasoned that the "merits of the negligent misrepresentation claim could also be determined only on a student-by-student basis" (Court of Appeal for Ontario,

2006, para. 30). Hickey-Button and Potter decided to take the matter to the Divisional Court, arguing that the motion judge's decision was flawed. The Court upheld Justice Manton's decision and dismissed the case, finding that the group of nursing students had no common issues and that the proper legal procedure would be to initiate individual claims. The Divisional Court noted: "It would be preferable for each claim to be determined in an ordinary action in which each student wishing to assert a claim would be named plaintiff in either one action or in separate actions to be tried together" (Court of Appeal for Ontario, 2006, para. 39). The students appealed this decision to the Court of Appeal for Ontario (2006). The Court of Appeal reversed the decision, holding that both the motion judge and the Divisional Court had made a legal error when applying s. 5 of the Act.[3] The Court concluded that the class action lawsuit could proceed to trial (Court of Appeal, 2006, para. 6).

After the case had been in the court system for many years, approximately 70 nursing students from the 1997 and 1998 classes were awarded legal costs and financial compensation from Loyalist College. According to Miller (2014), the first three students in the class action lawsuit received damages of approximately $200,000 per claim. Subsequently, Loyalist College argued that Queen's University had unilaterally withdrawn from an agreement to provide the programming, and Loyalist College sought damages from Queen's University (Fernandez-Blance, 2011). Whether or not Loyalist College would receive such compensation was unknown at the time of this writing.

Similarly, the case of *Olar v. Laurentian University* (2008) required Laurentian University to award compensatory damages to Alvin Olar based on misrepresentation of the transferability of courses, as indicated by the university's recruitment officers, and in the academic calendar, liaison department brochure, student guide, website, and other promotional materials. The Laurentian University calendar affirmed that students who had passed the first two years of the program "may proceed into the third year in mining engineering or extract metallurgical engineering at Laurentian University, or may transfer to the third year of other universities in Ontario if they wish to pursue chemical, civil or

---

3 The Act referrers to the *Class Proceedings Act*, 1992, S.O. 1992, c.6.

mechanical engineering" (Ontario Superior Court of Justice, 2003, para. 1). In this case, Laurentian University, located in Sudbury, Ontario, had admitted the student in the fall of 1994, with him understanding that he would complete the first two years of an engineering degree at Laurentian University and then transfer to another institution to complete the last two years of the 4-year engineering degree program.

After successfully completing the first and second year of the Laurentian program, Olar applied, and was accepted, for transfer into the civil engineering program at the University of Windsor (Ontario Superior Court of Justice, 2003, para. 9). At the time of the transfer, the student found that not all of his courses from Laurentian were in fact transferable, and that he would be required to complete an additional year of study to complete the degree program in civil engineering. Olar filed a class action lawsuit against Laurentian University alleging negligent misrepresentation with respect to the transfer of credits to another university.

Justice Patterson, relying on the Ontario Superior Court of Justice's decision in *Hickey-Button and Potter v. Loyalist College of Applied Arts and Technology* (2003), dismissed the class action lawsuit, finding that each student would have to "prove that he or she had completed the two year program in civil, chemical or mechanical engineering at Laurentian, and intended to transfer to another university to complete a four year engineering degree" (Ontario Superior Court of Justice, 2003, para. 33). In addition, Justice Patterson noted that the students would have to show that they "would not have attended Laurentian" if they had "not read or heard one of the several different alleged misrepresentations made in the Calendar" (Superior Court of Justice, 2003, para. 33).

After the Court dismissed Olar's class-action lawsuit, he pursued his own individual claim against Laurentian University (Dobrovnik, 2008). The presiding Ontario Court of Appeal judges unanimously upheld an April 30, 2007 decision finding that Laurentian University owed a special duty of care to its "students with respect to statements made in promotional materials intended to be used by students to make program and course selections" (Pellerin, 2013). On October 10, 2008, the Ontario Court of Appeal ordered Laurentian University to pay the student compensation in the amount of $350,000 for legal fees, extra tuition, and loss of potential wages for the additional year of study (Dobrovnik, 2008).

Both the cases of *Hickey-Button and Potter v. Loyalist College* (2006) and *Olar v. Laurentian University* (2008) indicated that the program information provided by post-secondary institutions is contractual by nature. However, in both cases, the courts ruled on individual student cases, essentially indicating that a review of individual circumstances was necessary in order to make a judgment, and that a judgment could not be made based on inaccurate representations published in the academic calendar alone, as doing so would not speak to the understandings and expectations of the individual students.

The published value of post-secondary educational credentials is another area where institutions must provide accurate information to the public. In the case of *Monckton v. C.B.S. Interactive Multimedia Inc. (c.o.b.[4] Canadian Business College)* (2012), the courts found that the for-profit career college had misrepresented and failed to disclose the accreditation status of its dental hygienist program (C.B.S. represents Canadian Business School, n.d.). The class action lawsuit was founded on the accusation that the Chief Executive Officer, Mazher Jaffery, and the college's General Manager, Roselyn Calapini, failed to make students aware of the implications of enrolling in a dental hygienist program that was not accredited by the Commission on Dental Accreditation of Canada (CDAC). First, all individuals who wish to practice as dental hygienists must pass the national exam administered by the National Dental Hygiene Certification Board. Graduates of a non-accredited program are not automatically eligible to write the exam. Second, if the institution is not accredited by the CDAC, individuals can experience a 9-to-10 month delay between graduation and registration with the College of Dental Hygienists (Ontario Superior Court of Justice, 2008, para. 3). Third, if the institution is not accredited by the College of Dental Hygienists, a student must pass a provincial clinical competency assessment in addition to passing the national exam (Ontario Superior Court of Justice, 2008, para. 11).

---

4 carrying on business.

Before classes started, students were required to make a deposit of $500.00 and sign a contract which did not indicate the implications of enrolling in a non-accredited program. Students were also sent a schedule outlining the fees for the program, in addition to a one-page brochure summarizing the particulars of the program. At para. 46, Justice Hoy of the Ontario Superior Court of Justice (2008) acknowledged that "none of the documents indicated that the program was non-accredited, and that the ability to write the Exam was therefore not guaranteed." The case was allowed to proceed as a class-action lawsuit because the Business College's misrepresentation was significant enough to harm a majority of students enrolled during a specific time frame. The plaintiffs alleged that the cause of action included negligent misrepresentation, breach of collateral warranty, breach of the *Competition Act* (1985), breach of the *Business Practices Act* (1990), and breach of the *Consumers Protection Practices Act* (2002).

Madam Justice Hoy affirmed that the class action proceedings could move forward. In this case, only the *Consumer Protection Act* (2002) was used to determine that the students were eligible for compensation of the costs associated with the program, because the students had paid for a service (education) with the understanding that they would be eligible to write examinations for the registration required to practice as a dental hygienist. The judge awarded the students damages in the amount of $103,500. In addition, the sum of $11,500 was paid to the Class Proceedings Fund of the Law Foundation of Ontario, as pursuant to Ontario Regulation Number 771/93, and $60,000 was paid to the plaintiff's lawyer.

In the case of *Gauthier c. Saint-Germain, Boudreau et L' Université d'Ottawa* (2010), a former doctoral student, Manon Gauthier, was granted the right to seek compensation from the University of Ottawa for an alleged breach of contract based on the former graduate student's claim that she had not been provided the kind of thesis supervision or amount of research funding that she had been promised (Knelman, 2012). This legal decision is important because post-secondary institutions, particularly universities, are generally allowed to control their own internal procedures and affairs. Canadian courts typically are reluctant to hear cases involving disputes between students and institutions.

Before examining the *Gauthier c. Saint-Germain, Boudreau et L' Université d'Ottawa* decision, which was released in French, the previous jurisprudence in this area will be briefly considered. The Appeal Courts in Ontario (e.g., *Dawson v. University of Toronto*, 2007; *Mulligan v. Laurentian*, 2008; *Wong v. University of Toronto*, 1992; *Zabo v. University of Ottawa*, 2005) have generally dismissed cases related to academic or scholastic matters. More recently, however, the judiciary in the cases of *Gauthier c. Saint-Germain, Boudreau et L' Université d'Ottawa* (2010) and *Jaffer v. York University* (2010) have reconsidered those earlier decisions. The Courts in Newfoundland (e.g., *Baxter v. Memorial University of Newfoundland*, 1992; *O'Reilly v. Memorial University of Newfoundland*, 1998), Nova Scotia (e.g., *Pacheco v. Dalhousie University*, 2005), New Brunswick (e.g., *Archer v. University of New Brunswick*, 1992), Manitoba (e.g., *Walia v. University of Manitoba*, 2013; *Warraich v. University of Manitoba*, 2003), Saskatchewan (e.g., *Bikey v. University of Saskatchewan*, 2009), Alberta (e.g., *Cruickshank v. University of Lethbridge*, 2010), and Québec have ruled that issues of an academic nature are beyond their jurisdiction, whereas the Appeal Courts in British Columbia (e.g., *Mohl v. University of British Columbia*, 2006) have ruled that they can adjudicate such matters (e.g., Hannah & Stack, 2015; Thompson & Slade, 2011).

As noted above, Gauthier alleged in her claim that the University of Ottawa was negligent and in breach of contract for failing to provide competent staff. Specifically, Gauthier asserted that her initial Ph.D. supervisor had acted inappropriately and caused her mental distress. Gauthier also asserted that her supervisor had told her that she would graduate with her doctorate in four years and would be automatically awarded a $50,000 admission scholarship and guaranteed a research assistantship (Black, 2012; Knelman, 2012). Gauthier maintained that her second thesis supervisor's inexperience, incompetence, and lack of a research strategy or sound advice for her had caused delays. She also alleged that additional delays had occurred because two members of her thesis committee had resigned. Gauthier began her Ph.D. program in the fall of 1999 and by the summer of 2006 she had still not graduated.

Gauthier launched a civil action against the university and sought general damages of $1,000,000 and special and punitive damages of $500,000 against the university.

The university's position was that since the matter was essentially academic in nature, the court did not have the authority or jurisdiction under the *Rules of Civil Procedures, RRO 1990, Reg. 194*; consequently, the claim should be dismissed. In 2008, Justice Hennessy of the Ontario Superior Court dismissed the action, finding it was primarily an academic issue: "It is well established in law that if the dispute is genuine in nature, the appropriate forum for resolving it is not the court but rather the internal procedures of the university" (Superior Court of Justice 2008, para. 23, unofficial translation). Justice Hennessy cited *Paine v. University of Toronto* (1981) where the court concluded that universities enjoy significant internal autonomy and that the court should be discouraged from "intervening when it is still possible for the university to correct its mistakes by resorting to institutional means" (Superior Court of Justice 2008, para. 24, unofficial translation).

Gauthier decided to take the matter to the Ontario Court of Appeal (2010), arguing that the Lower Court Judge's decision was flawed. The Court of Appeal overturned the decision, finding that the case could proceed and indicating that this matter was a contractual issue rather than an academic one. The court also concluded that jurisprudence used in this case did not support the legal principles advanced by the university (Court of Appeal, 2010, para. 29, unofficial translation). At para. 46, the Court of Appeal found that the Lower Court had the inherent jurisdiction to hear disputes in the area of tort or breach of contract law, "even if the dispute is academic in nature and arises out of the academic activities of the university" (Court of Appeal, 2010, unofficial translation). The Court of Appeal also noted that the Lower Court's jurisdiction can be limited only by clear and expressed "statutory legislation or contractual provisions" (Court of Appeal, 2010, para. 29, unofficial translation). Moreover, the Court of Appeal granted Gauthier leave to amend her statement of claim "to show what the university had agreed to and what standards of conduct and performance are to be expected in a supervisor" (Knelman, 2012). Justice Rouleau (2010), speaking on behalf of the majority Court, declared that "I would change the statement in almost its entirety by deleting paragraphs 6-141 with leave to amend" (Court of Appeal, 2010, para. 61, unofficial translation).

This decision was appealed to the Supreme Court of Canada, to provide direction with respect to universities having exclusive jurisdiction to deal with issues of an academic nature; however, in March 2011 the application for leave was dismissed. "One never really knows what to make of the Supreme Court's refusal to rule on matters," said Mr. Kiligman,[5] "but it might be taken to mean that the Court did not think it necessary to revisit the ruling by the appellate court" (cited by Knelman, 2012).

Jaffer v. York University (2010) is another Ontario case where the court indicated that the matter was contractual, allowing Jaffer to make his claim to the court. Ashif Jaffer was a 19-year-old student at York University's Glendon College Campus in the 2006-2007 academic school year. Jaffer had previously graduated from high school as an Ontario scholar (i.e., a student with an overall average of 80% or above), where he received an Independent Education Plan (IEP) accommodation for his Trisomy 21 Down Syndrome disability. After being accepted by York University, Jaffer disclosed his condition to student services and sought accommodation. Jaffer and the university attempted to determine what accommodations should be made, but did not reach a formal decision in his freshman year.

In April 2007, Jaffer failed a research paper; however, his professor apparently granted him a deferred grade standing and said that he could resubmit his paper in the future. Because the university had failed to provide an accommodation plan for his disorder, Jaffer interpreted the professor's decision to mean that he would be given deferred status in all his courses instead of failing grades. Eventually, the university informed him that he would not be permitted to continue his studies because of his insufficient academic standing (i.e., below a D+ average).

In April 2008, Jaffer then sought legal damages of three million dollars against the university, based on the legal theory that the university

5 Bob Kligman "is an expert on university case law with the Toronto law firm Cassels Brock" (Knelman, 2012).

should be held liable for not providing appropriate resources for his accommodation and for failing "to properly investigate, assess, and evaluate his claim for accommodation" (Court of Appeal, 2010, para. 6). Specifically, Jaffer claimed breach of contract, breach of a duty of good faith, negligence, and negligent misrepresentation by the university. York's defence was that this case was beyond the authority and jurisdiction of the Superior Court of Justice because the case dealt with issues of an academic nature. In addition, York noted that Jaffer had initiated a human rights complaint against the university, and that such a complaint had to be handled by the Ontario Human Rights Commission (OHRC) and not the courts.

In 2009, Justice Pitt of the Ontario Superior Court of Justice found in favour of York University for two reasons:

> There are two parts to the plaintiff's argument. First, he asserts that the school failed to accommodate him. Second, he asserts that this failure to accommodate led to his unjust expulsion from the program. Failure to accommodate belongs to the OHRC, and a dispute about expulsion is within the university's internal resolution process (para. 20).

The Lower Court judge further reasoned that although the broader claim might have involved contractual or tortious issues, "if the pith and substance of the impugned conduct is academic in nature, the action cannot be continued in the court" (para. 24).

Jaffer decided to take the matter to the Ontario Court of Appeal, arguing that the Lower Court judge had erred in his finding. The Court of Appeal dismissed Jaffer's claim in part. In its ruling, the Court noted that it did not have inherent jurisdiction to hear Jaffer's case based on the university's failure to accommodate his disability. The Court of Appeal affirmed that the Lower Court judge was "correct in his view that whether or not the university had failed to comply with its duty to accommodate under the Code was a matter for the OHRC" to decide (para. 40). Further, Jaffer did not have a reasonable cause of action for breach of contract, including breach of duty of good faith. Justice Karakatsanis was clear in stating that, "I conclude that the motion judge did not err in dismissing the claim for breach in contract, as pleaded, although I do so for different reasons" (para. 51). Also, Jaffer did not have a reasonable cause of action for negligent misrepresentation. The court acknowledged that "again, Jaffer's pleadings were too vague to make out such a claim: In my view, Jaffer has not made out a claim for negligent misrepresentation. The professor's offer to permit Jaffer to redo a paper in his course cannot reasonably be found as an action in negligent misrepresentation of the facts as pleaded" (para. 57). Justice Karakatsanis, however, delivered the opinion of the Court of Appeal that the basis of the claim was contractual rather than academic, indicating that the court could rule on the matter. Citing the case of *Gauthier c. Saint-Germain* (2010), Justice Karakatsanis noted the following:

> Judicial review is the proper procedure when seeking to reverse an internal academic decision. However, if a plaintiff alleges the basis for a cause of action in tort or contract and claims damages, then the court will have jurisdiction even if the dispute arises out of an academic matter (para. 26).

However, at the time of the claim, Jaffer had failed to provide sufficient contractual evidence for the court to conclude "exactly what accommodations York's implicit contract with him promised, what accommodations he was offered, and what further accommodations he required" (Knelman, 2012).

This decision was appealed in the Supreme Court of Canada, but the application for leave was dismissed. Knelman (2012), in summing up the *Jaffer* case, concluded that that "universities will still have exclusive jurisdiction over academic disputes in which students seek higher grades or reinstatement, but now students in Ontario who are seeking monetary damages may have their day in court."

The Requirement to Provide Due Process

Typically, the courts will not hear cases on post-secondary institution matters because the academic freedom granted to the institutions also allows for autonomy in governance. Institutions are expected, and in many instances required, to have policies and procedures in place to address, fairly and transparently, any matters which may arise. However, the courts may intervene when a complainant has not been afforded the benefit of due process and procedural fairness. Such was the case in *Spiegel v. Seneca College of Applied Arts & Technology* (2005). Seneca College had required Roland Spiegel to withdraw from his academic program on February 21, 2003, without giving him the requisite documents used to determine the decision soon enough for him to prepare to appeal it. Spiegel appealed this decision on March 2, 2003, and was notified by the College the following afternoon that his appeal date would be March 7, 2003. Spiegel received the College's investigative report on March 4, 2003 (Ontario Superior Court of Justice, 2005, para. 2). Spiegel sought adjournment on two occasions to prepare a defence for his case, but the College denied his requests. Spiegel filed a lawsuit against Seneca College, alleging procedural unfairness.

In this case, Spiegel was not afforded due process. The Ontario Superior Court of Justice (2005) sent the matter back to the College to be reviewed by a newly-constructed appeal panel. The Court did not consider the academic issues in the case, but rather, only the matters of due process. Justice Jarvis (2005), speaking on behalf of the majority court, affirmed that "We are all of the view that, in these circumstances, the refusal to grant a short adjournment to allow Mr. Spiegel to respond to the report was a denial of natural justice and procedural fairness" (para. 2).

Post-secondary educational institutions would be wise to consider previous court cases and legal decisions when creating, reviewing, and revising policies and procedures. Additionally, policies and procedures need to be regularly reviewed and updated because the rapid rate of technological change is creating new challenges and considerations.

The case of *Harelkin v. University of Regina* (1979) had some significant similarities to the *Spiegel* (2005) case. George Harelkin was a student in the School of Social Work at the University of Regina. After the 1975 fall semester, Harelkin was required to discontinue his studies because of his unsatisfactory academic performance. The student appealed the decision of the University of Regina Council Committee but was not allowed to review the information against him or to be involved in the appeal process. "The committee heard one side—the university—and decided adversely to the student, all in the absence of the student," noted Justice Dickson (Supreme Court of Canada, 1979, p. 598). Although Harelkin had the right to a further appeal within the university (i.e., by the Committee of the Senate), he filed an application for judicial review against the University of Regina, alleging failure to apply the principles of natural justice.

The trial judge overturned the decision of the Council Committee and granted a new hearing, allowing Harelkin "to be present, to be heard, to present evidence and to be represented by counsel, with respect to the refusal of the School of Social Work to allow him to pursue further studies" (Supreme Court of Canada, 1979, p. 561). The Court of Appeal of Saskatchewan overturned that decision, holding that, "where there is a right of appeal, *certiorari* should not be granted except under special circumstances," but no special circumstances had been established (Supreme Court of Canada, 1979, p. 561).[6] The *Harelkin* case ultimately went to the Supreme Court of Canada (1979), which determined that not allowing the student to be party to the initial appeal was incorrect. Justice Beetz delivered the opinion on behalf of the majority, noting that "the power exercised by the committee of the university council was quasi-judicial in nature and the committee had a statutory duty to hear the appellant, which duty was not complied with" (p. 567).

In *King v. University of Saskatchewan* (1969), Robert King had not succeeded in obtaining the academic standard required to be awarded a Bachelor of Law degree (LL.B.)[7] from the University of Saskatchewan.

---

6 Certiorari: "A means of achieving judicial review." An order "issued from a superior court to one of inferior jurisdiction, inquiring into the validity of the proceedings of the later" (Yogis, 1995, p. 134).

7 This was "the undergraduate law degree conferred by Canadian law faculties" (Yogis, 1995, p. 134).

King appealed the decision repeatedly, ultimately appealing to the University Senate, who refused to grant the law degree. At the previous university discussions and hearings, King had not been present, but at the senate hearing, he was both present and also represented by legal counsel (Supreme Court of Canada, 1969, p. 678). All of King's appeals to the University bodies were denied. King decided to take the matter to Court, indicating that he had been denied due process.

The Court of Appeal for Saskatchewan upheld the decision of the Court of Queen's Bench and dismissed the appeal. The Supreme Court of Canada (1969) received the chronology of the situation and ruled that although the initial appeals had not afforded King due process, the ultimate and final appeal to the University Senate had done so. Therefore, King's claims were deemed irrelevant, and the case was dismissed. The Supreme Court of Canada (1969) noted that even if the inferior tribunals had not applied the principles of natural justice, the senate appeal committee had done so (p. 679).

Bikey v. University of Saskatchewan (2009) is another case where a student was academically unsuccessful in his first year of a degree program, and the University required the student to discontinue his studies. Dyar Bikey was a student in the College of Dentistry at the University of Saskatchewan during the 2008/2009 academic school year. After his second semester in the program, Bikey received a letter from the Associate Dean of the College of Dentistry, requiring him to discontinue his studies because he had failed three courses (MED 109.19; DENT 288.3; DENT 208.3). The letter also advised Bikey that "many faculty voiced concern over issues of 'professionalism.' As such, the Executive Committee recommended you not be allowed to repeat Year 1" (The Saskatchewan Court of Queen's Bench, 2009, para. 1).

Bikey made several unsuccessful attempts to appeal the decision of the University of Saskatchewan, including requests to have his case re-examined, to be promoted to year two, and to have his grades reviewed. In addition, he also disagreed with the allegation of unprofessionalism (The Saskatchewan Court of Queen's Bench, 2009, para. 2). Simultaneously, Bikey tried to persuade the Saskatchewan Court of Queen's Bench (2009) to hear his case, but the Court, citing *Harelkin v. University of*

Regina (1979) and *King v. University of Saskatchewan* (1969), declined to interfere with authority and proceedings of the university (Shibley Righton, 2009) because the case was primarily academic in nature, and the University had sufficient policy and process measures in place to address the issue, pursuant to the *University of Saskatchewan Act* (1995). Instead, the Court required the University to render internal decisions on all outstanding matters before classes started again in September (The Saskatchewan Court of Queen's Bench, 2009, para. 15).

In *Ghaniabadi v. University of Regina* (1997), Hossein Ghaniabadi had failed a required fourth-year engineering course (ER 415). In order to graduate, Ghaniabadi needed a passing grade in ER 415 or a similar class approved by the Faculty of Engineering. The student had requested and been granted a re-read on the course paper, but the failing grade was upheld by the Committee on Student Appeals of the University of Regina Council (The Saskatchewan Court of Queen's Bench, 1997). Ultimately, the student tried to appeal to the University Senate, but it refused to hear the appeal. Ghaniabadi's solicitor wrote a letter to the University Senate, appealing the decision with respect to ER 415. The University responded to Ghaniabadi's lawyer, noting that "based on the foregoing, it is our view that there is no right reposed in Mr. Ghaniabadi to have a hearing in front of the Senate" (The Saskatchewan Court of Queen's Bench, 2009, p. 2).

The matter went to the Saskatchewan Court of Queen's Bench, and the Senate was ordered to hear the appeal, as hearing appeals was one of its mandated duties, pursuant to the *University of Regina Act* (1978). Section 33(1)(c) of the *Act* reads as follows: the Senate shall "appoint a committee to hear and decide upon, subject to an appeal to the senate, all applications and memorials by students or others in connection with any faculty of the university." As with most cases involving academic institutions, the court did not consider any academic matters, stating that the case was simply a matter of a governing body of the university refusing to provide a service to which the student was entitled. The Court concluded that the University of Regina Senate "is hereby ordered to hear and decide upon the appeal of the applicant from the decision of the University of Regina Council" (The Saskatchewan Court of Queen's Bench, 2009, p. 3).

Freedom of Speech and Expression Considerations

In the case of *Pridgen v. University of Calgary* (2012), ten undergraduate students, including twin brothers Keith and Steven Pridgen, posted negative and pejorative comments on a social networking site about one of their University of Calgary professors. The Facebook page, entitled "I no longer fear hell, I took a course with Aruna Mitra," was accessible to anyone searching the Internet and included comments such as "Somehow I think she just got lazy and gave everybody a 65....that's what I got. Does anybody know how to apply to have it remarked?" (The Court of Appeal, 2012, para. 7). The Court of Appeal (2012) described other comments as "highly critical of the professor's qualifications, teaching skills, and assessment practices" (para. 10). The course instructor was also described on Facebook as "inept," "awful," "illogically abrasive," and "inconsistent." Another post suggested the professor should be "drawn and quartered during a special presentation at Mac Hall" (para. 10).

The course instructor, Professor Aruna Mitra, found out about the Facebook posts from colleagues and reported them to the Interim Dean of the Faculty of Communication and Culture at the University of Calgary. The students were found guilty of non-academic misconduct under the university code of conduct and placed on probation for 24 months, ordered to issue a mandatory letter of apology to Professor Mitra, and informed that they were not to circulate or produce any similar material that could be defamatory to Professor Mitra or any member of the University of Calgary community. The students were also advised that failure to comply with the sanctions could result in suspension or expulsion from the university.

Keith and Steven Pridgen appealed the decision of the Dean to the University of Calgary's General Faculties Council Review Committee, and, as a result, the probation periods were changed to six and four months, respectively. A further appeal to the University of Calgary's Board of Governors Review Committee was rejected because under university policy the nature of the sanctions did not involve a fine, a suspension, or expulsion, so the Pridgens took the matter to Alberta Court of Queen's Bench. The main issues before the Court included whether there had been a lack of procedural fairness or denial of natural justice, whether the *Canadian Charter of Rights and Freedoms* applied to disciplinary proceedings taken by the University of Calgary, and also whether the students' *Charter* rights had been violated (The Court of Appeal of Alberta, 2012, para. 36).

The Pridgens cogently argued that their right to freedom of expression, as guaranteed by section 2(b) the *Canadian Charter of Rights and Freedoms*,[8] had been infringed by the university. The University of Calgary argued that the *Charter* did not apply to the university, as universities are afforded some exemptions from the *Charter* for the purpose of acting autonomously and allowing academic freedom. The application of the *Charter* (see section 32.(1)[9]) in respect to postsecondary institutions can be traced to the 1986 Supreme Court of Canada decision of *RWDSU v. Dolphin Delivery Ltd.*, where the court noted that the *Charter* was "only applicable to government actors and government action, not to private activity" (*Pridgen v. University of Calgary*, 2012, at par 34).

After an extensive *Charter* analysis, Justice Strekaf found that the students' *Charter* rights had been violated, as had administrative law procedures. The Lower Court Judge[10] remarked that, "I am satisfied that the University is not a *Charter* free zone. The *Charter* does apply in respect of the disciplinary proceedings taken by the University against the Applicants" (para. 69) pursuant to the *Post-secondary Learning Act* (2003). The Alberta Court of Queen's Bench (2010) overturned the

---

8 Section 2 of the *Canadian Charter of Rights and Freedoms*, which addresses *Fundamental Freedoms*, reads as follows: Everyone has the following fundamental freedoms:
   (a) freedom of conscience and religion;
   (b) freedom of thought, belief, opinion and expression, including freedom of the press and other media of communication;
   (c) freedom of peaceful assembly; and (d) freedom of association.

9 Section 32.(1) of the *Canadian Charter of Rights and Freedoms*, which addresses the *Application of the Charter*, reads as follows: This *Charter* applies:
   (a) to the Parliament and government of Canada in respect to all to all matters within the authority of Parliament including all matters related to the Yukon Territory and Northwest Territories; and
   (b) to the legislature and the government of each province in respect to all matters within the authority of the legislature of each province.

10 Also referred to as a Judicial Review Judge.

decision of the General Faculties Council Review Committee and removed the student probation orders. Justice Strekaf's decision was then appealed by the university and eventually went on to a three-judge panel of the Alberta Court of Appeal.

The Alberta Court of Appeal unanimously upheld the Lower Court decision on administrative law grounds. The majority (Justice McDonald and Justice O'Ferrall concurring) held that administrative law, and not *Charter* application, dictated that the punishment imposed on the brothers was too severe, as no evidence showed that the students' comments had harmed the professor. The majority stated that, "While it may be time to reconsider whether or not universities are subject to the Charter, it was unnecessary for the judicial review judge to do so in this case. And, in my respectful view, this Court ought not to compound that error by undertaking such an analysis now" (para 132). As noted above, Justice Paperny also agreed with the majority ruling that the decision of the Board of Governors Review Committee "was unreasonable from an administrative law perspective" (para. 128). However, Justice Paperny took a different approach than the majority with respect to the application of the *Canadian Charter of Rights and Freedoms*. She embarked on a detailed section 2(b) *Charter* analysis, ruling that the Pridgen brothers had the right to free expression within the university environment. Justice Paperny reasoned that "in exercising its statutory authority to discipline students for non-academic misconduct, it is incumbent on the Review Committee to interpret and apply the Student Misconduct Policy in light of the students' Charter rights, including their freedom of expression" (The Court of Appeal of Alberta, 2012, para. 112). However, since this opinion was a minority ruling, Justice Paperny's decision, with respect to the *Charter*, is a non-binding legal precedent.

The University of Calgary was involved in another case related to a breach of fundamental freedoms under section 2(b) of the *Canadian Charter of Rights and Freedoms*. In *Wilson et al. v. University of Calgary* (2014), the university found that several students had committed non-academic misconduct. In this case, the university had directed the members of a registered pro-life group on campus to display their contentious materials in a way that they could not be seen by the campus community walking by the display. The University of Calgary posted its own signs in this high-pedestrian-traffic area, indicating that the exhibit's extremely graphic images might be "offensive to some" and that the exhibit was "protected under the relevant section of the Charter Rights and Freedoms related to freedom of expression" (Alberta Court of Queen's Bench, 2014, para. 3). Moreover, the university was concerned that the display could cause major security issues on campus between members of the campus pro-life group and other students, including pro-choice advocates (Brief of Argument, 2013, para. 12).

The seven tuition-paying students, including Cameron Wilson, refused to turn their Genocide Awareness Project (GAP) signs inwards and were charged with trespassing and violating the university's non-academic misconduct policy. In 2009, shortly before trial, the Crown stayed the trespassing charges because the university could not prove that any university rule, regulation, or policies had been violated (Carpay, 2014). However, in 2010, the U of C charged the students with committing a "Major Violation" of the Non-Academic Misconduct Policy, namely "failure to follow the directions of a Campus Security officer in the legitimate pursuit of his/her duties" (Origination Application, 2011, para. 6). The students were found guilty of non-academic misconduct under the university code of conduct and issued formal written warnings for intentionally disobeying campus security directives (Brief of Argument, 2013, para. 7).

The students appealed this decision to the Board of Governors; however, it refused to hear the appeal, affirming a guilty verdict, so Wilson et al. took the matter to the Alberta Court of Queen's Bench. In 2014, the Court overturned the university's decision, holding that it was "unreasonable" for the Board of Governors not to hear the students' appeal. The Court also ruled that the decision lacked "justification, transparency and intelligibility within the decision-making process" (Alberta Court of Queen's Bench, 2014, para. 140). On April 1, 2014, the Alberta Court of Queen's Bench (2014) delivered its decision, sending the matter back to the university to be fully reviewed and given proper consideration by the Board of Governors. It eventually overturned its previous decision and removed the non-academic misconduct charges from the students' files (Abortion No, 2016).

Conclusion

In Canada, post-secondary institutions, particularly universities, are generally allowed to control their own internal procedures and affairs. Canadian courts typically will not hear cases involving disputes between students and institutions. This paper explained when, where, and why some cases may be heard and possibly determined in a court of law.

After almost any incident, a post-secondary institution can avoid litigation from students by simply ensuring that the institution's governance, policies, and processes adhere to the principles of due process and natural justice. Essentially, they require institutions to conduct their activities in the manner prescribed by their governing bodies.

References

Amdiss and the University of Ottawa, Ltd., 2010 ONSC 4738 (CanLII). Retrieved from https://www.canlii.ca/t/2c7xx.

Archer v. Université de Moncton (1992), 129 NBR (2nd) 289 (QB).

Baxter v. Memorial University of Newfoundland, 166 Nfld & PEIR 183, [1998] NJ No 222 (QL) (SC(TD)) [Baxter].

Bikey v. University of Saskatchewan, 2009 SKQB 340 (CanLII).

Black, D. (2012, April 23). Disgruntled university students can sue their school for breach of contract. *The Toronto Star*. Retrieved from https://www.thestar.com.

Brief of Argument (2013). *Wilson v. University of Calgary*, 2014 ABQB 190. Retrieved from https://www.jccf.ca/our-cases/wilson-v-university-of-calgary.

Business Practices Act, R.S.O. 1990, c. B.18.

Carpay, J. (2014). University of Calgary's war on free speech. *National Post*. Retrieved from https://www.nationalpost.com.

Class Proceedings Act, 1992, S.O. 1992, c.6.

Competition Act, R.S., 1985, c. C-34.

Consumer Protection Act, 2002, S.O. 1992, c.6.

Cruickshank v. University of Lethbridge, 2010 ABQB 186.

Davis, B. (2015). Governance and administration of postsecondary institutions in Canada. In T. Shanahan, M. Nilson, & L. Broshko (Eds.), *Handbook of Canadian higher education law* (pp. 57-78). Kingston, ON: McGill-Queen's University Press.

Dawson v. University of Toronto, 2007 ONCA 875 (CanLII). Retrieved from https://ww.canlii.ca.

Dobrovnik, F. (2008). Sault man wins lawsuit against Laurentian University. *The Sault Star.* Retrieved from https://www.saultstar.com/2008/10/23/sault-man-wins- lawsuit-against-laurentian-university.ca.

Fernandez-Blance, K. (2011). Lawsuit filed against Queen's. *The Queen's Journal, 139*(17). Retrieved from https://www.queensjournal.ca/story/2011-10-28/news /lawsuit-filled-against-queens.

Gauthier c. Saint-Germain, 2008 CanLII 43576 (ONSC). Retrieved from https://www. canlii.ca.

Gauthier c. Saint-Germain, Boudreau et L' Université d'Ottawa, 2010 CanLII 11057 (ONCA). Retrieved from https://www.canlii.ca.

Ghaniabadi v. University of Regina, 1997 CanLII 11057 (SK QB). Retrieved from https://www.betacanlii.org/t/lnsx8.

Hannah, D., & Stack, D. (2015). Students. In T. Shanahan, M. Nilson, & L. Broshko (Eds.), *Handbook of Canadian higher education law* (pp. 125-166). Kingston, ON: McGill-Queen's University Press.

Harelkin v. University of Regina, 1979 2 S.C.R. 561. Retrieved from https://www. scc.lexum.org/decisia-scc-cse/scc-cse/scc-cse/en/item/2633/index.do.

Ha-Redeye, O. (2010). *SCJ jurisdiction over academic disputes.* Retrieved from https://www.slaw.ca/2010/10/10/scj-jurisdiction-over-academic-disputes/.

Hickey-Button and Potter v. Loyalist College of Applied Arts & Technology, 2003 CanLII 3772 (ON SC). Retrieved from https://www.canlii.ca.

Hickey-Button and Potter v. Loyalist College of Applied Arts & Technology, 2006 CanLII 20079 (ON CA). Retrieved from https://www.canlii.ca.

Jaffer v. York University, 2009 ONSC 60086 (CanLII). Retrieved from https://www. canlii.ca.

Jaffer v. York University, 2010 ONCA 654 (CanLII). Retrieved from https://www. canlii.ca.

King v. University of Saskatchewan, 1969 CanLII 89 (SCC), [1969] SCR 678. Retrieved from https://www.beta.canlii.org/t/lxd7c.

Knelman, J. (2012). Court rules students may sue universities in some cases. *University Affairs.* Retrieved from https://www.universityaffairs.ca/court-rules-students-may-sue-universities-in-some-cases.aspx.

MacIsaac, A. (2014). *This student is not just a number: The Ontario Court of Appeal Recognizes jurisdiction over academic disputes in Jaffer v. York University.* Retrieved from http://canliiconnects.org/en/commentares/35052.

Miller, J. (2014). Loyalist college nursing students settle in legal case. The Belleville Intelligencer. Available at: http://www.intelligencer.ca.

Mohl v. University of British Columbia (2006), 2006 BCCA 70 (CanLII), 52 BCLR (4th) 89 (CA).

Monckton v. C.B.S. Interactive Multimedia. (2012), 2012 ONSC 06-CV-310529CP (CanLII). Retrieved from https://www.canlii.ca.

Mulligan v. Laurentian University, 2008 ONCA 523 (CanLII). Retrieved from https://www.canlii.ca.

Musgrove, J. (2011). *Recent trends in misleading advertising enforcement.* Toronto, ON.

Olar v. Laurentian University, 2003 ONSC 10008 (CanLII). https://www.canlii.ca.

Olar v. Laurentian University, 2007 ONSC 20787 (CanLII). https://www.canlii.ca.

Olar v. Laurentian University, 2008 ONCA 699 (CanLII). https://www.canlii.ca.

O'Reilly v. Memorial University of Newfoundland, 166 Nfld & PEIR 327, 1998 Carswell Nfld 200 (WL Can) (SCTD)).

Origination Application (2011). *Wilson v. University of Calgary, 2014 ABQB 190.* Retrieved from https://www.jccf.ca/our-cases/wilson-v-university-of-calgary.

Pacheco v. Dalhousie University, 2005 NSSC 222, 238 NSR (2nd) 1 [Pacheco].

Paine v. University of Toronto and al. (1981) CanLII 1921 (ONCA), [1981] OJ No. 3187.

Pellerin, S. (2013). *College sued for negligent misrepresentation of program.* Retrieved from http://mmmlawyers.ca/uncategorized/college-sued-for- misrepresentation.

Post-secondary Learning Act, S.A. 2003, c. P-19.5 (Alberta).

Pridgen v. University of Calgary, 2010 ABQB 664 (CanLII). Retrieved from https://www .canlii.ca.

Pridgen v. University of Calgary, 2012 ABCA 139 (CanLII). Retrieved from https://www .canlii.ca.

Queen's University Human Rights Office (n.d). *Jaffer v. York University, 2010 ONCA 654.* Retrieved from https://www.queensu.ca/humanrights/hrlg/meeting-headlines.

Rules of Civil Procedures, RRO 1990, Reg. 194.

RWDSU v. Dolphin Delivery Ltd., [1986] 2 S.C.R. 573, 33 DLR (4th) 174.

Shibley Righton. (2009). *Education law e-bulletin: A newsletter for educators.* Retrieved from https://www.shibleyrighton.com.

Spiegel v. Seneca College of Applied Arts & Technology, 2005 ON SCDC 3233 (CanLII). Retrieved from https://www.canlii.ca.

Thompson, M.J., & Slade, T. (2011). *Gauthier v. Saint-Germain: A forthcoming lesson from the Supreme Court of Canada on Educational Malpractice?* Lang Michner LLP and McMillian LLP.

University of Regina Act, R.S.S. 1978, c. U-5.

University of Saskatchewan Act, 1995, S.S. 1995, c. U-6.1.

Walia v. University of Manitoba, 2013 MBCA 61.

Warraich v. University of Manitoba, 2003 MBCA 58.

Wilson v. University of Calgary, 2014 ABQB 190 (CanLII). Retrieved from https://www .canlii.ca.

Wong v. University of Toronto, (1992), 4 Admin. L.R. (2nd) 95 (O.N.C.A).

Yogis, J.A. (1995). *Canadian law dictionary* (3rd ed.). Hauppauge, NY: Barron's Educational Series.

Zabo v. University of Ottawa, [2005] O.J. No. 2664 (O.N.C.A.).

CHAPTER 18

Understanding Pre-service Teachers' Legal Literacy and Experiences with Legal Issues in Practicum Settings

Benjamin Kutsyuruba and James Murray

Abstract

There is a dearth of research that examines legal literacy among pre-service teachers in Canada. Pre-service teachers' legal literacy refers to the knowledge level that teacher candidates in teacher education programs have with respect to educational law and policy and how it affects their preparation for entering the teaching profession. This chapter presents findings from an exploratory qualitative study that examined teacher candidates' (n=744) reflections that detailed observations of and experiences with legal issues while on practicum placements in a teacher education program in one southeastern Ontario university (during the 2014-2015 academic year). In this chapter, we identify the most frequently occurring aspects of school law and policy; analyze teacher candidates' awareness of school laws and policies pertaining to those aspects; and explore their perceived preparedness to deal with legal issues occurring in their practicum placements. We conclude with the discussion of findings and research implications for teacher education programs.

Introduction

Research suggests that teaching is becoming increasingly complex, requiring increased teacher competencies in applying a range of practices for varying purposes, incorporating and integrating different kinds of knowledge, building up a sophisticated pedagogical repertoire, and adapting to learner diversity and shifting contextual forces (Gambhir, Broad, Evans, & Gaskell, 2008). The goal of pre-service teacher education programs in Canada has been to prepare students to become effective educators in both elementary and secondary classrooms by providing teacher candidates with opportunities to gain the knowledge and skills needed to teach all children. Provincial legislation sets out the content of pre-service teacher education in very broad terms in most provinces, generally including such components as orientation toward curriculum and pedagogy, a practicum in the schools, and some discussion of child development, law and social issues (Gambhir et al., 2008). In addition to learning about preparing lesson plans, teaching classes, encouraging students in their studies, evaluating work and progress, maintaining classroom discipline, demonstrating good citizenship, and acting as advisors by connecting students to their career goals, teacher candidates are expected to be literate in school law and policy. Pre-service teachers' legal literacy refers to the knowledge level that teacher candidates in teacher education programs have with respect to educational law and policy and how it affects their preparation for entering teaching profession.

It is not surprising that during instructional and practicum components, pre-service teachers are primarily encouraged to explore and begin to understand their personal pedagogy and to apply instructional approaches and methods they have explored during their teacher education courses. Consequently, minimal time is available for pre-service teachers to develop a comprehensive understanding of, and appreciation for, their complex roles within educational law and policy. Yet, research found that legal issues are the third most essential area of teacher preparation (Garner, 2000). To be more responsive to a society that is becoming more legally complex, and to better serve children's interests, future teachers require a firm understanding of the law related to children

(Sametz, 1983). Most of the time, teacher education programs offer an education law course in order to develop pre-service teachers' legal and policy literacy (Gullatt & Tollett, 1997).

Although the need for increased attention to the development of legal literacy has been voiced in the literature (Bain, 2009; Gullatt & Tollett, 1997; Littleton, 2008; Schimmel & Militello, 2011), most of the research has been conducted in the United States. There is a dearth of research that examines perceptions of legal literacy among pre-service teachers across Canada. Thus, we embarked on the exploratory study with the purpose of examining teacher candidates' reflections that detail observations of and experiences with legal issues while on practicum placements in a teacher education program in one southeastern Ontario University during the 2014-2015 academic year. We set out to identify the most frequently occurring aspects of school law and policy; analyze teacher candidates' awareness of school laws and policies pertaining to those aspects; and explore their perceived preparedness to deal with legal issues occurring at their practicum placements. Upon the review of the literature on legal literacy, we describe the context of the course within which these reflections occurred, detail research methodology, discuss the research findings, and offer research implications for teacher education programs.

Review of the Literature

Due to the limited research on teacher candidates' legal literacy and preparation to deal with legal and policy issues and procedures during the teacher education programs, we reviewed the relevant literature entailing such topics as teachers' knowledge of law and legal literacy, with specific focus on the need for teacher candidates' awareness and understanding of the importance of legal and policy matters in education. While the majority of the literature on the legal literacy of teachers comes from the United States, some Canadian studies have been conducted on this topic in the past. Both of these strands of literature are discussed here, as much of the American perspective is highly congruent with the Canadian context (Delaney, 2008).

Why the Need for Teachers' Legal Literacy?

A substantive reason why educators in general, and teacher candidates in particular, ought to develop their understandings of the law and the legal system lies in a "singular and fundamental fact about modern education: the education system, its structures, operations, interactions, and finance are all governed by a complex and extensive collection of laws" (Kutsyuruba, Burgess, Walker, & Donlevy, 2013, p. 4). With this in mind, educators must understand the legal parameters within which they work in order to guide their professional actions and to protect themselves from legal concerns. As professionals, educators must be aware of the law as it relates to professional codes of ethics; conduct and misconduct; standard of care and treatment of pupils; protection of physical, mental and emotional wellbeing of students; confidentiality of information; and educational policies, among other areas. As employees, teachers must be aware of issues relating to collective agreements and collective bargaining, union membership, and teaching contracts (Bezeau, 2007). Overall, the law determines conditions of teaching and guides teaching practices in virtually every aspect, from the treatment of students with exceptionalities to issues pertaining to curriculum.

Traditionally, teachers have been fairly immune from examination under the microscope of the law; yet, as the law becomes increasingly involved in education, so too are teachers swept into the legal process (MacKay, Sutherland, & Pochini, 2013). Understanding the laws surrounding professional conduct and interactions with students is of particular importance for educators, as ignorance of such laws may lead to legal complications and ultimately may provide employers with grounds for dismissal. Indeed, teachers may be susceptible to litigation, and an inadequate understanding or misunderstanding of laws and policies, rules and regulations, rights and responsibilities could potentially result in negative repercussions for teachers (Posocco, 2016). Manos (2007) noted that, "ignorance of the law is never an excuse for improper or unlawful behaviour, but that ignorance can have extremely harmful repercussions for an educational employee—loss of license, livelihood, and even liberty" (p. x). In fact, litigation in the United States has tended to target teachers (Gullatt & Tollett, 1997), and one can expect a similar phenomenon in an increasingly litigious society in Canada as well. In sum, legal literacy is not only essential to creating a legally educated public school workforce, it can also offer educators ways to arm themselves with the appropriate legal knowledge to protect themselves and their students (Schimmel & Militello, 2007). The law touches virtually every aspect of teachers' professional lives, and, as such, it is crucial that educators develop a working knowledge and understanding of the legal parameters within which they function (Kutsyuruba et al., 2013).

What is the State of Teachers' Knowledge of Law?

Despite the fact that law affects educators in every area of study, at every level of education, both US and Canadian research pointed out that teachers do not perceive themselves as legally literate (Gullatt & Tollett, 1997; Peters & Montgomerie, 1998). However, the fact that legal knowledge and training of educators remain low may not be the fault of their own (Schimmel & Militello, 2007). This should not come as a surprise, due to the absence of a systematic education about school law in the vast majority of teacher certification and professional development programs. Additionally, educators typically regard the law with anxiety, misunderstanding, and a sense that it is there to trap them (Wagner, 2007), fearing "an invisible monster lurking in the shadows of the classroom, hallways, or playground, waiting to ensnare any educator who makes an innocent mistake" (Schimmel & Militello, 2007, pp. 257-258). Based on their extensive national survey of U.S. teachers, they found that over 75 per cent of those surveyed had taken no course in school law and 50 per cent of respondents were uninformed or misinformed about teacher and student rights. Moreover, the majority of respondents identified "other teachers" as the primary source of legal knowledge in schools, although most of these teachers, too, had had no formal course in educational law and were similarly misinformed about legal issues. Therefore, achieving legal literacy requires a change in consciousness, knowledge, and behaviour in pre-service and in-service education (Militello & Schimmel, 2008). These same authors later have gone even as far as suggesting that the failure of pre-service and in-service programs to address the legal illiteracy of teachers could be considered educational malpractice (Schimmel &

Militello, 2011), as legal illiteracy carries a high emotional, administrative, and financial price.

We assume that the state of legal literacy among the Canadian teachers is not very different. Almost two decades ago, Peters and Montgomerie (1998) found that in some Canadian jurisdictions educators revealed an extremely high level of uncertainty, already referred to as self-confessed ignorance, concerning rights in educational matters based on the *Canadian Charter of Rights and Freedoms* (1982) and found in the provincial statutes. Leschied, Lewis, and Dickinson (2000) similarly noted that Canadian studies on teachers' knowledge of the law are scanty, and have yielded results consistent with those in the United States. "Although few studies assess teachers' knowledge of the law affecting their practice, those that do exist support the notion that teachers have a poor comprehension of education law" (p. 3). More recently, the review of the literature revealed a scarcity of Canadian studies in the areas of educators' legal literacy, suggesting the need to augment them with content generated from studies and data gathered elsewhere pointing out that the lack of legal knowledge amongst educators is a condition of worldwide proportion (Davies, 2009). In discussing the value to practicing teachers of understanding educational law, Delaney (2009) found four main themes:

- the heightening of awareness, understanding, and sensitivity with respect to the various legal issues confronted by educators in today's schools;
- the facilitation of sound and responsible decision-making when dealing with various legal issues in schools;
- the fostering of a certain degree of professionalism; and lastly,
- the raising of teachers' self-confidence levels. (p. 123)

For busy teachers, decisions must be made during the course of unfolding of events. Keeping this in mind, to whom do those in schools turn for legal advice in difficult situations? Clearly for teachers, school administrators are the first source of information. In that regard, findings from a recent Canadian study indicated that school administrators failed 50% of the time to correctly answer legal questions, thus suggesting that school-based administrators lack knowledge of school law principles, feel uncertain or lack confidence when making decisions involving legal issues, and may require further education in education law (Findlay, 2007).

How Teacher Candidates are Prepared at the Pre-Service Teacher Education Level?

Leschied et al. (2000) argued that their research findings have direct implications for teachers' and administrators' preparation and continuing education programs:

1. Educators have a high frequency of involvement with legal issues.

2. Educators have a considerable lack of confidence in their ability to respond in an informed way to situations requiring knowledge of the law pertaining to children. Their lack of confidence appears justified given their low level of self-assessed knowledge of relevant areas of the law. Not surprisingly, they are somewhat to moderately concerned about their legal liability.

3. The areas in which educators have concerns vary according to the level of school at which they work (i.e., elementary vs. secondary), their gender, and their legal experience; however, all groups report matters relating to school safety as their greatest legal concern.

4. Educators rely on their supervisors or peers within the education system for the bulk of their information and advice about legal matters.

5. Educators believe they have inadequate opportunities for learning about relevant laws and legal issues, and desire more such opportunities (pp. 4-5).

At the most pedestrian level, understanding of key aspects of school legislation and policy will ultimately assist teacher candidates in transition from teacher education programs into teaching careers. In the practicum settings, teacher candidates focus on gaining practical teaching experience within the prescribed duties and responsibilities of school teachers. Therefore, significant legal problems germane to the profession at large are the same as those affecting student teaching (Garner, 2000). According to Fischer, Schimmel, and Stellman (2003), student teachers are held to the same duties of care as full-time teachers. Therefore, addressing legal literacy at the pre-service level is no longer optional, but obligatory. However, in the U.S., literature pointed out that coursework in educational law is fairly minimal in, or noticeably missing from, the curriculum of teacher preparation programs, and lack of knowledge of the law is prevalent (Gullatt & Tollett, 1997; Reglin, 1990; Sametz, McLoughlin, & Streib, 1983; Schimmel & Militello, 2011). In regards to the legal literacy in pre-service teacher education programs in Canada, several authors advocated that teacher education programs need to provide pre-service teacher candidates with a sound theoretical and practical background in education law (Davies, 2009; Delaney, 2008; Kitchen, 2010; Leschied et al., 2000; Sydor, 2006; Young, Kraglund-Gauthier, & Foran, 2014). Researchers have suggested that there needs to be enhanced and meaningful legal training at the teacher education level for teachers to develop capacity to best protect themselves and their students at school (Kitchen, 2010; Littleton, 2008; Schimmel & Militello, 2011).

Typically, this is achieved through stand-alone courses, or by addressing legal issues as part of a broader survey course (Young et al., 2014). From a practical standpoint, Sydor (2006) argued that the knowledge that teachers gain in the study of school law contributes to an efficient and orderly functioning of schools because they accept responsibility for their practice as professionals, and not simply as employees. Similarly, Young et al. (2014) emphasized that it is incumbent upon pre-service teacher education programs to disseminate legal and educational information. This can be done by creating spaces to analyze policy and equip beginning teachers with the knowledge to deal with the complex issues that emerge in the planning and practice of teaching. However, these authors also argued that the amount of legal literacy teaching and learning varies widely across Canada, pointing to a lack of agreed-upon standards. We share their concern about the disparate student outcomes of such learning in light of the complexity of the tensions in legal dilemmas (teacher to teacher, teacher to student, teacher to school authorities, teacher to parent, and teacher to the community), and advocate for the need to understand teacher candidates' legal literacy by exploring what legal issues they most frequently deal with and how aware and prepared they are to address them in their practicum settings.

Context of the Research

This exploratory study was situated and conducted in one south-eastern Ontario university, where a course on school law and policy is being taught to primary-junior and intermediate-senior teacher candidates within the undergraduate teacher education program. This course provides an overview of the legal aspects of teaching in Ontario. While the attention is focused on key legislation like the *Education Act*, the *Teaching Profession Act*, and selected regulations supporting these statutes, teacher candidates also receive basic information about the legal duties of education personnel; the teacher's contract of employment and related job security procedures; and the purposes, structure and practices of the teacher associations in Ontario. As this course is mandatory under the *Teaching Profession Act* for all teacher candidates, its purpose is to ensure that each student receives a basic introduction to the laws and regulations most relevant to teacher candidates and beginning teachers. The primary purpose of this course is to help prospective teachers integrate the knowledge and experience acquired in coursework and practicum by examining the components of governmental, administrative, legal, ethical, and professional aspects of public education in Ontario and Canada. Major topics for discussion include (but are not limited to) the role of law and policy in teaching; legal bases of education; constitutional/*Charter* considerations; organization of education at the local and provincial levels; professionalism and ethical behaviour; teacher organizations and contracts; legal rights and duties of teachers, administrators and students; legal liability of teachers (e.g., negligence); and discipline. All teacher candidates must complete this course in order to receive Bachelor of Education or Diploma in Education degrees and an Ontario Teacher's Certificate.

Research Methodology

To explore the perceptions of legal literacy among pre-service teachers, a mixed-methods design was used to allow for elaboration on themes and triangulation of data (Johnson & Onwuegbuzie, 2004). It included quantitative and qualitative research strategies to elicit teacher candidates' perceptions, as evidenced by their reflection papers. As part of the school law and policy class, candidates are required to submit a culminating summary paper with a reflection on their practicum experiences. Legal and professional issues, dilemmas, and challenges occur frequently within the school context, and manifest themselves in many ways. Therefore, in this paper, teacher candidates are required to detail personal observations of how legal issues discussed in the course readings, presentations, and group conversations were helpful during their practicum placements in schools. Teacher candidates: (1) identify one or more aspects of education law and policy; (2) give enough detail so that readers can get an understanding of the teacher candidate's experience with or observation of the law/policy issue in the context in which it occurred; and (3) demonstrate an appreciation for the complex legal issues in the teaching profession. Confidentiality is maintained and no real names of people or places are ever identified (pseudonyms are appropriate). Gender and/or ethnicity are only included if either plays an important role in which the incident occurred. These papers are in no way to be a criticism of a particular teacher's or school's practices.

After the ethical clearance was granted, all archived reflection papers from two sections (PJ and IS) were accessed. The working samples used in the study were: N=430 for the Primary-Junior section and N=344 for the Intermediate-Senior section. All identifying information was removed so that researchers received a collection of reflection papers without the student name, number, or year of completion. The data from the reflection papers were analyzed using the combination of etic (based on the themes covered in the course and evident from the literature) and emic (based on the emergent themes from participants' responses) codes. Frequency of mention tables (see Figure 4. *Appendix*) and thematic descriptions with pertinent quotes were produced as part of this data analysis. It should be noted that many reflection papers had mentions of more than one legal issue. Furthermore, we are cognizant of the research limitations of this exploratory study; data were elicited from course participants' reflection papers indirectly and in a post hoc manner, as opposed to the direct observations, surveying, and possible interviews with teacher candidates about the legal issues, their perceived awareness of them, and preparedness to deal with them as a result of completing the course.

Research Findings

The data analysis is presented below as it pertains to two sections in line with the three research questions: (1) identification of the frequencies of mention and types of legal and policy issues in those reflection papers; (2) awareness of school laws and policies pertaining to those aspects; and (3) perceived preparedness to deal with legal issues occurring at their practicum placements.

Frequency of Legal Issues

As noted in Figure 2 below, the five most frequently mentioned legal issues by the Primary-Junior teacher candidates were: (a) student safety and wellbeing or safe schools (n=132); (b) no-touch policies and reasonable use of force (n=106); (c) liability of teachers and risk management (n=70); (d) teacher duties, roles, and responsibilities (n=61); and, (e) special needs, at-risk, and ELL learners (n=39).

In comparison, Figure 3, below, shows that the five most frequently mentioned legal issues by the Intermediate-Senior teacher candidates were: (a) student safety and wellbeing or safe schools (n=72); (b) liability of teachers and risk management (n=72), and teacher duties, roles, and responsibilities (n=72); (c) digital technology and social media issues (n=60); (d) no-touch policies and reasonable use of force (n=55), and professional and ethical standards of licencing and professional associations (n=55); and (e) student discipline, suspension and expulsion (n=39).

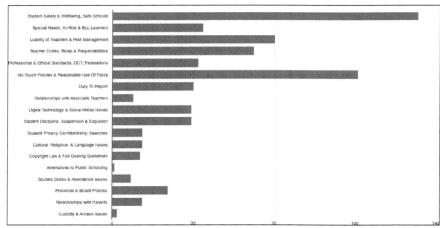

Figure 2. *Frequency of Legal Issues (Primary-Junior, N=430)*

Noteworthy were both the similarities and differences in the legal issues experienced and chosen to be discussed by the teacher candidates from different teaching streams. It is reassuring that the issue of student safety, health and wellbeing, including safe and accepting schools, was identified most often by teacher candidates from both sections. Teacher duties, roles and responsibilities and liability of teachers and risk management were the second most cited issues for the Intermediate-Senior group. This is not surprising given that secondary teachers tend to engage in more inherently risky activities such as shop, design, and technological education, science experiments, athletics, outdoor education, and extended field trips. The issue of "no-touch policies and reasonable use of force" was also considered important, particularly at the Primary-Junior level where closer contact between teacher and student is more prevalent due to having to deal with students of very young ages. However, it was also seen as problematic by Intermediate-Senior teachers as it related to the teaching of specific courses (e.g., dance, drama, physical education) or school athletics where contact is often required. It appears that the use of digital technologies, particularly social media, by both teachers and students was viewed as a significant topic at the secondary level, where educators are struggling with balancing the inherent potential of such technology as a learning tool against student safety, welfare, and privacy, in an age of increased cyber-bullying. Also, relationships with parents and the issue of custody and access were prevalently noted in the Primary-Junior data.

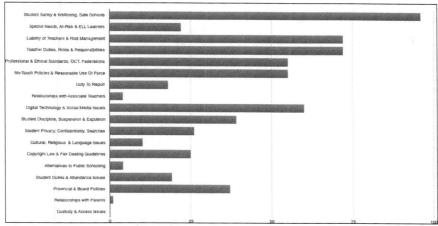

Figure 3. *Frequency of Legal Issues (Intermediate-Senior, N=344)*

Perceived Awareness of the Issues

Overall, the participants in both sections noted that having completed (and even during the process of completing) the school law and policy course, they felt that their level of awareness of the nature, frequency, and types of legal issues that typically arise in everyday teaching practice increased considerably. Generally, the majority commented that after taking this course they had much more awareness of what is acceptable and not acceptable for a teacher. For many of the teacher candidates, there seemed to be an element of "surprise" or "revelation" about the multitude of legal issues during the practicum placements that served as the "starting point" or antecedent to their increased awareness and understanding of why law matters to educators:

- I was surprised by how often potential legal issues were discussed. I, therefore, found that the course readings and discussions were quite relevant and helpful in the active school environment. Although I was not necessarily able to answer any questions, as my understanding of the complex legal system is quite surface-level, it was reassuring that I was aware of these issues at all (IS).

- This course has served as a tremendous foundation of beneficial resources pertaining to various rights, obligations and legislation that are integral to the teaching profession. To be honest, I was taken aback by all the content and issues that a teacher can find themselves dealing with on a daily basis and I was further surprised during my first practicum when most of these ideas and theories were put into practice. In a sense I guess I did not appreciate the gravity of the law and its dynamic relationship within the teaching profession (PJ).

- I found that having some background knowledge from taking [the course] was extremely valuable while out on practicum as it made me aware of what had to be mindful of. Though it is rather intimidating just how much we are responsible for as teachers and the standard for which we are held to, it is incredibly useful to now know what these standards and responsibilities are (PJ).

- This course has opened my eyes to the omnipresence and complexity of law, and made me cognizant of the legal responsibilities, and potential pitfalls, surrounding every action I take in my capacity as a teacher. During my practicum I encountered a number of situations where a more solid understanding of the law guided me in making the correct decisions ... In my (short) experience teaching, I have already noticed the complex web of legal responsibilities that teachers must navigate as part of their day-to-day duties (PJ).

Most of the teacher candidates observed or were directly involved in a number of situations and circumstances that, prior to having taken the course, they might not have viewed as "legal" in nature. For example, one teacher candidate noted: "We took many classes regarding policy and curriculum, but nothing would prepare you for the real thing of being in the classroom. The same thing goes for the content learned in [school law and policy course]; anything we read in the text [book] would not mean much until I saw it in action during practicum" (PJ). Others noted that it was during the practicum placements that they gained a better understanding and appreciation of the potential challenges and problems that could arise for both students and teachers as a result of legal unawareness.

For many students, awareness of how laws apply to issues within the school buildings or classroom walls was insufficient; they argued for the need to know the complex internal and external factors affecting educators:

- Having to learn about technology-mediated issues in schools and cyber-bullying made me realize the growing problems teachers have to deal with. At one time, it seemed like all behavioural or student-related issues could be solved in the classroom but now the internet has given people an alternative outlet for bullying others anonymously (IS).

- Sometimes issues within a school between staff cannot be solved internally, and as a member of the college there are rights and procedures to follow for guidance and assistance. As a teacher you have the right to a safe working environment with colleagues. Having taken this law and policy course, I feel I am more aware of my rights and responsibilities as a teacher (IS).

For many of the teacher candidates (especially in the Primary-Junior section), the use of the course textbook was instrumental in getting to know and recognize the different legal issues:

- The school law and policy course has been integral to my teaching practice by creating awareness towards potential legal issues that I may run into in the classroom. I found the discussion board really helpful in reflecting on potential classroom issues. The use of the course book however was especially useful during my first practicum placement (PJ).

- I often found myself referring to "A Guide to Ontario School Law" as it is such a healthy resource for my next placement, and as I move forward in my career. It is an immeasurable asset to know the rights of myself and of my students (PJ).

It is also important to note that participants recognized that they did not have, nor did they need to have, all of the answers to legal questions as they set out on their professional practice. Several of them commented that they realized that they "were not expected to be lawyers or experts" in the field. Simply being aware of potential legal issues and knowing whom to turn to or how to learn more about how to deal with them was seen as comforting and reassuring to them:

- The lessons learned in this class were very helpful, not necessarily because anything horrible happened over my two blocks of practicum requiring me to act as my own lawyer, but rather because I took a great deal of comfort knowing generally where I stood legally in my daily interactions with students (IS).

- During my ten-week period in various classrooms, I saw many of the different laws and policies we have learned about in action. It is comforting to know that these laws and policies are in place to protect not only the students, but also the teachers. This course has provided me with an abundance of information about the different laws and policies in schools that I must abide by. This information is crucial to my success in the teaching field, and now that I have this information I will be able to become the best teacher I can be (IS).

- The course taught me a lot about using my professional judgment with grey areas. As a teacher, it is vital to thoroughly understand my rights and responsibilities under the Education Act. If it was not for this course, I might have tried to pull the students apart without thinking about the repercussions or even the slightest chance that students might have accused me of touching them. A teacher's key responsibility is to create a healthy and safe environment for students.

As was evident from numerous reflections, the increased teacher candidates' awareness of the laws and policies led to increased confidence and improved capacity to deal with issues that arose:

- I am cognizant that it will not be as easy to deal with bullying in the older grades. However, now that I am aware of the policies on bullying and the *Safe Schools Act*, I am more confident that I will be able to manage whatever is thrown at me during my next practicum (PJ).

- My understandings of these and other topics of school policy and law are for more enriched then before. There are some areas that I still need to research and understand a bit more such as *social media for teachers,* but I feel that upon completion of this course I am more prepared and confident when given the opportunity to teach my own class (IS).

Most notably, seeing legal issues in action in practicum settings allowed students to reflect on the importance of being aware of different concerns that may affect their classroom teaching and being ready to confidently deal with those situations.

Perceived Preparedness to Deal with Legal Issues

Overall, teacher candidates reported that after completing the course on school law and policy, they felt less uncertain and anxious about the legal issues they were likely to face, both on practicum and in their future teaching careers. Many indicated that they were now more prepared for making decisions relating to education law and policy:

- Although this is my first notable encounter with the complexities and complications of legal issues in the teaching profession, this experience has prepared me for those that will inevitably arise throughout my career in education (IS).
- I feel that through the online modules, the textbook readings and the discussion forums, this class helped prepare me for the role of teacher during my practicum placements. It was interesting to read about various policies and situations and then apply them during my 6-week placement in October/November... the content of this class helped me to better understand how to deal with a variety of incidents while out in the school environment (PJ).
- I am looking forward to my second placement, as I feel better equipped with the knowledge of laws and policies. Being familiar with these important issues not only protects me, but will protect my students as well (PJ).
- Going in to my next practicum, I now have a clearer picture of how to set boundaries. I will actually practice this with peers prior to having to do it with students so it is clear in my mind. I think my position has changed since my practicum (PJ).
- After [this course], I feel like I have a better understanding of the difference between "No-Touch" and "Reasonable Force" and will

not be as hesitant to react in these situations that will arise in the future (IS).

- If it were not for the knowledge I acquired through the course readings, presentations, and group conversations, I would not have known the duties of a teacher in a situation like this...this situation served to remind me not only of the many duties teachers are responsible for outside the curriculum, but also of all the legal gray areas that can arise with student-teacher relationships. While one can think theoretically, conceptually and hypothetically about the many legal issues which impact the teaching profession, I found that it was not until I encountered these issues in the real world that the multifaceted, complex and dynamic nature of the intersection of law and teaching became clear to me (IS).

Teacher candidates also indicated that they now realized and understood the seriousness of these matters, the potential to get into legal and professional difficulty, and the need to always act in a prudent, reasonable, and judicious manner. They also noted that preparedness meant developing "professional judgment" based on the high professional and ethical standards that are placed on educators today:

- In my future practice as an educator, I will always take the necessary precautions to ensure that I never find myself in a compromising situation where there can be any interpretations of inappropriateness (IS).
- Learning about the case studies from this course about professional issues, student issues, and liability issues has definitely encouraged me to adapt the mindset of erring on the side of caution (PJ).
- In the end, we need to exercise careful professional judgment in response to these situations. Fortunately, there are policies and laws... that provide educators with a better understanding of how we can act in these situations (IS).
- Through the [school law and policy] course, I have gained a deeper understanding of the school policies and the legal framework surrounding education and teaching in general. Looking back to my experiences in previous practica, there are many instances I can

think of where I would have looked at situations and actions differently had I known more about the various laws and policies in place. I also realized how prominent professional judgment is in a lot of issues that occur in schools (IS).

Some participants, particularly at the secondary level, indicated that they were now thinking and planning in a more proactive fashion, with a view to minimizing risk and the possibility of legal problems. They acknowledged the importance of looking forward, thinking things through and planning in preventative ways, particularly in circumstances where the level of risk was higher and in the use of social media:

- I found [the section on risk in location and activities] very relatable to my practicum experience. On several occasions, I found myself assessing for potential risks that may be present during a certain demonstration that I was performing or a certain lab activity that students were performing...I performed demonstrations with much thought given to safety of the students and myself...Risk management is especially important in the science classroom, where the environment is potentially more hazardous compared to regular classrooms (IS).

- Social media and [related] "grey areas" in teaching are important for teachers to be aware of as there are repercussions for what is shared in the digital world. Teachers need to be conscious of not only what they are sharing on social media, but of what students may be sharing as well (IS).

Finally, although participants felt that they had learned a great deal in the course, and felt better prepared to enter the teaching profession, they also acknowledged that they were at an early stage of learning in this area. They realized the importance of continuing to learn more about education law and policy following teacher certification, with many committing to doing this once they became practicing teachers:

- There were so many direct parallels between the coursework and the real professional practice...there are such a vast variety of details we have to be familiar with as future educators, and I am aware that mastering all that information will not come overnight, or even in the three months we have spent looking at it. Like developing professional practice, learning and keeping up with our legal obligations will be a life-long commitment, but I feel that I have developed the skills to think critically, comprehend, and read legal documents for meaning (PJ).

- Now that I am better versed on the laws surrounding this issue, I will certainly inquire at each school that I am teaching at what their procedure is for protecting anaphylactic students, and whether I will have any of these students in my class. Particularly as a newly hired occasional teacher, I feel that it is my responsibility to ensure that all of my students are protected to the best of my ability, and that includes being as well-informed as possible (IS).

Overall, the sentiments among many of the teacher candidates reflected those of one of the Intermediate-Senior participants, who noted: "In my future career as an educator, I hope to continue my practice and active discussion in Ontario school law and policy, as it can and does have an enormous impact on the daily life of everyone in the education system."

Discussion

Our findings showed both similarities and differences in the issues that teacher candidates have observed or dealt with at their practica. For teacher candidates in both sections combined, the most cited issues overall were:

1. Student Safety and Wellbeing, Safe Schools;
2. Liability of Teachers and Risk Management;
3. No-Touch Policies and Use of Reasonable Force;
4. Teacher Duties, Roles and Responsibilities;
5. Digital Technology and Social Media Issues.

Similarly, Leschied et al. (2000) found that topics like school safety (with its constituent concerns about accidents, violence, youth crime, etc.), teacher conduct (comprising concerns about allegations of civil and criminal liability), children in need of protection (essentially the duty to report child abuse), and custody and access (involving access to children and their school records) were the most frequently reported areas of legal concern in their study. There is remarkable agreement between their findings and our study, despite the passage of fifteen years. As for the differences, we found that issues most frequently mentioned by teacher candidates in different teaching streams were attributed to the nature of their teaching contexts. Teacher supervisory duties, liability, and risk management were prioritized in the secondary school context due to inherently risky activities. Discussing the legal issues that art teachers may face in their classrooms, Bain (2009) highlighted the need for increased awareness of potential liability and equipment use risks for art teachers. The issues like no-touch policies, reasonable force, and custody and access were seen at the elementary level due to closer contact between teachers and students of very young ages. However, scholars warned against excessively cautionary rhetoric that can result in disadvantageous consequences for student learning (e.g., delete outright banning of teacher-student contact, or the no-touch policy), thus sadly subduing the natural impulse of elementary students to innocently hug their teachers (Davies, 2009).

Analyzing teacher candidates' perceived awareness of legal issues, we found that the school law and policy course learning generally contributed to the initial awareness of what is acceptable and not acceptable for a teacher. Indeed, it is preferable for teacher candidates to learn the law by foresight, rather than hindsight (Dunklee & Shoop, 1986) because legal unawareness may lead to potential violation of students' constitutional rights (Schimmel & Militello, 2007). Interestingly, it was not until they observed, or were directly involved in, situations and circumstances of legal nature during their practicum experiences that they started to notice legal issues, and grow in their awareness of why law matters to educators. These findings contrast those of Young et al. (2014) who noted that many of the B.Ed students in their classes dealing with law admitted that the material they were being exposed to was nothing they have encountered in their teaching practica. In our study, teacher candidates' practicum placements were also the time when they developed a greater appreciation of the potential challenges and problems that could arise for both students and teachers as a result of legal unawareness. We whole-heartedly agree that "the knowledge of education law is more effective as a protector than as a healer and it is better to have a solid understanding of education law than it is to study the relevant statutes after the fact" (Reglin, 1990, p. 17). Aspiring educators must indeed become aware of requirements and mandates and take adequate precautions to avoid potential disciplinary actions and litigation (Gullatt & Tollett, 1997). Results of our study show recognition on the part of teacher candidates that they did not have, nor did they need to have, all of the answers to legal questions, and also that they needed to become neither lawyers nor legal experts in the field. Similarly, others contended that the goal for teacher preparation should not be for teacher candidates to obtain law degrees, but rather to become educators with sufficient legal content, knowledge, skills, and training to perform their tasks well (Clear, 1983; Davies, 2009).

In terms of teacher candidates' perceived preparedness to deal with legal issues, we found that completing the course on school law and policy contributed to decreased feelings of uncertainty and anxiety about the legal issues they were likely to face both on practicum and in their future teaching careers. This is encouraging in light of other findings that educators often approach the law with uncertainty, anxiety, misunderstanding, and fear that contribute to a growing concern among educators about negligence, liability, and litigation (Fischer et al., 2003; Wagner, 2008). Reglin (1990) noted that at times, educational developments seem to outpace educators' abilities to cope, thus resulting in confusion, frustration, stress, and even hostility toward the law. Overall, the reflections indicated that teacher candidates perceived to have more confidence to deal with legal issues and felt better prepared to enter the teaching profession. Gullatt and Tollett (1997) found that many of respondents to their questionnaire about the undergraduate preparation in school law expressed a concern about being "underprepared in all legal areas of education" (p. 133). Therefore, these authors argued that the ultimate goal of a pre-service educational law course specific to classroom teachers should be to prepare new teachers for the responsibilities of a professional educator. Critical for this espoused perception of preparedness in our study was realization of the seriousness of legal matters, the potential to get into legal and professional difficulty, and the need to always act in a prudent, reasonable, and judicious manner. Sydor (2006) posited that when teacher education includes instruction about the legal context of schooling, teachers are better prepared to do their work, have a better understanding of what is required of them from a legal perspective, and are consequently less likely to misstep in their professional duties. Sydor continued, "Teachers who understand the boundaries of their roles with pupils, parents, colleagues and administrators are less likely to be intimidated by the actions of others and more likely to exercise their authority with reason and perspective" (p. 936). Although there was a general acknowledgement of being at an early stage of learning in this area, teacher candidates were committed to proactive and preventative thinking, particularly in circumstances where the level of risk was higher. As this was notably observed in an intermediate-senior teaching context, one such area may be related to the social, ethical, and legal implications of computer use in their lessons (Koc & Bakir, 2010) and misconstrued representation of professional identity through online social networking websites (Burgess & Newton, 2008). Commitment to continuous development of legal literacy among our participants is inspiring, because, in addition to knowing what is appropriate in classroom conduct, being well-informed practitioners of preventive law can empower teachers to protect their students, schools, and their own interests (Mead, 2008; Schimmel & Militello, 2011).

Conclusions and Implications

We would like to conclude with an encouraging quote from one of the Intermediate-Senior teacher candidates from our study, as someone who clearly "gets it" in regards to legal literacy: "The teaching profession – in addition to knowledge of curriculum and pedagogy – requires a sort of 'legal literacy.' This implies that a teaching professional should be aware of the multi-faceted set of laws and policies that both affect and inform their practice." Legal literacy of teachers needs to include awareness (or knowledge) of the law and policy and understanding of the level of preparedness for dealing with legal issues in teaching practice.

We believe that awareness directly counteracts ignorance, which sometimes can be compared to "bliss." However, we know that according to the courts, ignorance of the law is not an accepted excuse (Garner, 2000); therefore, ignorance of educational law is no excuse for teachers acting unprofessionally or inappropriately (Delaney, 2008). As evidenced by our exploratory study, courses on school law and policy in teacher education programs can be effective in addressing legal ignorance and increasing awareness of legal issues and preparedness to deal with them among teacher candidates. Thus, gaining a better understanding of what teachers know, what they want and need to know about school law, and determining the best methods of providing both pre-service and ongoing training are essential to creating a legally educated public school workforce (Schimmel & Militello, 2007). By addressing the legal literacy of teacher candidates in a systematic manner, teacher education programs will help them "use the law as a source of guidance to avoid unconstitutional actions, to bring legal violations to the attention of colleagues and administrators, and to improve the educational experience of students by ensuring that their rights are understood and respected" (Schimmel & Militello, 2011, p. 55).

Legal literacy has the potential to not only guide teachers candidates' actions in terms of prevention of negative behaviours, but also inform them of actions which are deemed to be legal necessities; in other words, legal literacy outlines what they as teachers must do, and not only what they must not do. Despite the research limitations, the implications of our exploratory study point out that possessing a strong knowledge and understanding of education law is crucial for educators at any level, especially for aspiring and beginning teachers, in an increasingly litigious society where legal issues can arise unexpectedly and at virtually any moment.

Finally, we encourage colleagues and researchers to explore the issues of legal literacy, awareness, and preparedness of teacher candidates through alternative methodologies that will contribute to the limited research in this field. Future research studies will do well to explore in more detail the occurrence of specific issues in practicum settings, their coverage in school law courses across Ontario (and in Canada), and perceived awareness and preparedness of teacher candidates through direct questionnaires and interviews.

References

Bain, C. (2009). Untangling legal issues that affect teachers and student teachers. *Art Education, 62*(5), 47-53.

Bezeau, L.M. (Ed.) (2007). *Educational administration for Canadian teachers [Electronic version]* (7th ed.). Fredericton, NB: University of New Brunswick.

Burgess, D., & Newton, P. (2008). *The representation of professional identity through online social networking websites.* Paper presented at the Annual Conference of the Canadian Association for Teacher Education, Vancouver, BC.

Canadian Charter of Rights and Freedoms, Part I of the *Constitution Act, 1982*, being Schedule B to the *Canada Act 1982* (U.K.), 1982, c. 11.

Clear, D. (1983). Malpractice in teacher education: The improbable becomes increasingly possible. *Journal of Teacher Education, 34*(2), 19–24.

Davies, T.A. (2009). The worrisome state of legal literacy among teachers and administrators. *Canadian Journal for New Scholars in Education, 2*(1), 1-9.

Delaney, J.G. (2008). The value of educational law to teachers in the K-12 school system. *The Morning Watch: Educational and Social Analysis, 36*(1-2), 1-23.

Education Act, R.S.O. 1990, c. E.2. (Ontario, Canada).

Findlay, N.M. (2007). In-school administrators' knowledge of education law. *Education Law Journal, 17*(2), 177-202.

Fischer, L., Schimmel, D., & Stellman, L.R. (2003). *Teachers and the law.* Boston, MA: Allyn & Bacon.

Gambhir, M., Broad, K., Evans, M., & Gaskell, J. (2008). *Characterizing initial teacher education in Canada: Themes and issues.* Toronto, ON: International Alliance of Leading Education Institutes.

Garner, D.R. (2000). *The knowledge of legal issues needed by teachers and student teachers.* Paper presented at the Annual Meeting of the Mid-South Educational Research Association, Bowling Green, KY.

Gullatt, D.E., & Tollett, J.R. (1997). Education law: A requisite course for preservice and inservice teacher education programs. *Journal of Teacher Education, 48*(2), 129-135.

Johnson, R.B., & Onwuegbuzie, A.J. (2004). Mixed methods research: A research paradigm whose time has come. *Educational Researcher, 33*(7), 14-26.

Kitchen, J. (2010). Making education law meaningful to beginning teachers: A narrative inquiry. *In Education, 16*(2), 108-121.

Koc, M., & Bakir, N. (2010). A needs assessment survey to investigate pre-service teachers' knowledge, experiences and perceptions about preparation to using educational technologies. *The Turkish Online Journal of Educational Technology, 9*(1), 13-22.

Kutsyuruba, B., Burgess, D., Walker, K., & Donlevy, J.K. (2013). *A guide to Ontario school law*. Kingston, ON: Turning Point Global.

Leschied, A., Lewis, W., & Dickinson, G. (2000). Assessing educators' self-reported levels of legal knowledge, law-related areas of concern and patterns of accessing legal information: Implications for training and practice. *Journal of Educational Administration and Foundations, 15*(1), 38–77.

Littleton, M. (2008). Teachers' knowledge of education law. *Action in Teacher Education, 30*(2), 71-78. doi:10.1080/01626620.2008.10463493.

MacKay, A.W., Sutherland, L.I., & Pochini, K.P. (2013). *Teachers and the law: Diverse roles and new challenges* (3rd ed.). Toronto, ON: Emond Montgomery Publications Limited.

Manos, M.A. (2007). *Knowing where to draw the line: Ethical and legal standards for best classroom practice*. Toronto, ON: Rowman & Littlefield.

Mead, J.F. (2008). Teacher litigation and its implications for teachers legal literacy. *Action in Teacher Education, 30*(2), 79-87. doi:10.1080/01626620.2008. 10463494.

Militello, M., & Schimmel, D. (2008). Toward universal legal literacy in American schools. *Action in Teacher Education, 30*(2), 98-106. doi:10.1080/016266 20.2008.10463496.

Peters, F., & Montgomerie, C. (1998). Educators' knowledge of rights. *Canadian Journal of Education, 23*(1), 29-46.

Posocco, S.C.L. (2016). *The importance of legal literacy in education*. (Master of Teaching Thesis), Ontario Institute for Studies in Education, University of Toronto.

Reglin, G. (1990). Public school educators' knowledge of selected Supreme Court decisions affecting daily public school operations. *Journal of Educational Administration, 7*(1), 17-22.

Sametz, L. (1983). Teacher certification programs should require knowledge of children and the law. *Contemporary Education, 54*(4), 263-266.

Sametz, L., McLoughlin, C., & Streib, V. (1983). Legal education for pre-service teachers: Basics or remediation? *Journal of Teacher Education, 34*(2), 10-12.

Schimmel, D., & Militello, M. (2007). Legal literacy for teachers: a neglected responsibility. *Harvard Education Review, 77*(3), 257-284.

Schimmel, D., & Militello, M. (2011). The risks of legally illiterate teachers: The findings, the consequences and the solution. *University of Massachusets Law Review, 6*(1), 37-55.

Sydor, S. (2006). *Teacher education needs more education law.* Paper presented at the 17th Annual Conference of the Canadian Association from the Practical Study of Law in Education (CAPSLE), Montreal, QC.

Teaching Profession Act, R.S.O. 1990, c. T.2.

Wagner, P.H. (2007). *An evaluation of the legal literacy of educators and the implications for teacher preparation programs.* Paper presented at the 53rd Annual Conference of Education Law Association, San Diego, CA.

Wagner, P.H. (2008). The legal preparedness of preservice teachers. *Action in Teacher Education, 30*(2), 4-14. doi:10.1080/01626620.2008.1046348 7.

Young, D.C., Kraglund-Gauthier, W.L., & Foran, A. (2014). Legal literacy in teacher education programs: conceptualizing relevance and constructing pedagogy. *Journal of Educational Administration and Foundations, 24*(1), 7-19.

Figure 4. *Appendix*

Type of Legal Issues	Frequency of Legal Issues' Mention (Primary/Junior, N=430)	Frequency of Legal Issues' Mention (Intermediate/Senior, N=344)
Student Safety & Wellbeing, Safe Schools	132	96
Special Needs, At-Risk & ELL Learners	39	22
Liability of Teachers & Risk Management	70	72
Teacher Duties, Roles & Responsibilities	61	72
Professional & Ethical Standards, OCT, Federations	37	55
No-Touch Policies & Reasonable Use of Force	106	55
Duty to Report	35	18
Relationships with Associate Teachers	9	4
Digital Technology & Social Media Issues	34	60
Student Discipline, Suspension & Expulsion	34	39
Student Privacy, Confidentiality, Searches	13	26
Cultural, Religious & Language Issues	13	10
Copyright Law & Fair Dealing Guidelines	12	25
Alternatives to Public Schooling	1	4
Student Duties & Attendance Issues	8	19
Provincial & Board Policies	24	37
Relationships with Parents	13	1
Custody & Access Issues	2	0

Educational Institutions' Legal Authority Over Students' Off-Campus Behaviours and Activities: A Case Study of Fanshawe College's Response to the 2012 Fleming Drive Riot

Vanessa Piccinin

Abstract

This paper examines a specific case of civil disobedience which occurred in the immediate vicinity of an Ontario community college. The case study approach was employed to critically examine and contextualize key issues pertaining to students' rights, particularly the right to due process. Specifically, to what extent can educational administrators enact policy to impose disciplinary measures over students' off-campus behaviours? Moreover, how is social media used to monitor/govern students? The competing interests of higher-level administrators, students, local police, and the greater community were also considered in discussing implications for future policy and practice.

> A man who lives in the country or in a small town is likely to be conspicuous, under surveillance by his community, so to speak, and therefore under its control. A city man is often invisible, socially isolated from his neighbourhood and therefore incapable of being controlled by it. He has more opportunities for crime. *(President's Commission on Law Enforcement and Administration, 1967a, p. 6 in Vago, 1993, p. 214)*

Introduction

History has repeatedly proven that once individuals gather as a collective they are more apt to behave differently. This 'mob mentality' often results in deviant acts which cause harm toward others and their property. This paper aims not to examine trends in student activism and other peaceful demonstrations or acts of civil disobedience (e.g., the Occupy Movement), but rather those which rapidly become uncivil, such as the display of unpatriotic behaviour seen at the 2011 Stanley Cup finals, when the Canucks lost and Vancouverites took to the streets, looting and vandalizing public and private property. In this case, social media played a role in identifying perpetrators and leading to their arrests, a tactic also employed by members of the public, educational administrators and law enforcement in the case discussed in this paper.

Stateside, civil disobedience has also resulted in substantial violence on campuses. As a result of the Fanshawe College riot, amendments and changes to current policies and delegated legislation (i.e., the Student Code of Conduct and municipal by-laws) underwent review. During this process, London, Ontario, Canada, considered East Lansing, Michigan's response as an example for effective future planning. In this case, more than 5,000 rioters took to the streets in anger over their university team's defeat in the 2009 NCAA Basketball Quarterfinals (also referred to as, ironically, 'March Madness') and caused over $150,000 (USD) damage (Cook, 1999). Therefore, this paper examines the various responses to students' involvement in acts which pose a threat to public safety. Moreover, it considers the role of social media in reporting, influencing, and even shaping the outcome of said events. By means of a case study approach, the riots are contextualized and considered from the legal perspective of educational administrators. Specifically, to what extent can educational institutions enact policy to impose disciplinary measures over students' off-campus behaviours? Implications and recommendations for future policy and practice are also discussed.

Context/Background

Located in east London, Ontario, Canada, the Fanshawe College of Applied Arts and Technology is the second largest post-secondary institution in the city, and grants certificates, diplomas, and applied degrees. Although Fanshawe College has two residences, the vast majority of students cannot be housed on campus and many choose to live in the sub-division adjacent to the east gates of campus. Figure 5 below provides a map of the Fleming Drive neighbourhood. Once a mixed housing neighbourhood comprised of families and students, in which many of the families owned their single-detached homes, the area experienced a recent shift in demographics. First, the largest townhouse complex, the Mews, became subject to large, destructive parties and numerous noise violation complaints, prompting Fanshawe College to purchase the property and make substantial repairs (Faust, 2011). These parties were not limited to the Mews but also to nearby Thurman Circle and Fleming Drive.

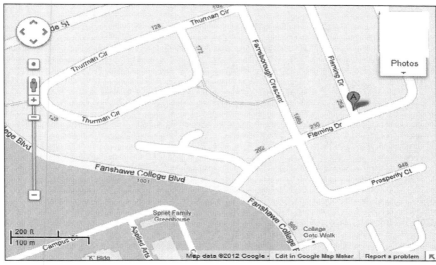

Figure 5: *Map of Fleming Drive Area*

Most notably, in 2007 a riot erupted, preventing paramedics from responding to a 911 call. Moreover, emergency and law enforcement vehicles were impeded from accessing the street when students dragged a couch into the middle of Fleming Drive and set it on fire. Many beer bottles were thrown at police, who were forced to retreat. The crowd of 200 to 300 was eventually dispersed, but one man had to be subdued with a Taser (Hayes, 2007). Although social media did not extensively cover these events, newspapers that had enabled comments on their on-line editions highlighted the public's plea that something be done.

This is not to say harmful behaviour was limited to the surrounding neighbourhood. The on-campus residence has also been subject to additional scrutiny; for instance, when 18 year old high school student Jason Mauti died in Fanshawe's Falcon residence during his 2006 March Break visit. Mauti allegedly had been drinking alcohol and smoking marijuana[1] before slipping and suffering blunt force head trauma, rendering him unconscious in a student's bed. Declared brain-dead upon hospital admission, he succumbed to his injuries two days later (McLay, 2006). Mauti was in London to tour Western University, and according to Fanshawe administration was required to sign into the residence (Dubinkski, 2006), yet it was not clear if Mauti did so. Under Section 3.4.11 of Fanshawe's Code of Conduct (a document which shall be further discussed in greater detail), "failure to properly monitor the activities of a visitor whom the student invited to a College facility and/or failure to report misconduct by the visitor" is a non-academic offence – "Failure to Comply" (2012, p. 10). Yet Fanshawe College's administration elected to claim they had no responsibility for the event and no students were subject to further investigation.

In comparison to Fanshawe College, Western University has no record of any major disruptions, fires, riots, or attacks on emergency service personnel. Nevertheless, Richmond Street, a major road which runs from north London past the main gates of the university and downtown to the bar/club/restaurant strip known as "Richmond Row," is subject to an enhanced police presence on weekends and other key dates during the academic year. It would seem, however, that additional factors, such as

1 Family friend stated the toxicology report found no traces of drugs and/
   or alcohol in his body. Further, Fanshawe representatives denied that excessive
   drinking could have taken place in the residence, which has its own security staff
   (Dubinkski, 2006).

increased enrolment at both institutions as well as an expansion of non-school owned student residences have resulted in more students partaking in public festivities.[2]

Pre-riot initiatives/regulations

In response to increased incidents of student-led public disobedience, London Police Services (LPS) initiated Project L.E.A.R.N. (Liquor Enforcement and Reduction in Noise). Aimed at reducing or preventing on-campus or near-campus incidents, Project L.E.A.R.N. is enacted at specific times of year - Orientation/Frosh Week, Homecoming, and St. Patrick's Day. In a 2011 press release, citizens were forewarned that "Police will maintain a high visible police presence to proactively dissuade unlawful or inappropriate behaviour that is disruptive to the community and to adequately respond to calls for service in a timely manner" (London Police Services, p. 1). Furthermore, Western University and Fanshawe College supported this initiative and warned that students may be subject to academic sanctions if arrested or fined.

The city also has a Town and Gown Committee comprised of residents, students, and politicians representing the Fanshawe and Western campuses and surrounding neighbourhoods. The committee's mandate is to serve "as a forum for the exchange of information on issues and initiatives involving the University of Western Ontario and Fanshawe College vis-à-vis The Corporation of the City of London and the local community and (to) recommend(s) potential responses related thereto" (City of London, 2012). Led by Orest Katolyk, Manager of Licensing and Municipal Law Enforcement Services for the City of London, the committee also informs future policy development for educational administrators and municipal politicians.

---

2 I also postulate that allowing drinking establishments to remain open an hour longer, and the inclusion of bus passes in Western and Fanshawe undergraduate tuition, may have also increased the number of students in the campus and downtown areas; however, I did not find data to support this claim and include it in my argument.

Upon admission, students are informed of Policy 2-G-01 (more commonly known as Fanshawe College's Student Code of Conduct), which was enacted in 1990 and most recently amended in early 2012. Although similar documents exist at other educational institutions, no school has publicly announced it will use them against their students involved in the Fleming Drive riot (this includes underage students from various school boards and of-age students from other post-secondary institutions), which merits further discussion below.

The Riot

As witnessed in previous years, residents of the Fleming Drive community and their guests began drinking early on St. Patrick's Day. As a pro-active response to the steadily growing (and inebriated) crowd, LPS began to assume a larger presence. Local news media were also on-site to cover the St. Patrick's festivities for the evening newscasts, including CTV London, the city's largest cable network station. By 10 p.m. crowds had grown fairly large and many people took to the streets. Only a few arrests were made during the day. A number of the participants used Facebook, Twitter, and YouTube to promote the uncivil behaviour and to encourage more people to come to the neighbourhood. Others began to upload pictures and videos, including a CTV News camera operator, who narrowly escaped his vehicle before it was overturned and set on fire.

Many eyewitness videos depicted people chanting, jeering, and encouraging the fire to spread. Bystanders became active participants and began to fuel the flames with private property including a couch, a barbeque, a basketball net, and the wooden panels of fences from many of the surrounding homes. A propane tank was also thrown into the fire but, fortunately, it was empty and did not cause a major explosion. The CTV news van, however, did, causing glass and debris to spread a fair distance, injuring many, including homeowners and other occupants who claim to have not been taking part in the riot. Unfortunately, emergency responders could not reach them - even with the support of LPS's tactical units who donned full riot gear. On-line videos best summarize the evening's events, which continued until nearly 5 a.m. Only once the crowd dispersed were law enforcement officers and first responders able to properly treat the injured and make arrests.

The Aftermath

While social media networks continued to transmit updates throughout the night and the following day, Fanshawe College's administration worked with LPS to organize a press conference. At 10 a.m. Monday, March 19, a preliminary report and statement was given. LPS Chief Brad Duncan expressed the severity of this incident:

> Last night London experienced the worst case of civil disobedience that our community has ever been subjected to. Never in my 32 years as a police officer have I observed behaviours that escalated to the point that there was risk that individuals could be seriously hurt or killed. (Lector, 2012)

In further describing clean-up costs, it was explained that repair efforts could not get underway until Fleming Drive's asphalt cooled. Specifically, the road could not be re-paved as it was still smoking from the CTV News van fire (CTV News, March 18, 2012). Additional street cleaners were dispatched and families began to gather evidence for insurance claims. Initial estimates pegged damage at over $100,000, including $55,000 to twenty-two police vehicles and fire trucks. These estimates did not account for incidents prior to police and fire rescue response, in which ambulances were pelted with beer bottles.[3] Nor did this figure include the hours and labour costs to repair the patrol cars that would be out of commission for up to eight weeks (Everest, 2012a, p.14). More recent estimates of property damage have surpassed $500,000 (MacQueen, 2012).

Of additional importance is how families and other non-student residents were affected by the riot. Among the most telling reactions was that of a 36-year-old single mother of six. She spent the night sheltered in her basement trying to keep her children calm. She had previously

---

3 My younger brother was a Fanshawe Paramedic student at the time and responded to two of these calls.

complained to the police, and had her windows broken only one week prior. She moved her family out of the home the following day (Warren, 2012). The overall consensus at this point was that those responsible needed to be identified and brought to justice.

Fanshawe College President Howard Rundle re-iterated the sentiment and announced that of the arrests made, six were Fanshawe students and all had been given an "Interim Suspension" – a sanction which "may be imposed on a student pending an investigation of a complaint of misconduct" (Fanshawe, 2012, p. 3). The Student Code of Conduct details the conditions of such as follows:

1.1.4. Interim Suspension

The CCA or Campus Security Services may impose an interim suspension on a student pending an investigation of a complaint of misconduct. The CCA or Campus Security Services will consult with the academic manager of the program in which the student is registered and with any other relevant stakeholders. Interim Suspension may be imposed where:

- it is reasonably necessary to ensure the safety and/or well-being of members of the College Community or to ensure the preservation of property of the College or a member of the College Community; or
- it is reasonably necessary to ensure the student's physical or emotional safety and/or well-being; or
- there are reasonable grounds to suspect that the student poses a threat to, disruption of, and/or interference with the normal operations of the College or the rights of members of the College Community to use and enjoy the College's learning and working environment and facilities.

During a period of interim suspension, a student may be denied physical access to specified College facilities, (including classes), and/or any other College activities or privileges for which the Student might otherwise be eligible, as the CCA may determine to be appropriate. Electronic access to College on-line services will be continued during this period unless the alleged misconduct involves the misuse of such electronic services, in which case the student's access may be suspended at the discretion of the College. (Fanshawe, 2012, pp. 15-16)

It is interesting to note how students maintained access to courses and professors. Since this riot occurred near the end of the academic term, many of the suspended students, had they previously been in good academic standing, were entitled to complete the semester. This raises the conflicting notions of the procedural fairness to which each student is entitled, and the public's perception of the students' entitlement to such.

Social Media: Judge, Jury, Executioner?

While Fanshawe College administrators enacted Policy 2-G-01 to begin imposing academic sanctions for students' non-academic offences, media 'buzzed' with extensive commentary and debate as to what consequences the rioters should face. For instance, in a London Free Press poll, 91% voted in favour of expelling any student convicted in the riots (QMI Agency, 2012). Fanshawe College alumni also expressed a similar view; one alumnus launched an on-line petition (below) the morning following the riots, which quickly surpassed its goal of 2000 signatures:

As graduates of Fanshawe College, it is our prerogative to protect the value and integrity of our degrees, diplomas, and certificates, which we worked so hard to obtain from your institution. We feel that Fanshawe College should do everything in their power to protect our interests in this regard. Acts of violence, such as the riot that recently occurred on St. Patrick's Day [sic] 2012 cannot be tolerated any longer - students involved in this unfortunate incident are an embarrassment to all alumni. We demand that any student found to have committed an act of violence or vandalism during this "riot," be immediately expelled from

Fanshawe College. We recognize that Fanshawe students are not entirely to blame for this incident, but that does not lessen the fact that our reputation is irreparably tarnished. We are furious. (Ayerhart, 2012)

Throughout the week following the riot, additional arrests were made and two more Fanshawe students were placed on interim suspensions. As of July 7, 2012, sixty-three individuals (including twenty-five Fanshawe students) faced 153 charges under the *Criminal Code of Canada* ranging from mischief to resisting arrest to assaulting a police officer (London Police Services, 2012). Yet most of those arrested were not Fanshawe students. As previously discussed, social networks had been used earlier in the day to encourage non-Fleming Drive residents to join the St. Patrick's festivities. Nevertheless, the negative impact of social media on the riots was lessened later in the night as rioters' actions were dutifully recorded; on-line confessions and live-streamed video quickly provided the necessary documentation and evidence for educational administrators and law enforcement alike. For instance, rioters' confessions via Facebook and Twitter were screen-captured then forwarded to media and LPS's Twitter accounts. Furthermore, extensive video (from on-site news crews and numerous cell phone videos) had been immediately uploaded to YouTube. The only negative aspect was the overwhelming quantity of materials being forwarded to Fanshawe College and LPS. Understandably, all of it could be carefully reviewed, but would require substantial resources. As Constable Dennis Rivest explained, "This will be a tedious and time consuming process that will require patience on behalf of the media and the public" (AM980, 2012). He went on to state that twenty officers would be assigned to this task.

Many mainstream media outlets used social media to inform their reporting styles; however, this raised a question of credibility as stories became fluid when news outlets invited public commentary, in turn causing many fact-based news reports to become speculative opinion pieces or editorial debate. Source material's reliability was also questioned. For instance, Smartphone applications enable one to place himself (or another) falsely at the riots. Similar to 'photo shopping,' some of the footage led to mistaken identity. Or, in more extreme cases, individuals claimed to be at the riot but were later found to have embellished the extent of their involvement (e.g., one man spoke with The Globe and Mail to retract his involvement, which he had boasted about on-line). Others had yet to be formally charged, like Ryan Stanhope who tweeted[4] "Im prob [sic] on the news for flipping that car" but also retracted that statement. Thus, while the public attempted to be helpful in forwarding evidence, determining consequences for the rioters had to be left to the professionals. President Rundle echoed this sentiment and asked those unqualified to investigate to remove themselves from the investigation (YouTube in Lector, 2012). In essence, he had to follow a stringent legal course of action to ensure due process to all those involved, while also assuring the public that justice would be served. Therefore, he placed all Fanshawe students charged under the *Criminal Code of Canada* under interim suspensions.

Fanshawe College's Disciplinary Powers

To best understand President Rundle's options one must closely examine the Student Code of Conduct, specifically the formal investigation protocol and the possible outcomes of such. Many of the examples of Prohibited Conduct are similar - or exact matches - to the charges rioters face under the *Criminal Code of Canada* such as Disruption; Misconduct Against Persons and Dangerous Activity; Misconduct Involving Property; Smoking, Alcohol and Drug Use; and Improper Use of Dangerous Objects and Substances; furthermore, all those fined or charged are also subject to the disciplinary action under the code as per Section 3.4.9. "Contravention of any provision of the Criminal Code or any other local, municipal, provincial, or federal statutes including without limiting the generality of the foregoing, all by-laws, regulations, and

---

4   Recently this verb has entered the English lexicon, from the social network Twitter, in which users can provide updates of a maximum of 140 characters including links to photos, videos and websites. When something is re-tweeted it is no longer protected, so even after one closes their account or increases security settings, the information can be used by others.

statutes" (Fanshawe, 2012, p. 10). Based on the severity and quantity of offences, as well as the student's disciplinary history, President Rundle could approve a variety of disciplinary sanctions, ranging from oral and written cautions and warnings to more formalized consequences such as behaviour contracts or conduct probation orders, before considering the most severe consequences of restitution orders, suspensions and expulsions (Fanshawe, 2012, pp. 10-11). Each of these three most serious outcomes are explained below

3.5.6. Restitution Order

... an order requiring the Student to compensate the College, a member of the College Community, or any other affected party for loss or damage to property. The Student's Academic Record is subject to an encumbrance until the CCA is provided with satisfactory evidence that order has been complied with or that arrangements satisfactory to the College have been made to comply with the Order.

3.5.7. Suspension

3.5.7.1. Short-term...:

... an order suspending the Student from participation in all or specified College activities, courses, or programs for ... 1 to 5 business days.

- Furthermore, with the exception of residence students, and unless otherwise specified, no student shall be allowed to physically access the College Campus and any contravention thereof may lead to more severe sanctions being imposed.
- Residence students will have limited access to the Residence and food services.
- Electronic access to College on-line services will be continued during this period unless the alleged misconduct involves the misuse of such electronic

services, in which case the student's access may be suspended at the discretion of the College.

3.5.7.2. Longer term...:

... an order requiring a Student to withdraw from an individual course or all courses in which the Student is enrolled and prohibits participation in any College activities or any combination of these for a period not less than the end of the current semester in which the Student is enrolled.

- ... result in automatic failing (F) grades in affected courses in which the Student is registered, and no fees will be refunded for that semester.
- ... opportunity to receive a "W" ("withdrawn") grade will also be forfeited. In some cases, the suspension may be deferred to the next semester and may extend up to one academic year.
- If the student is currently in Residence, the student will usually be removed from Residence with no refund of Residence fees for that semester.

3.5.8. Expulsion order..:

- immediately terminates the Student's contractual relationship with the College.
- expels the Student from all College programs, courses, and activities.
- results in automatic failing (F) grades in all courses in which the Student is registered, and no fees will be refunded for that semester.
- denies the student the opportunity to receive a "W" ("withdrawn")
- If the student is currently in Residence, the student will usually be removed from Residence with no refund of Residence fees for that semester.
- is issued by the Registrar.

- Formal communication to the student of the expulsion, on the recommendation of the CCA and the student's Program Academic Manager, will be issued by the Registrar detailing the conditions of the expulsion.
- A Student who is expelled under this provision may reapply to the College as defined in policy 2-A-03 Admission of Students to College Applied. Degree, Diploma, and Certificate programs (Fanshawe, 2012, pp. 11-13).

In consideration of the time authorities require to gather evidence and proceed in their investigations, President Rundle (or designate) might not have enough time to fully consider the circumstances prior to rendering ultimately serious decisions.

Potential conflicts arising from expulsions due to off-campus conduct are to be expected. Yet, to what extent can the outcomes of the school's investigations influence the decisions rendered in the criminal courts? President Rundle stated he would expel any students convicted for their involvement in the riots. But what if the student only needed to write final exams? Or, what if the investigation concluded after the student had formally completed his/her studies? Can the college deny a student the opportunity to graduate prior to a guilty verdict in a criminal proceeding? Can they retroactively revoke a conferred academic achievement? In a CBC Radio interview, President Rundle was asked what would happen if a suspended student was later found innocent in a court of law. Acknowledging that the student may lose a year or more of his education awaiting criminal proceedings, he replied "that's a risk we're willing to take" (CBC, 2012). Additional guests of the broadcast, including Canadian Federation of Students National Chairperson Roxanne Dubois, denounced the "two-tier justice system" that educational institutions' Codes of Conduct were creating, and pointed to the University of Ottawa's failed attempt to propose a Code that would permit administration significant authority over students' off-campus behaviours (CBC, 2012). Addressing these issues is key to future proceedings, particularly in determining if post-secondary institutions should (and to what extent) police their students.

Conclusion: Where Do We Go From Here?

One might assume that after the riots, civil disobedience and behaviours contrary to the Code would be non-existent. Sadly, this was not the situation in this case, as students and their guests continued to cause public disturbances. In the six days following the riot, LPS distributed an additional "178 provincial offenses notices in the Fleming Drive area for offenses ranging from open liquor to someone lighting a fire on their driveway" (Everest, 2012b, p.14). Moreover, numerous opinion editorials and on-line discussions continued to place blame on a variety of groups: Fanshawe students, renters who reside in the Fleming Drive area, and in the case of the underage perpetrators, their parents. The call for action was loud and strong. Fanshawe College, LPS and the City of London were expected to respond swiftly and efficiently.

Perhaps Fanshawe College could have sought more opportunities to be involved in municipal planning initiatives, or could have re-examined LPS's proposed satellite station at Fanshawe College, which they had rejected. Moreover, City of London by-laws could have been amended earlier. Mayor Joe Fontana quickly admitted this and called for an immediate revision and expansion to curfew and zoning by-laws. Council agreed and an emergency planning session was called to discuss potential amendments to the city's by-laws. On Monday, April 2, 2012, City Council held a public forum to help determine if municipal by-laws should expand to include the following definitions of nuisance:

> disorderly conduct; public drunkenness or public intoxication; the unlawful sale, furnishing, or distribution of alcoholic beverages or controlled substances; the deposit of refuse or litter on public or private property; damage to or destruction of public or private property; pedestrian traffic, vehicular traffic, or illegal parking that obstructs the free flow of traffic or could interfere with the ability to

provide emergency services; unreasonable noise, including loud music, talking, singing or shouting; unlawful open burning or fireworks; public disturbances, including public brawls, fights, quarrels or threats; outdoor public urination or defecation or any other conduct or activity a social gathering or party that is carried on so as to constitute public nuisance (Martin, 2012).

Interestingly enough, the East Lansing riots were credited as the major influence on this by-law, which is based on the municipality's public nuisance ordinances (Katolyk in Martin, 2012). It should also be noted that in this case East Lansing banned students from the town itself, drawing the ire of the American Civil Liberties Union (Cook, 1999). Before such drastic methods are considered perhaps Fanshawe College should enact certain measures to promote the pro-active role they play in monitoring student behaviour and administering consequences of the Code. Specifically, three recommendations merit consideration for future planning:

i). Maintain collaborative ties with the community

To achieve this, Fanshawe College's administration should encourage off-campus students who reside in the area to apply for vacancies on the Town and Gown Committee. Students should also be encouraged to promote positive behaviour and choices, and even be consulted when shaping future policy regarding consequences for serious acts of disobedient behaviour. This could be achieved in a variety of accessible means: focus groups, surveys, on-line discussions and Wikis. Prior to St. Patrick's Day 2014, LPS partnered with Western and Fanshawe Student Council Presidents to produce a YouTube public service announcement. Such initiatives exemplify best practice.

ii). Encourage students and the community to report Code infractions

Fanshawe College's administration should maintain a secure email account to which students and the public can send tips. Additional media sources, including Crime Stoppers' phone line and LPS's Twitter feed or tips email account, should also be promoted as means to support students who are following Fanshawe College's administration's focus that students be encouraged to report infractions. For instance, LPS Chief Duncan maintains his own Twitter account and goes on foot patrol tweeting warnings, infractions and party busts on St. Patrick's Day, all the while thanking the community for their support. The response has been overwhelmingly positive as residents' fears are assuaged.

iii). Continue to promote Fanshawe College

Moreover, promote the positive actions and initiatives undertaken by the vast majority of students, including the 500+ who volunteered at the College's Open House, held Saturday, March 24, just one week after the riot. Many parents interviewed acknowledged the potential danger for their children but were satisfied Fanshawe College was a positive choice for their children (Maloney, 2012). Again, LPS should continue to partner via social media with student leaders to promote and enhance community presence.

Perhaps when the Student Code of Conduct is reviewed, procedures taken to respond to the 2012 riot can be re-examined to influence future policy and code development. Outcomes from other post-secondary institutions' attempts to impose and to enact code violations should also be considered.

Fanshawe's immediate yet cautious response can also serve to influence other post-secondary institutions. For instance, just days following the Fleming Drive riot, a similar event took place in Kentucky. Cars were overturned and fires started (once again a response to their team NCAA team's loss in the 'March Madness' basketball tournament). This reminded me of Fanshawe College's "It's About Choices" statement:

> You've made your choice and now you're pursuing your dream to succeed. You chose Fanshawe College ... and we chose you because we believe in your success. The choices you make while you're here determine your success. The College has expectations about the conduct of each of our

students. How you handle your responsibilities during your time with us is your choice. Let's work together to ensure your success, and in future years you can look back and be proud of the choices you made.

Fanshawe College made international headlines for its riot; now educational administrators, municipal politicians and law enforcement have the chance to put the school back in the headlines, this time for making the right choices... choices they can look back on and be proud (and authorized) to have made.

References

AM980. (2012, March 28). *Police preach patience as Fleming Drive Riot investigation continues.* Retrieved from http://www.am980.ca/channels/news/local/story.aspx?I D=1677537.

Ayerhart, S. (2012, March 18). *Fanshawe College: Expel students involved in rioting.* [On-line petition]. Retrieved from http://www.change.org/petitions /fanshawe-college-expel-students-involved-in-rioting.

Balganesh, S. (2013). The uneasy case against copyright trolls. *Southern California Law Review, 86*(4), 723-780.

CBC (Canadian Broadcasting Corporation). (2012, March 21). *The Current.* [audio file]. Retrieved from http://www.cbc.ca/video/news/audio-player.html?Clipid=2213294 533.

City of London. (2012). Town and Gown Committee. Retrieved from http://www.london.ca/d.aspx?s=/CommitteesandTaskForces/TGC.htm.

Cook, J. (1999, April 19). East Lansing bans some Michigan State students from town after riots. *The Guardsman.* Retrieved from http://www.theguardsman.com/s9904 26/uwire03.shtml.

CTV. (2012, March 18). 6 p.m. newscast. *CTV London.*

Dubinkski, K. (2006, March 14). Student's organs help at least five. *The London Free Press.* Retrieved from http://pbdba.lfpress.com/cgi-bin/publish.cgi?p=12698&s= massacre.

Everest, P. (2012a, March 29). Riot costs add up for police in repairs, overtime. *The Londoner*, p. 14.

Everest, P. (2012b, March 29). Fleming Drive remains problem spot for police. *The Londoner*, p. 14.

Fanshawe College. (2012, January 18). Student Code of Conduct. *Fanshawe College Policy Manual*. Retrieved from http://www.fanshawec.ca/sites/defult/files/assets/p olicies/pdf/2g01.pdf.

Faust, E. (2011, March 21). Off-campus residence extends Fanshawe's campus. *Interrobang*. Retrieved from http://www.fsu.ca/interrobang_article. asp?storyID=6 897&sectionID=1&issueID=171.

Hayes, M. (2007, September 11). Fleming Dr. fracas: Fanshawe students riot. *The Gazette, 101*(6). Retrieved from http://www.gazette.uwo.ca/article.cfm?section=fr ontPage&articleID=1014&month=9&day=11&year=2007.

Lector. H. (2012, March 20). Fanshawe riot leads to serious consequences. *The Eyeopener*. Retrieved from http://theeyeopener.com/2012/03/fanshawe-riot-leads- to-serious-consequences/.

London Police Services. (2012, July 7). Fleming Drive Investigation – Update. Retrieved from http://www.police.london.ca/d.aspx?s=/Newsroom/20122444.htm.

London Police Services. (2011, August 29). Project L.E.A.R.N. (Liquor Enforcement and Reduction in Noise). Retrieved from http://www.police.london.ca/d.aspx?s =/New sroom/2011549.htm.

MacQueen, K. (2012, November 2). Inside the war against drinking on campus.

Maclean's on campus. Retrieved from http://oncampus.macleans.ca/education/ 2012/11/02/battling-the-binge/.

Maloney, P. (2012, March 26). Riots fail to faze parents of students. *The London Free Press*. Retrieved from http://www.lfpress.com/news/london/2012/03/25/19547221 .html.

Martin, C. (2012, March 29). It's another fine mess. *The London Free Press*. Retrieved from http://m.lfpress.com/news/london/19568951.

McLay, D. (2006, March 15). Student dies in residence. *Interrobang*. Retrieved from http://www.fsu.ca/interrobangarticle.asp?storyID=5709&sectionID=1&issueID=0QMI Agency. (2012, March 18). At least 11 arrested for St. Patrick's Day riot. *The London Free Press*. Retrieved from http://cnews.canoe.ca/CNEWS/Canada/2012/ 03/18/19518116.html.

Vago, S. (2003). Law and social control. *Law and Society*. New Jersey: Prentice Hall.

Warren, D. (2012, March 21). After the riot. *The Ottawa Citizen*. Retrieved from http://www.ottawacitizen.c om/life/After+riot/6333522/story.html.

Table of Cases

---

1   "r" signifies that the case is cited in the reference section.
2   "f" signifies that the case is cited in the footnotes.

E

Evans-Marshall v. Board of Education (2010), 222, 243r.

G

Garcetti v. Ceballos (2006), 222, 243r.
Gauthier c. Saint-Germain, Boudreau et L' Université d'Ottawa (2010), 442, 423, 427, 437r, 439r.
Ghaniabadi v. University of Regina (1997), 431, 437r.

H

Harelkin v. University of Regina (1979), 428, 429, 430, 437r.
Hazelwood School District School District v. Kuhlmeier (1988), 229, 229f, 243r.
Hickey-Button and Potter v. Loyalist College (2003), 417, 420, 437r.
Hickey-Button and Potter v. Loyalist College (2006), 421, 437r.

I

Irwin Toy Ltd. v. Quebec (1989), 226, 243r.

J

Jaffer v. York University (2010), 423, 425, 427, 437r, 438r, 439r.
Jubran v. Handworth (2005), 351, 374r.

K

Keefe v. Geanakos (1969), 231, 232, 243r.
Kempling v. British Columbia College of Teachers (2005), 235, 243r.
King v. University of Saskatchewan (1969), 429, 431, 438r.

L

Lacks v. Ferguson Reorganized School District (1998), 233, 243r.
Loyola High School v. Quebec (Attorney General) (2015), 2, 5, 171-202.

M

Mahmoodi v. Dutton and the University of British Columbia (1998), 374r.
Mailloux v. Kiley (1971), 230, 231, 232, 243r.

Mayer v. Monroe County Community School Corp (2007), 222, 231, 243r.
Miles v. Denver Public School Board (1991), 229f, 243r.
Mohl v. University of British Columbia (2006), 423, 438r.
Monckton v. C.B.S. Interactive Multimedia (2012), 421, 438r.
Morin v. Regional Administration Unit #3 (2002), 222, 230, 231, 239, 243r, 244r.
Morse v. Frederick (2009), 351, 374r.
Mpega v. Université de Moncton (2001), 374r.
Mulligan v. Laurentian University (2008), 414, 415, 416, 423, 438r.
Multani v. Commission scolaire Marguerite-Bourgeoys (2006), 187, 187f, 188, 190.

N
Nazik Amdiss and the University of Ottawa, Ltd. (2010), 416, 436r.

O
Olar v. Laurentian University (2008), 419, 421, 438r.
O'Reilly v. Memorial University of Newfoundland (1998), 423, 438r.

P
Pacheco v. Dalhousie University (2005), 374r, 423, 438r.
Paine v. University of Toronto (1981), 424, 438r.
Pridgen v. University of Calgary (2012), 352, 374r, 432, 433, 439r.

R
R. v. Big M Drug Mart Ltd (1985), 180, 180f, 186.
R. v. B.W.P. (2006), 32f, 33, 40r.
R. v. D.W.H (2001), 352, 374r.
R. v. Elliott (2016), 374r.
R. v. Ewanchuk (1999), 375r.
R. v. Ghomeshi (2016), 375r.
R. v. Jones (1986), 190, 190f.
R. v. Keegstra (1990), 227, 230, 243r.
R. v. M. (M.R.) (1998), 15, 40r.
R. v. Mabior (2012), 375r.

Contributors

Dr. Fiona Blaikie is a Professor in the Faculty of Education at Brock University, St. Catharines, Ontario, Canada. Her scholarship in visual arts education has evolved from a focus on aesthetic values inherent in criteria for assessment of studio art to arts informed research. Situated in social, cultural, political, gender and class contexts, her recent work on the body and clothing investigated the aesthetics of scholarship, evolving to the aesthetics of youth culture in which the body and clothing are examined through visual images and texts as connected and situated. Fiona is a former President of Canadian Society for Education through Art. She has served as a university administrator for 15 years, most recently as Dean of the Faculty of Education at Brock University. Currently, Fiona is the Chief Examiner of Visual Arts for the International Baccalaureate Organization, and she is an elected World Councillor for the International Society for Education through Art. She can be reached at fiona.blaikie@brocku.ca.

David Boulding, B.A. Hons. English/Native Studies (Trent University), M.A. Poetry/Rhetoric and Law at the University of British Columbia (1987), has a Diploma in Counselling (Haven Institute) and is a former trial lawyer with a practice restricted to writing, speaking, and training about fetal alcohol. For 10 months a year, at the Strathcona Park Lodge Outdoor Education Centre on Vancouver Island, British Columbia, Canada, David works at selective logging, and mills beautiful beams on his band saw mill. All his papers are available for free at www.david boulding.com. His films and videos are on YouTube, and he answers emails: dmboulding@gmail.com.

Ken Brien, Ed.D., is an Associate Professor of Educational Administration and Leadership at the University of New Brunswick, Fredericton, New Brunswick, Canada. He worked previously as a high school teacher and administrator in Northern Ontario. He has served as president of the Canadian Association for the Study of Educational Administration (CASEA) and the Commonwealth Council for Educational Administration and Management (CCEAM). His teaching and research interests include educational law, policy, governance, administration, and leadership in provincial, national, and international settings. Ken can be reached at kbrien1@unb.ca.

Dr. Dawn Buzza is a Professor of Education at Wilfrid Laurier University, Waterloo, Ontario, Canada. She holds a M.A. in Education (Counselling) and a Ph.D. in Educational Psychology from Simon Fraser University. Her areas of research interest include adolescent development, social-cognitive perspectives on learning and motivation, and self-regulated learning (SRL). Her research involves working with secondary teachers to develop and test strategies for supporting students during the transition to high school. She is currently serving as Acting Dean of the Faculty of Social Work at Wilfrid Laurier University. Dawn can be reached at dbuzza@wlu.ca.

Dr. Paul T. Clarke is a Professor of Educational Law and Leadership at the University of Regina, Saskatchewan and the Associate Dean of Faculty Development and Human Resources in the U of R's Faculty of Education. He holds a Ph.D. and LL.M. from the University of Saskatchewan. His areas of research focus on school law with specific interests in freedom of religion, freedom of speech, and the rights of sexual minorities. Paul may be reached at clarkep@uregina.ca.

Kelly Clement is the college secretary for governance matters in the College of Graduate and Postdoctoral Studies at the University of Saskatchewan, Saskatoon, Saskatchewan, Canada. Her main area of interest is policy revision and development to provide clarity in decisions and processes. She has a sincere interest and commitment to natural justice. Kelly can be contacted at kelly.clement@usask.ca.

José R. da Costa is the Digital Services Librarian employed by the Kamloops Public Library, Kamloops, British Columbia, Canada. His main area of interest is digital literacy, specifically how it intersects with the intellectual property interests of rights holders and addressing the digital divide: the barrier that is stratifying our society based on who is and is not capable of using technology in professional and personal capacities. Through the Kamloops Public Library he provides technology instruction and support for seniors, newcomers, teens, and children. He holds a Masters degree in Library and Information Studies and an undergraduate Arts degree in History and Classics, both from the University of Alberta. José can be contacted at jdacosta@tnrd.ca.

Dr. José L. da Costa is a Professor of Educational Administration and Leadership in the Department of Educational Policy Studies, Faculty of Education at the University of Alberta, Edmonton, Alberta. He holds a Doctorate of Education in Educational Administration (University of British Columbia), a Master of Arts in Technology Education (California Polytechnic University, San Luis Obispo), and a Bachelor of Education (Honours, University of British Columbia). His research focuses on how educational programming, teacher learning, and administrative structures impact student success in school. José teaches courses in educational administration and leadership, generally, and supervision of instruction, specifically. He has also taught a variety of graduate-level introductory and advanced research methods courses. José also teaches educational law and ethics to 4th year pre-service teacher-education students. José can be contacted at jdacosta@ualberta.ca.

Yvette Daniel, Ph.D., is an Associate Professor in Educational Leadership and Policy Studies at the Faculty of Education, University of Windsor, Canada. Dr. Daniel has extensive experience in teacher education as course instructor and faculty advisor. She teaches Educational Foundations and Law courses in the pre-service program and administrative and policy courses at the graduate level. She has developed a new service-learning program for teacher candidates. She is Principal Investigator on a three-year Social Sciences and Humanities Research Council of Canada (SSHRC) and University of Windsor funded cross-cultural research and partnership development project that explores youth civic engagement for healing and reconciliation (*Tikkun*) in their communities. Yvette can be contacted at ydaniel@uwindsor.ca.

Jerome G. Delaney, Ph.D. (University of Alberta), is an Associate Professor of Educational Administration in the Faculty of Education at Memorial University of Newfoundland, St. John's, Newfoundland, Canada. He teaches B.Ed. courses in Effective Teaching and Educational Law, and graduate courses in Legal Foundations of Educational Administration, Educational Administration: Theory & Practice, and the Social Context of Educational Leadership. Dr. Delaney spent 30 years as a high school teacher and principal (3 principalships) in the K-12 public school system in Newfoundland. He welcomes correspondence at jdelaney@mun.ca.

Nora M. Findlay, Ph.D. (Western University), served more than twenty-five years as an educator and school-based administrator in Saskatchewan, Canada. She is the author of a number of journal articles, book reviews, policy analyses, and book chapters at both the national and international levels. Her scholarly interests include student rights, school law, school safety, educational administration, and Indigenous education. Nora may be reached at findlay.nora@gmail.com.

Tatiana Gounko, Ph.D. (University of Alberta), is an Associate Professor in the Department of Educational Psychology and Leadership Studies at the University of Victoria, British Columbia, Canada. She teaches graduate courses on educational policy and higher education and is involved in the Learning and Teaching in Higher Education (LATHE) Certificate program offered to doctoral students who aspire to become academics. Her research interests include international comparative higher education, policy and law, and educational reforms. Tatiana can be reached via email at tgounko@uvic.ca.

André P. Grace, Ph.D., is Canada Research Chair in Sexual and Gender Minority Studies (Tier 1) in the Faculty of Education, University of Alberta, Edmonton, Alberta, Canada. He served as an external reviewer for the Chief Public Health Officer's Reports Unit on the State of Public Health in Canada for the 2011 and 2012 national reports, which include foci on the comprehensive health, educational, and cultural concerns of sexual and gender minority youth. Dr. Grace's work advancing the need for greater synchronicity in research, policy, and practice informs his book *Lifelong learning as critical action: International perspectives on people, politics, policy, and practice* (Canadian Scholars' Press, Toronto, 2013), for which he is the 2014 recipient of the American Association for Adult and Continuing Education (AAACE) Cyril O. Houle Award for Outstanding Literature in Adult Education. His latest book, is entitled *Growing into resilience: Sexual and gender minority youth in Canada* (University of Toronto Press, 2015). For mor information, please visit https://www.andregrace.com and http://chewproject.ca

Dr. Luigi Iannacci is an Associate Professor in the School of Education and Professional Learning at Trent University in Peterborough, Ontario, Canada. He teaches and coordinates courses that focus on language and literacy and special needs learners. He has taught mainstream and special education in a range of elementary grades in Ontario. His research interests and publications are focused on first and second language and literacy learning, critical multiculturalism, critical dis/ability studies, early childhood education, critical narrative research and ethics. He is the past president of LLRC (Language and Literacy Researchers of Canada) and the past president of ISEB (International Society for Educational Biography). Dr. Iannacci can be reached at luigiiannacci@trentu.ca. Website: http://people.trentu.ca/luigiiannacci/index.html.

Terry Kharyati, after struggling through high school and CEGEP, began his university training with the goal of becoming a teacher, and was inspired by the leaders and teachers who had helped and mentored him. His drive and passion for helping a range of students and staff to learn and grow were demonstrated early on, and he seized leadership opportunities whenever they presented themselves. Terry was a teacher, vice-principal, and principal for 23 years, and is now working as the Director of Human Resources at the Western Quebec School Board. He has recently graduated from the M.Ed. program at Queens University, where he immersed himself in the study of the impact of leadership on school climate and student and staff efficacy, and he believes that effective systems need to support and nurture all school leaders. He is a proud husband and father of three beautiful girls and lives in the community he proudly serves. Terry can be contacted at tkharyati@gmail.com.

Benjamin Kutsyuruba, Ph.D., is an Associate Professor in Educational Policy, Leadership, and School Law and an Associate Director of Social Program Evaluation Group (SPEG) in the Faculty of Education at Queen's University, Kingston, Ontario, Canada. Throughout his career, Benjamin has worked as a teacher, researcher, manager, and professor in the field of education in Ukraine and Canada. His research interests include educational policymaking; educational leadership; mentorship and development of teachers; trust, moral agency, and ethical decision-making in education; international education; school climate, safety, well-being, and flourishing; and, educational change, reform, and restructuring. His areas of teaching include educational leadership, school law and policy, educational policy studies, and policymaking in education. Benjamin can be contacted at ben.kutsyuruba@queensu.ca.

Dr. Bruce Maxwell is Associate Professor of Education at the University of Quebec at Trois-Rivières, Quebec, Canada. Previously a humanities teacher at the college level, Bruce now teaches ethics and law for educators, educational foundations, and preparatory courses relating to Quebec's statutory ethics and religions curriculum. His research and writings focus on professional ethics teaching, ethical issues in education and schooling, and ethical development through teaching and learning in schools. He has written a number of articles, chapters and books on these topics including, most recently, the co-authored *Questioning the classroom: Philosophical perspectives on Canadian education* (Oxford University Press). Bruce can be contacted at bruce.maxwell@uqtr.ca.

Dr. Kevin McDonough is Associate Professor of Philosophy of Education at McGill University, Quebec, Canada. He is co-editor (with Walter Feinberg) of *Citizenship and education in liberal-democratic societies: Teaching for collective identities and cosmopolitan values* (Oxford, 2003). He has published numerous scholarly articles and book chapters on issues at the intersection of political philosophy, moral philosophy, and education. Kevin can be reached at kevin.mcdonough@mcgill.ca.

Danielle S. McLaughlin was Director of Education of the Canadian Civil Liberties Association and Education Trust (CCLA/CCLET) from 1988 to 2016. During this period, she developed the "Teaching Civil Liberties" and "Civil Liberties in the Schools" programs, reaching thousands of students, teachers, and teacher-candidates across Ontario. Between 1997 and 2001, Danielle represented CCLA on the Toronto Police Services Board sub-committee on Race Relations. The Law Foundation of Ontario named Danielle the 2010-2011 Law Foundation of Ontario Community Leadership in Justice Fellow. This appointment took her to the Faculty of Education at the University of Windsor, where she had the opportunity to collaborate with Drs. Yvette Daniel, Karen Roland, and Andrew Allen on projects dealing with teaching in a democratic society. In 2016, The Ontario Justice Education Network awarded Danielle the Hux-Kitely Exemplary Justice Education Award. Danielle blogs regularly for Huffington Post Canada, The Centre for Freedom of Expression at Ryerson University, and is heard weekly on her Know Your Rights segment on AMI.ca's *Kelly and Company.* She is also the author of *That's not fair! Getting to know your rights and freedoms,* Kids Can Press, Toronto, Citizen Kid selection for 2016. Danielle can be reached at Danielle@daniellesmclaughlin.com.

Frank Muia is a teacher in the Dufferin-Peel Catholic District School Board in Ontario. He has been a mainstream and Special Education Resource Teacher at the elementary and secondary level and is presently a high school Department Head of Special Education and Academic Resources. Frank has been involved with various curriculum writing initiatives including the development of Special Education Additional Qualification courses for Trent University, where he continues to work as a part-time instructor. His professional interests include effective programming practices and building literacy programs for students with diverse learning needs. Frank can be reached at frank.muia@dpcdsb.org.

Dr. Jacqueline Muldoon is currently the Provost and Vice President Academic at Trent University, Peterborough, Ontario, Canada. She has been a professor at Trent University since 1983 and served three terms as the Dean of Education at Trent University's School of Education and Professional Learning. She served as an executive member and Chair of the Ontario Association of Deans of Education. Dr. Muldoon earned her B.Sc. from Brock University (Mathematics and Economics), her M.A. in Economics at the University of Guelph, and her Ph.D. in Economics from McMaster University. Dr. Muldoon believes in academically rigorous and collaborative learning, through the use of innovative technologies, and exposure to critical research in education, whereby students can tackle contemporary issues about society, environmental sustainability and social justice in the education system. She also believes that effective teacher education is a partnership involving the whole community as a community of learners. Jacqueline can be reached at jamuldoon@trentu.ca.

James Murray is currently in his fourth year of the Ph.D. program at the Faculty of Education at Queen's University. He holds a M.Ed., L.L.B., and B.A. Honours (Political Studies) from Queen's University. Prior to returning to Queen's University, James was an elementary school principal for sixteen years, a vice-principal, special education resource teacher and elementary classroom teacher. He also practiced law for a number of years prior to entering education. James's academic and professional interests are in the areas of education law and policy, leadership, ethics and special education. His current research focuses on exploring the trust dynamic between the principal and parents of students with special needs. James can be reached at 3jwm@queensu.ca.

Blair Niblett, Ph.D., is an Assistant Professor in the School of Education at Trent University in Peterborough, Ontario, Canada. His research explores social justice, activism, and experiential education. Blair can be contacted at blairniblett@trentu.ca.

Vanessa Piccinin is a doctoral candidate in Educational Leadership and Policy, within the School of Leadership, Higher, and Adult Education, at the Ontario Institute for Studies in Education (OISE), University of Toronto, Ontario, Canada. Her research examines various perspectives in policy and legal issues affecting institutional leaders and the rights of students of all ages throughout the education system. She has taught at the elementary, secondary, and post-secondary levels in a variety of subjects. She is also a certified guidance counsellor and principal who has recently returned to the high school classroom to teach French Immersion. She was also awarded the 2015 Fellowship by the Canadian Association for the Practical Study of Law in Education (CAPSLE) for her work entitled *Beyond gay-straight alliances: LGBTQQIP2SAA students in Canadian schools.* She can be reached at vanessa.piccinin@utoronto.ca.

Mauro Porco is a Special Education and Resource Teacher in the Simcoe Muskoka Catholic District School Board and an Instructor of Special Education Additional Qualification Courses at Trent University. He has taught mainstream and special education classes at the elementary and secondary level in Ontario, Canada. He has also held leadership positions within the Simcoe Muskoka Catholic District School Board as a Special Education Consultant and Coordinator of Special Education Services. His teaching and research interests are focused on developing and implementing equitable and inclusive practices through relationship building and the use of assistive technologies. Mauro can be reached at mporco@smcdsb.on.ca.

Dr. Carole Richardson is the Dean of the Schulich School of Education at Nipissing University in North Bay, Ontario, Canada. Prior to becoming Dean, she served as Associate Dean and taught music methods for eight years. Before coming to Nipissing, Dr. Richardson taught classroom music in middle schools and conducted choirs in Ontario, Canada and in the Cayman Islands. Her research focuses on the importance of arts experiences in the lives of preservice teachers and the role of autobiographical and collaborative narrative inquiry in preservice education. Carole may be reached at caroler@nipissingu.ca.

Dr. Shaheen Shariff is an Associate Professor at McGill University. Her work is grounded in the intersection of law and education, with a focus on human rights and constitutional issues, diversity, legal pluralism and civil society. She is an Associate Member of the Center for Human Rights and Legal Pluralism at McGill's Law Faculty and Affiliate Scholar at Stanford University Law School's Center for Internet and Society. She is best known for her expertise on cyberbullying, sexting, and sexual violence on university campuses, and advocates for a balance between free expression, privacy, safety, protection, and regulation. Her research and teaching are centered in the study of law as it impacts educational policy, pedagogy and practice. Professor Shariff served as expert witness at several Canadian House of Commons committees relating to proposed legislation and testified at the Senate Standing Committee on Human Rights in 2012. She is currently on an advisory board for Quebec's Premier Philippe Couillard to develop a provincial strategy on cyberbullying; and was an invited panelist at a conference on cyberhate at the United Nations Headquarters in New York, chaired by Secretary General Ban Ki Moon. She also testified at the Nova Scotia Task Force on cyberbullying and was key advisor to the Quebec English School Board Association's task force. She served on the Board of Directors of Kids' Help Phone, and provided expert witness testimony that informed a landmark Supreme Court of Canada ruling on protection of children's privacy rights. The Social Sciences and Humanities Research Council of Canada (SSHRC) and the Quebec Ministry of Education have awarded her several research grants. She is currently the Project Director and Principal Investigator of a $2.6 million Partnership grant awarded by the SSHRC for a term of 7 years. She also serves on SSHRC grant review committees. She is also one of four recipients globally of Facebook's Inaugural Digital Citizenship Grant. Her work has culminated in 7 books (translations into Portuguese and Italian); and numerous journal articles and book chapters; resources and videos found at www.mcgill.ca/definetheline. She also earned the Queen's Diamond Jubilee Medal for her public policy contributions to Canada. Shaheen may be reached at Shaheen.shariff@mcgill.ca.

About the Editor

William T. Smale, Ph.D. (University of Alberta); H.B.P.E; B.Sc; B.Ed; M.Ed, is an Associate Professor in the School of Education and Professional Learning at Trent University in Peterborough, Ontario (Canada). He teaches and coordinates undergraduate courses in Educational Law, Ethics and Professional Conduct, and graduate courses in Research Methods and School Law. His research interests include school law, educational administration, early school leaving, deviance, and early childhood interventions. William may be reached at williamsmale@trentu.ca.

Made in the USA
Lexington, KY
10 July 2018